CLOSER

SEEING THE WORLD IN DETAILS

CLO

SER

MICHAEL CLINTON

First published in 2015 by

Glitterati Incorporated

Glitterati Incorporated
New York | London

New York Office:
630 Ninth Ave, Ste 603
New York, NY 10036
Telephone: 212 362 9119

London Office:
1 Rona Road
London NW3 2HY
Tel/Fax +44 (0) 207 267 9739

www.GlitteratiIncorporated.com | media@GlitteratiIncorporated.com
for inquiries

First edition, 2015

Library of Congress Cataloging-in-Publication data is available from the publisher.

Hardcover edition ISBN 13: 978-0-9905320-1-9
Design: Liz Trovato
Printed and bound in China by C P Printing, Limited
10 9 8 7 6 5 4 3 2 1

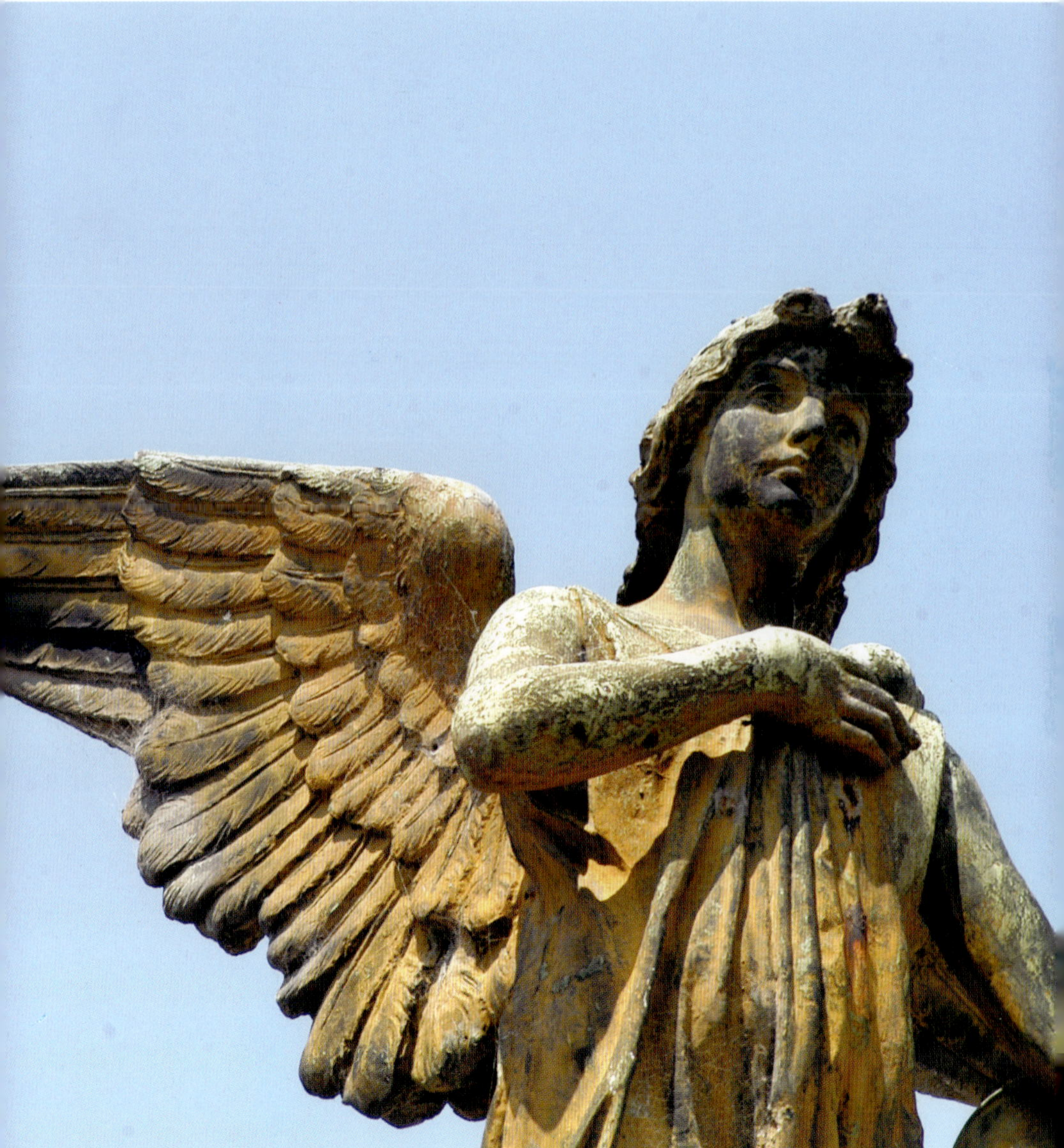

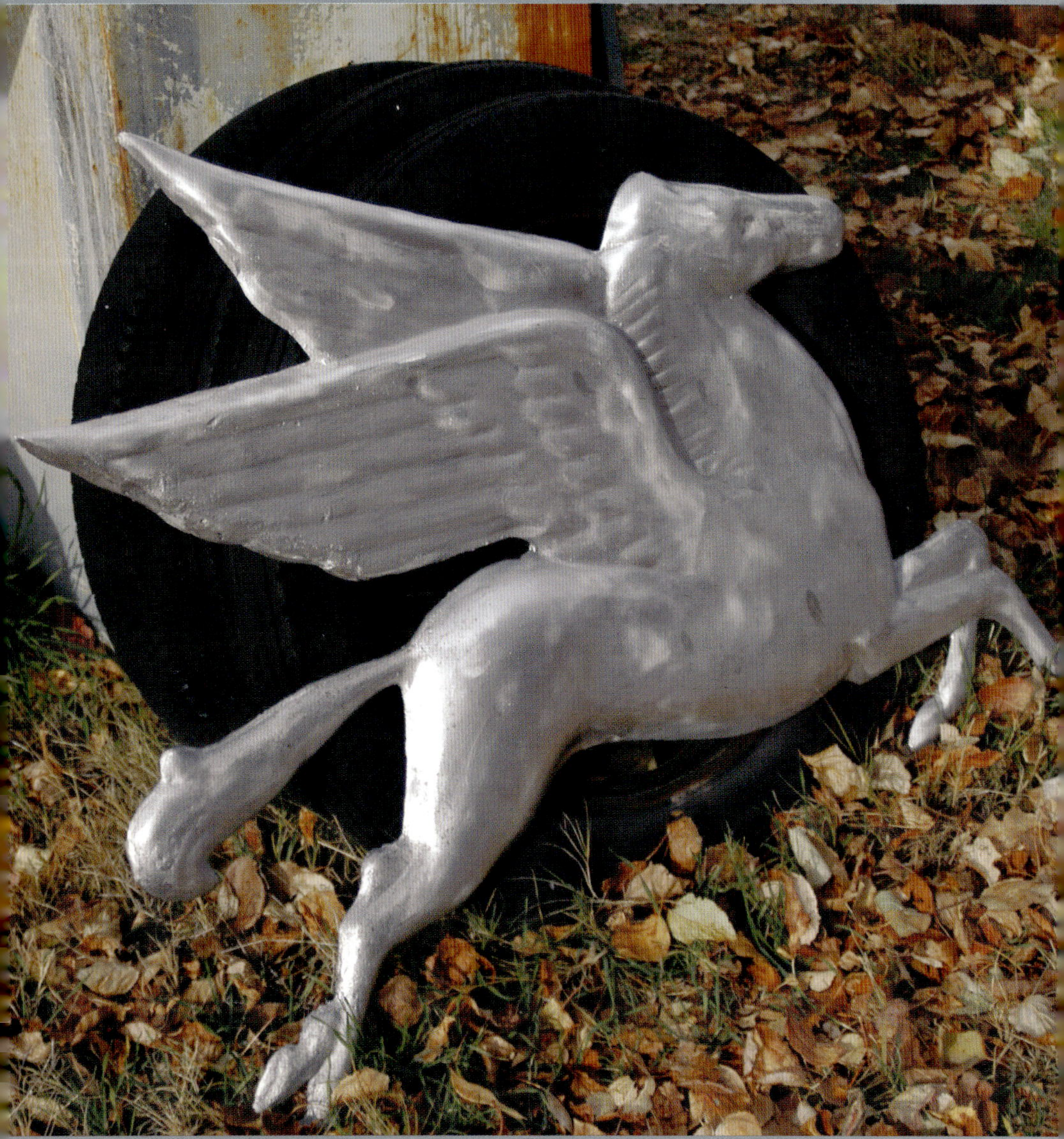

For Nicolas and Emerson. Never forget to focus on the details of your life,
as brothers, sons, nephews, and men.

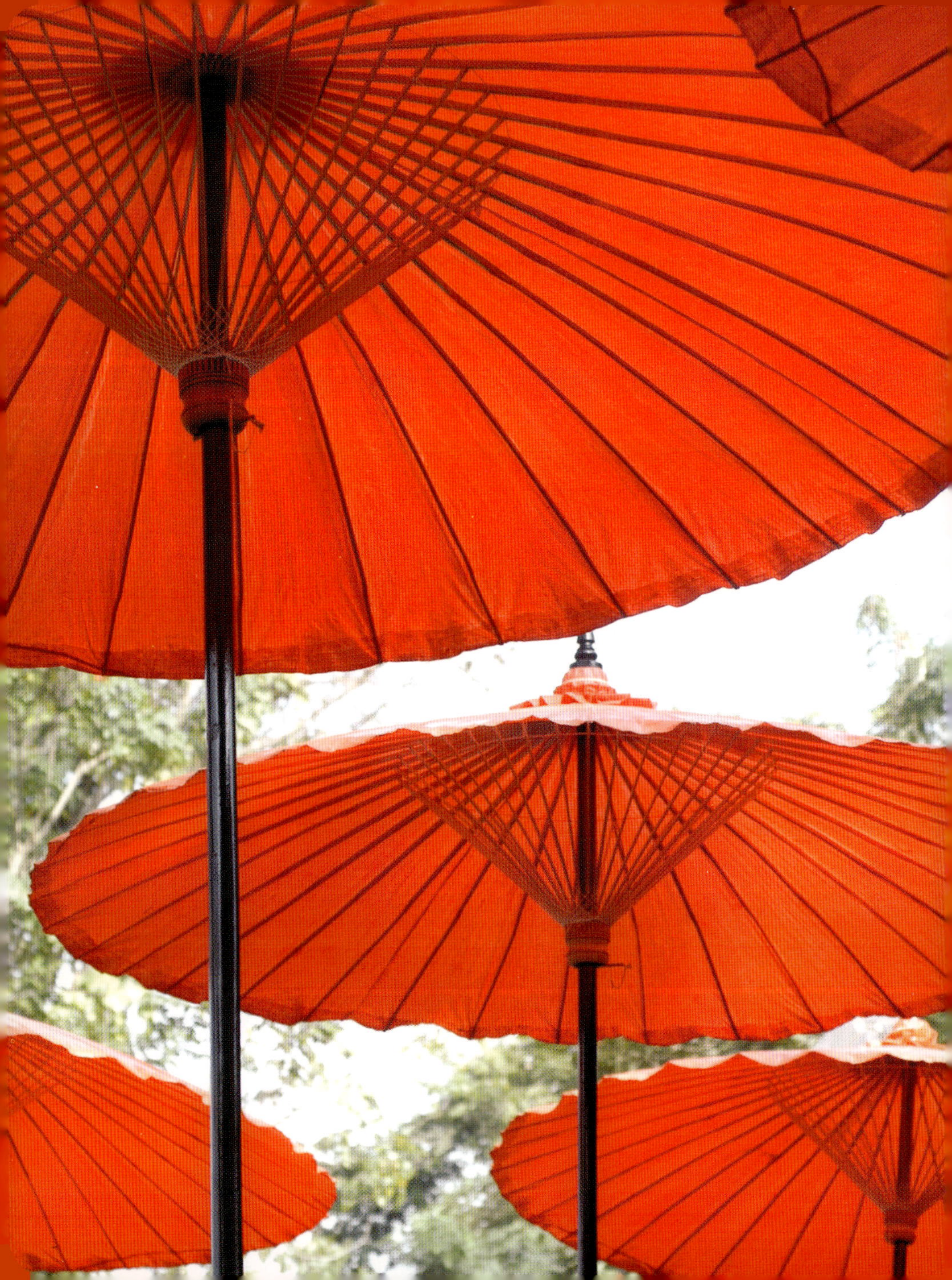

CONTENTS

Introduction

We live in a fast world. Click, swipe, ping, touch, tweet, delete. These have become the actions of our lives. As we stay fixated on our devices, we begin to miss the human nuances that can make all the difference to us: a smile, a friend's hand on your shoulder, a child's hug. In so many ways, the digital world enhances our lives and in so many ways it endangers the important moments that help to define us.

In *The Art of Stillness*, writer Pico Iyer reminds us how stillness opens us up in a way that counters the madness of modern life. For me, it is the concept of getting closer, or seeing the world in details, whether it is at home, or while traveling the world. Stay still and look at the world around you.

This approach can take on many forms: a family dinner without smartphones, which makes us concentrate on the conversation and hear what is important in our loved ones' lives, and reminding us that nonverbal cues are as important as verbal ones; noticing that someone at work is struggling a bit, allowing you to lend a quiet and helpful hand; or something as simple as offering a nice gesture to a stressed-out stranger. Being closer to the details of our lives keeps us connected to our world in a way that a digital device never can.

One of my favorite moments is waking up at my house and walking around the yard, looking at the trees and flowers and shrubs. That 20-minute ritual with latte in hand is the magic of the day. It is then that I get to look at the wonders of nature and how they envelop our house in a way that is both comforting and secure. After that walk, it seems that every problem can be solved, once I know that my favorite Atlas tree is thriving and that the peonies will bloom once again.

A friend once asked me, "What brings you joy?" Give a quick response, he said, don't linger too much on your answer. Well, certainly the people (and animals, too) who are important to me fill me up. But my answer was running in Central Park, skiing down a slope on a crisp winter day, hiking in the hills above Santa Fe, gazing at a sunset in any Western sky, reading great literature, looking at art and photography, finding ways to give random acts of kindness through a foundation that some friends and I started, called Circle of Generosity. They all bring me joy.

My career has afforded me a big New York life with fancy dinners, events, red carpets, and celebrities. And while I wouldn't trade it for anything, more and more I realize that the simple details of everyday life can bring so much pleasure.

As an adventurer and traveler, I've been fortunate enough to visit more than 120 countries, run seven marathons on seven continents, and meet incredible people. Standing atop Mt. Kilimanjaro, in Tiananmen Square, or at the Pyramids of Giza all bring a wonder that stays with us forever.

But as time has gone on, I've also come to realize that while the big sweeping views are grand and exhilarating, it is the small details in the world that have made my travels richer over time. Walking past a small shop in Place des Vosges in Paris, my eye caught some small figurines of French dance-hall girls. I pulled out my camera and took some wonderful photos of these girls. While taking the elephant ride to the Red Fort in Jaipur, India presents a scene that is spectacular and chaotic, it is the whimsical multicolors applied to the elephant's trunk in exquisite detail that will mesmerize you. Plates of food, local posters, statues and their details, signs, flora, local handicrafts—all add up to getting closer to a place, a culture, and its people.

During my travels, I find myself taking in the big picture, but more often I get still in a scene and I take it all in, getting down to the most granular level possible. It adds a completely different level of experience.

You don't have to travel halfway around the world to get closer. In fact, you can practice this in your everyday life. Put down your device and concentrate on the people around you, your surroundings, and all of the details that are in your house or neighborhood or office or favorite place to visit. You'll be surprised at how much depth it adds to your day.

We are surrounded by memories, sensory stimuli, and the specifics of our lives that help to define who we are as people. Seeing the world in details is the message of this book. The photos inside take you on a journey that is closer than most. There are no sweeping landscapes or familiar landmarks and monuments. Instead, there are moments of discovery.

The cover photo is a good example. While walking through a park in Oslo, I came across this small metal sculpture of a man doing something basic in life—simply drinking water, a universal experience that is shared by every other human on the planet. Around me, many people didn't even notice the statues as they went about their business. For me, it was a beautiful detail in the park that deserved some attention. Using my macro lens allowed me to see it in even greater detail.

As you flip through this book, I hope it will inspire you to take out your own macro lens, literally and figuratively. Get closer to your own life. The rewards will astonish you.

—Michael Clinton

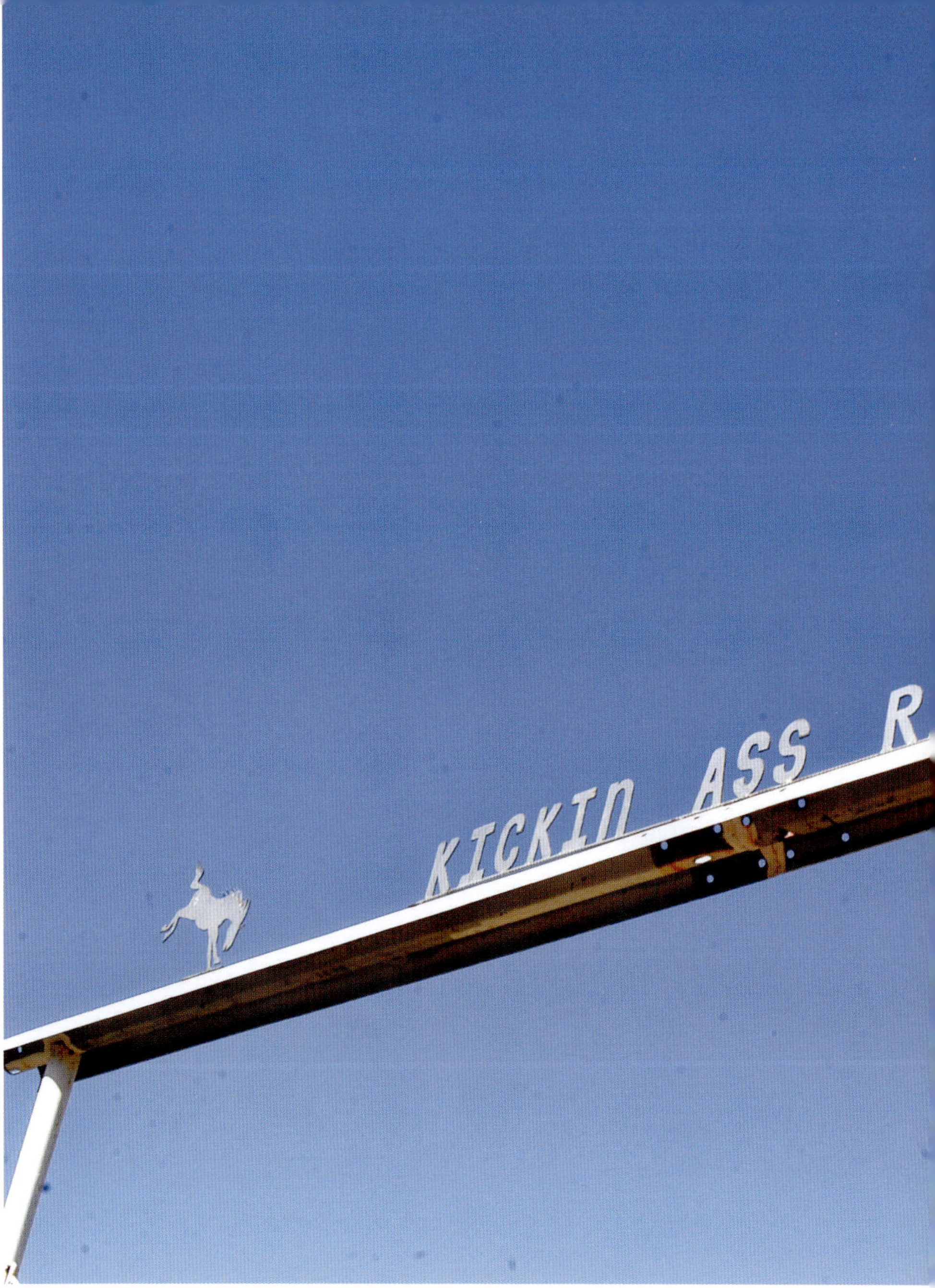
KICKIN ASS R

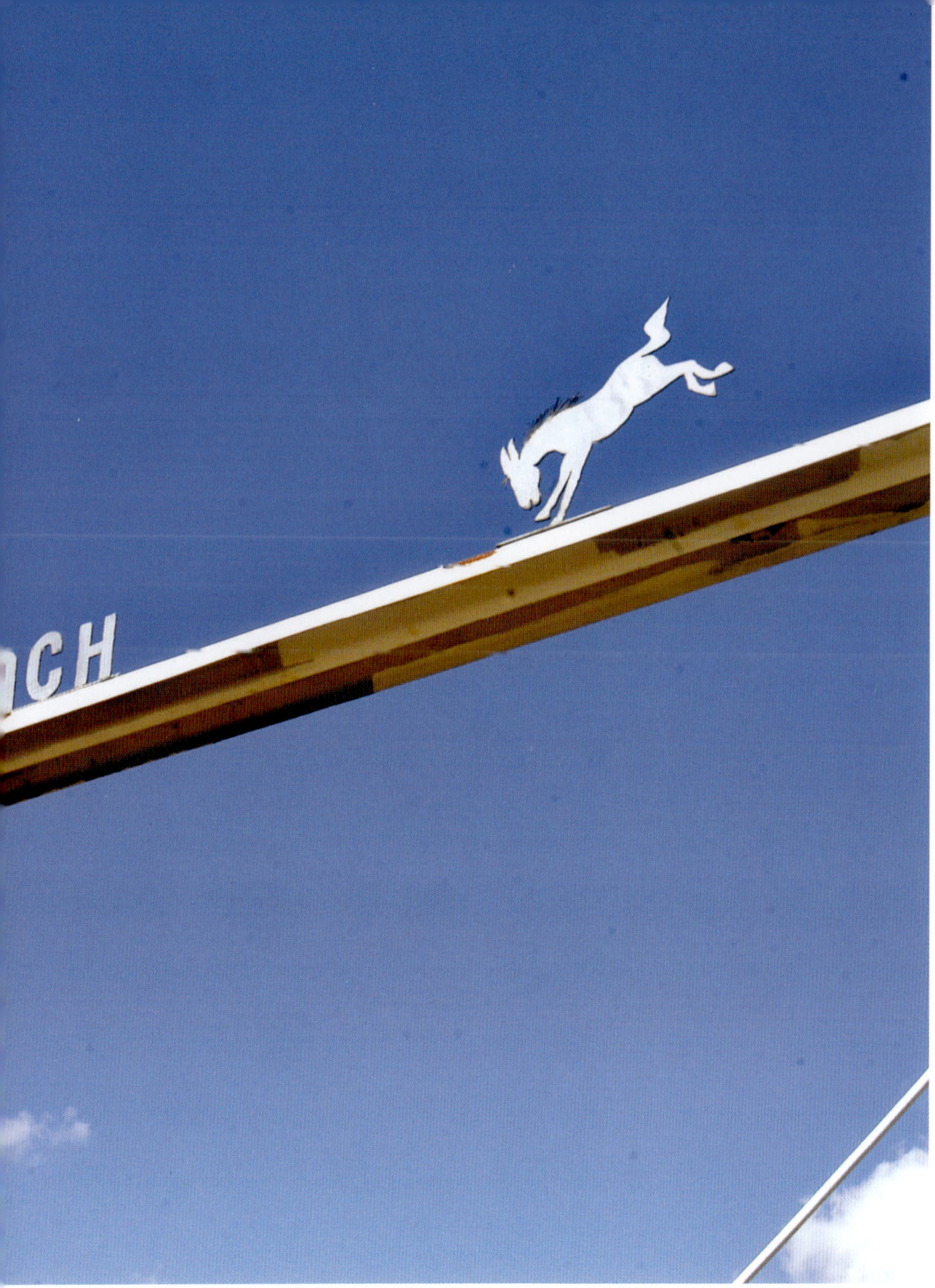
CH

GOING

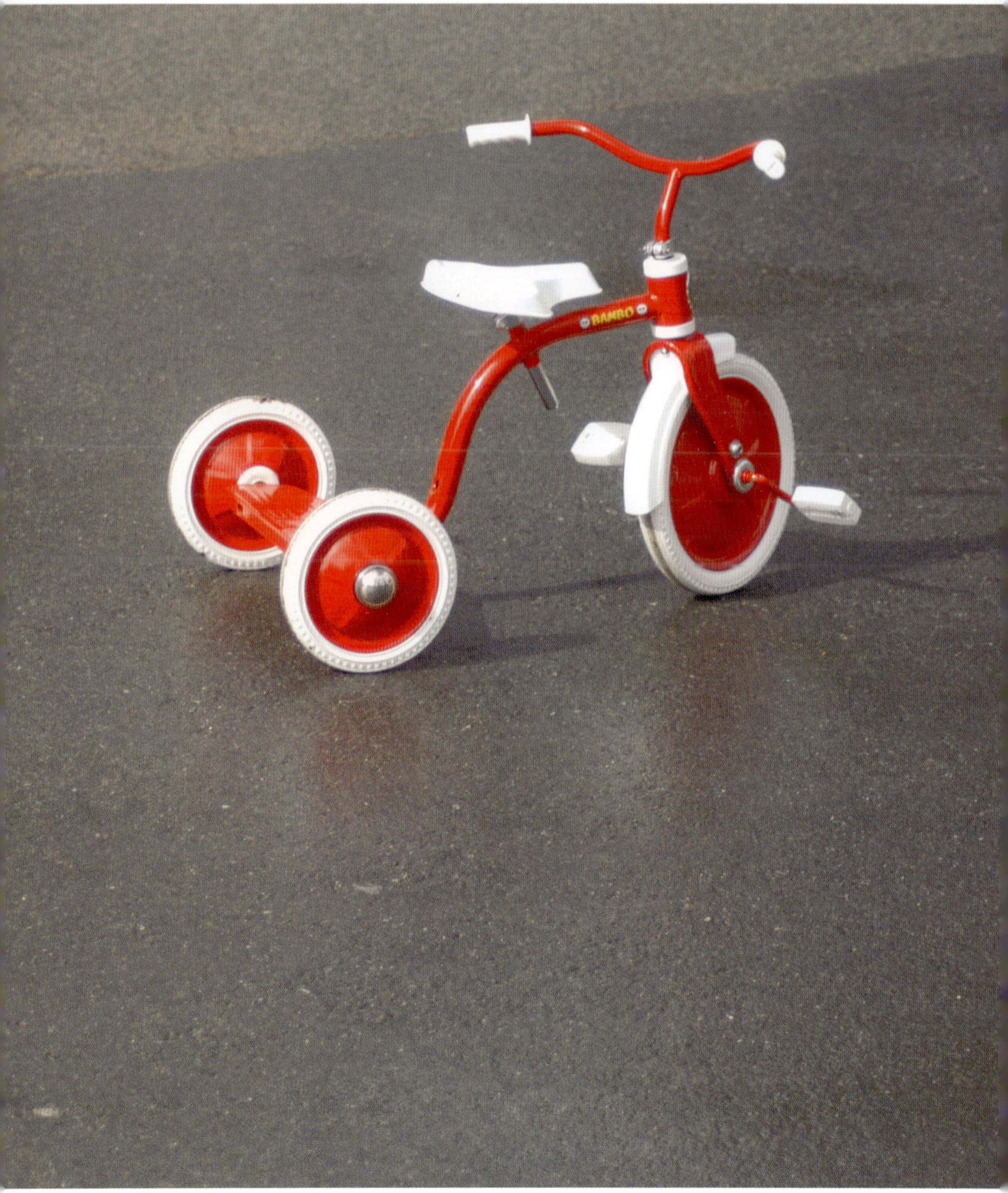
BAMBO

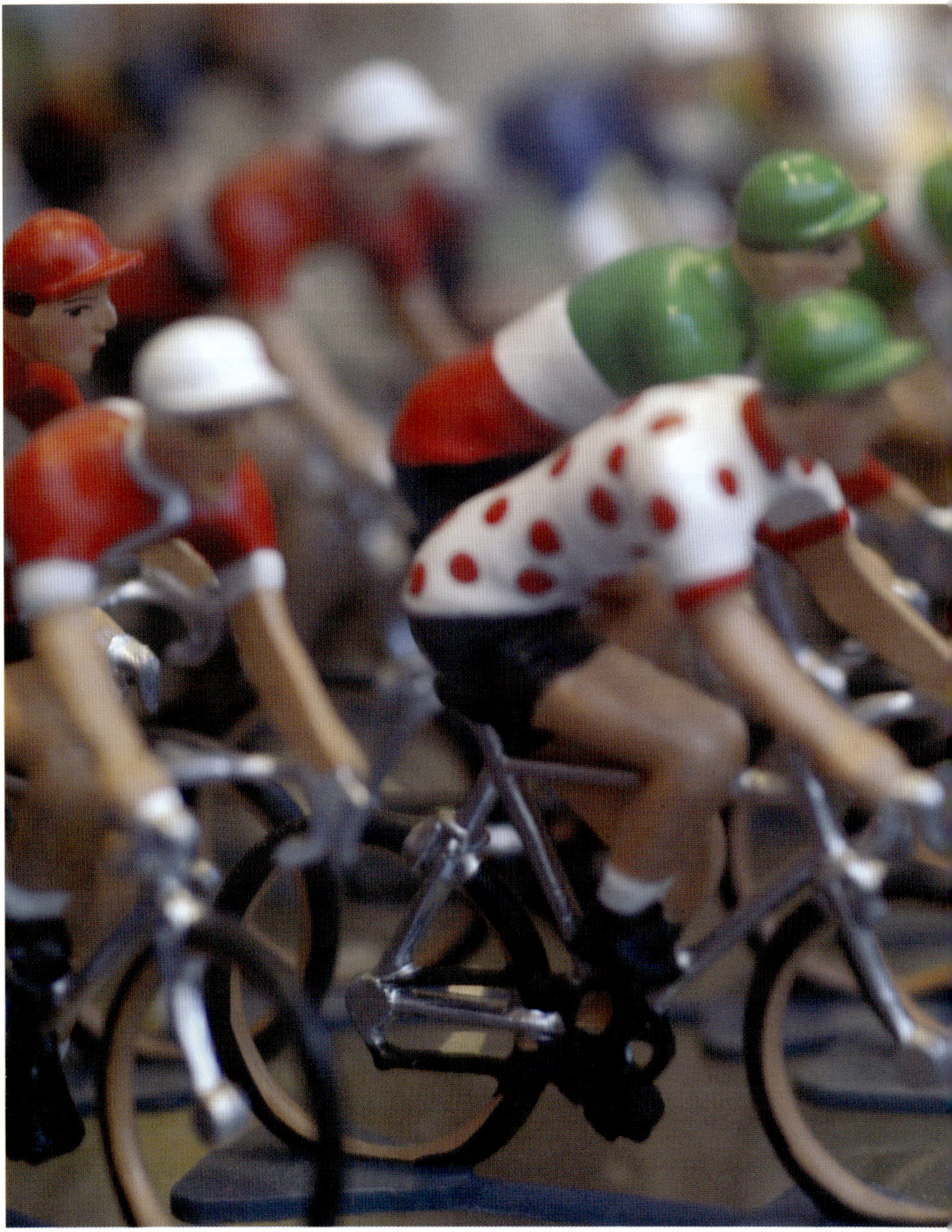

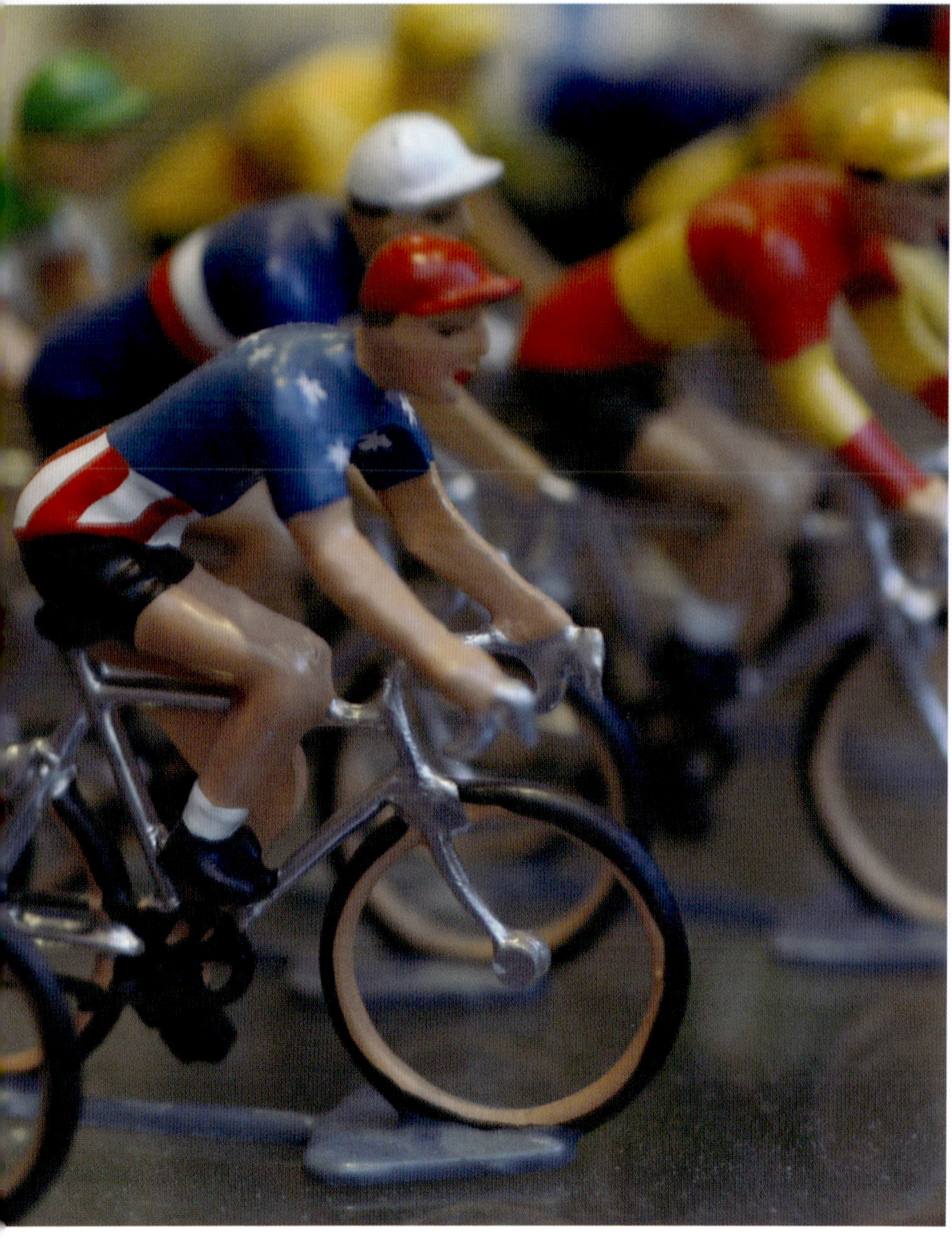

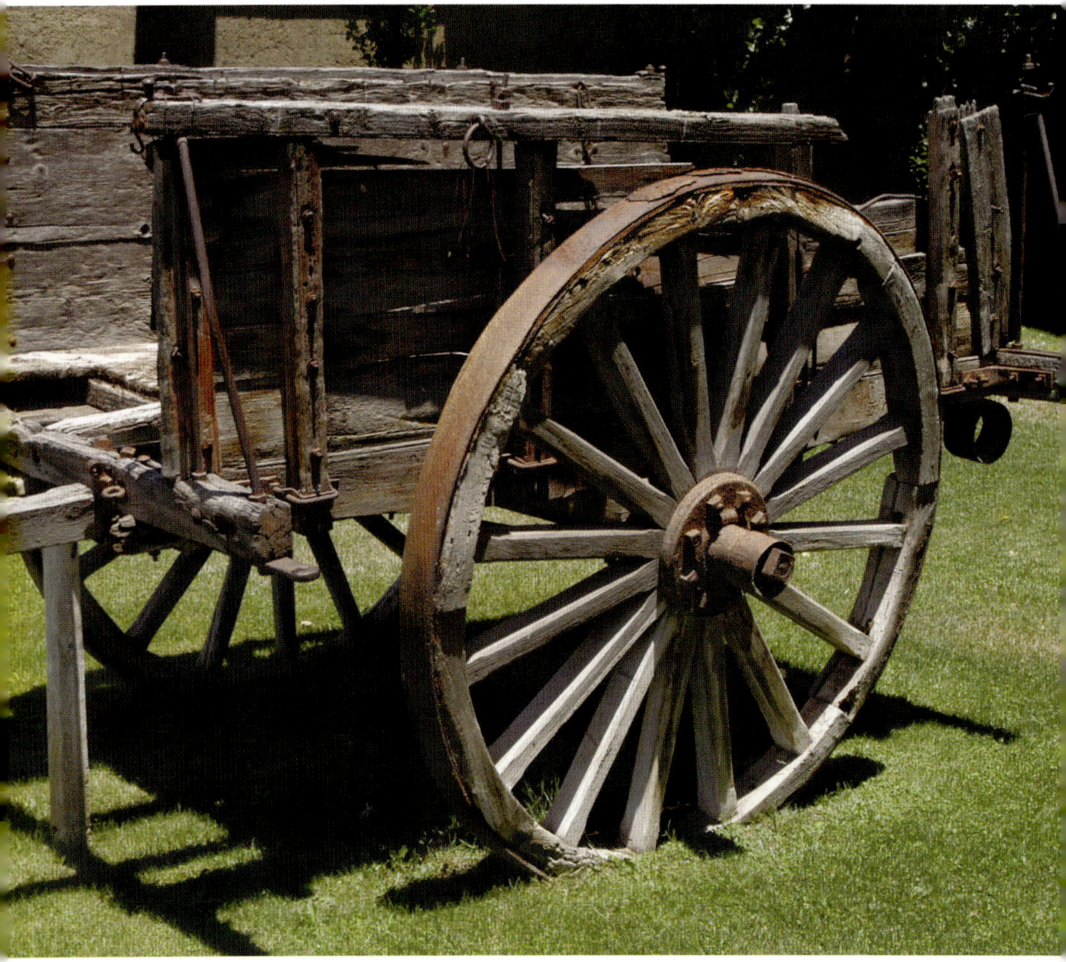

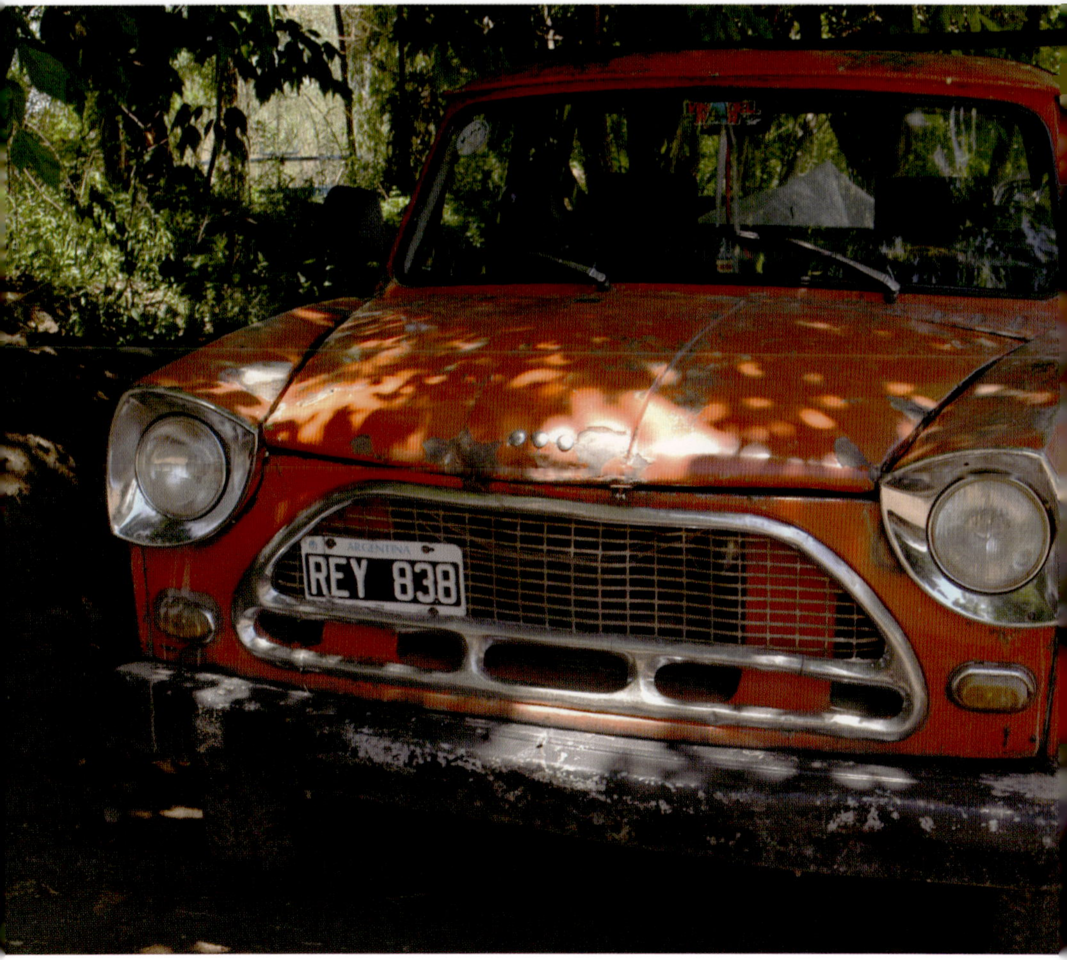
ARGENTINA
REY 838

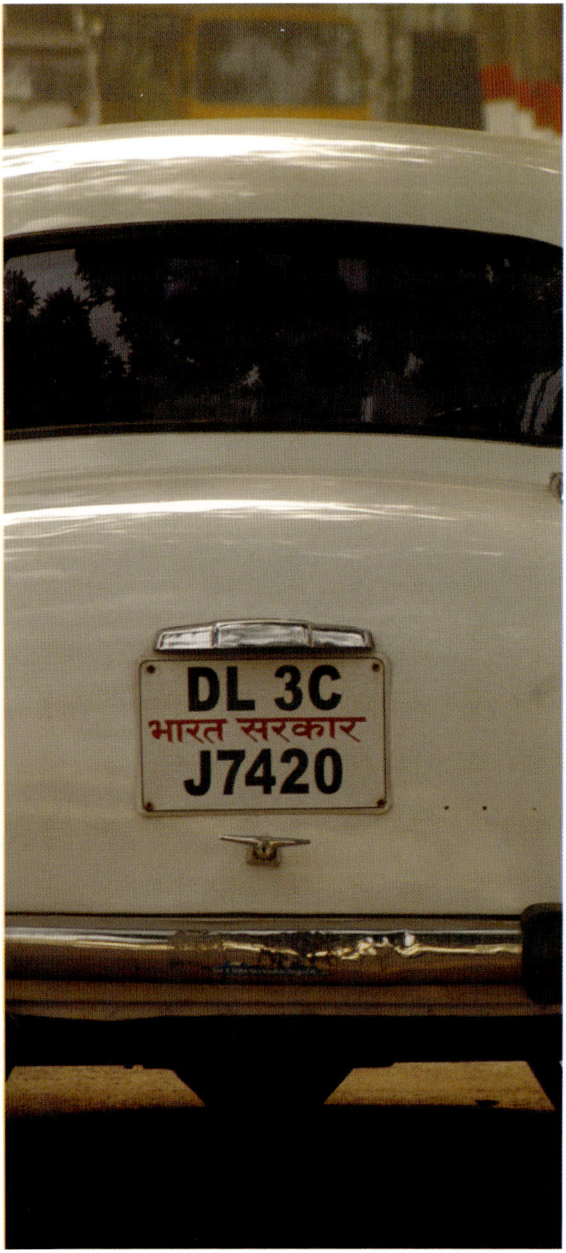
DL 3C
भारत सरकार
J7420

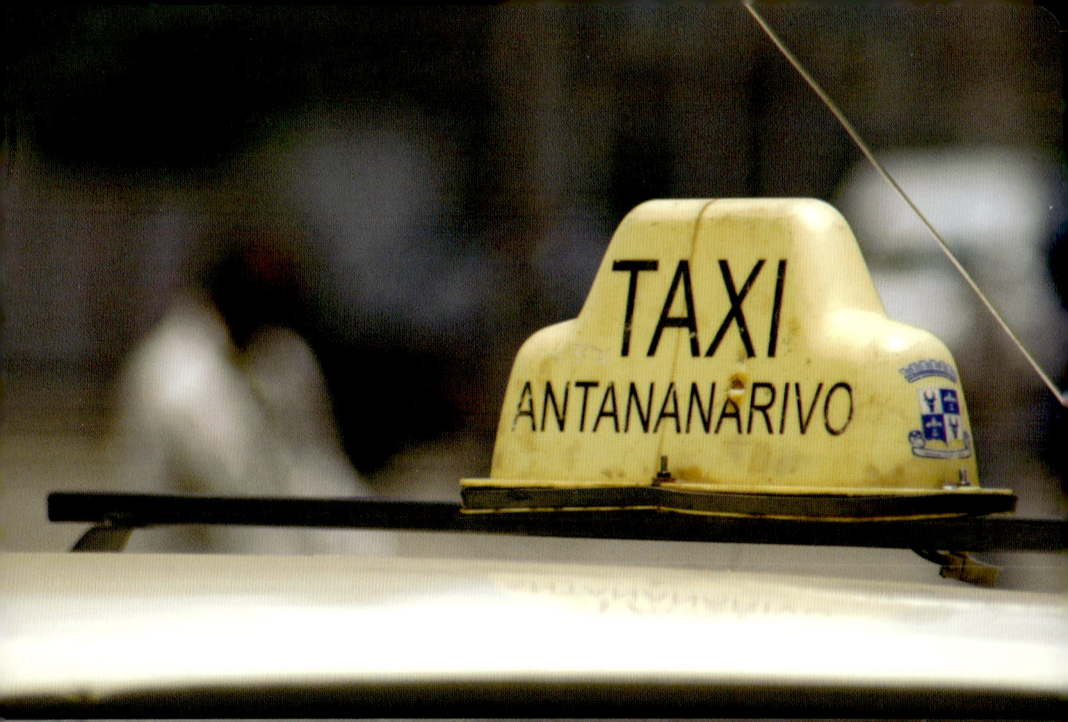
TAXI
ANTANANARIVO

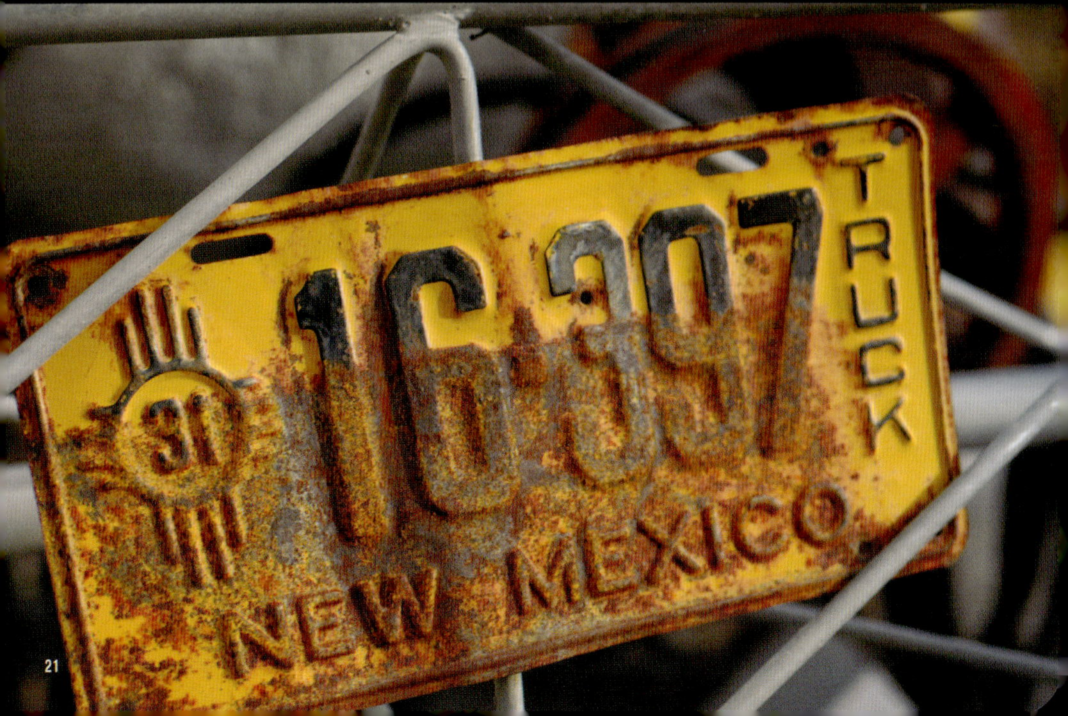
31
16397
TRUCK
NEW MEXICO

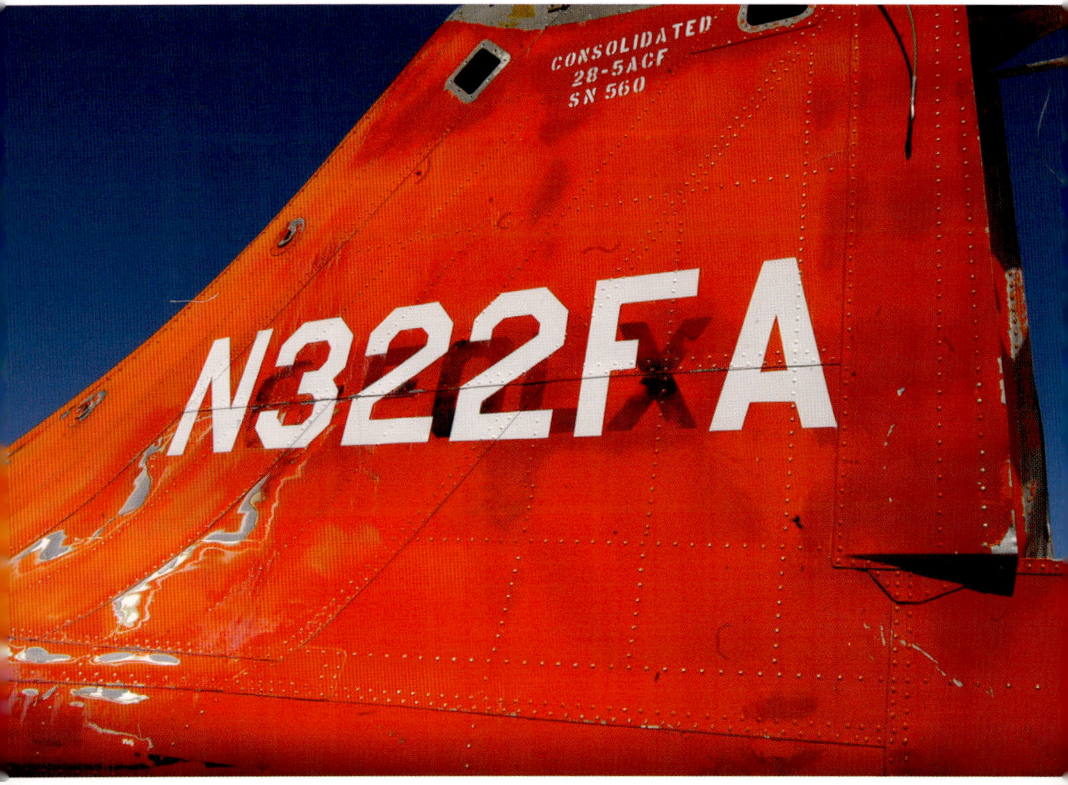
CONSOLIDATED
28-5ACF
SN 560
N322FA

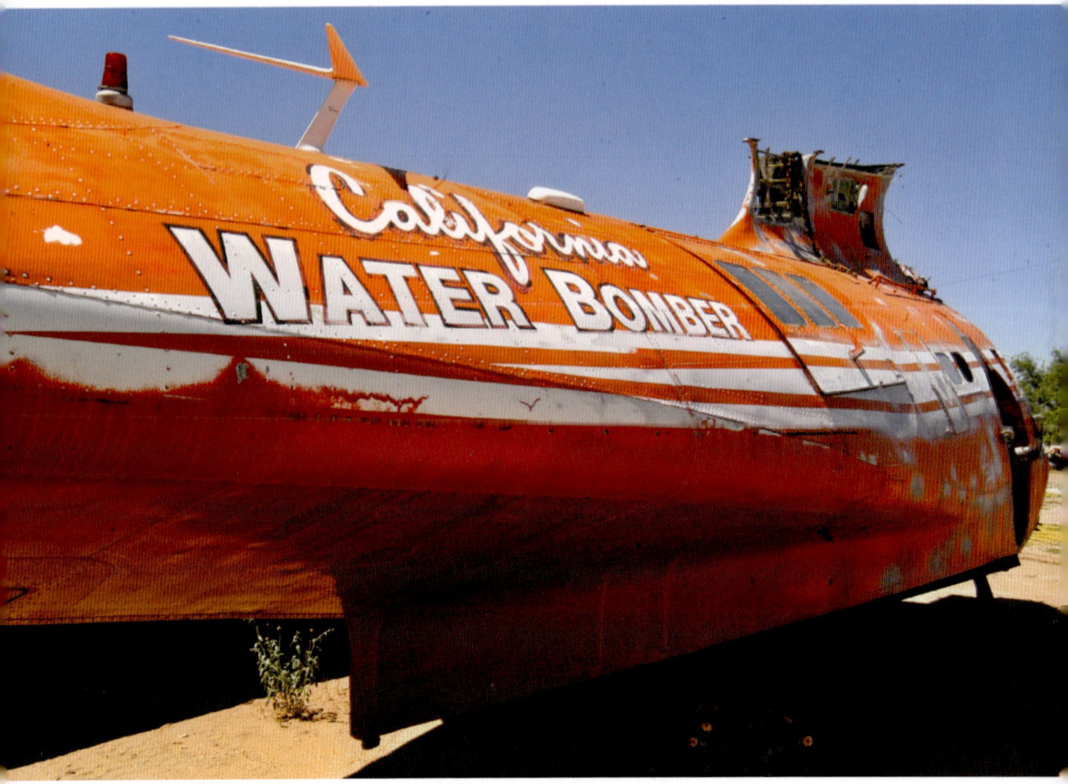
California
WATER BOMBER

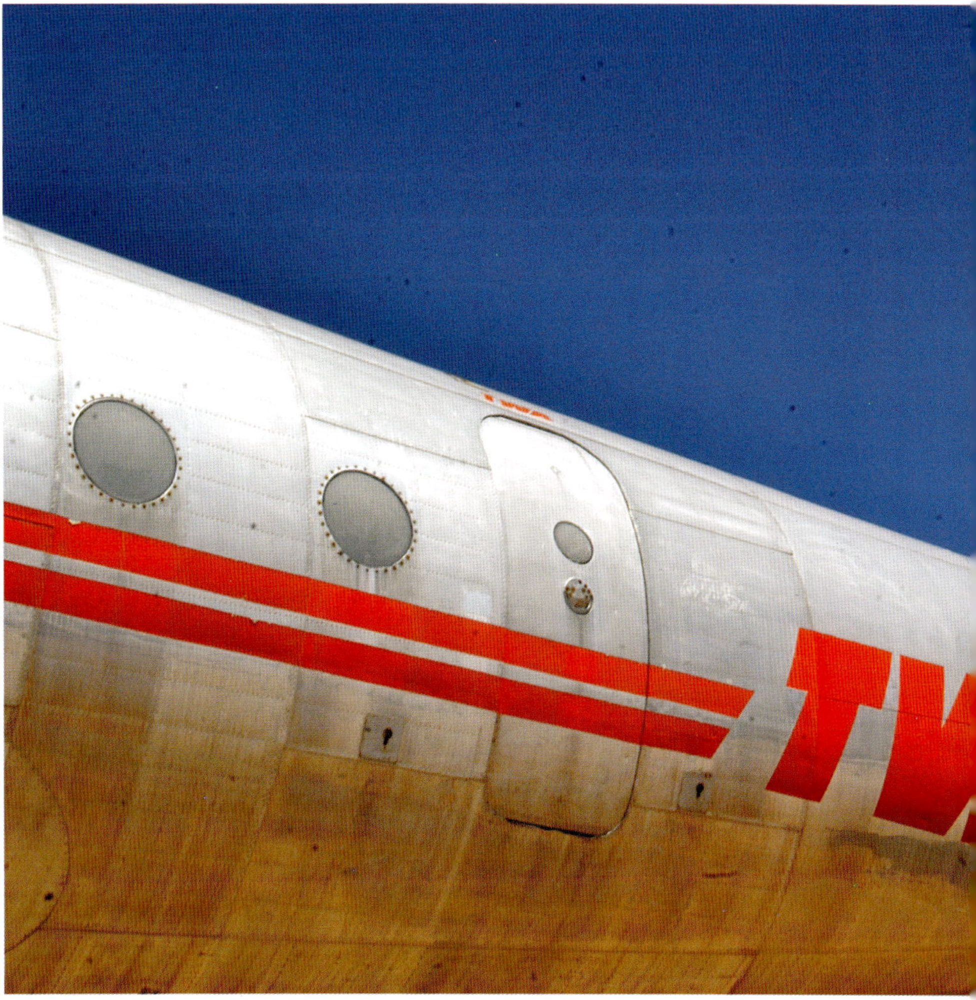
TWA

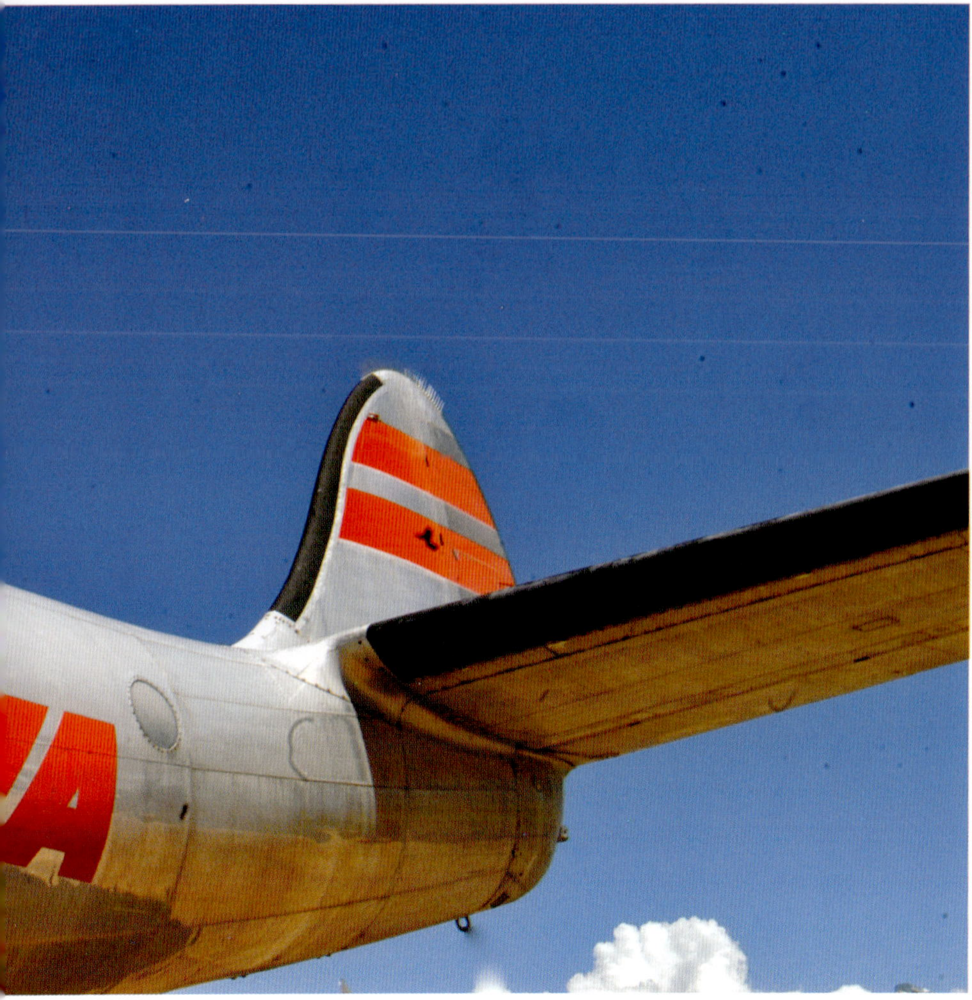

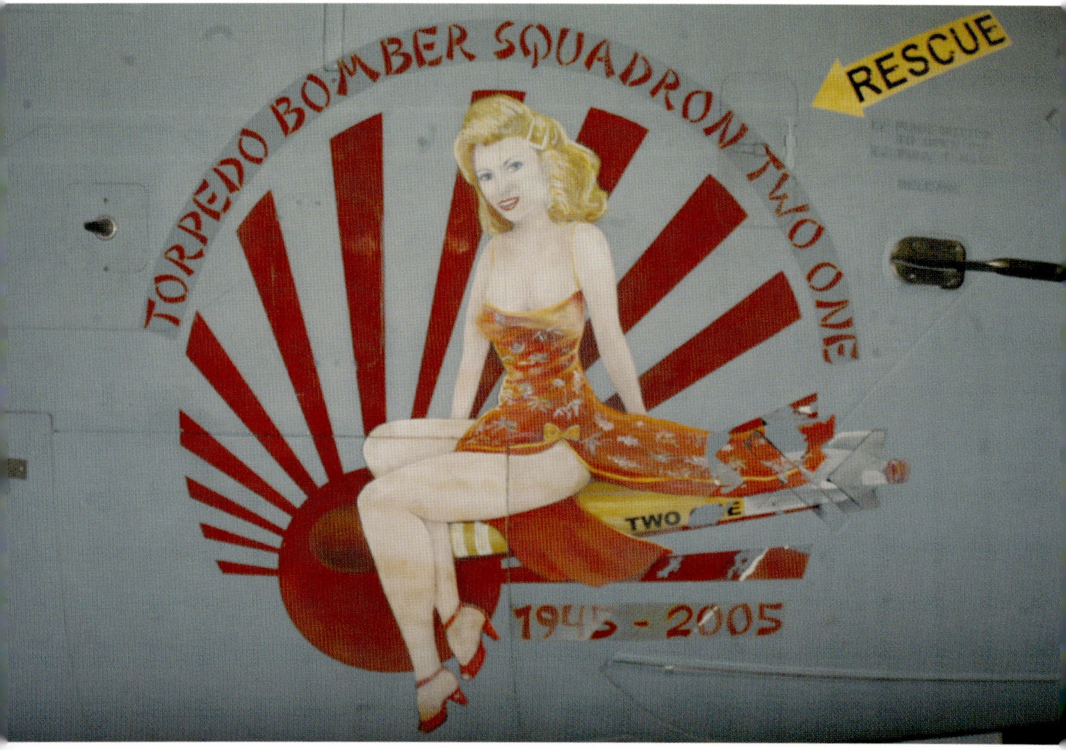
TORPEDO BOMBER SQUADRON TWO ONE
RESCUE
1945 - 2005

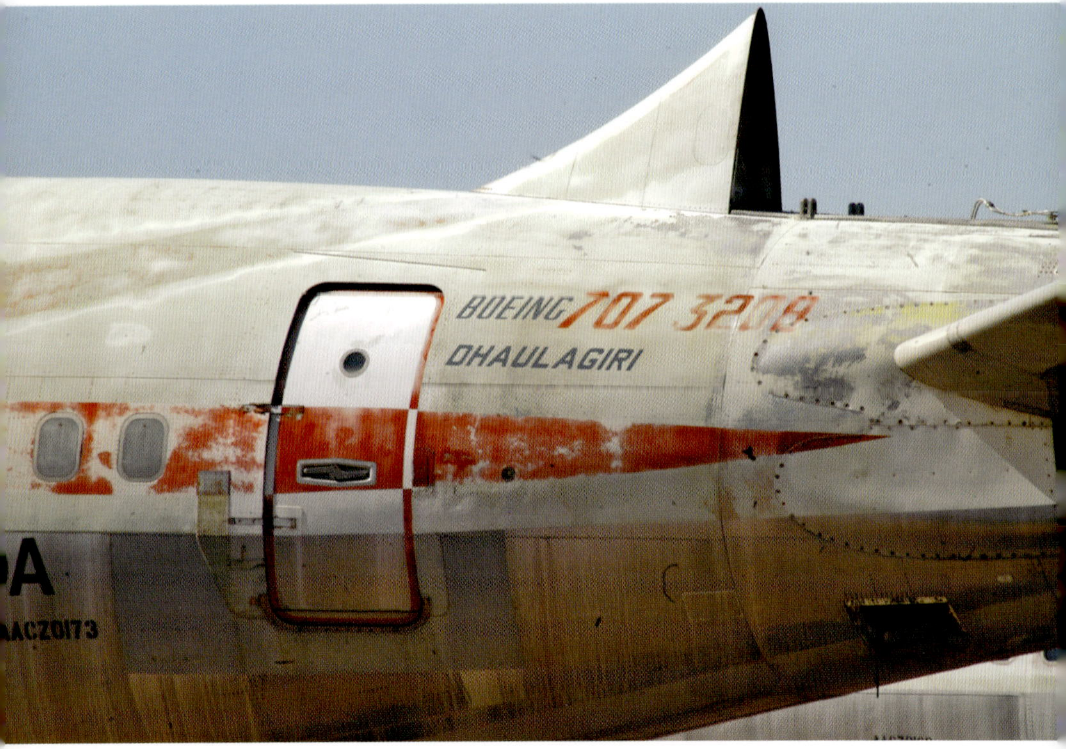
BOEING 707 320B
DHAULAGIRI

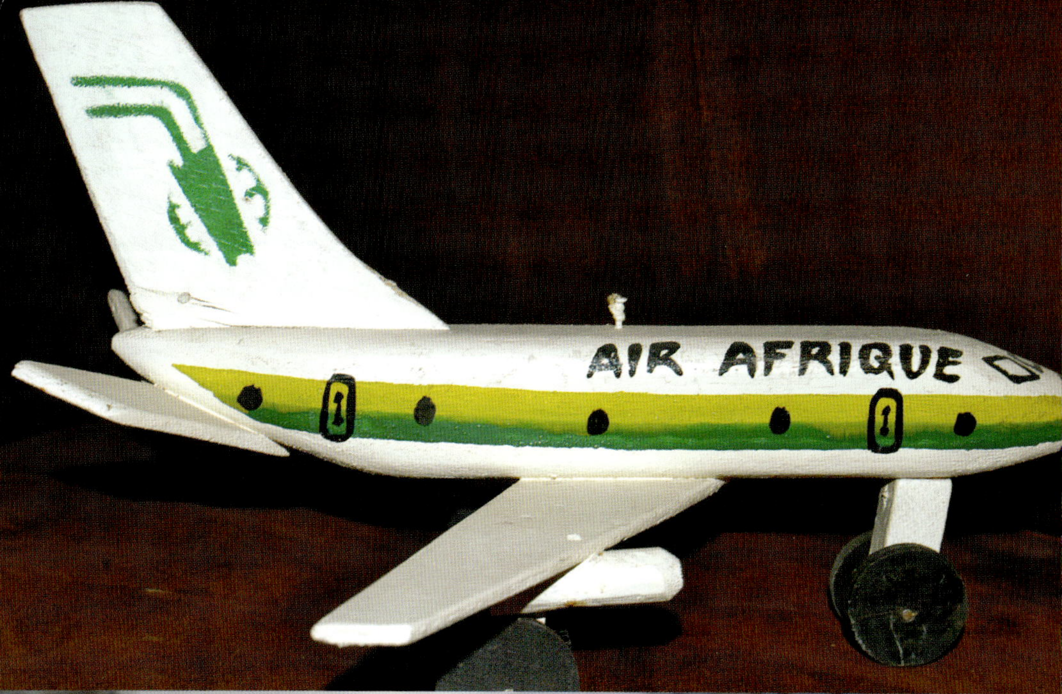
AIR AFRIQUE

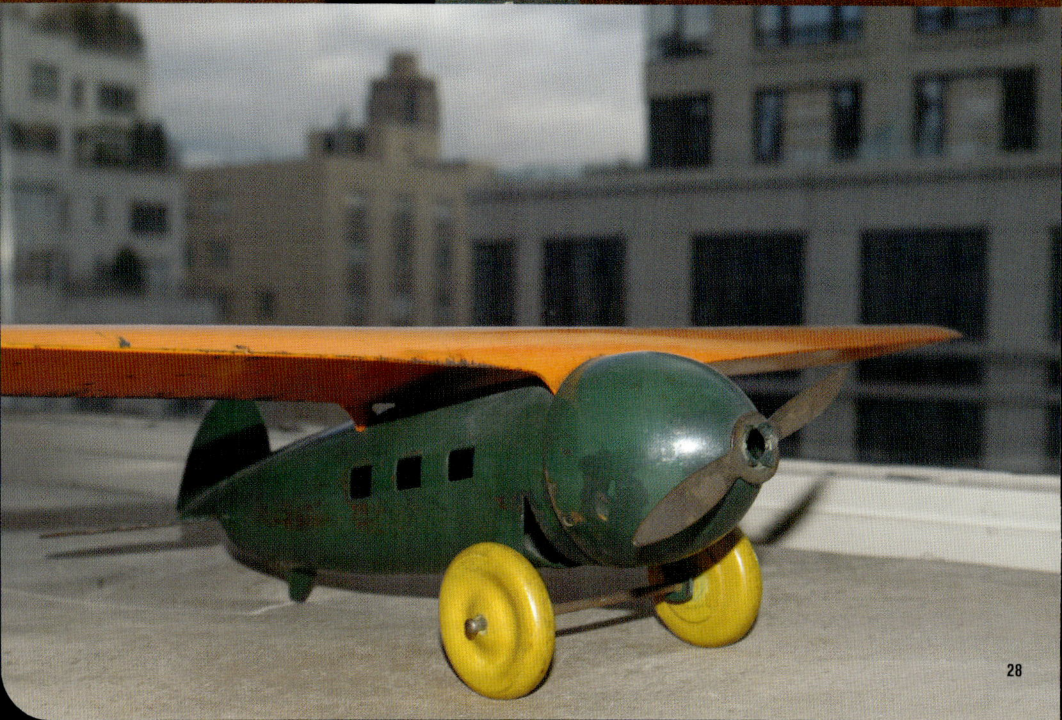

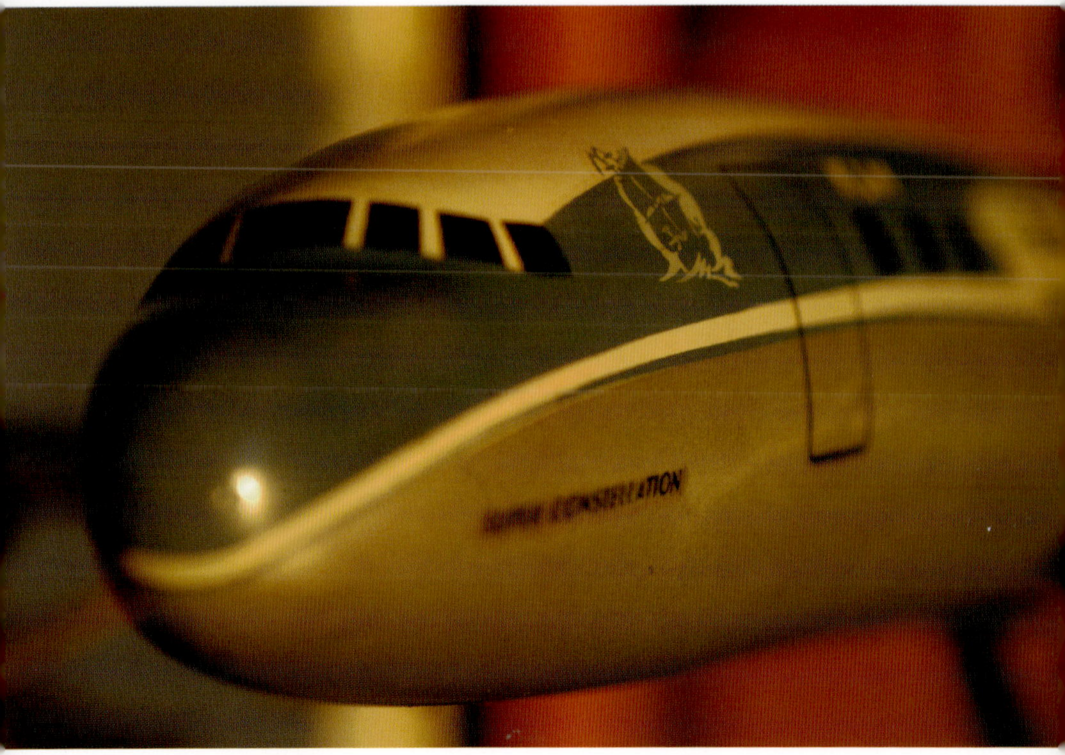

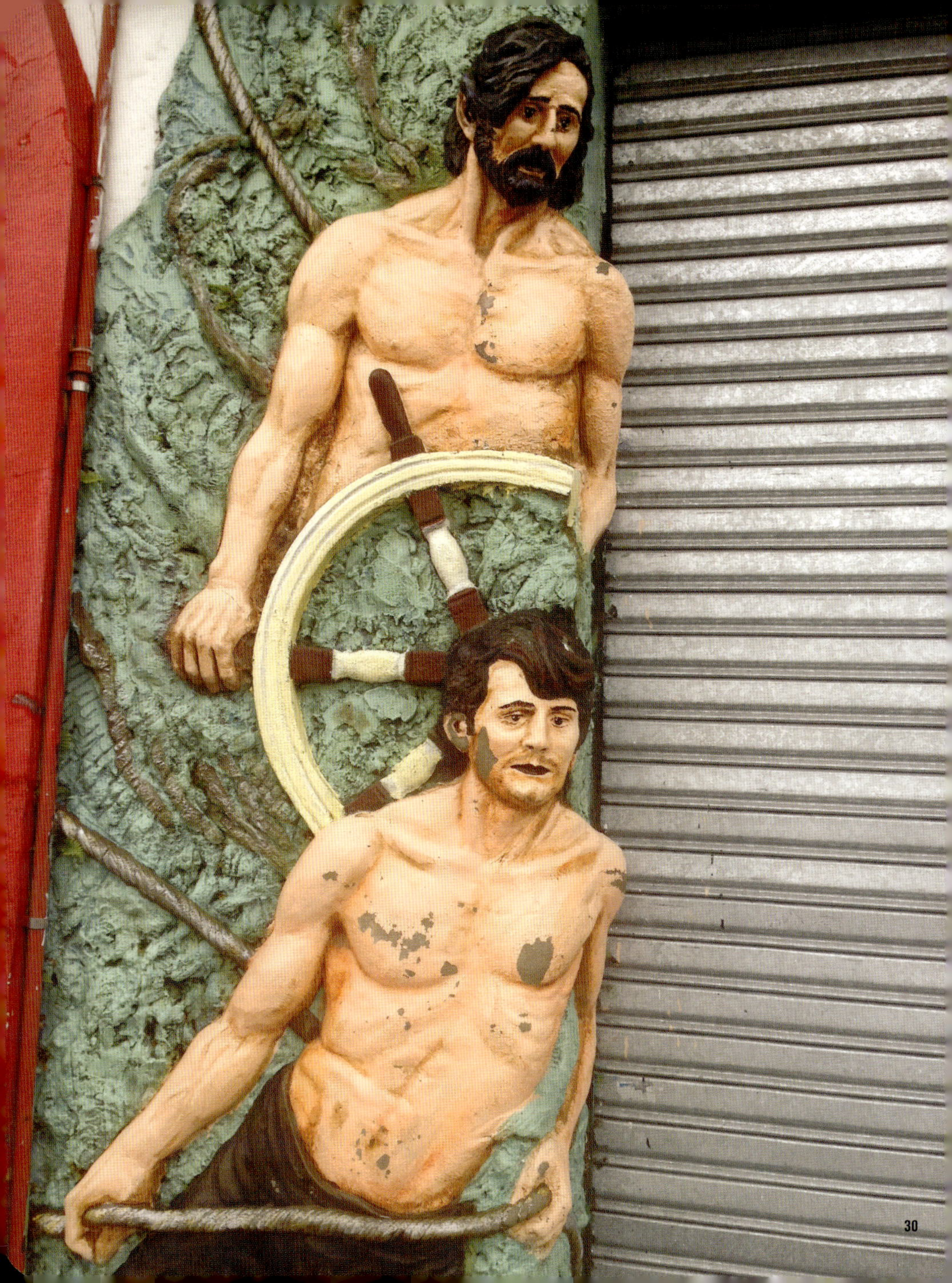

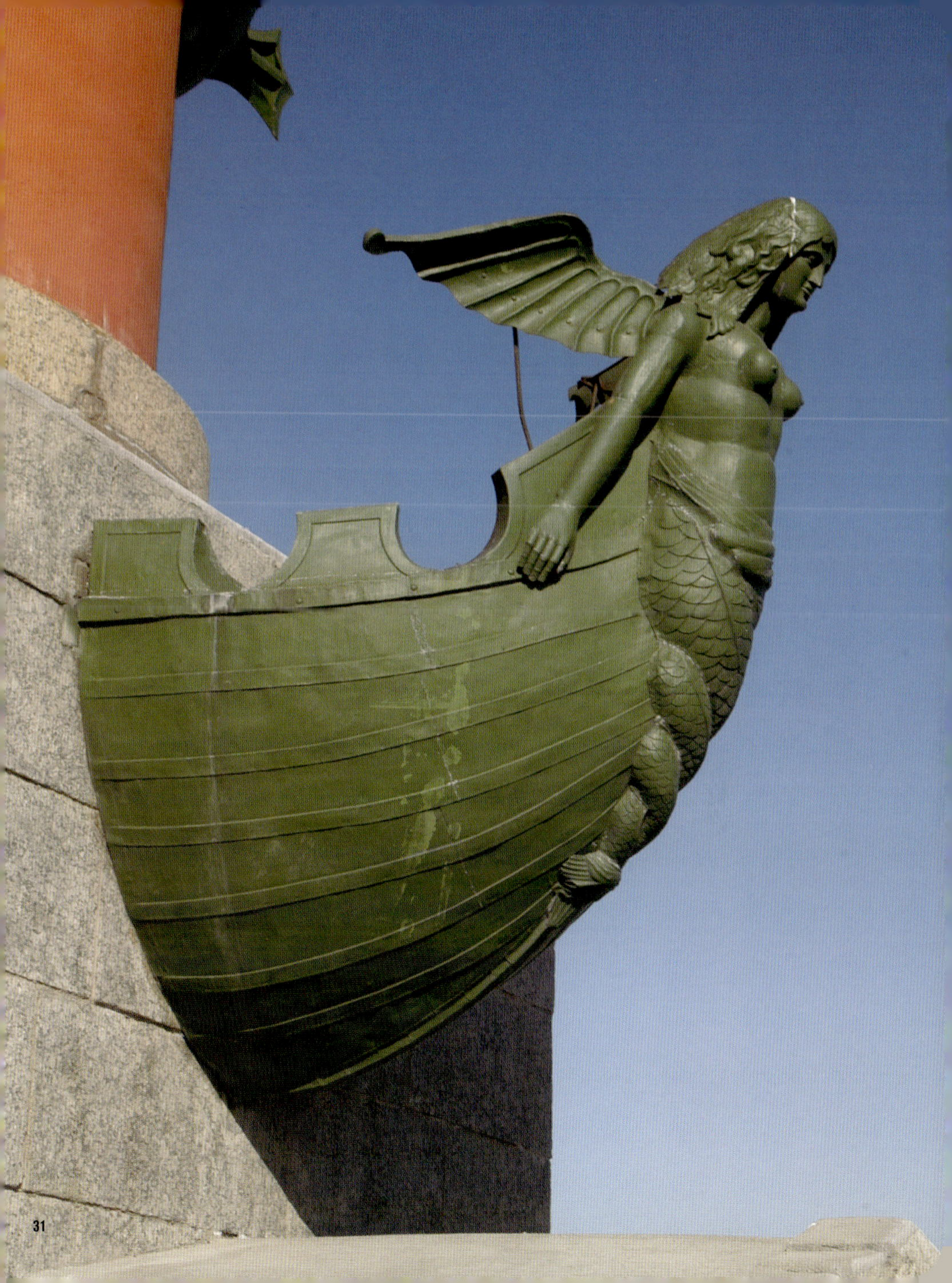

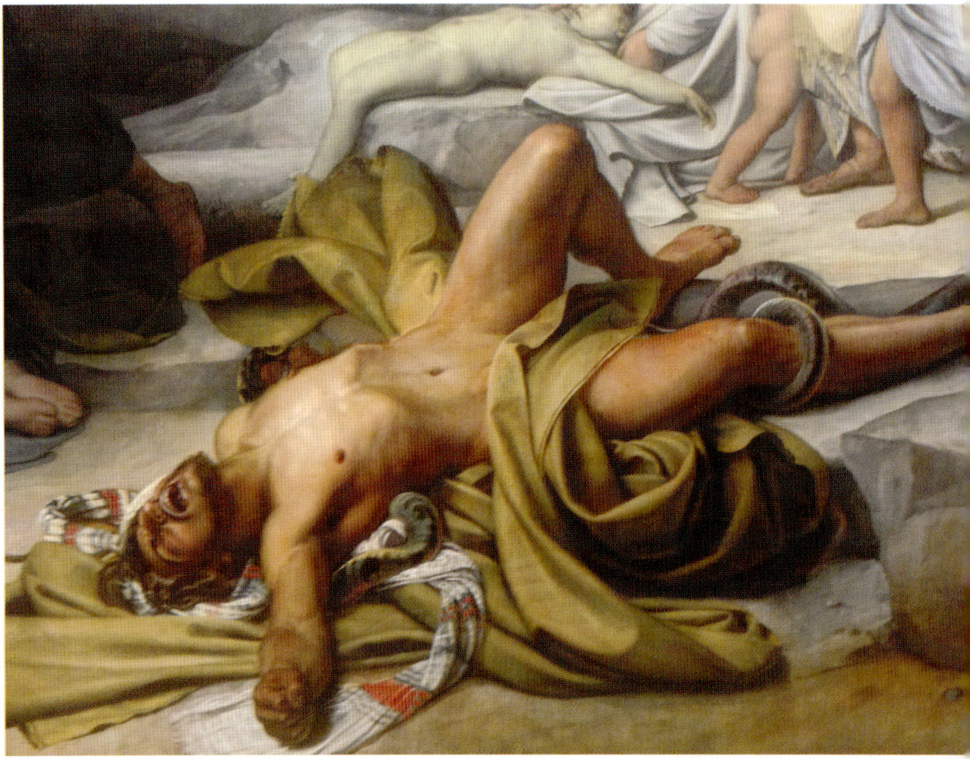

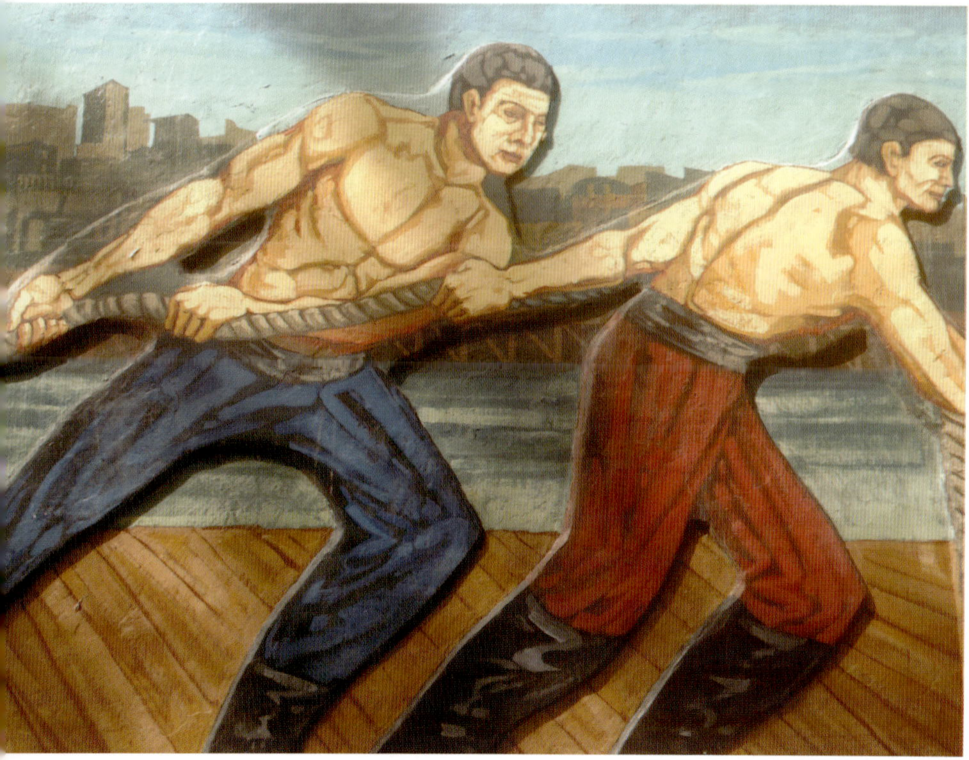

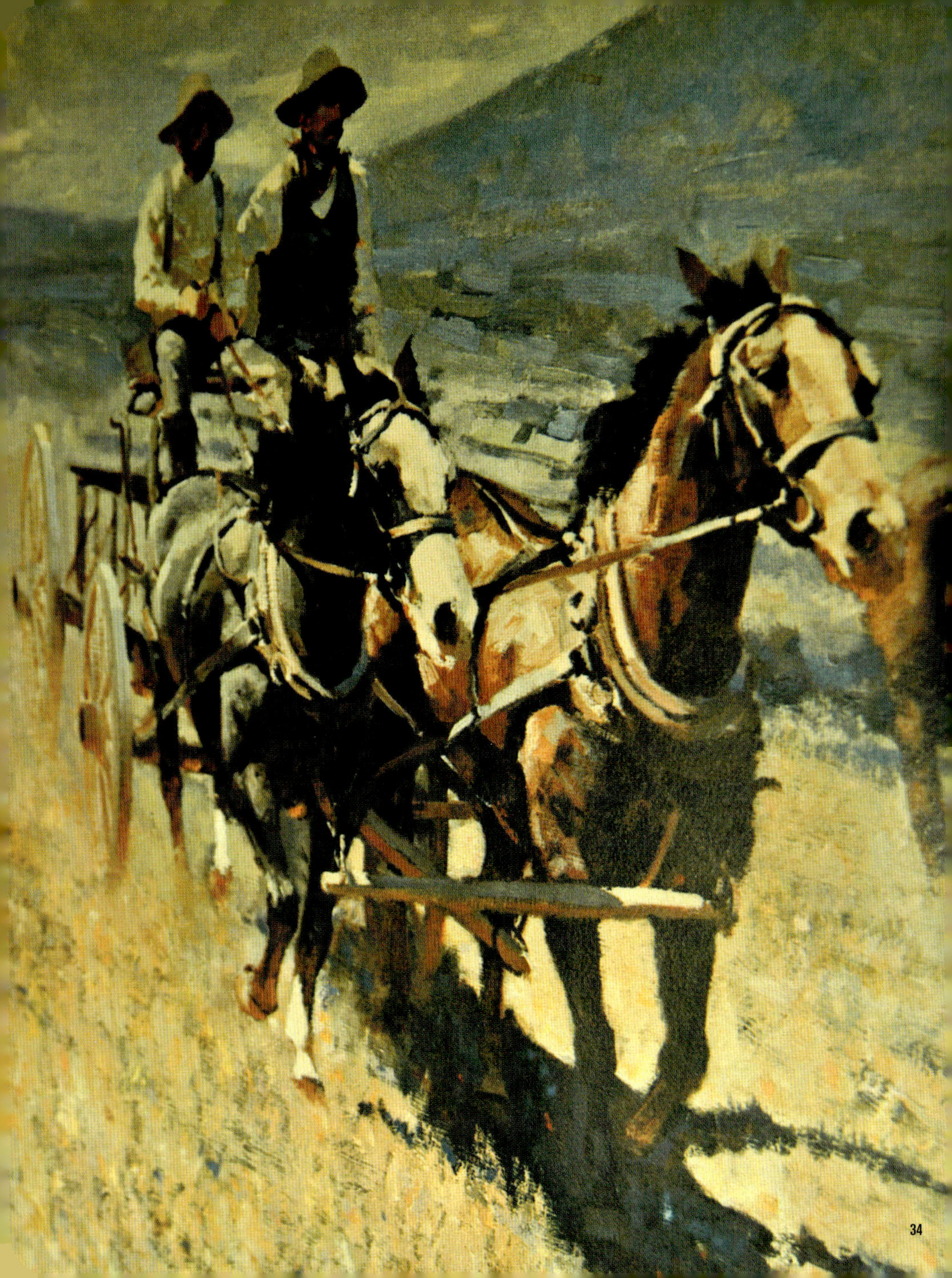

SHOWING

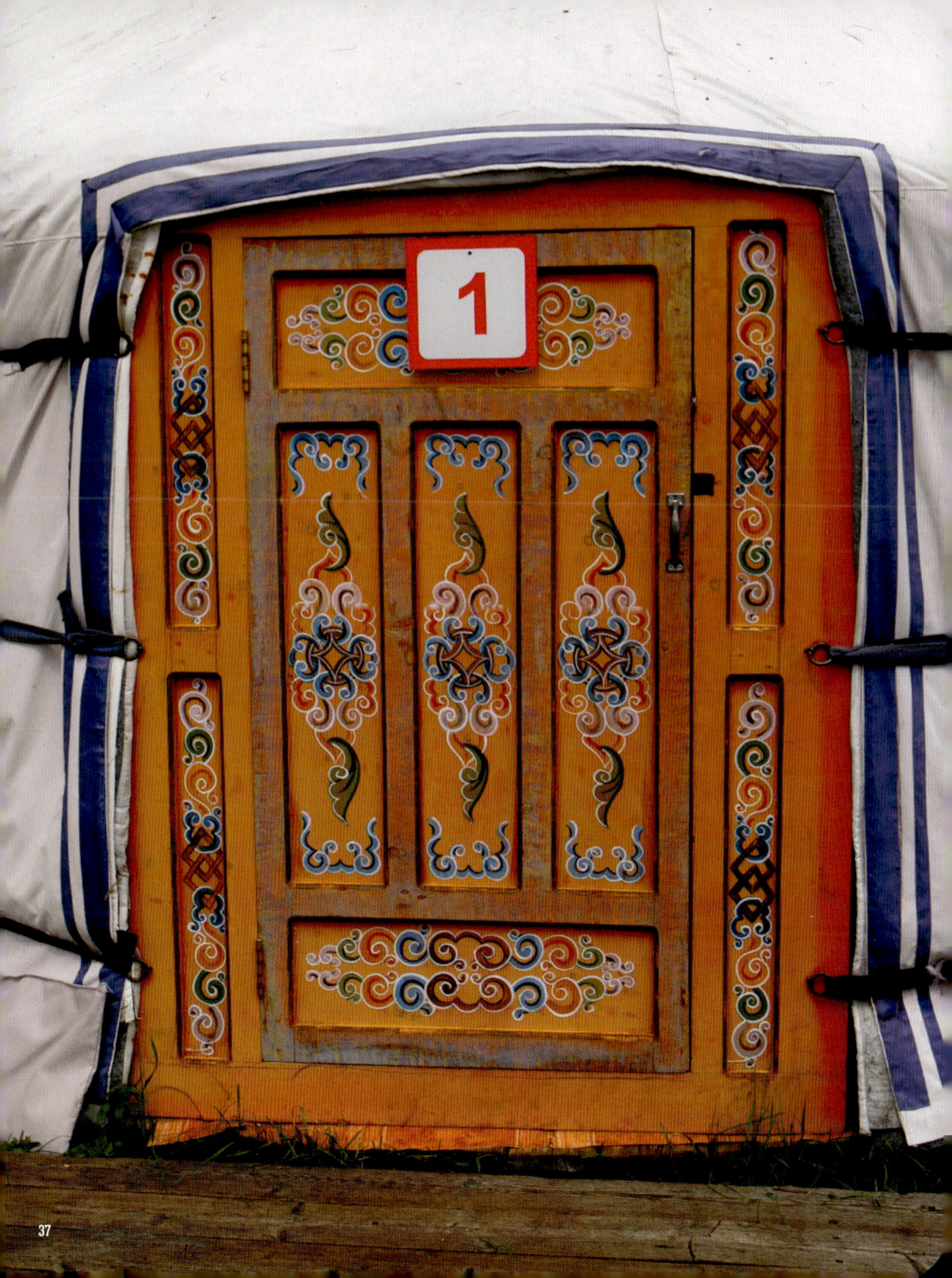
1

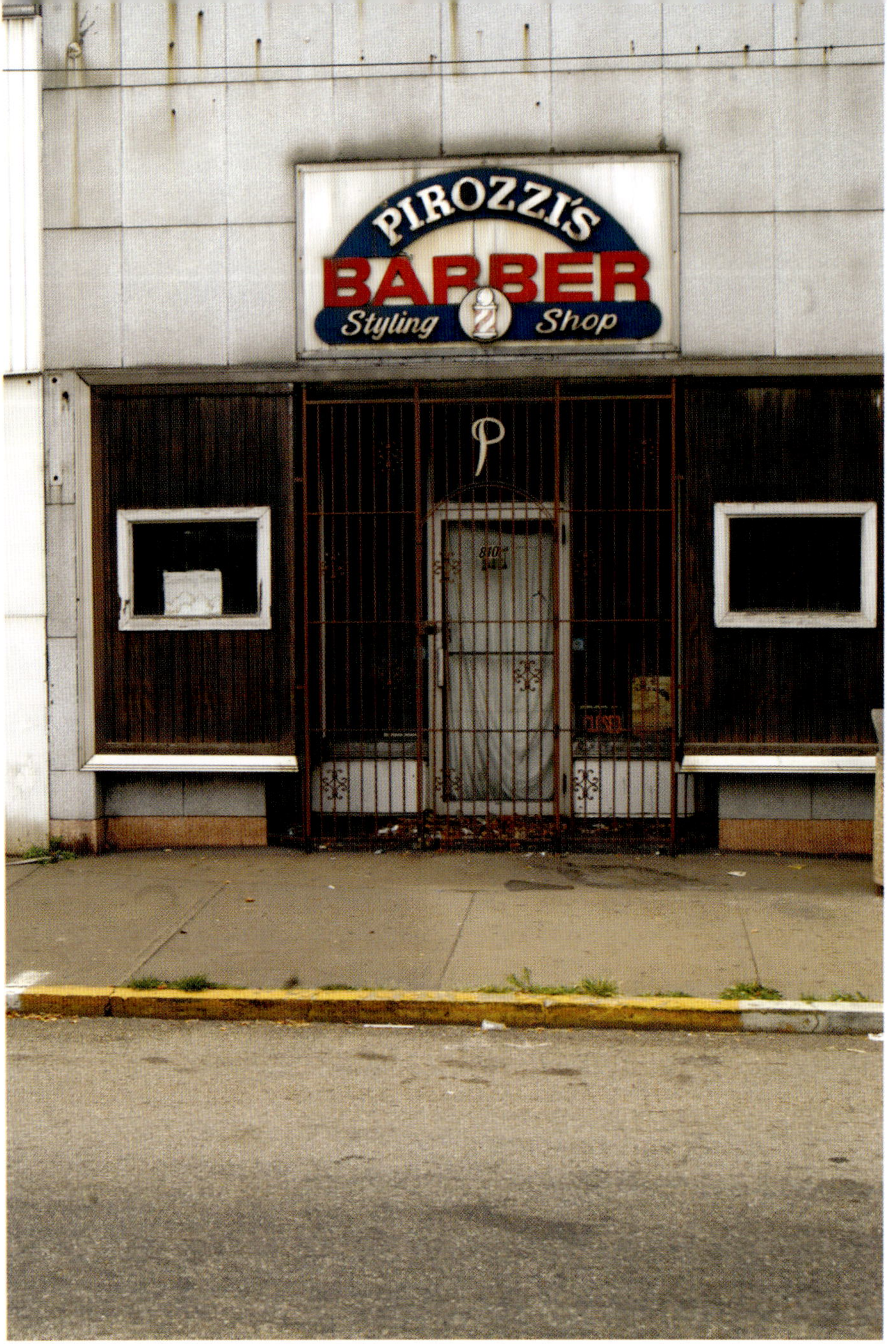
PIROZZI'S
BARBER
Styling
Shop
P
CLOSED

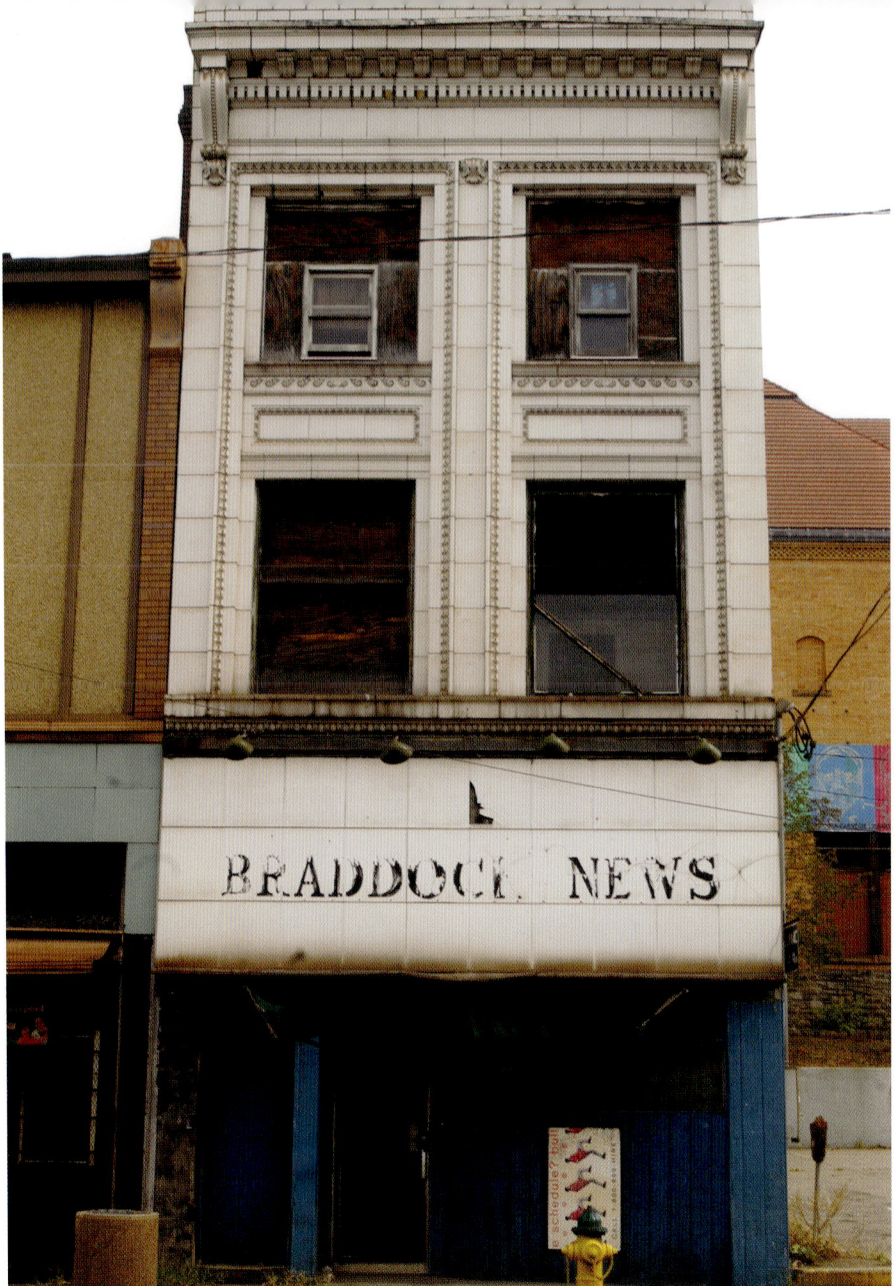
BRADDOC NEWS

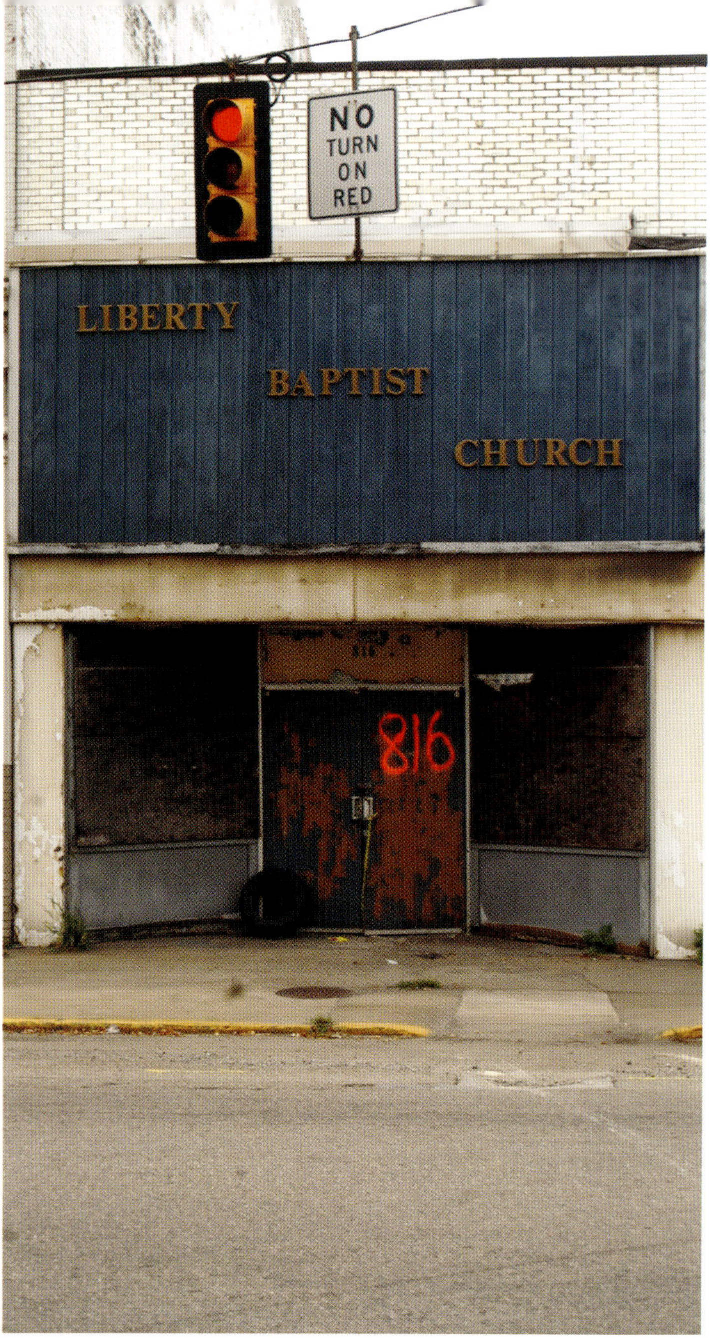
NO TURN ON RED
LIBERTY BAPTIST CHURCH
816

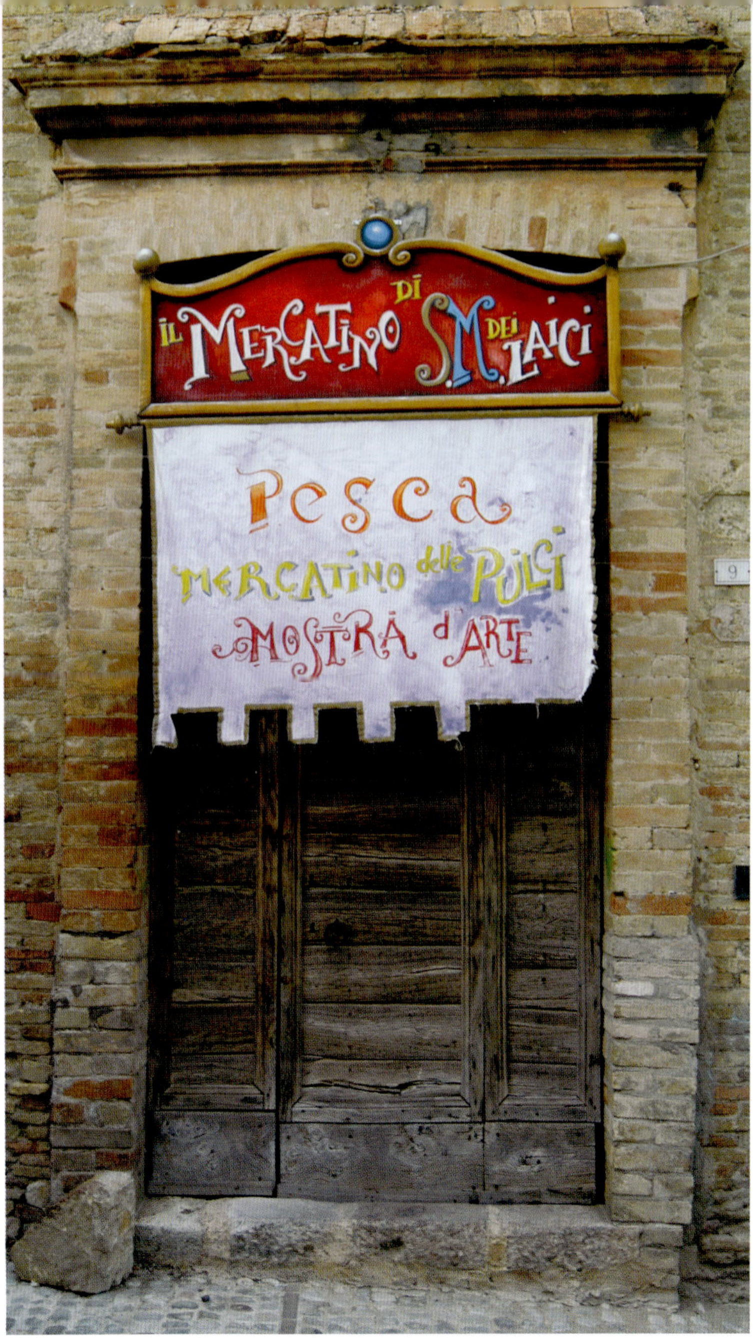
IL MERCATINO DI S.M. DEI LAICI
Pesca
MERCATINO delle PULCI
MOSTRA d'ARTE
9

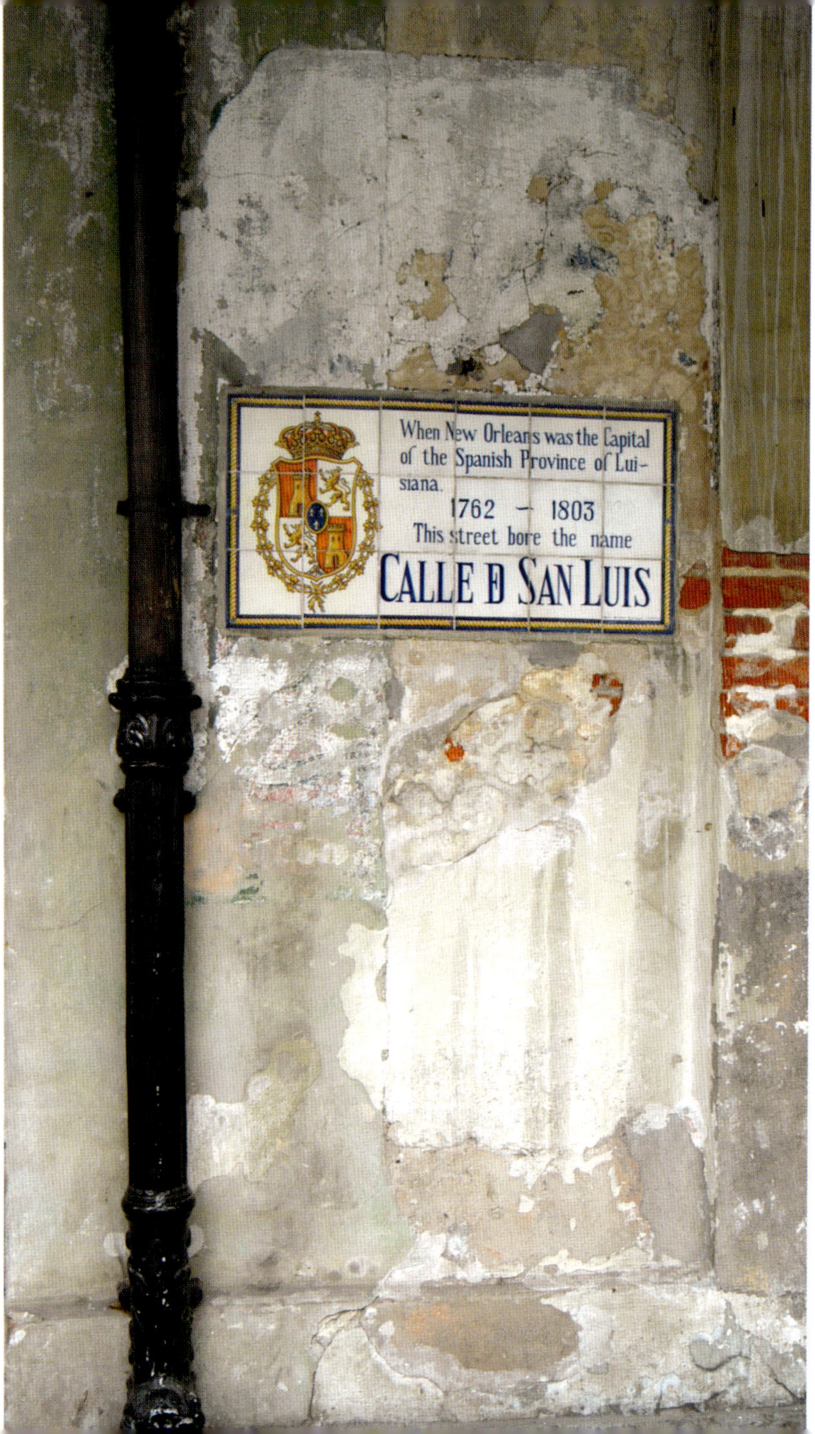
When New Orleans was the Capital
of the Spanish Province of Lui-
siana.
1762 – 1803
This street bore the name
CALLE D SAN LUIS

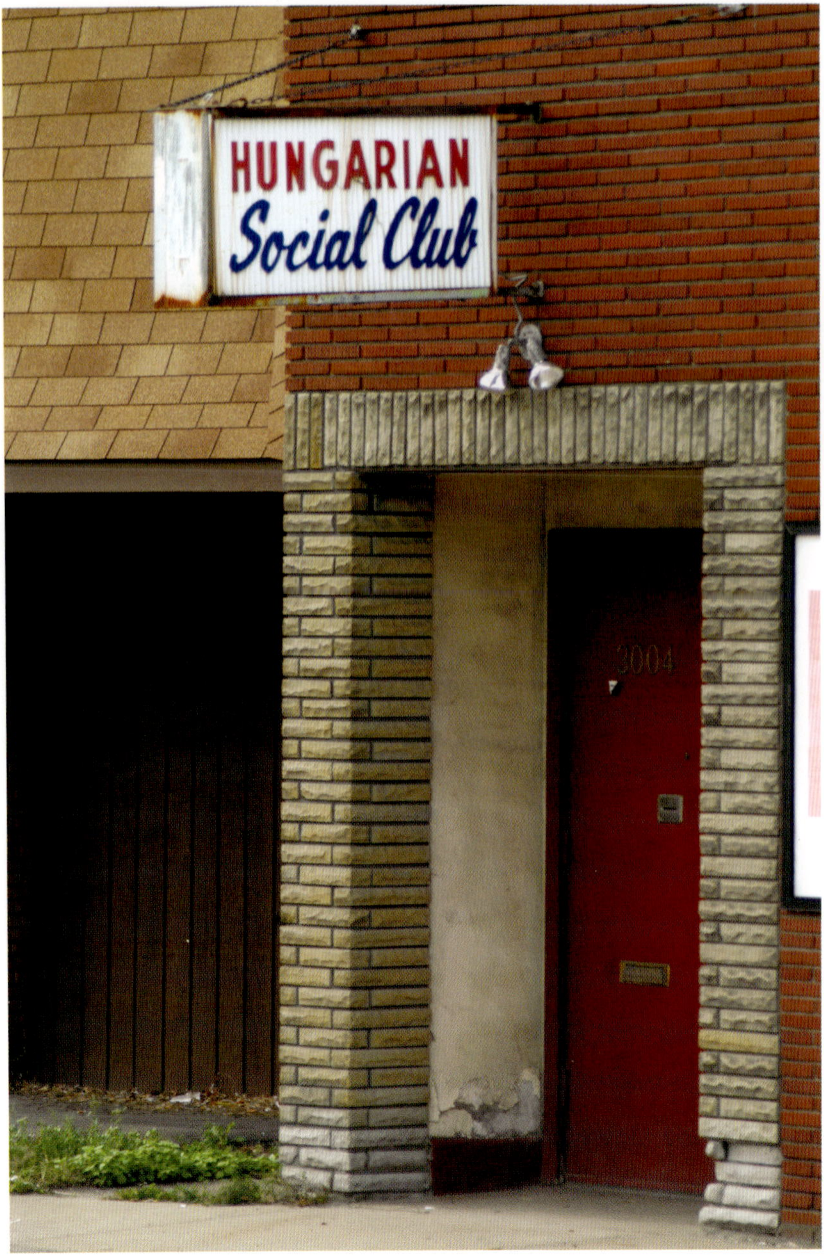
HUNGARIAN
Social Club
3004

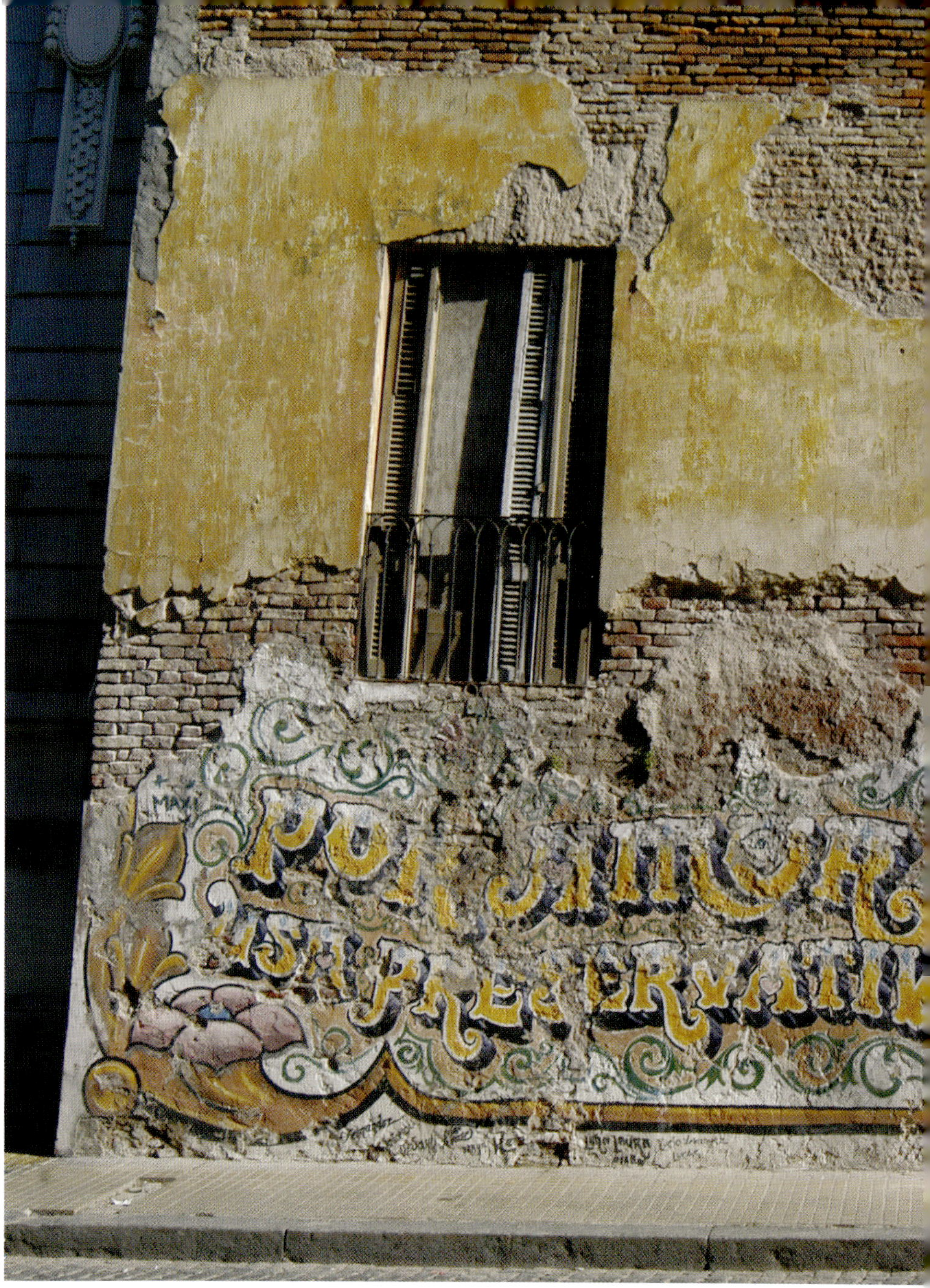
MAXI

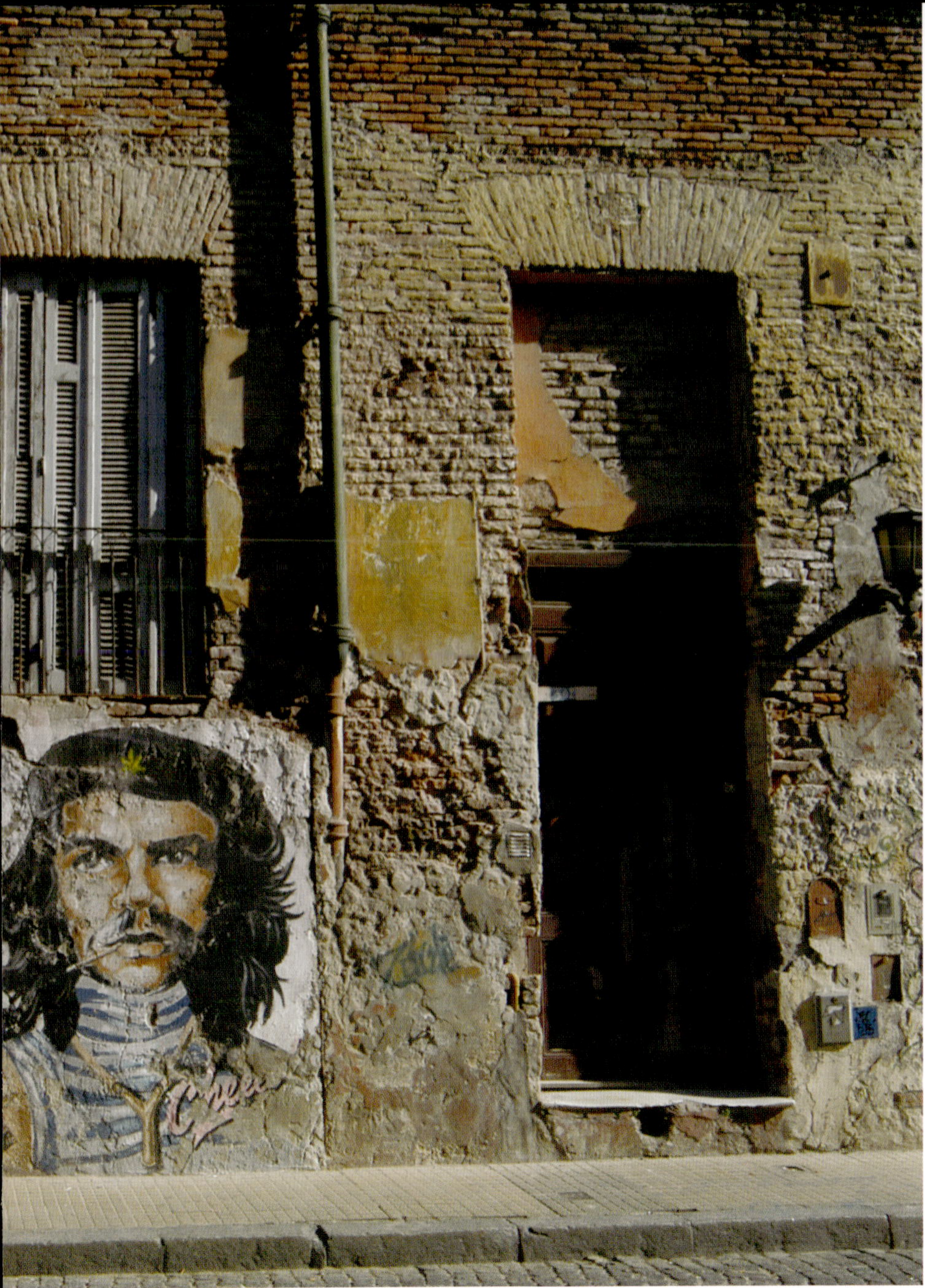

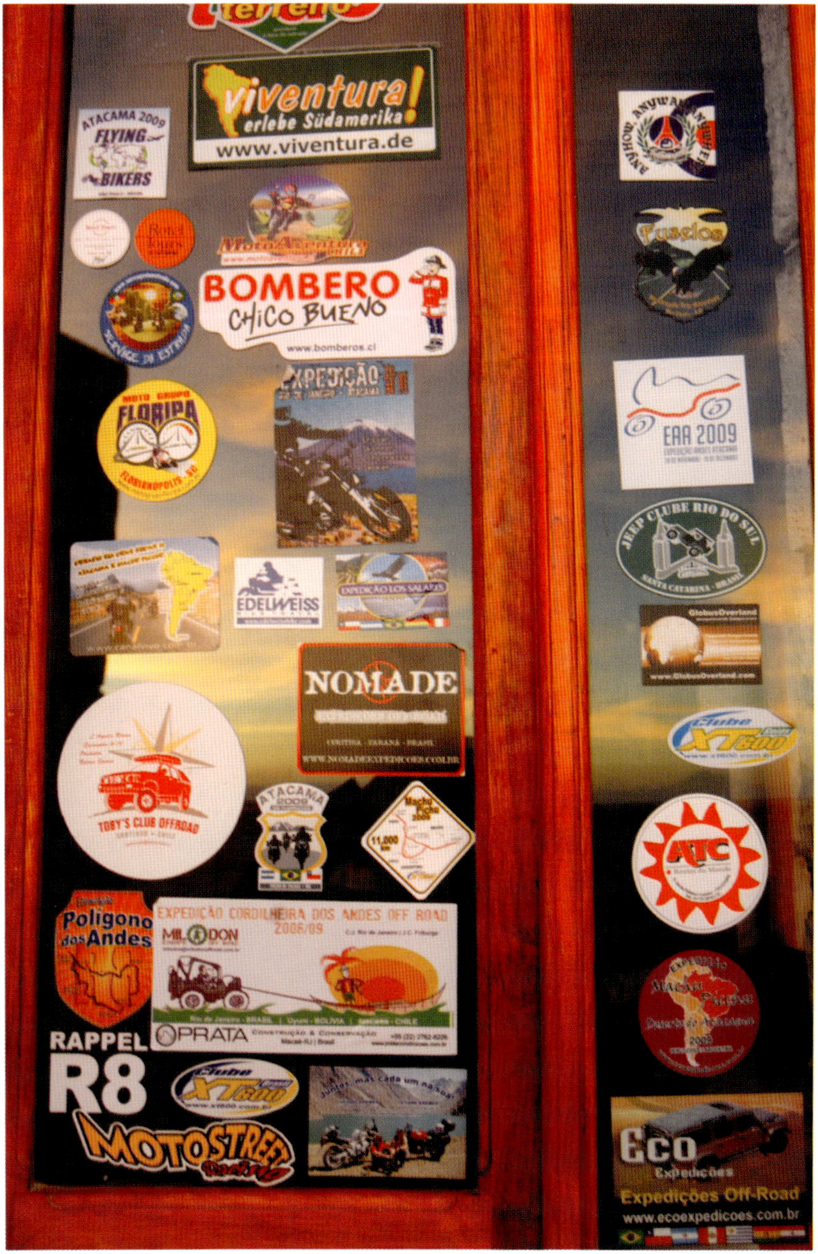
viventura!
erlebe Südamerika
www.viventura.de
ATACAMA 2009
FLYING
BIKERS
BOMBERO
CHICO BUENO
www.bomberos.cl
Fuselos
EXPEDIÇÃO
MOTO GRUPO
FLORIPA
EAA 2009
JEEP CLUBE RIO DO SUL
SANTA CATARINA - BRASIL
EDELWEISS
EXPEDIÇÃO LOS SALARES
GlobusOverland
NOMADE
WWW.NOMADEEXPEDICOES.COM.BR
Clube XT600
TOBY'S CLUB OFFROAD
ATACAMA 2009
ATC
Poligono dos Andes
EXPEDIÇÃO CORDILHEIRA DOS ANDES OFF ROAD
2006/09
PRATA
RAPPEL
R8
Clube XT600
MOTOSTREET
Eco
Expedições
Expedições Off-Road
www.ecoexpedicoes.com.br

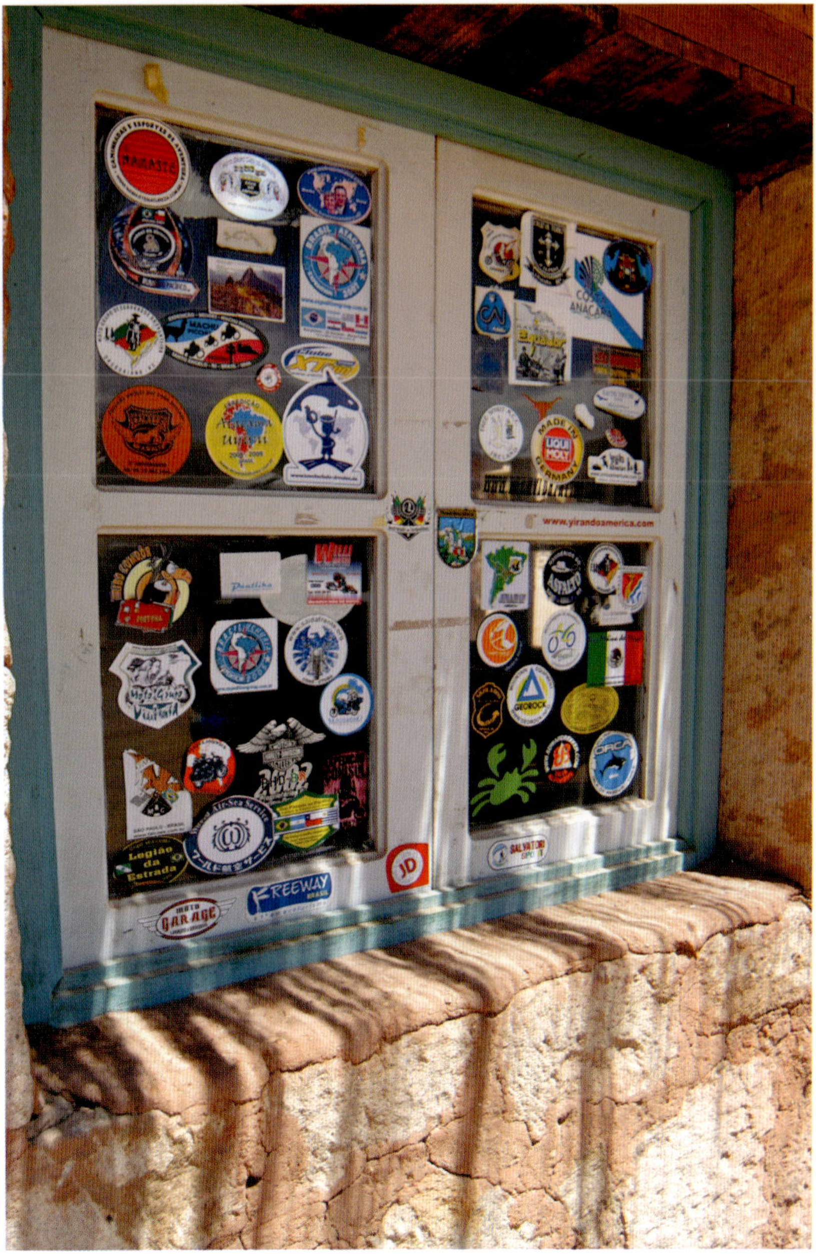
www.yirandoamerica.com
MADE IN GERMANY
LIQUI MOLY
GEOROCK
ORCA
Legião da Estrada
FREEWAY
GARAGE
SALVATORI

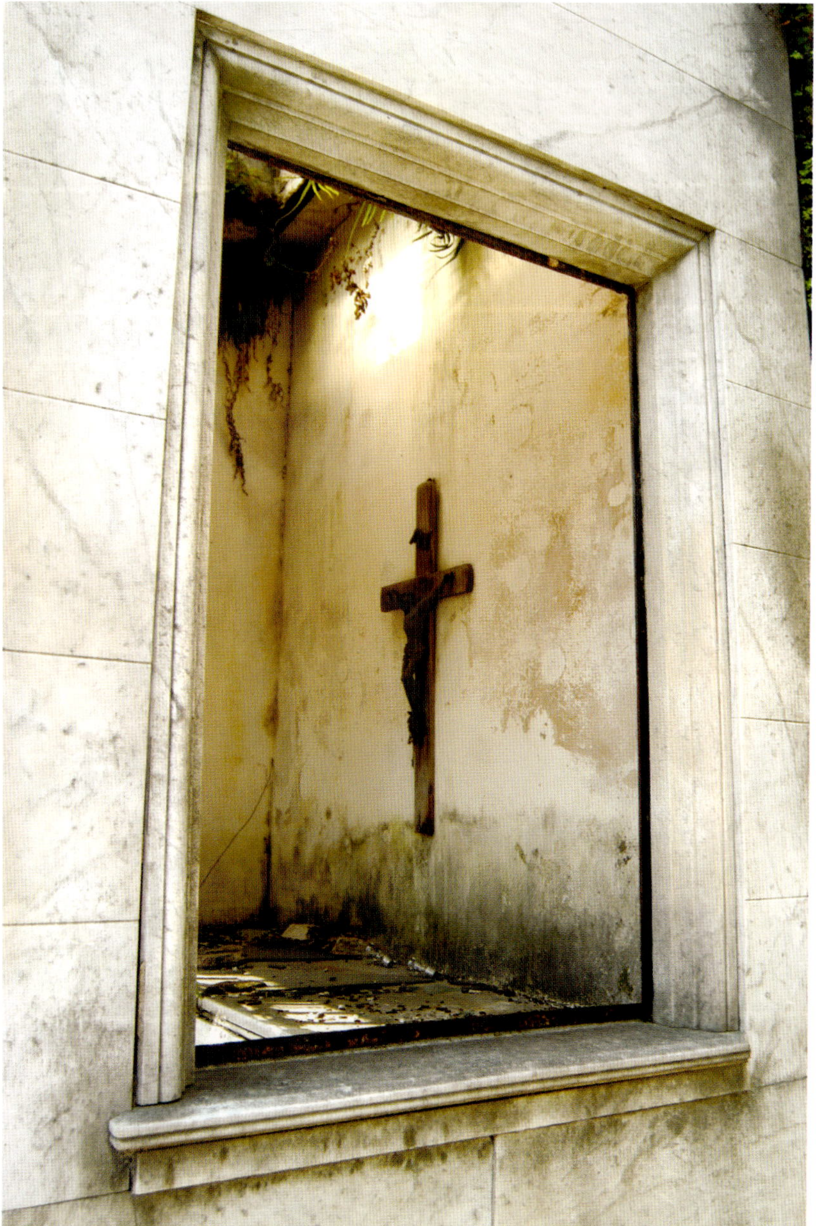

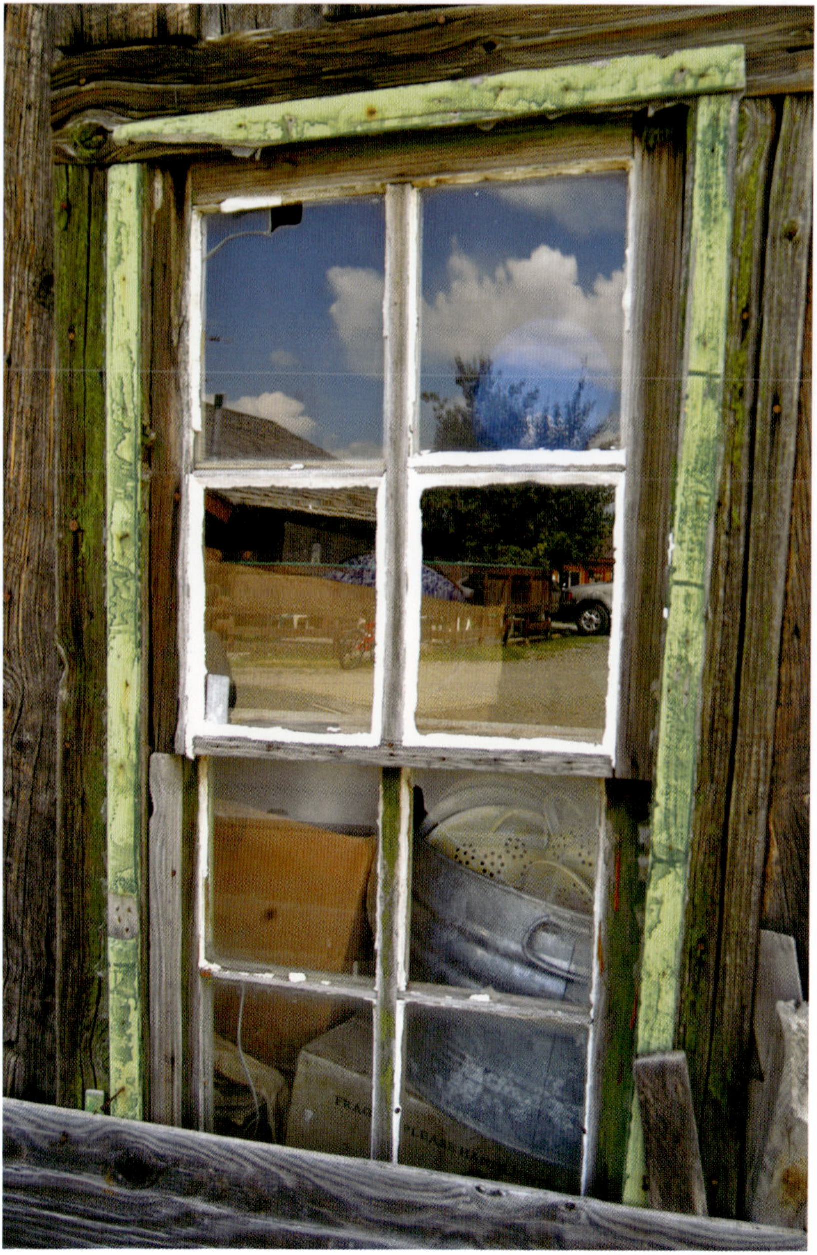

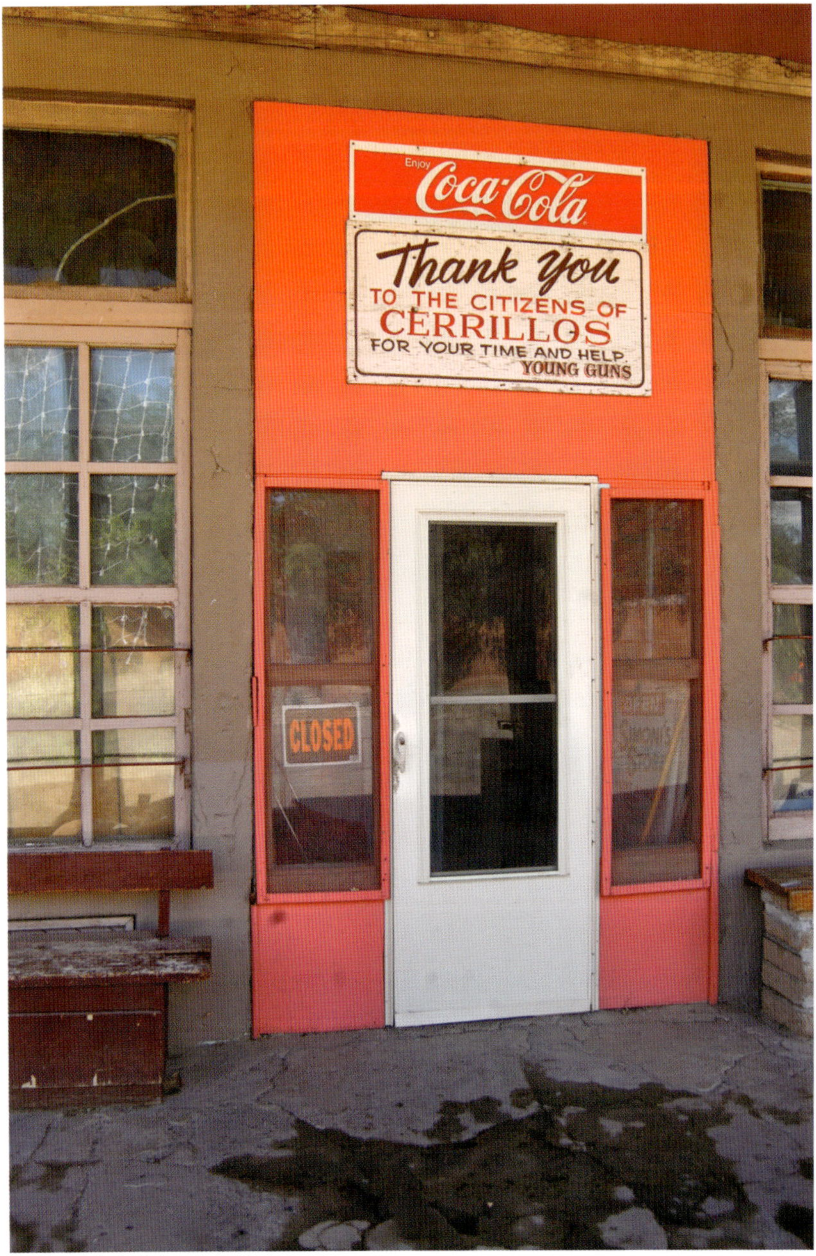
Enjoy
Coca-Cola
Thank You
TO THE CITIZENS OF
CERRILLOS
FOR YOUR TIME AND HELP.
YOUNG GUNS
CLOSED

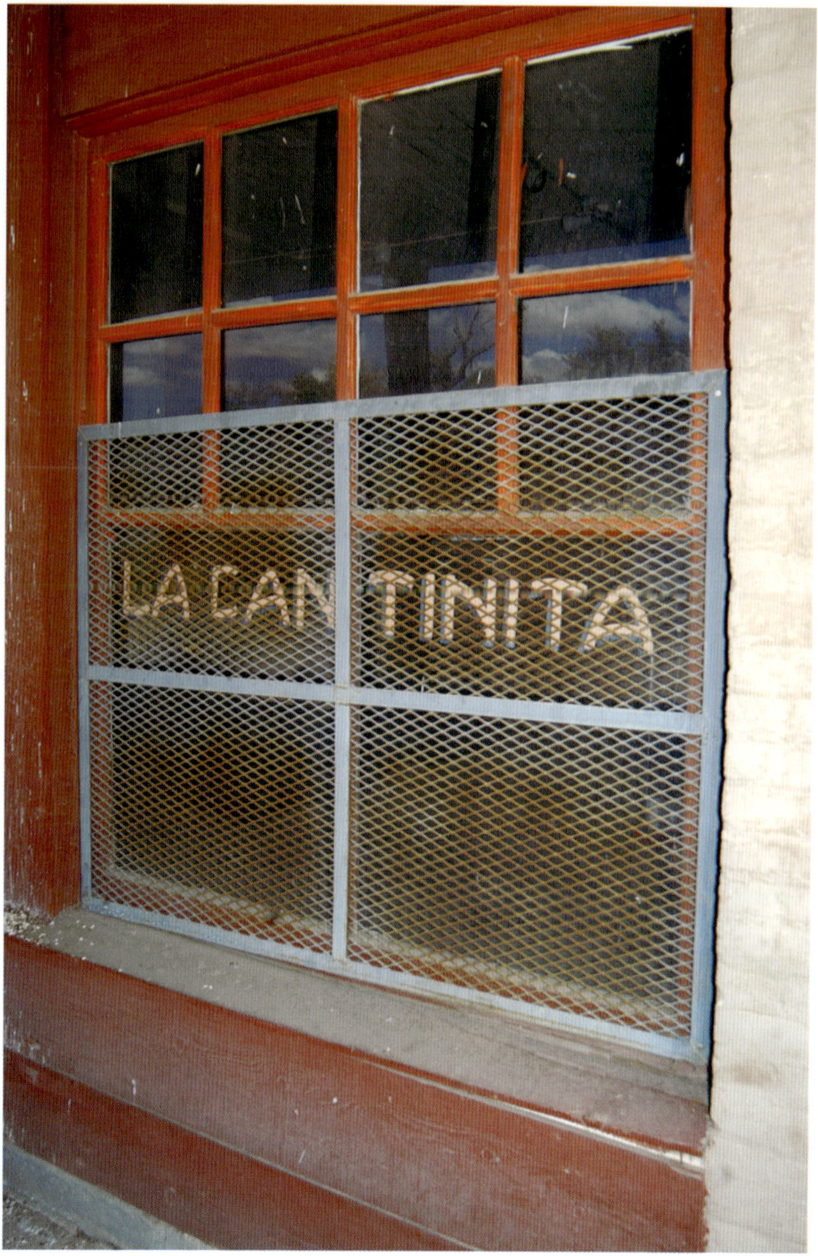
LA CAN TINITA

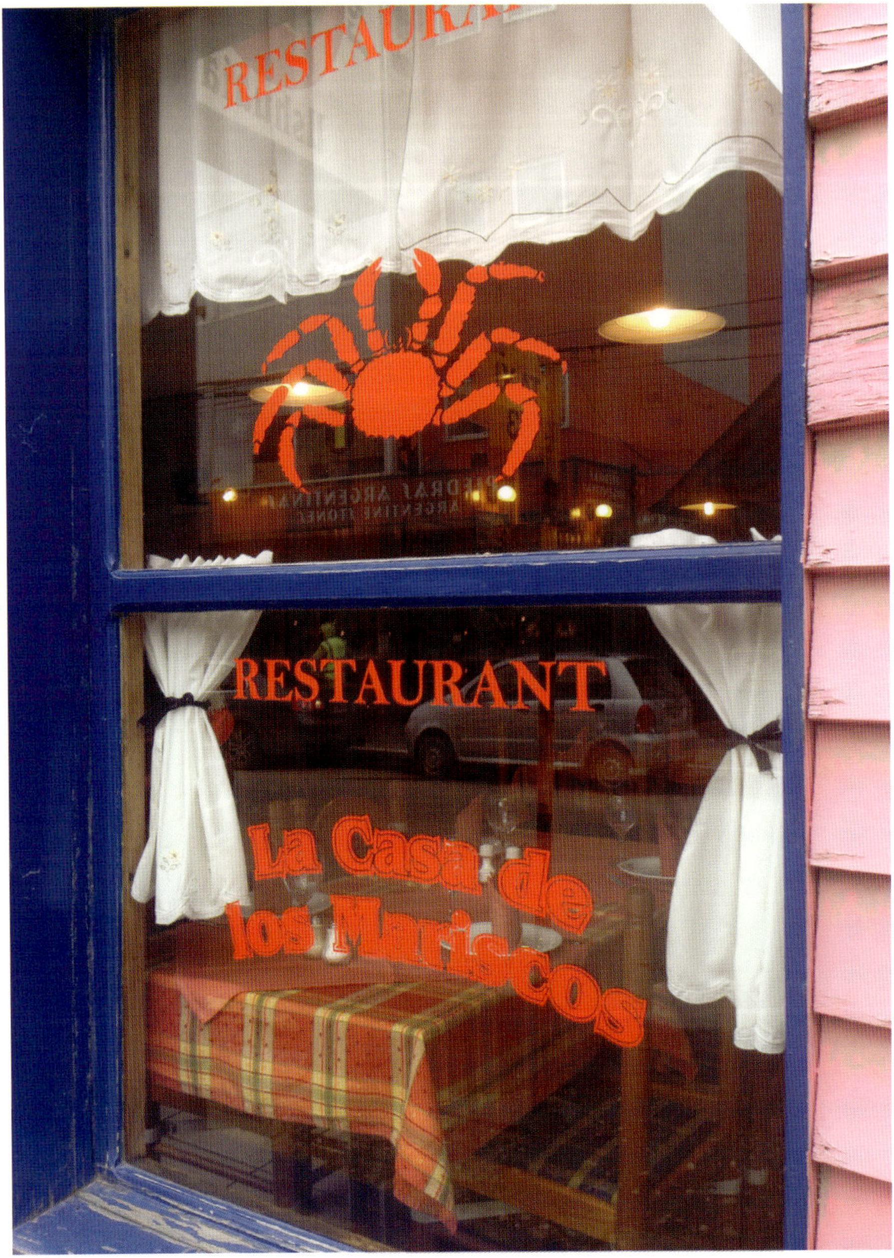
RESTAURANT
La Casa de
los Mariscos

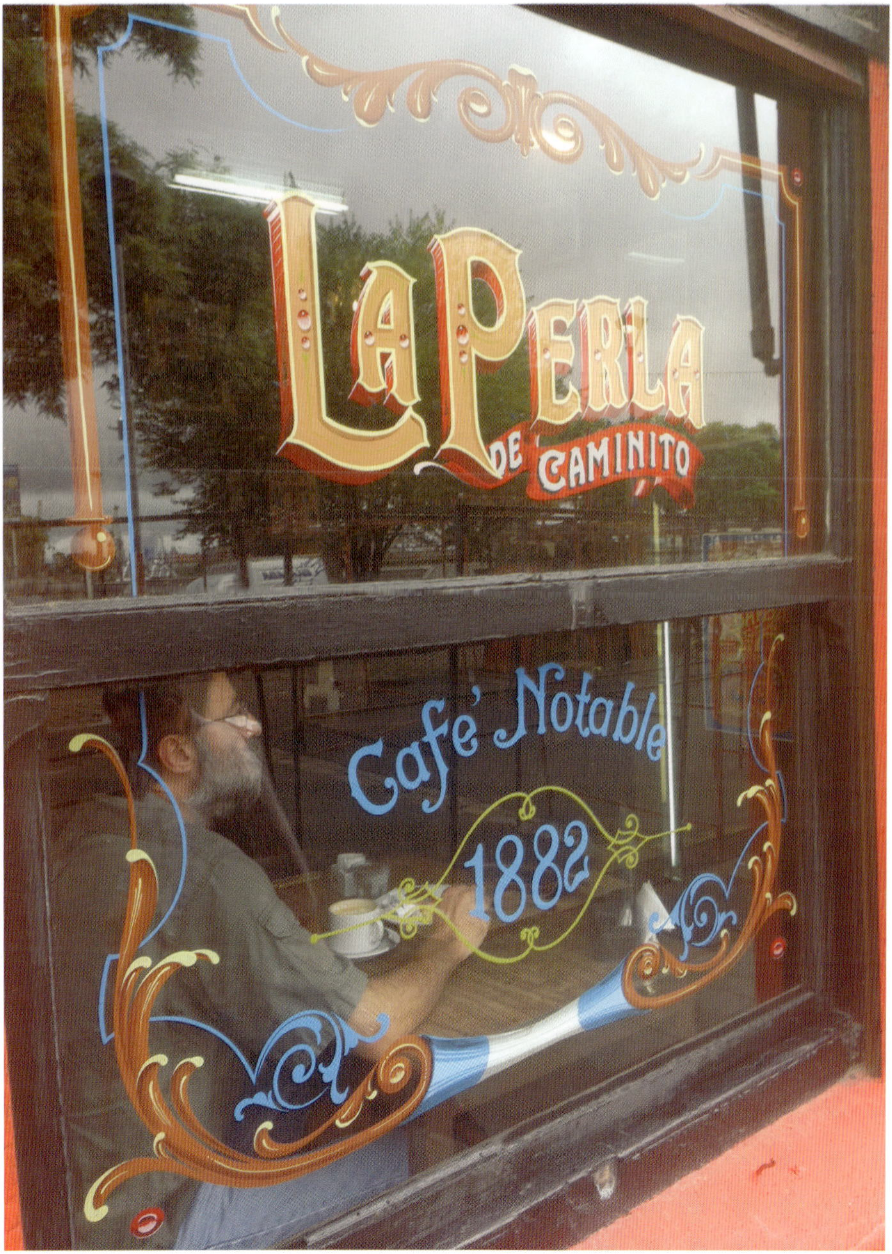
La Perla
de Caminito
Café Notable
1882

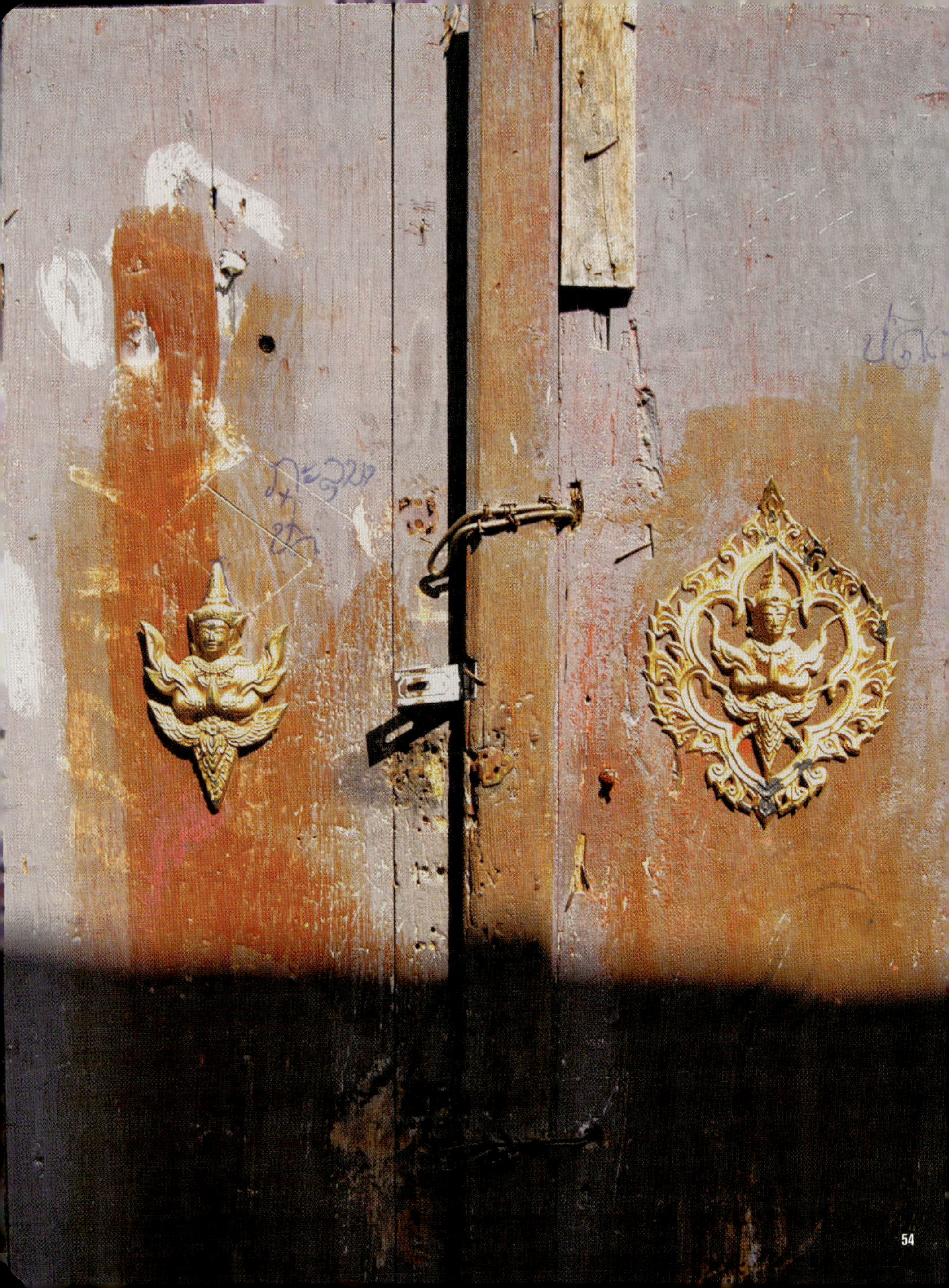

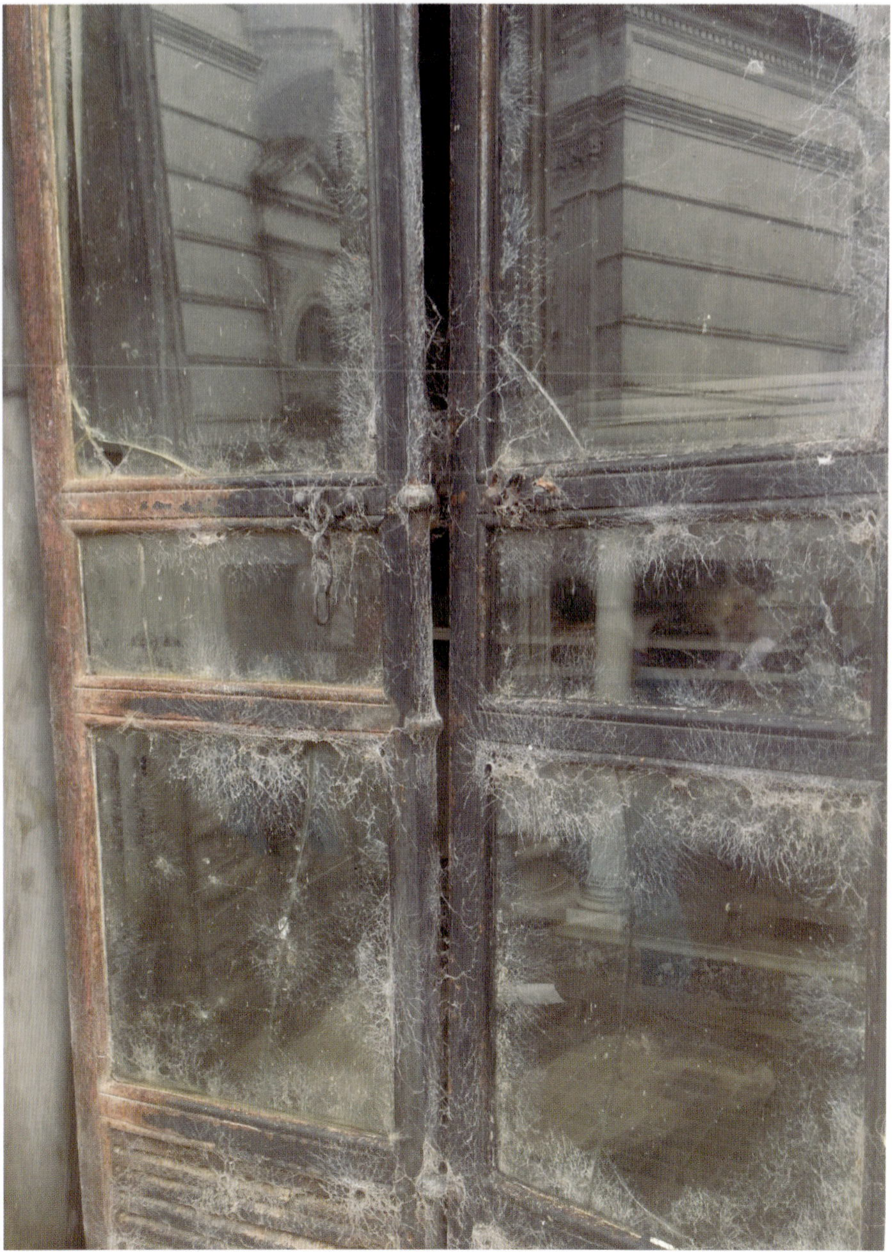

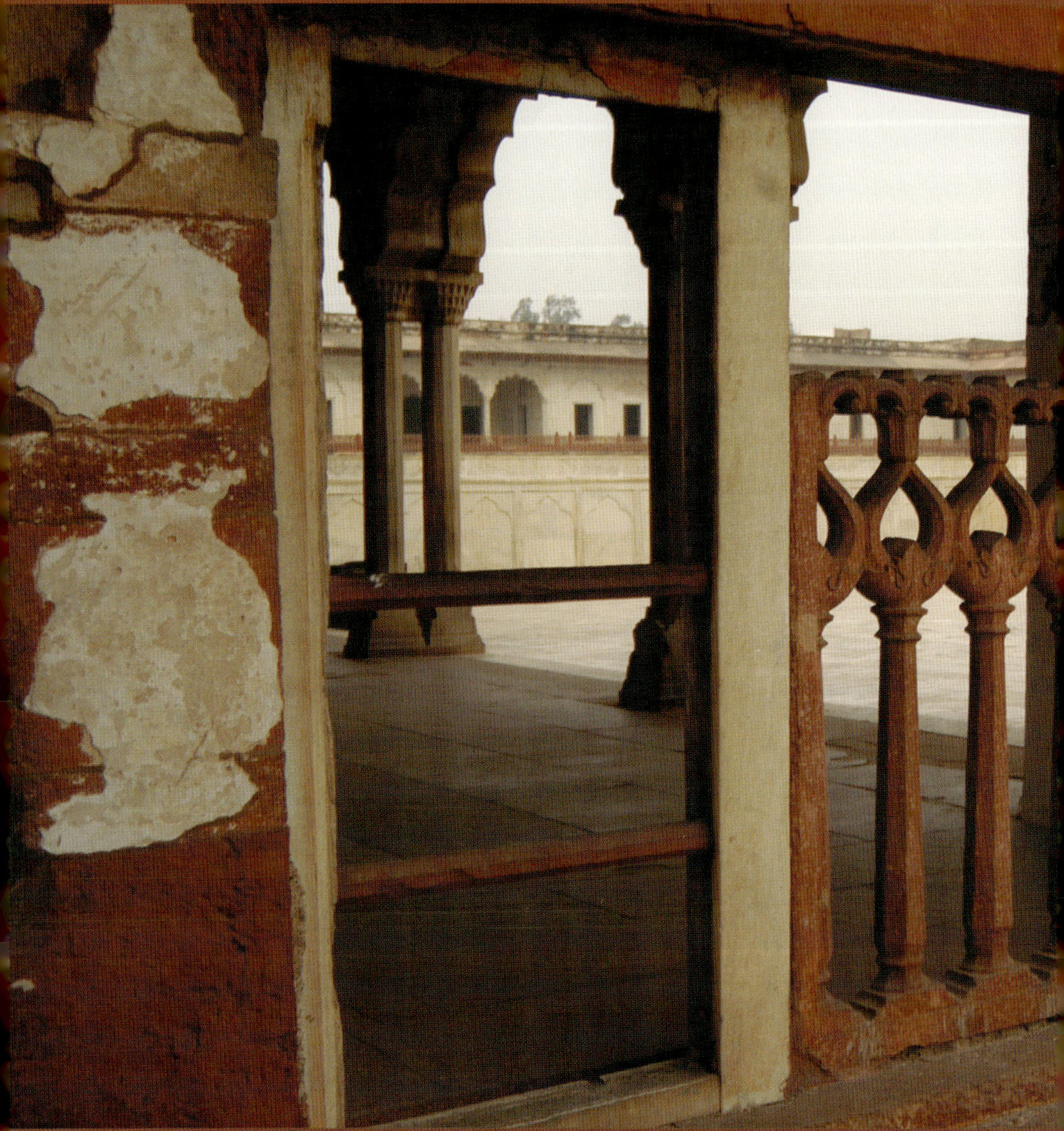

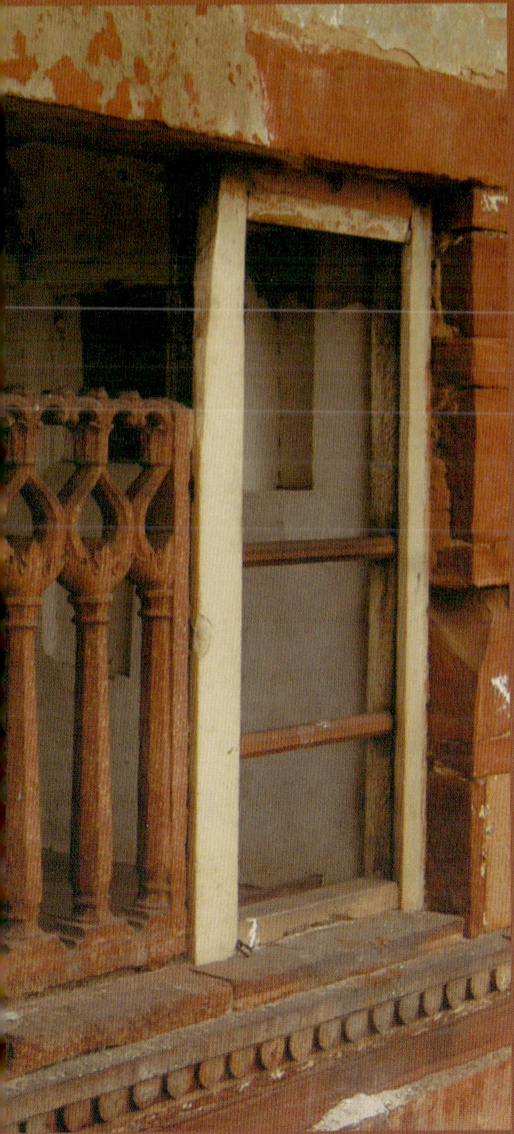

TELLING

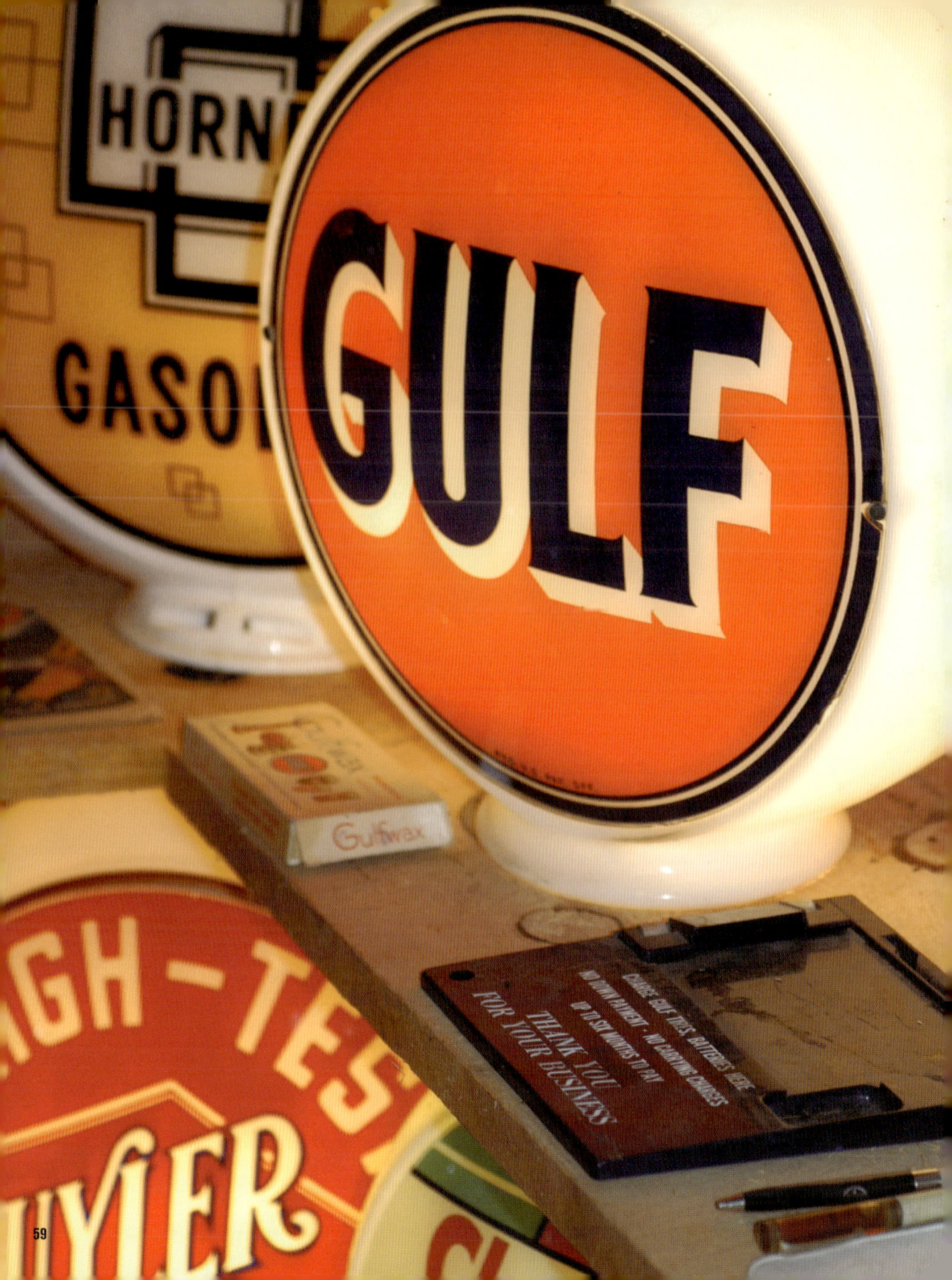
GULF
Gulfwax
CHARGE GULF TIRES, BATTERIES HERE
NO DOWN PAYMENT · NO CARRYING CHARGES
UP TO SIX MONTHS TO PAY
THANK YOU
FOR YOUR BUSINESS

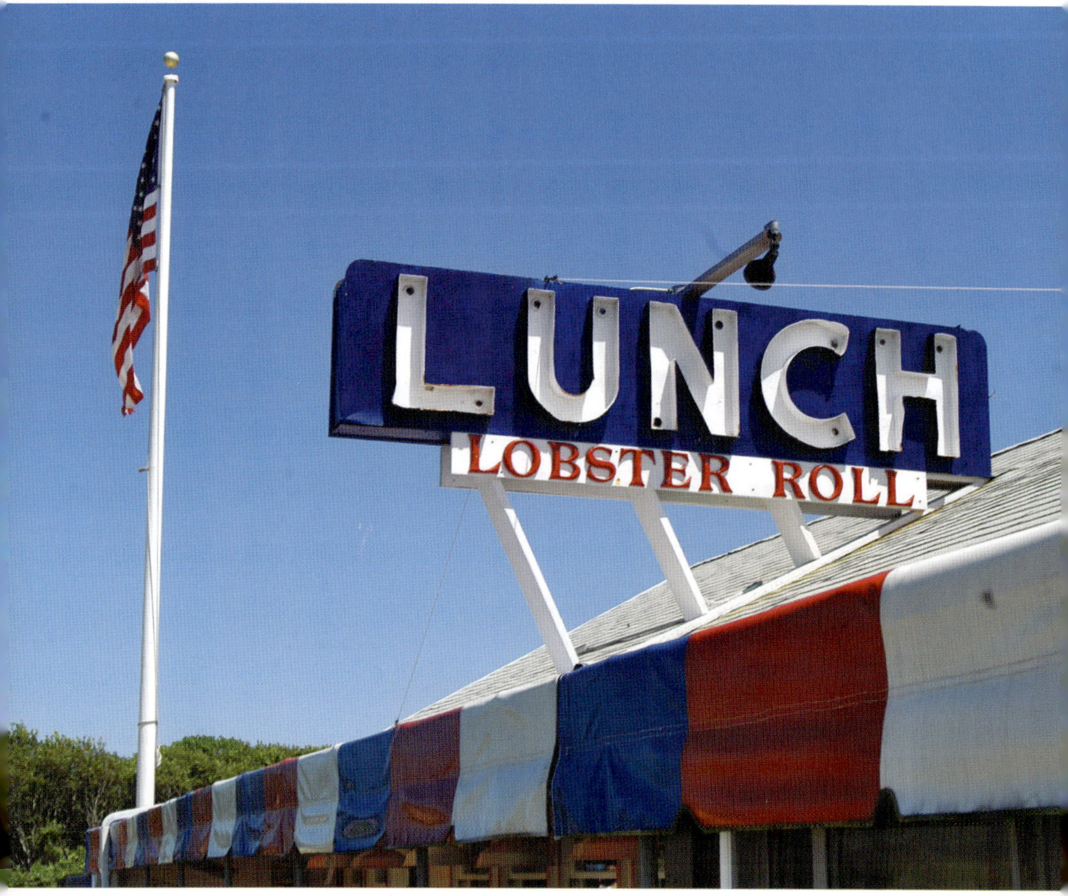
LUNCH
LOBSTER ROLL

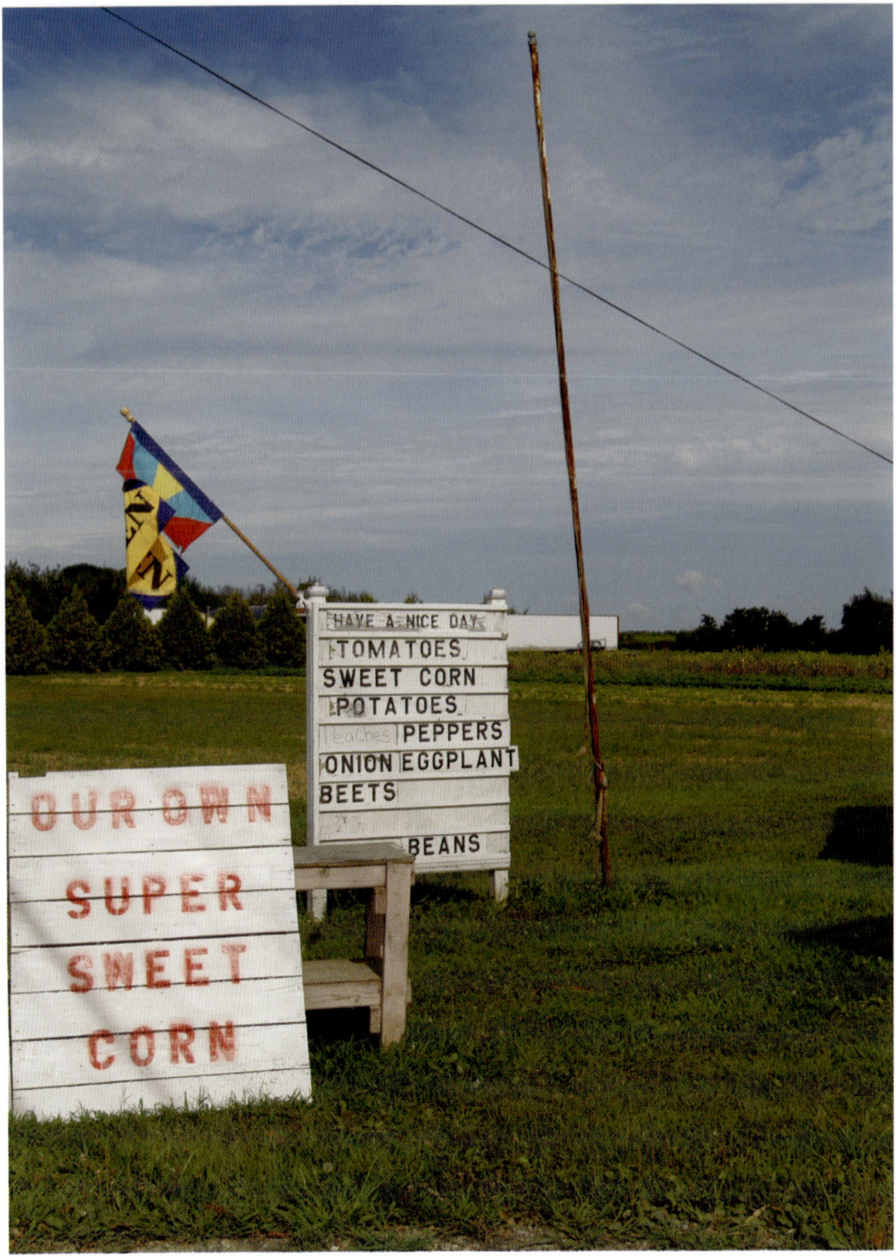
HAVE A NICE DAY
TOMATOES
SWEET CORN
POTATOES
Peaches
PEPPERS
ONION EGGPLANT
BEETS
BEANS
OUR OWN
SUPER
SWEET
CORN

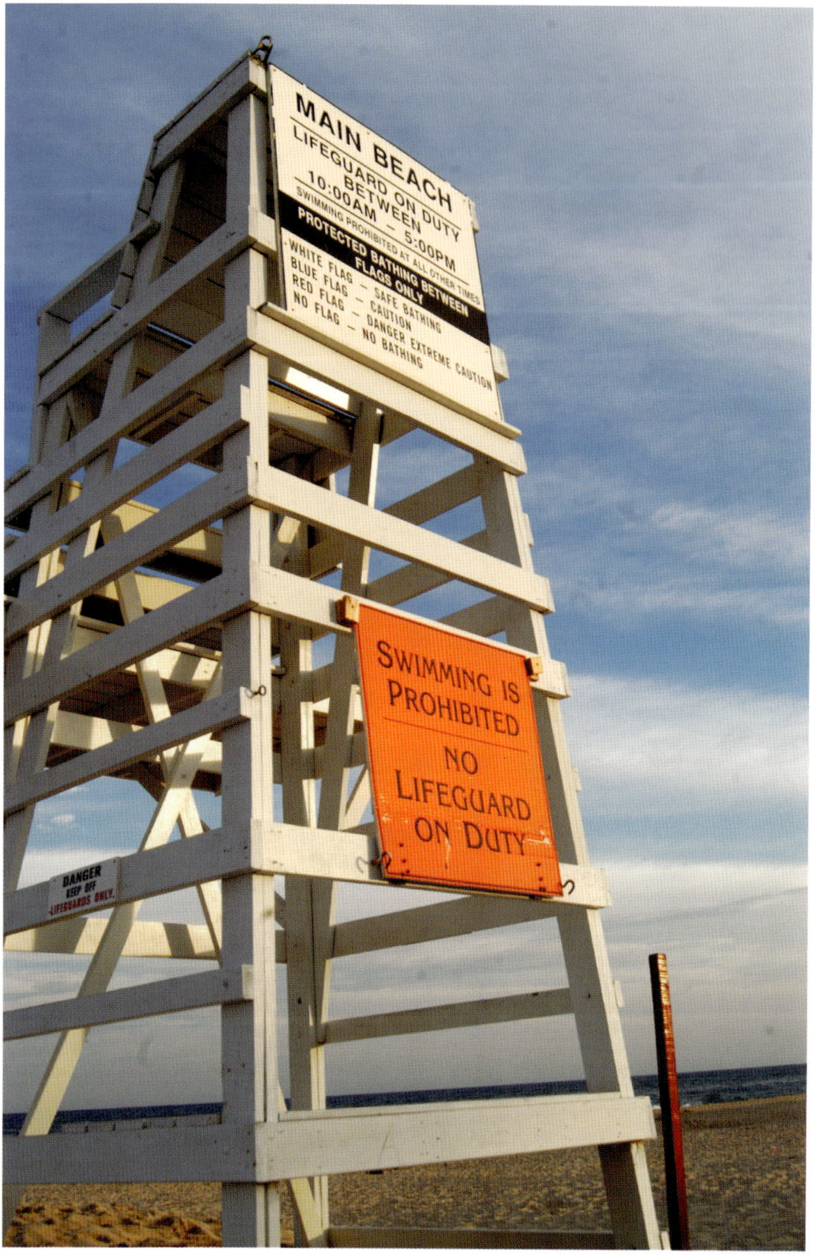
MAIN BEACH
LIFEGUARD ON DUTY
BETWEEN
10:00AM – 5:00PM
SWIMMING PROHIBITED AT ALL OTHER TIMES
PROTECTED BATHING BETWEEN
FLAGS ONLY
WHITE FLAG – SAFE BATHING
BLUE FLAG – CAUTION
RED FLAG – DANGER EXTREME CAUTION
NO FLAG – NO BATHING
SWIMMING IS PROHIBITED
NO LIFEGUARD ON DUTY
DANGER
KEEP OFF
LIFEGUARDS ONLY.

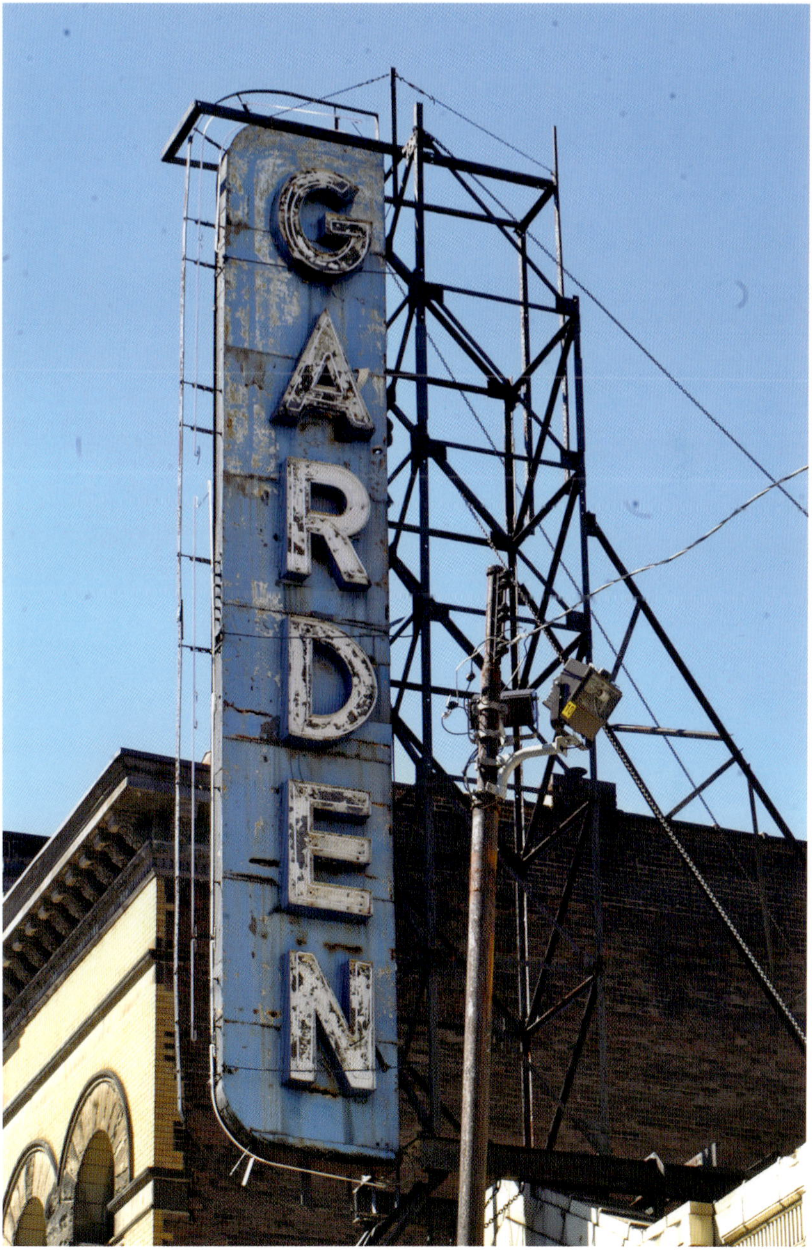
GARDEN

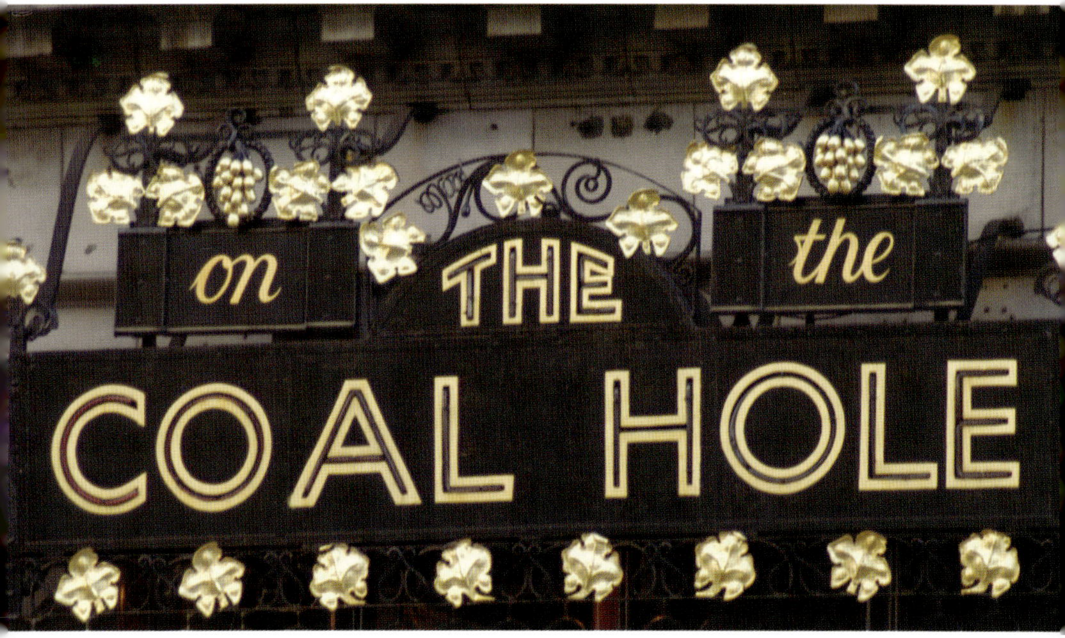
on THE the
COAL HOLE

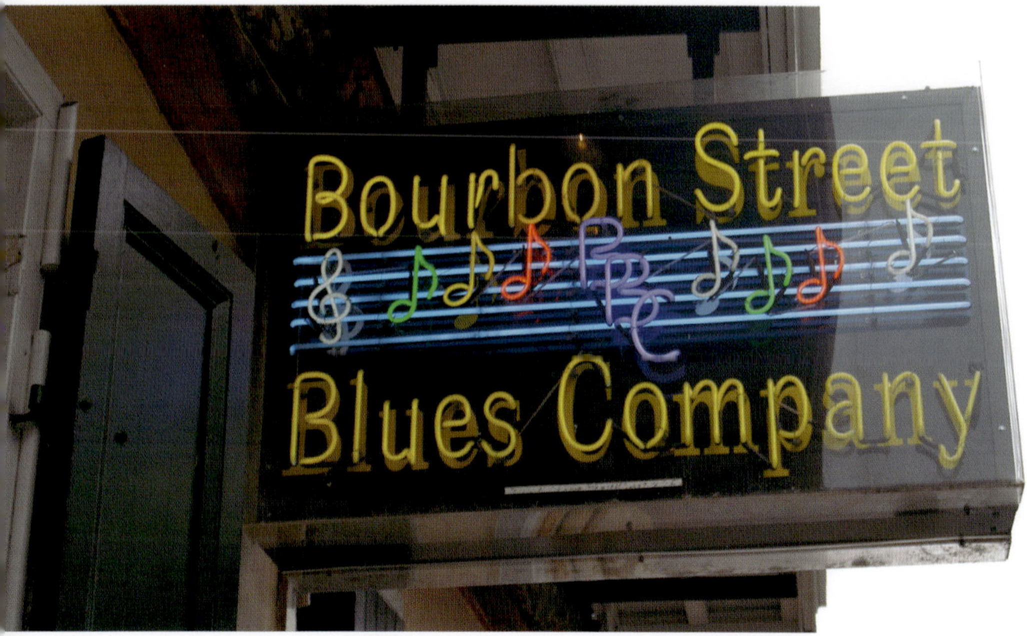
Bourbon Street
Blues Company

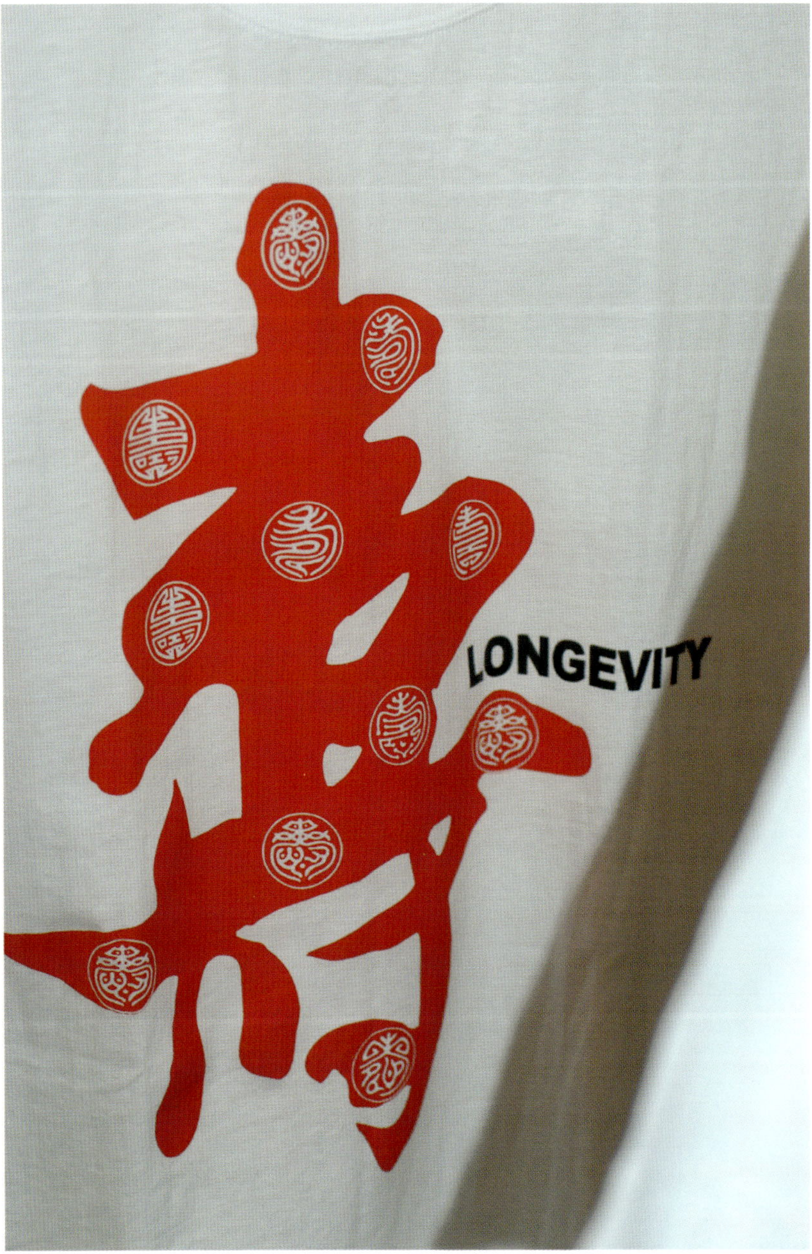
LONGEVITY

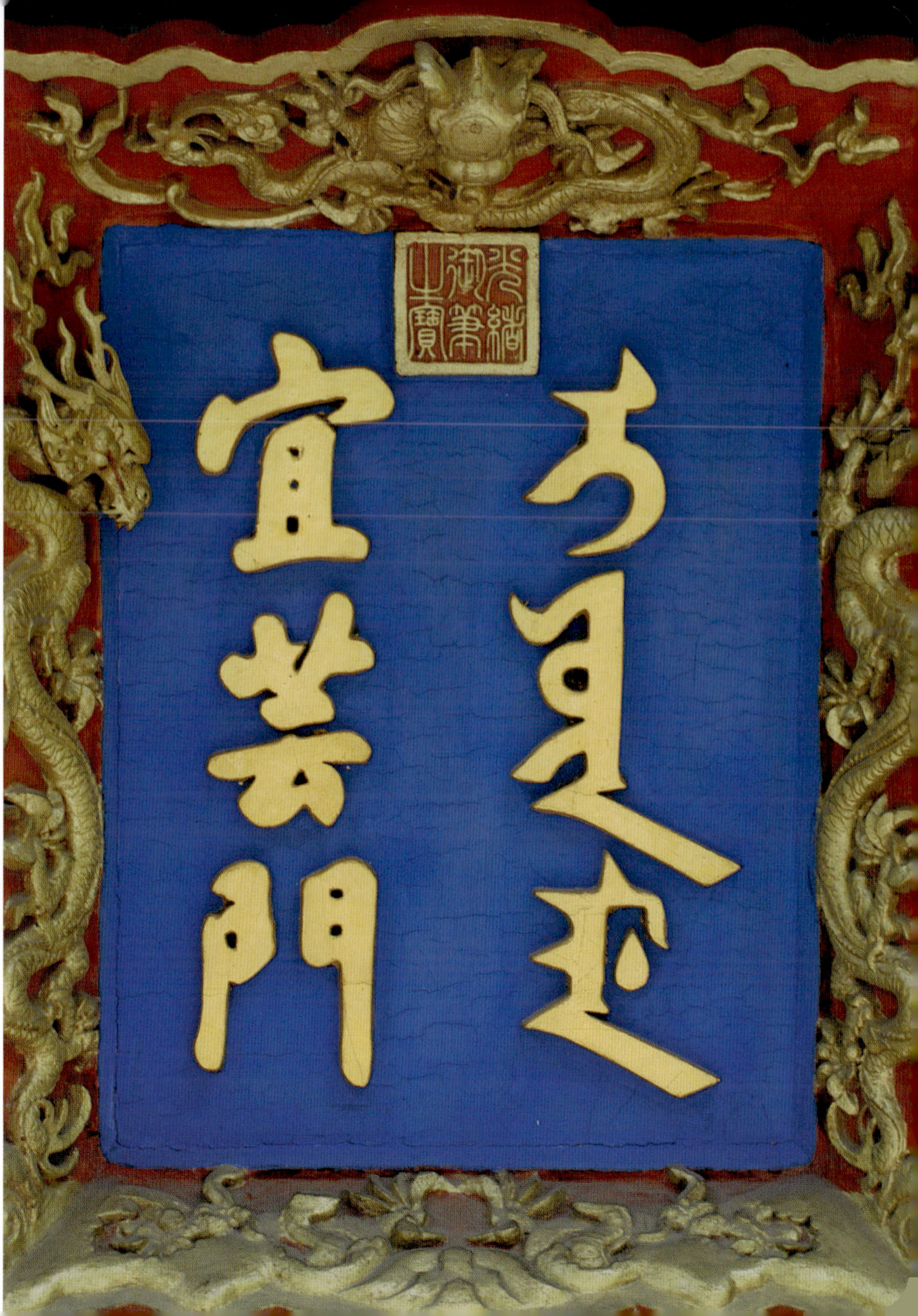
光緒御筆之寶
宜芸門

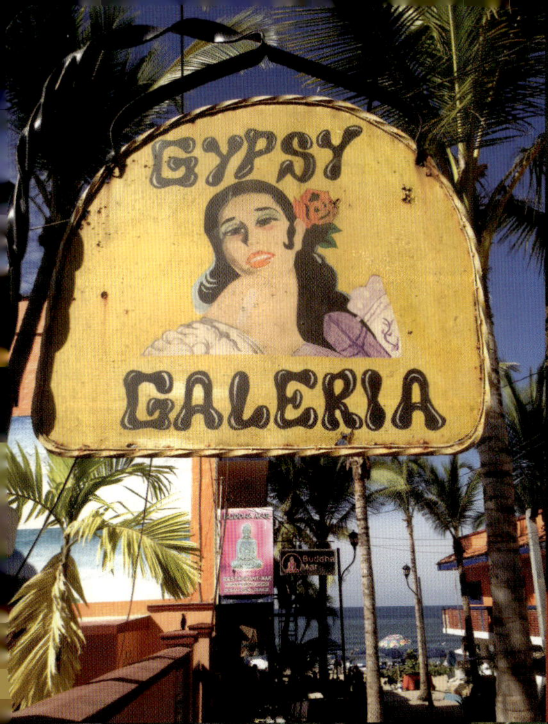
GYPSY
GALERIA

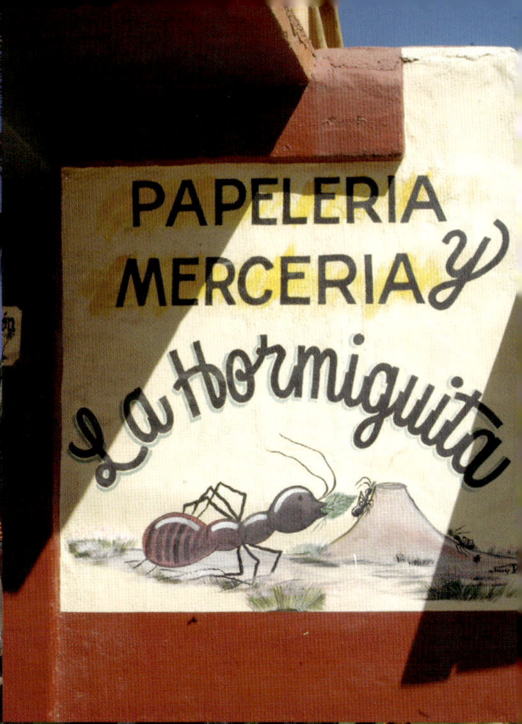
PAPELERIA
MERCERIA y
La Hormiguita

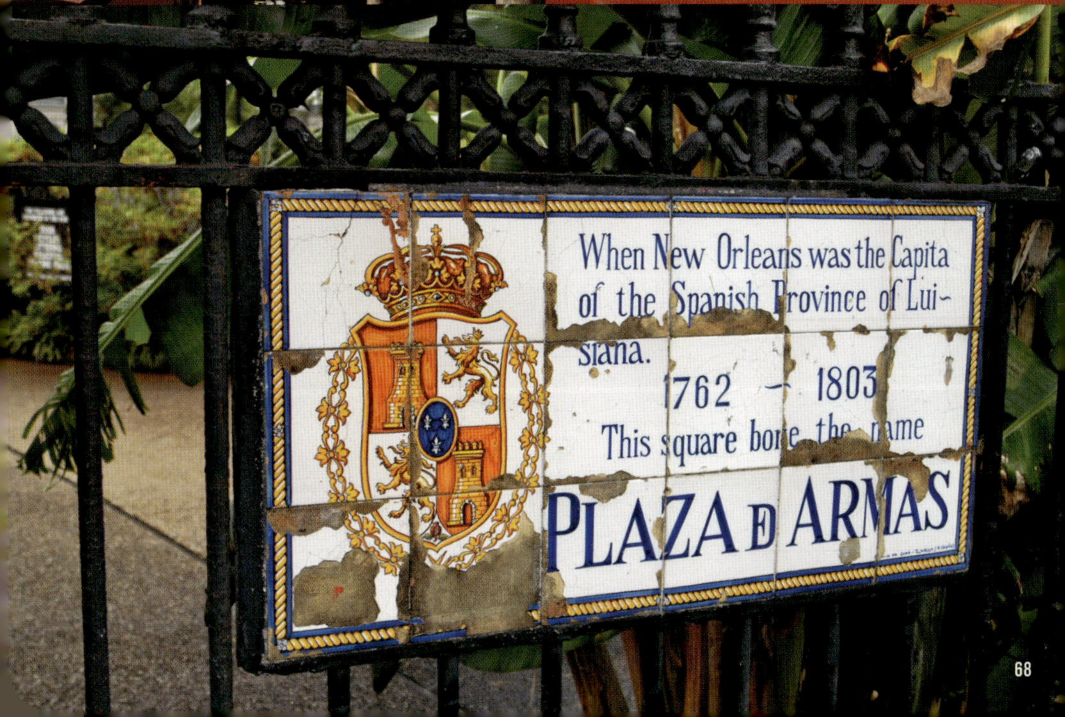
When New Orleans was the Capita
of the Spanish Province of Lui-
siana.
1762 - 1803
This square bore the name
PLAZA DE ARMAS

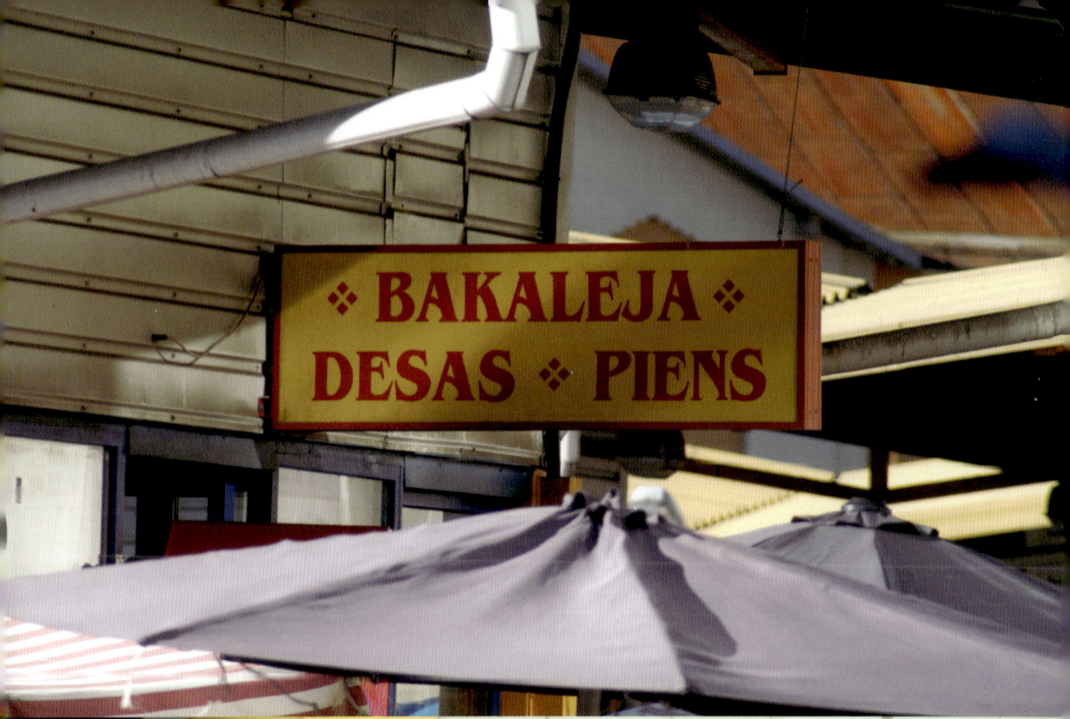
BAKALEJA
DESAS PIENS

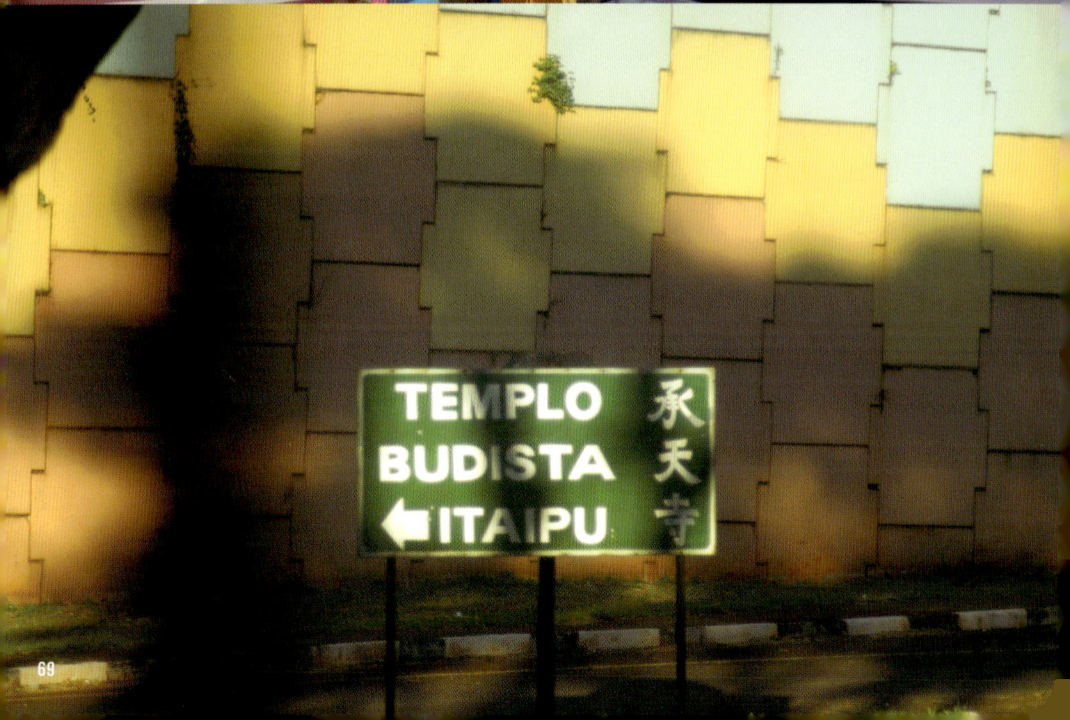
TEMPLO
BUDISTA
ITAIPU
承天寺

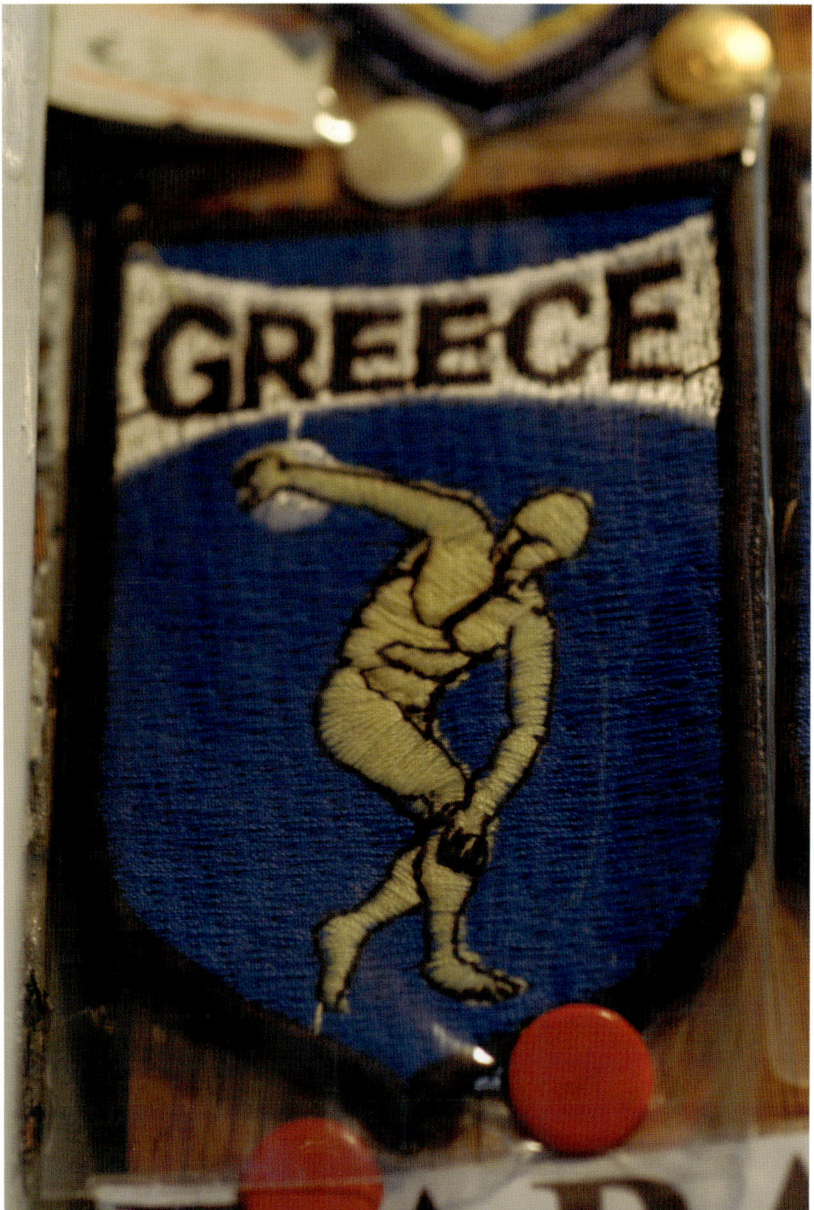
GREECE

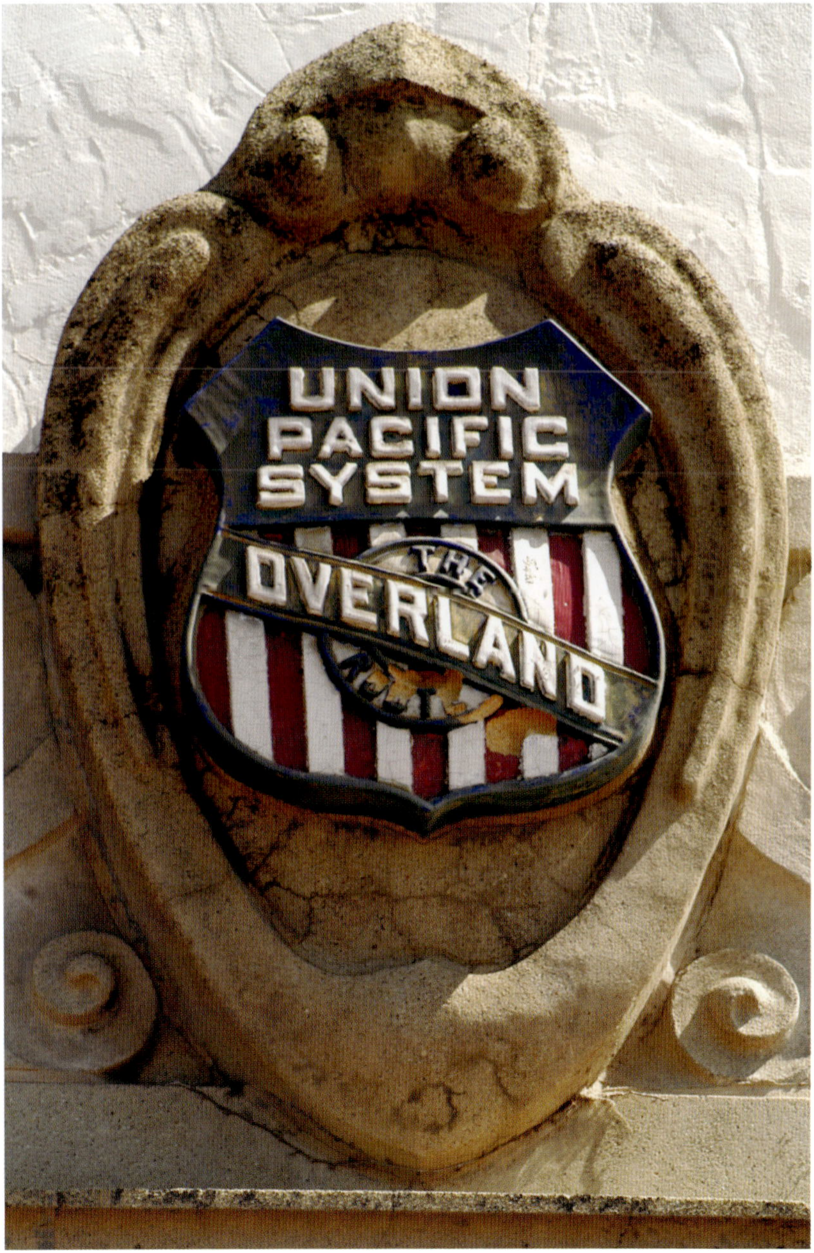
UNION
PACIFIC
SYSTEM
THE
OVERLAND

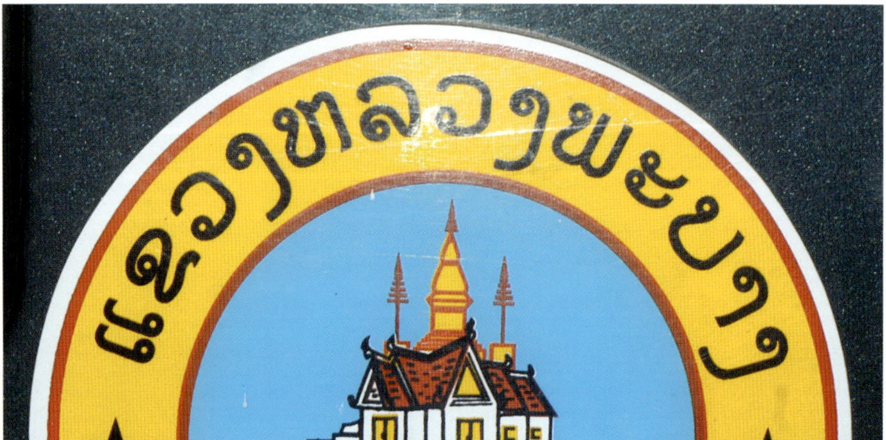
ແຂວງຫລວງພະບາງ
ອະນຸຍາດດໍາເນີນ
ທຸລະກິດຂົນສົ່ງ
ພະແນກ ຄ.ຂ.ປ.ກ

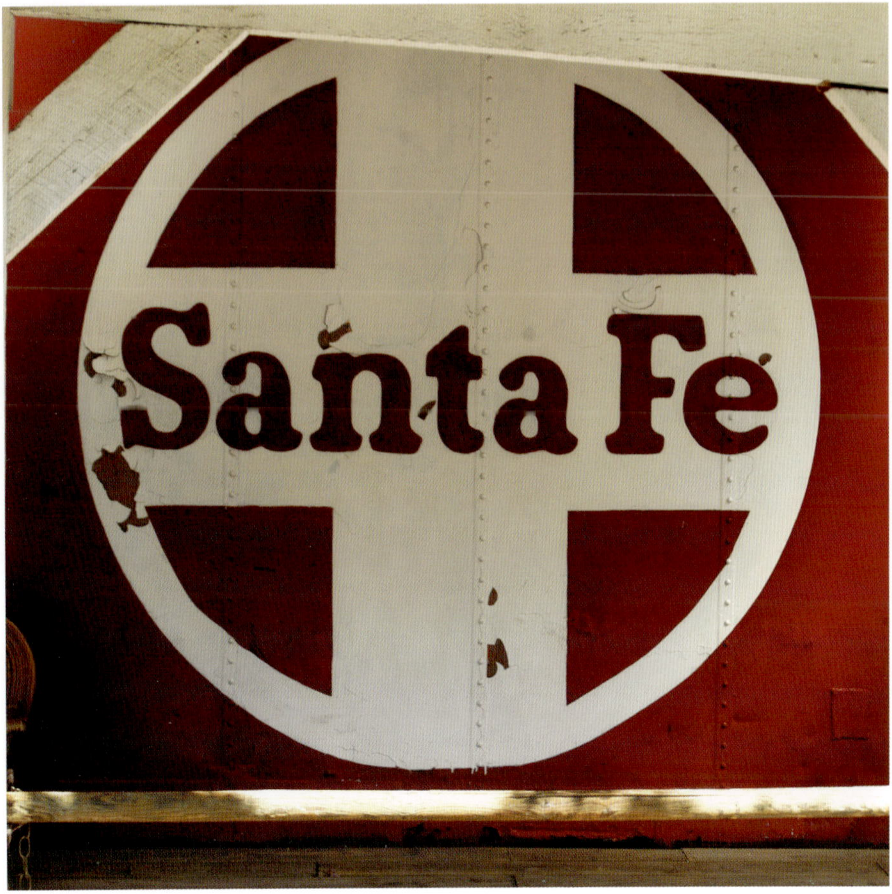
Santa Fe

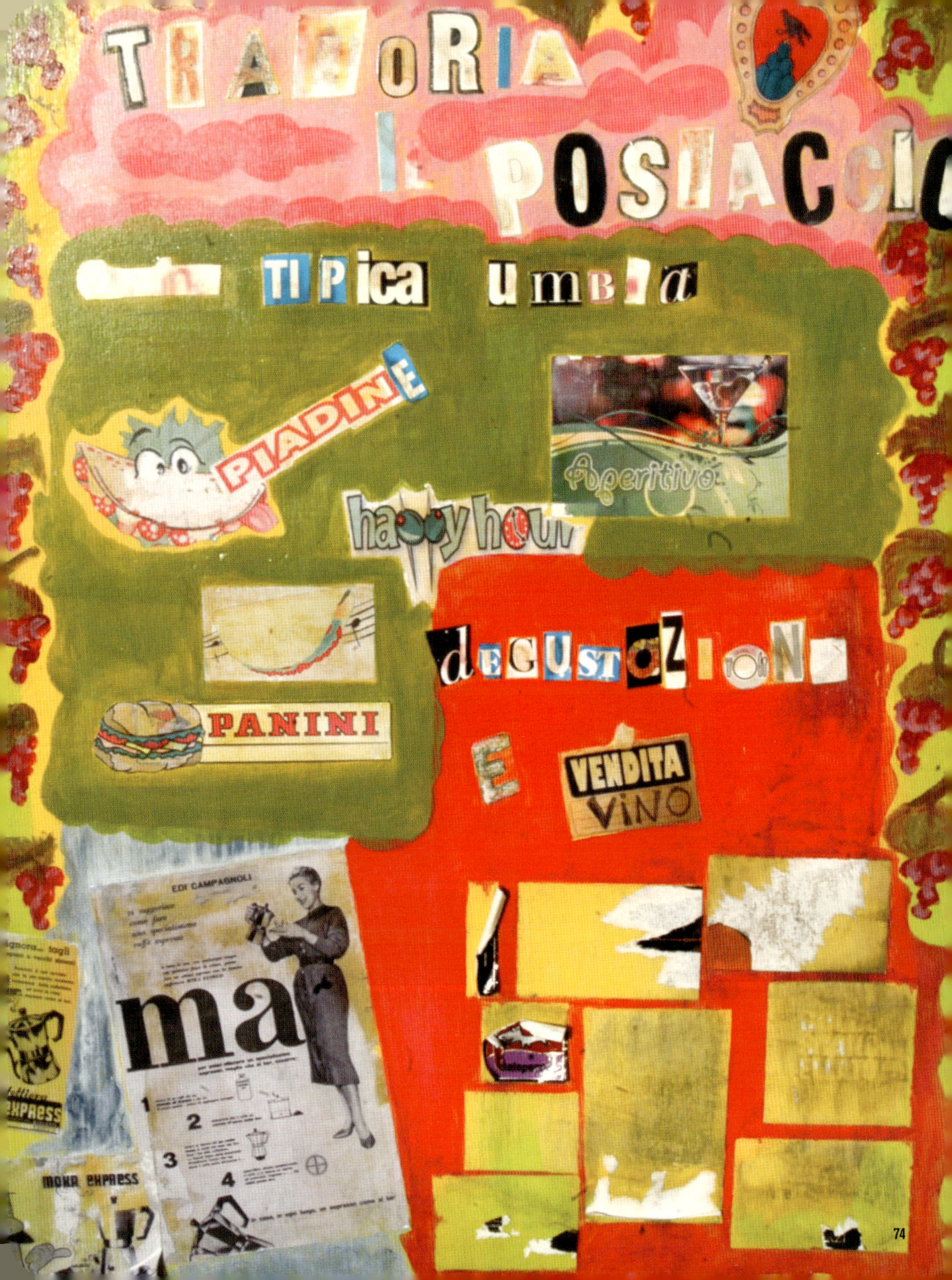
PIADINE
Aperitivo
PANINI
VENDITA
VINO
EDI CAMPAGNOLI
ma
MOKA EXPRESS

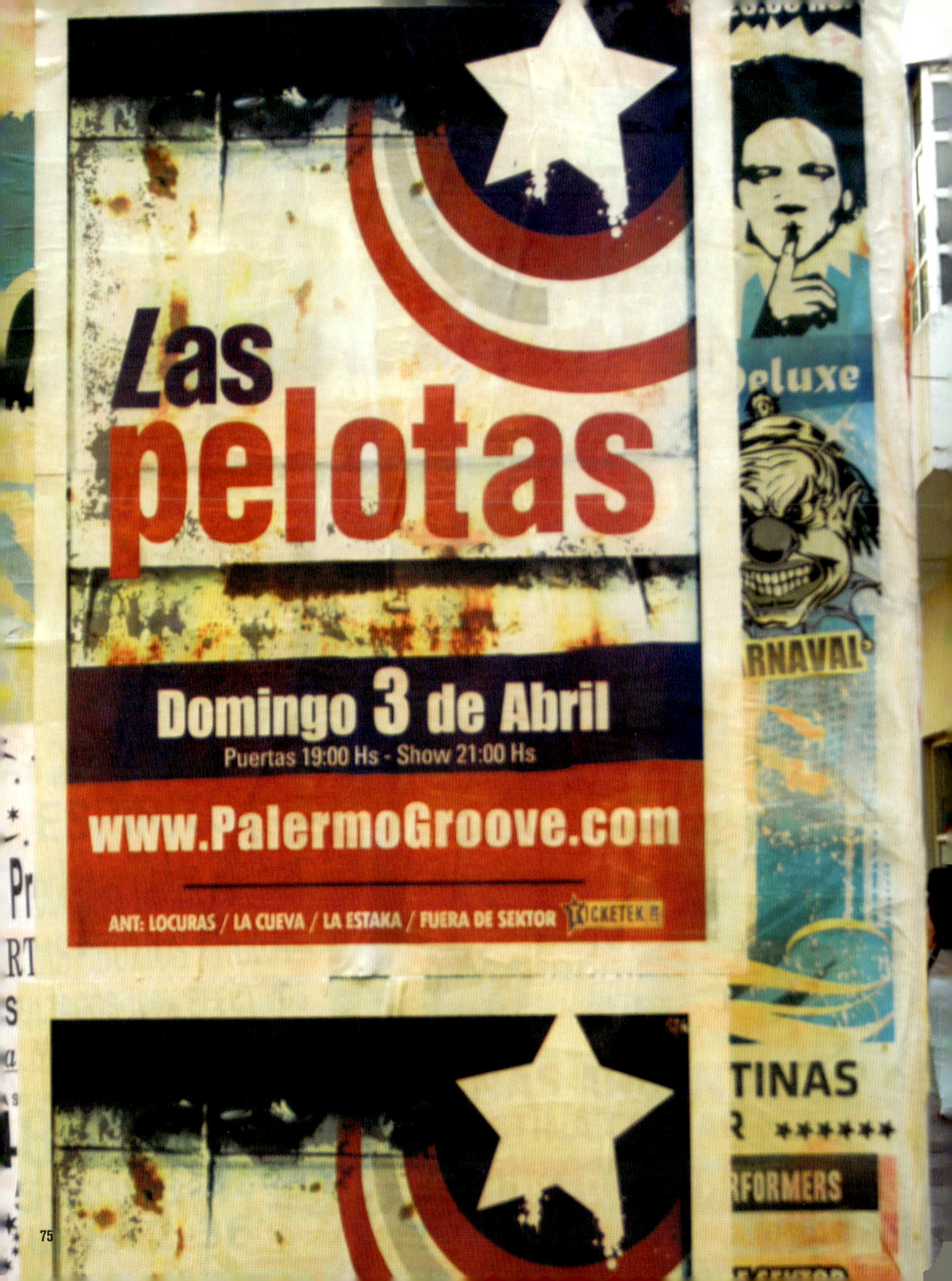
Las pelotas
Domingo 3 de Abril
Puertas 19:00 Hs - Show 21:00 Hs
www.PalermoGroove.com
ANT: LOCURAS / LA CUEVA / LA ESTAKA / FUERA DE SEKTOR
TICKETEK
Deluxe
ARNAVAL
TINAS
RFORMERS

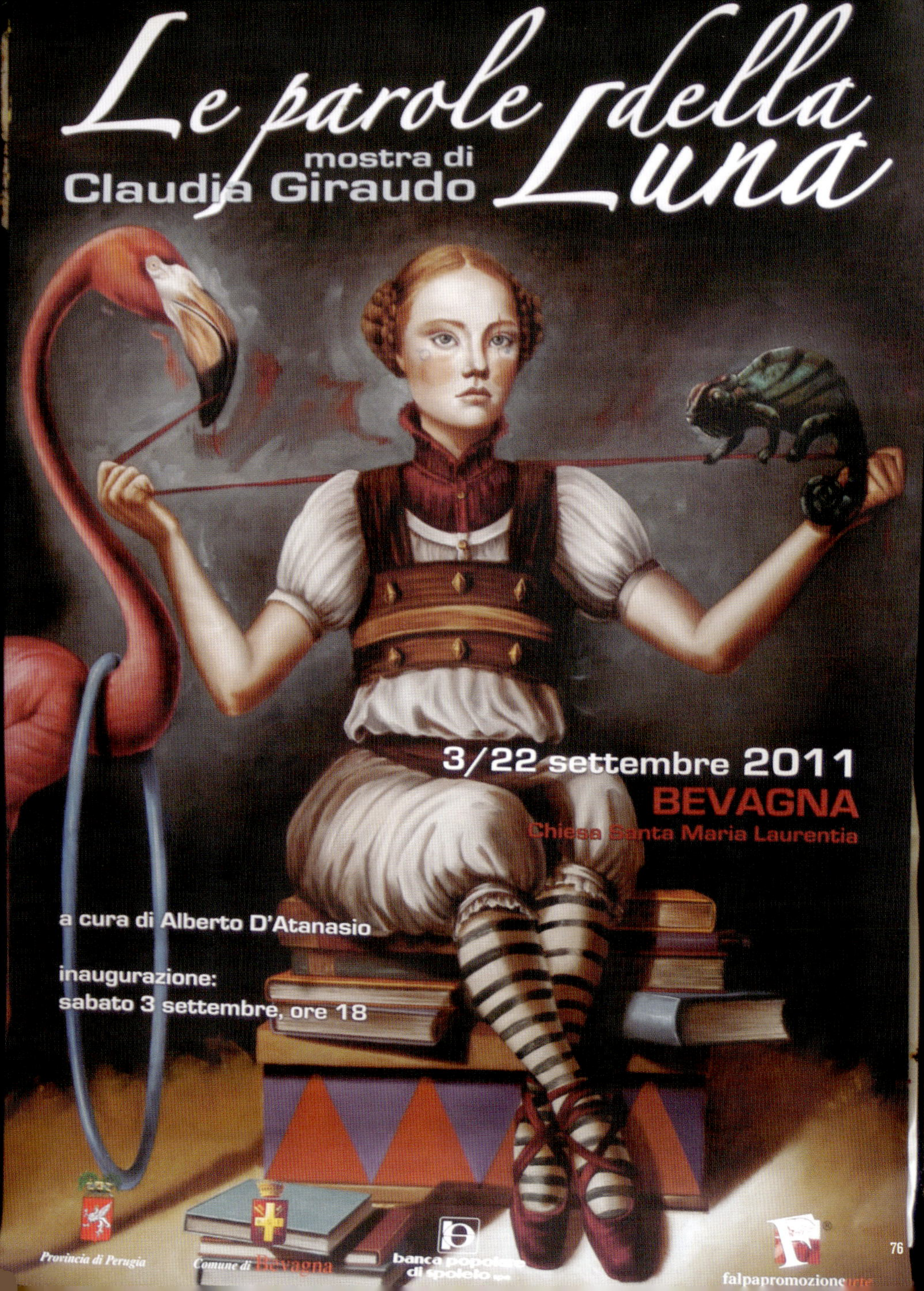
Le parole della Luna
mostra di
Claudia Giraudo
3/22 settembre 2011
BEVAGNA
Chiesa Santa Maria Laurentia
a cura di Alberto D'Atanasio
inaugurazione:
sabato 3 settembre, ore 18
Provincia di Perugia
Comune di Bevagna
banca popolare di spoleto spa
falpapromozionearte

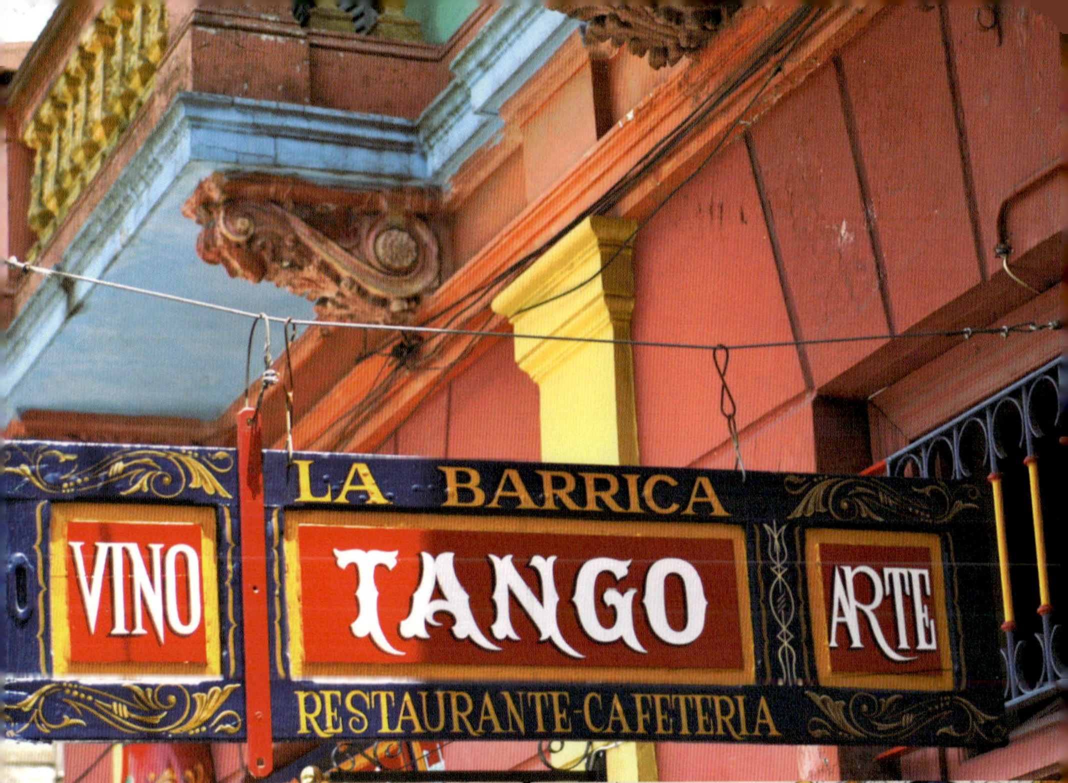
LA BARRICA
VINO
TANGO
ARTE
RESTAURANTE-CAFETERIA

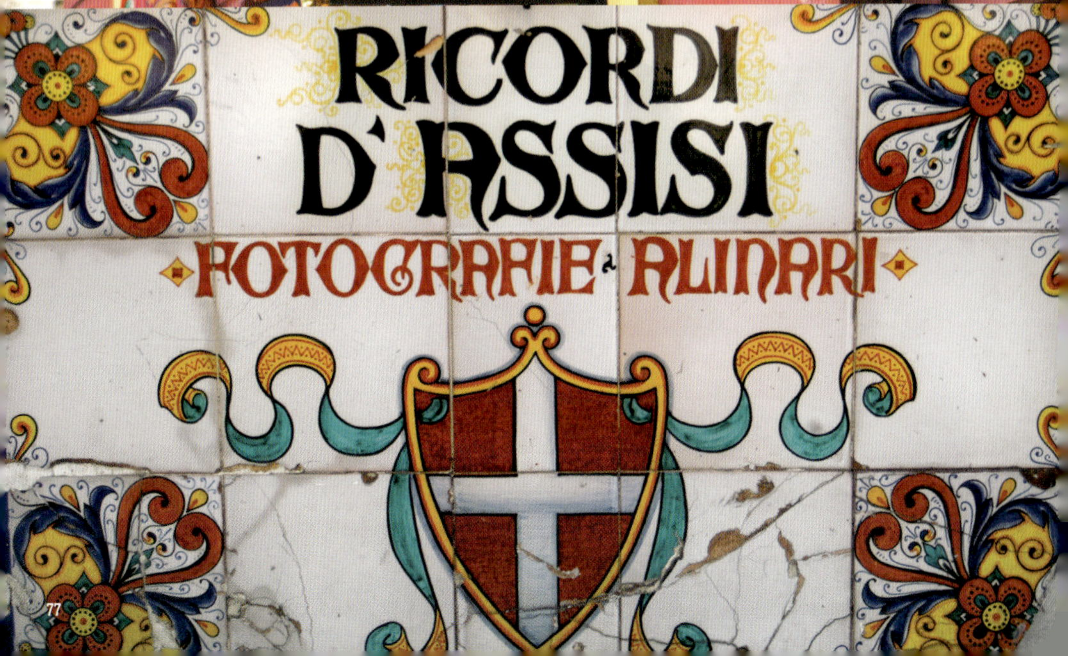
RICORDI
D'ASSISI
FOTOGRAFIE ALINARI

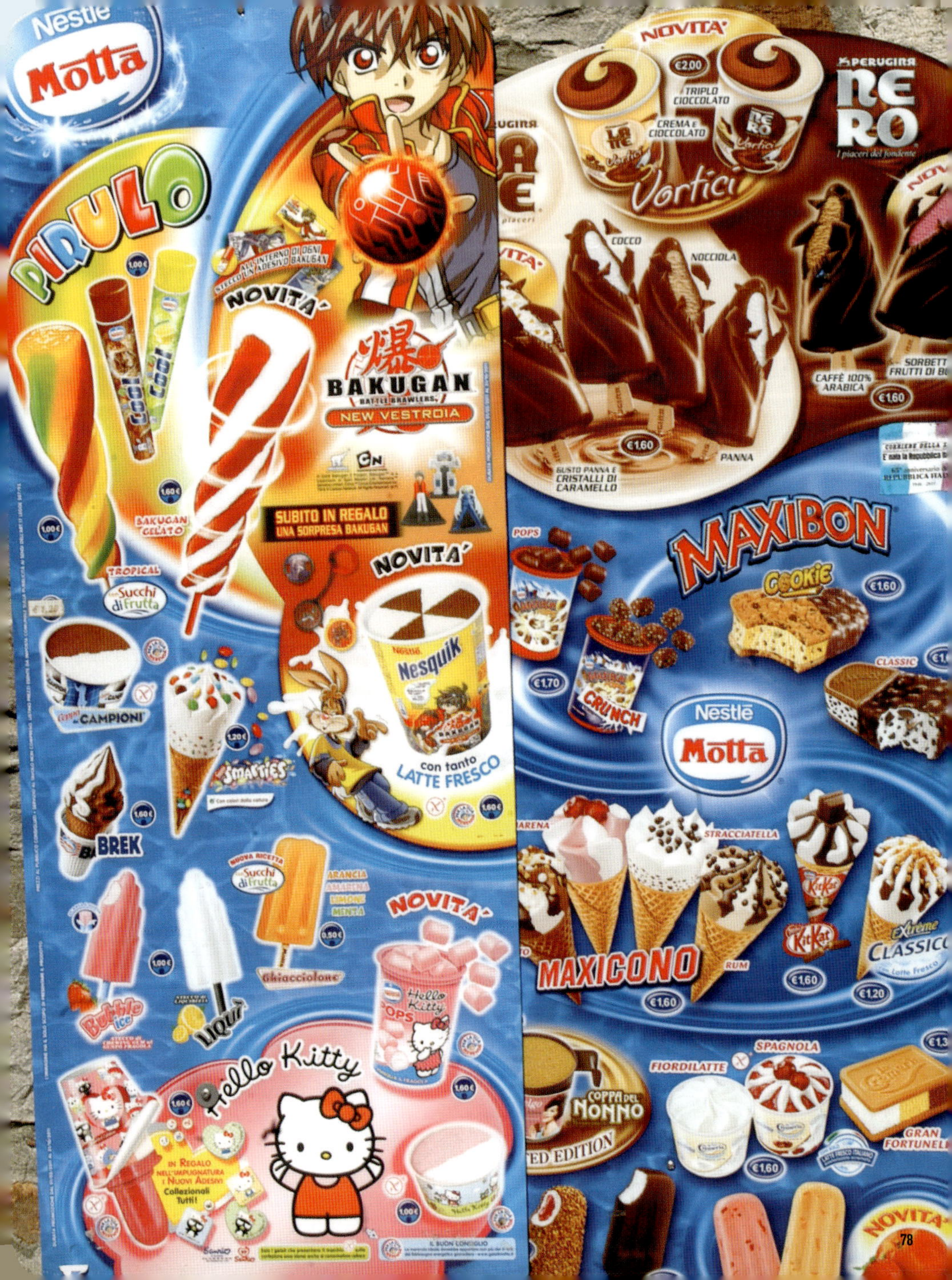
Nestlé
Motta
PIRULO
1,00 €
Cool
Cool
1,60 €
1,00 €
BAKUGAN GELATO
TROPICAL
Succhi di Frutta
NOVITA'
ALL'INTERNO DI OGNI STECCO UN ADESIVO BAKUGAN
BAKUGAN
BATTLE BRAWLERS
NEW VESTROIA
SUBITO IN REGALO
UNA SORPRESA BAKUGAN
NOVITA'
Nesquik
con tanto LATTE FRESCO
1,60 €
CAMPIONI
1,20 €
SMARTIES
BREK
1,60 €
NUOVA RICETTA
Succhi di Frutta
ARANCIA
AMARENA
LIMONE
MENTA
0,50 €
Ghiacciolone
1,00 €
LIQUI
NOVITA'
Hello Kitty
POPS
1,60 €
Hello Kitty
1,60 €
IN REGALO NELL'IMPUGNATURA I NUOVI ADESIVI
Collezionali Tutti!
1,00 €
IL BUON CONSIGLIO
NOVITA'
€2,00
TRIPLO CIOCCOLATO
CREMA E CIOCCOLATO
PERUGINA
NERO
I piaceri del fondente
Vortici
COCCO
NOCCIOLA
CAFFÈ 100% ARABICA
SORBETTO FRUTTI DI BOSCO
€1,60
€1,60
GUSTO PANNA E CRISTALLI DI CARAMELLO
PANNA
POPS
€1,70
CRUNCH
MAXIBON
COOKIE
€1,60
CLASSIC
Nestlé
Motta
STRACCIATELLA
MAXICONO
RUM
€1,60
€1,60
KitKat
Extreme
CLASSICO
€1,20
FIORDILATTE
SPAGNOLA
COPPA DEL NONNO
LIMITED EDITION
€1,60
GRAN FORTUNELLO
NOVITA'

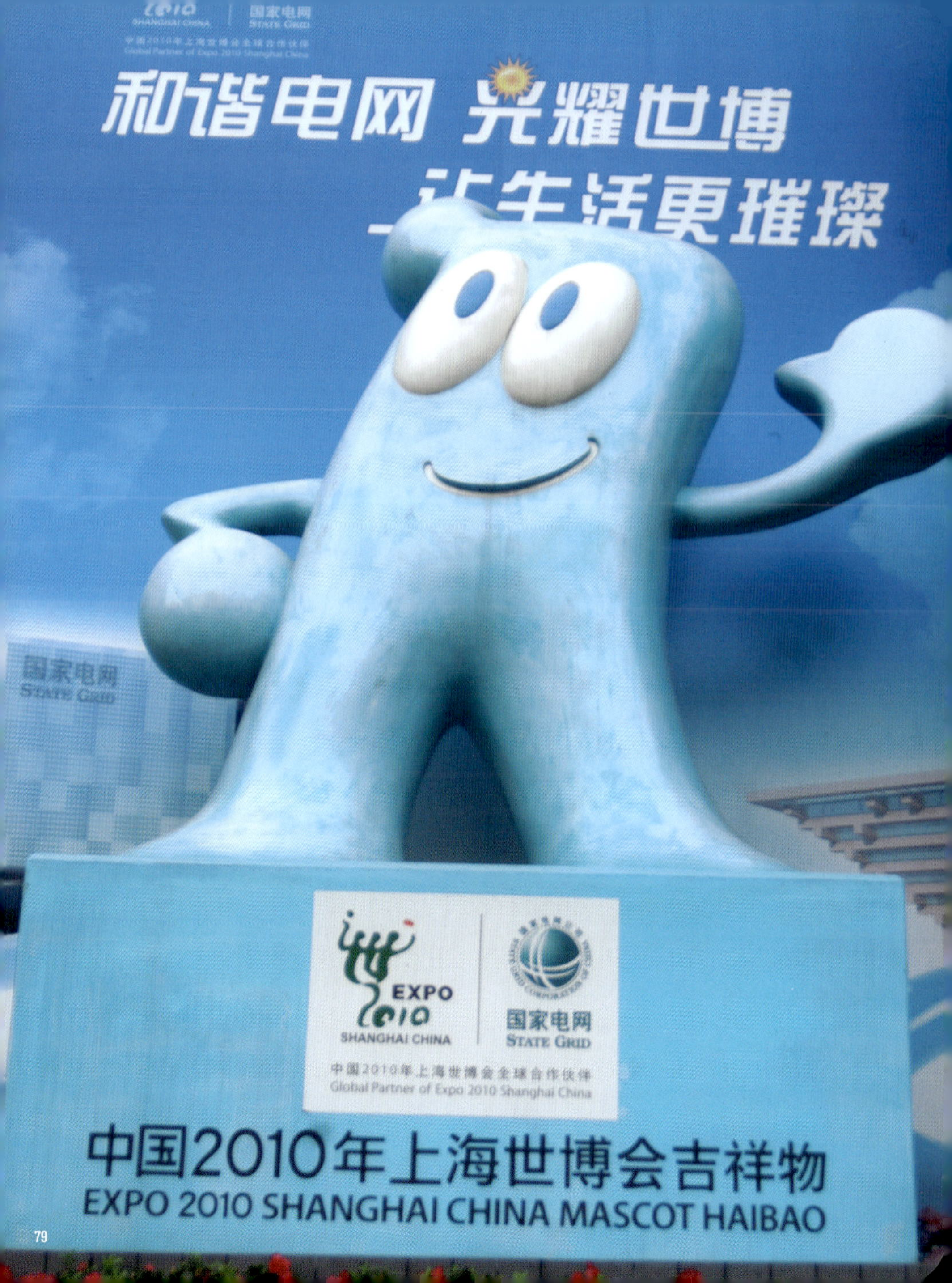
和谐电网 光耀世博
国家电网
STATE GRID
EXPO
2010
SHANGHAI CHINA
国家电网
STATE GRID
中国2010年上海世博会全球合作伙伴
Global Partner of Expo 2010 Shanghai China
中国2010年上海世博会吉祥物
EXPO 2010 SHANGHAI CHINA MASCOT HAIBAO

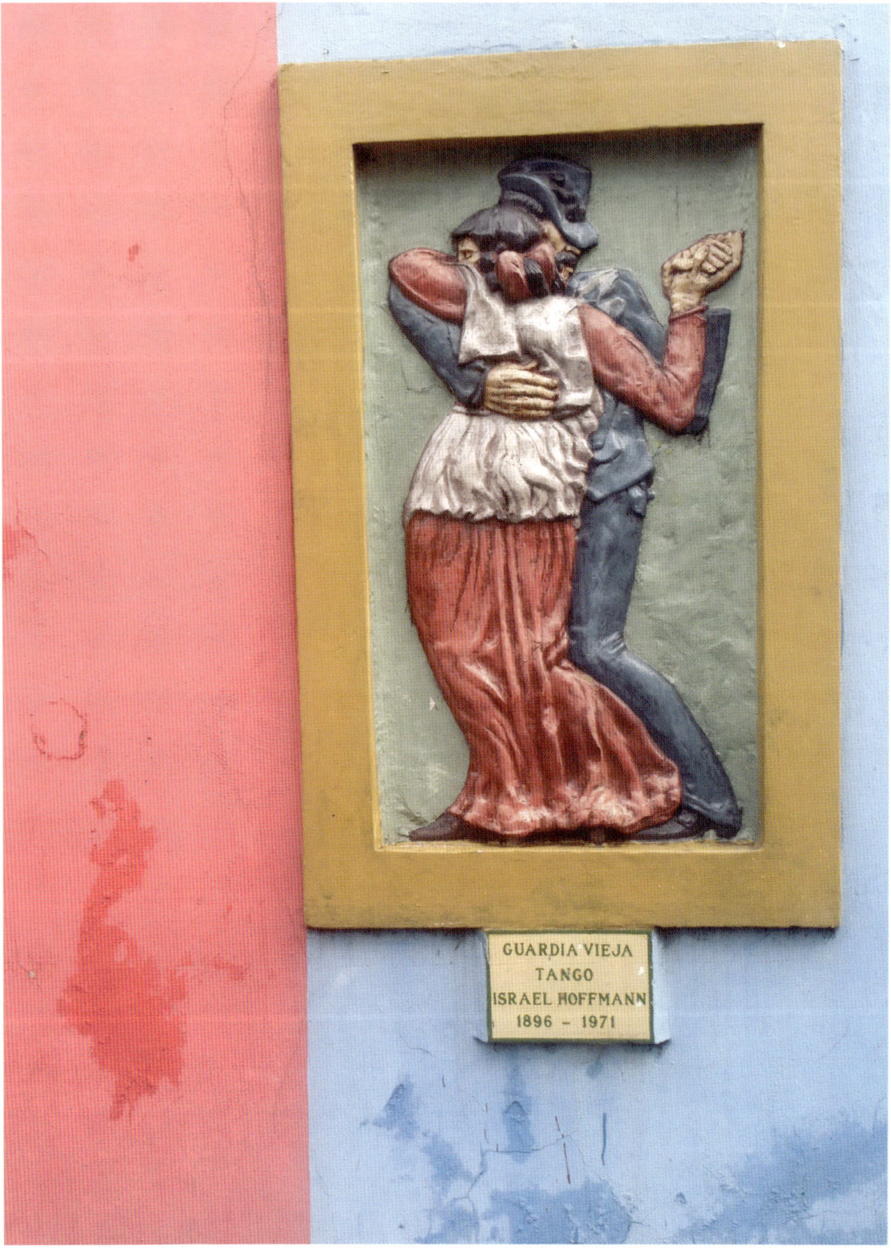
GUARDIA VIEJA
TANGO
ISRAEL HOFFMANN
1896 - 1971

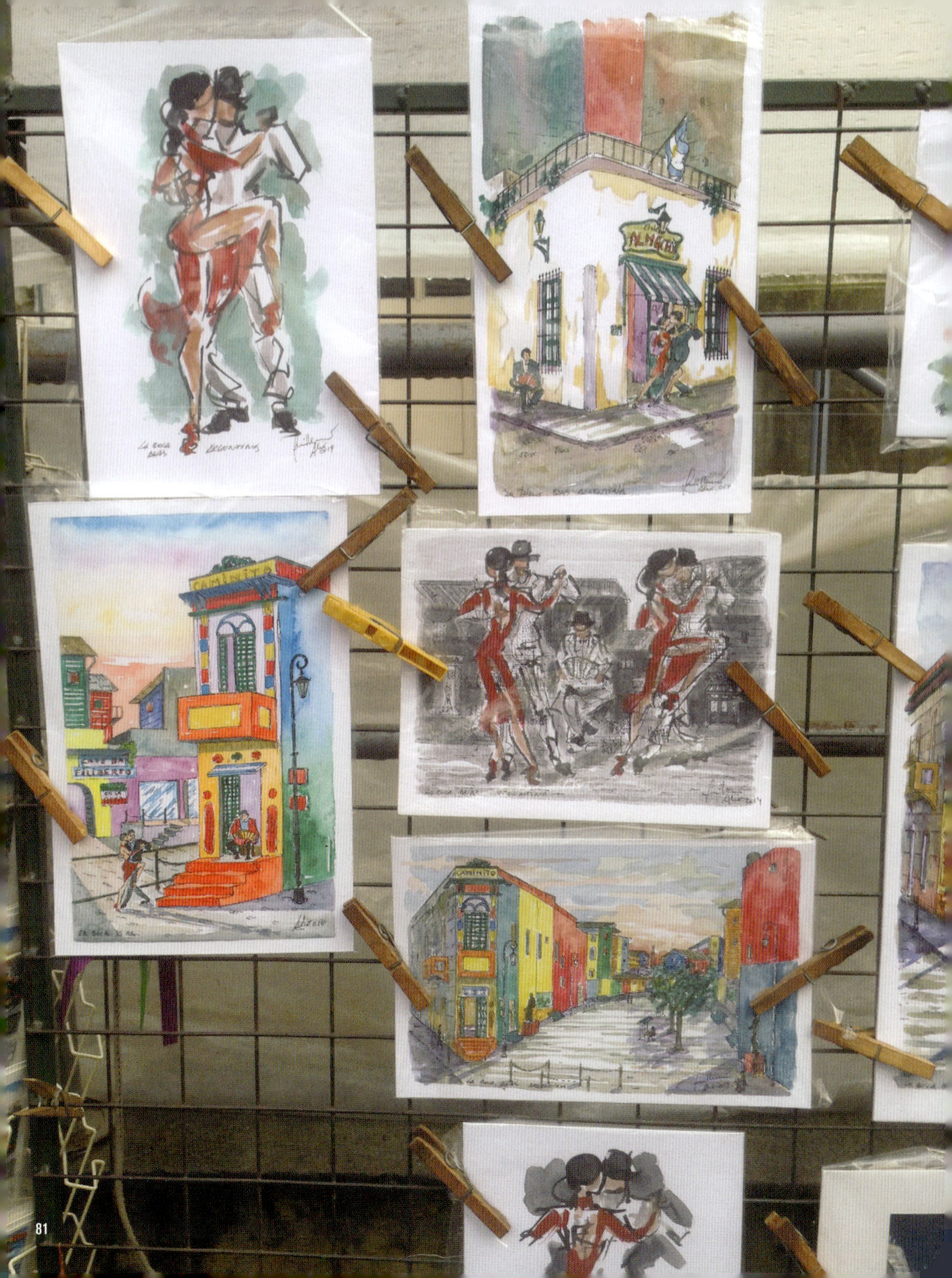

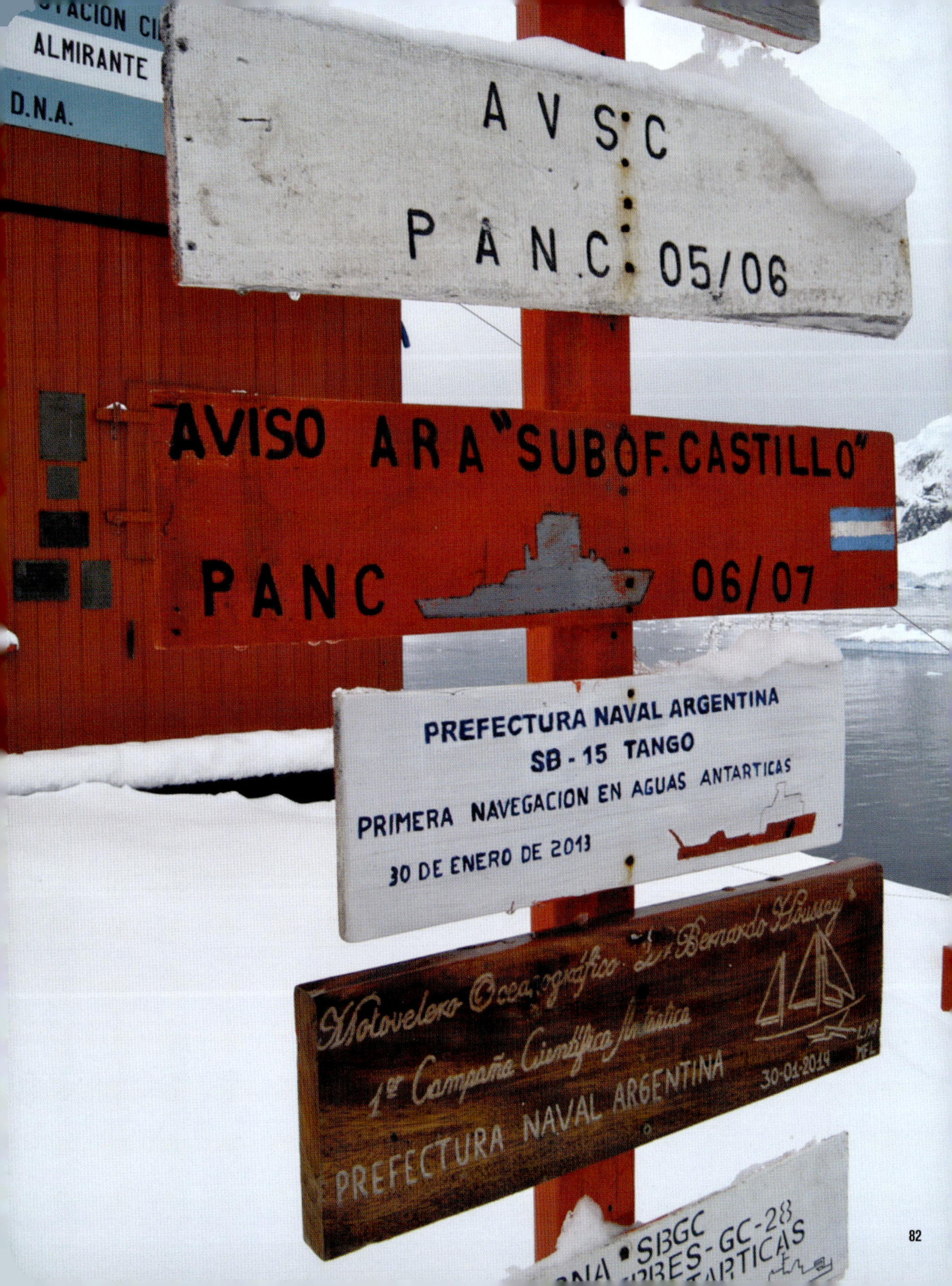
ALMIRANTE
D.N.A.
AVSC
PANC 05/06
AVISO ARA "SUBOF. CASTILLO"
PANC 06/07
PREFECTURA NAVAL ARGENTINA
SB - 15 TANGO
PRIMERA NAVEGACION EN AGUAS ANTARTICAS
30 DE ENERO DE 2013
Motovelero Oceanográfico Dr. Bernardo Houssay
1er Campaña Científica Antártica
30-01-2014
PREFECTURA NAVAL ARGENTINA

LOOKING

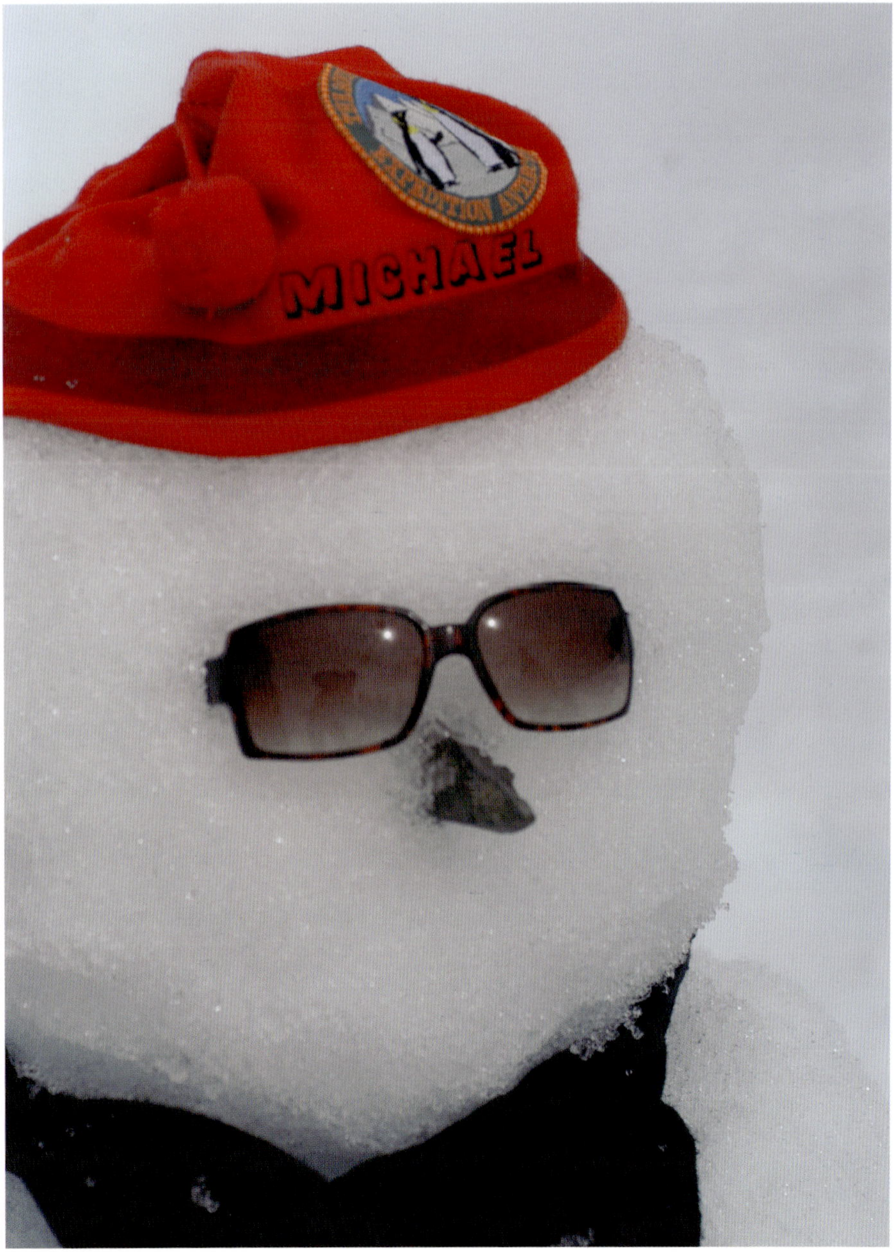
MICHAEL

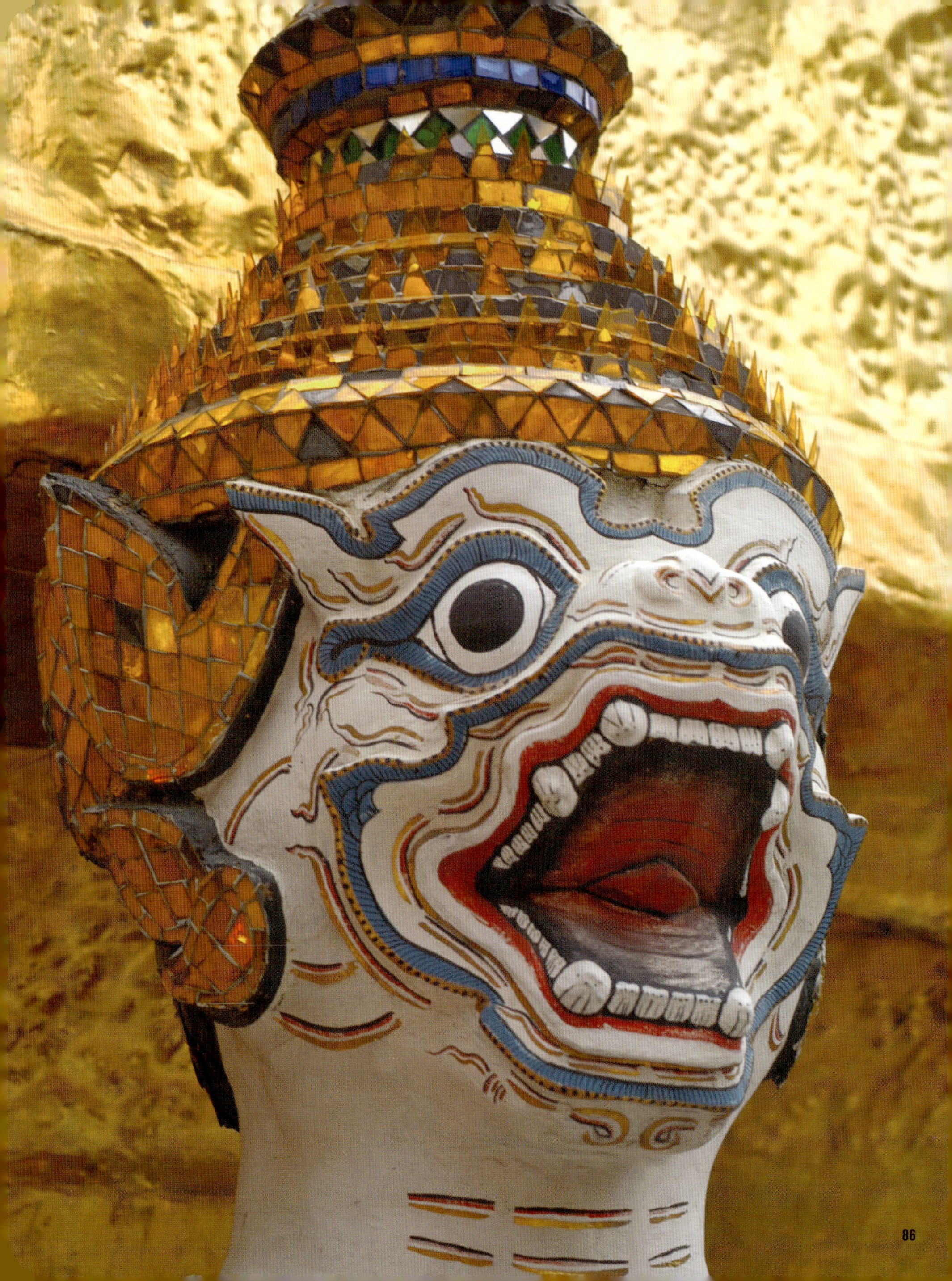

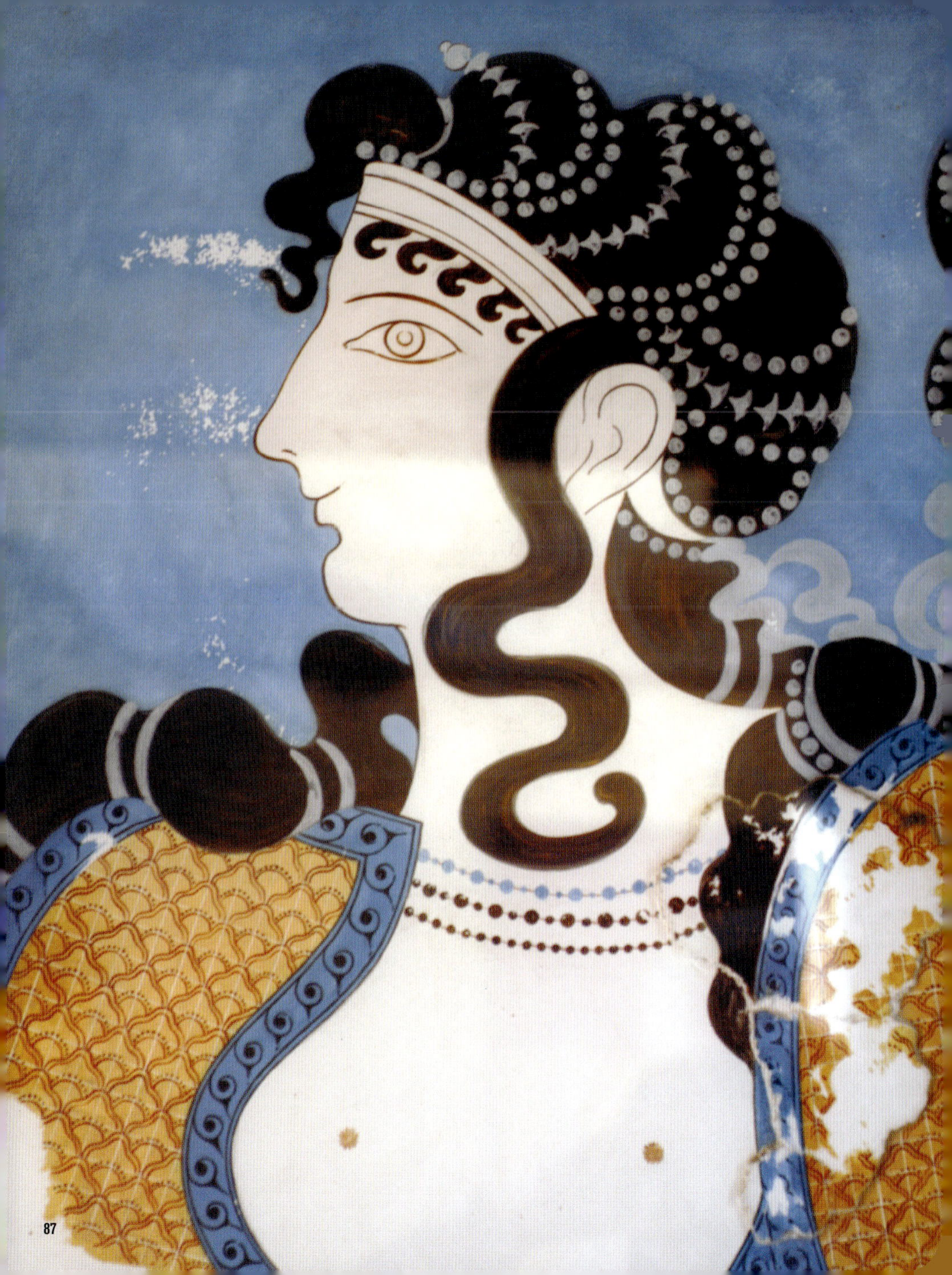

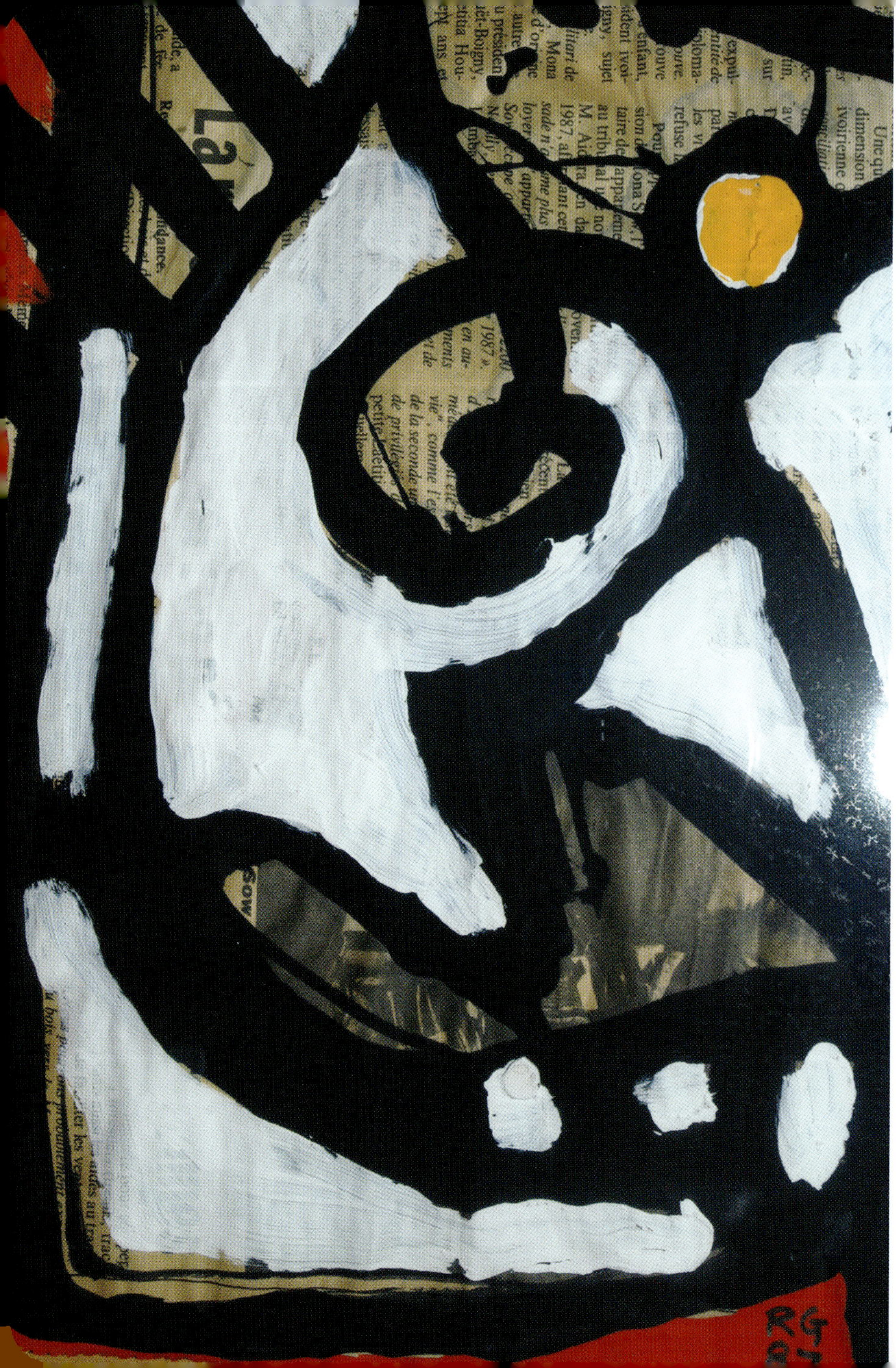

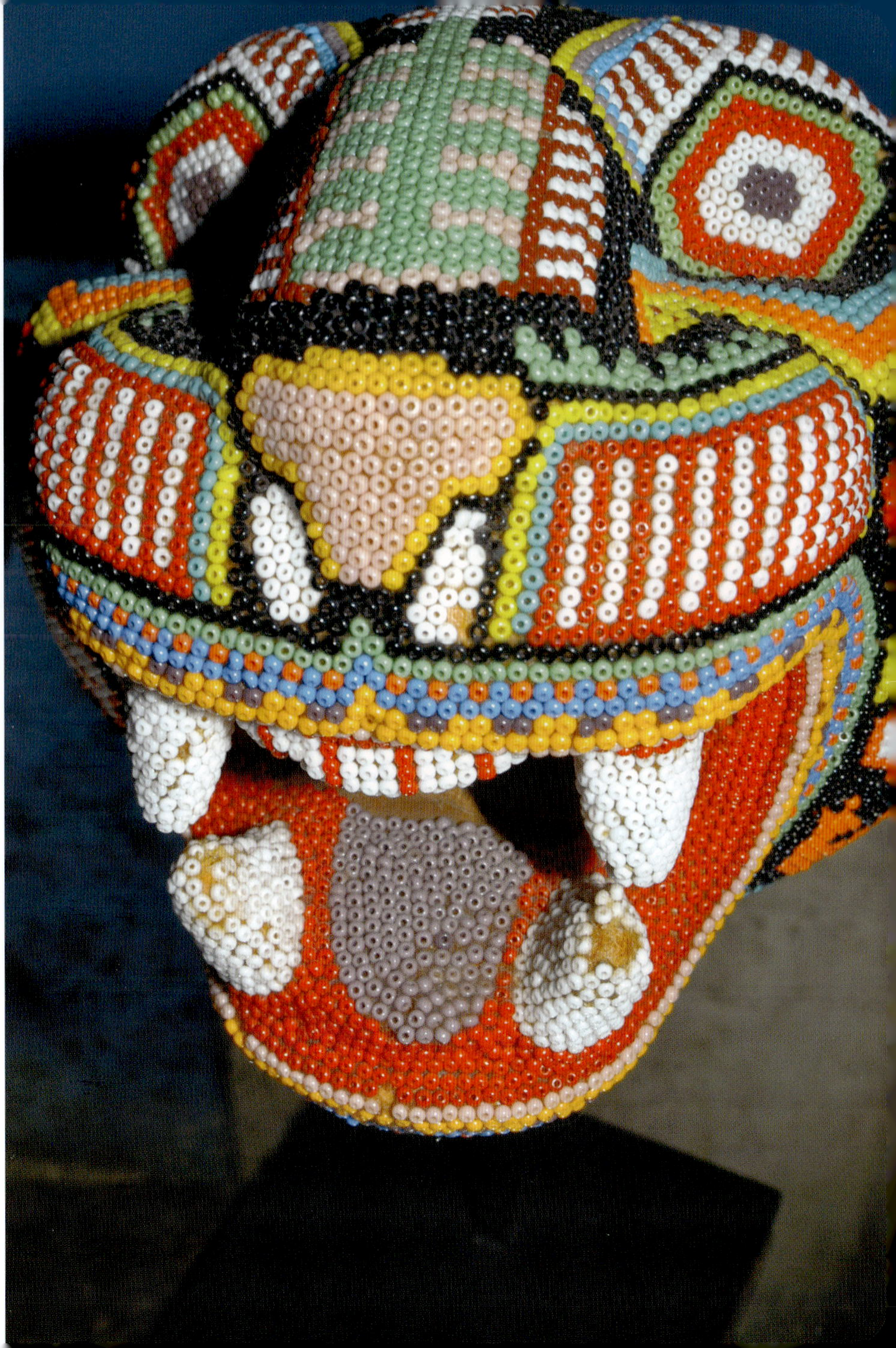

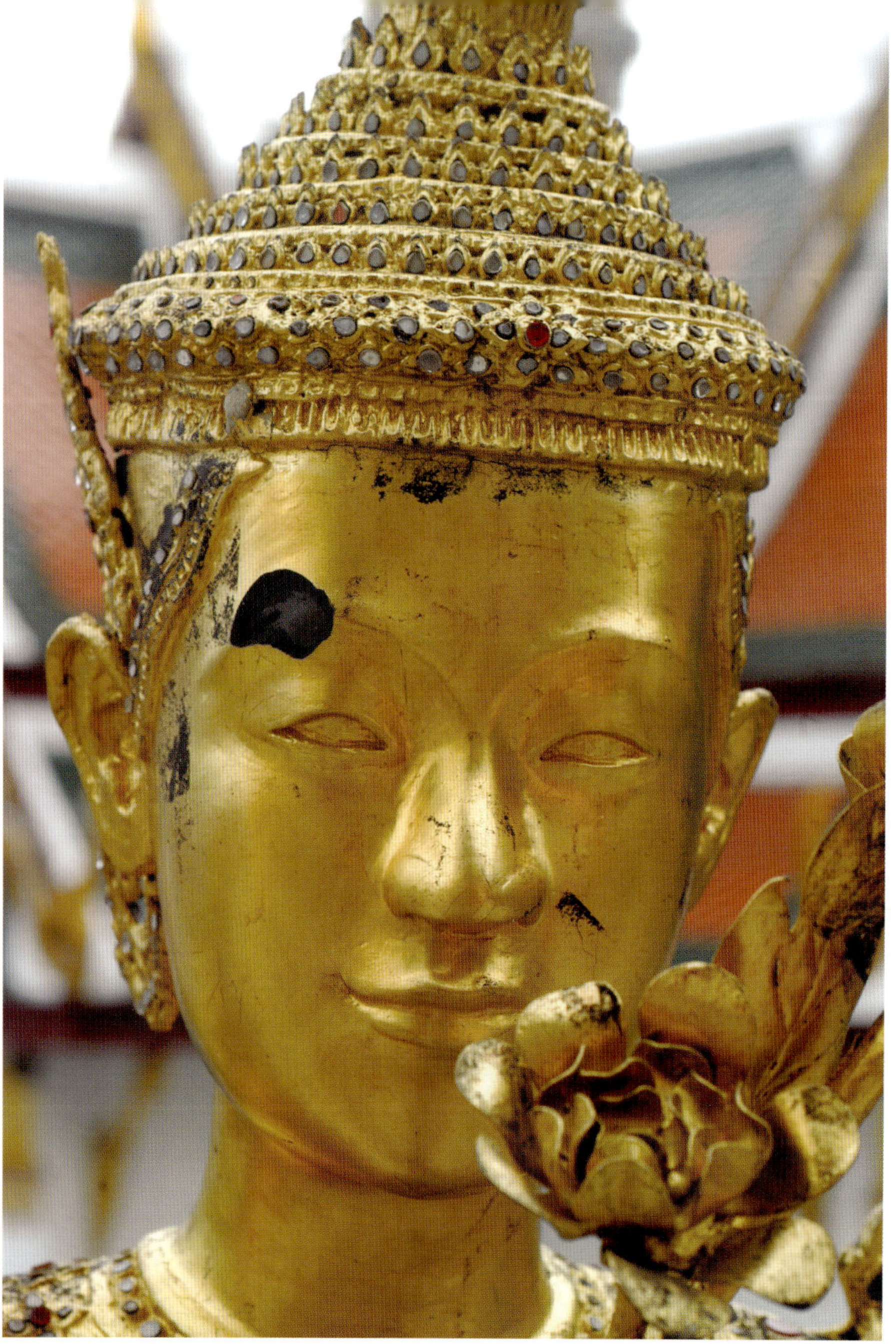

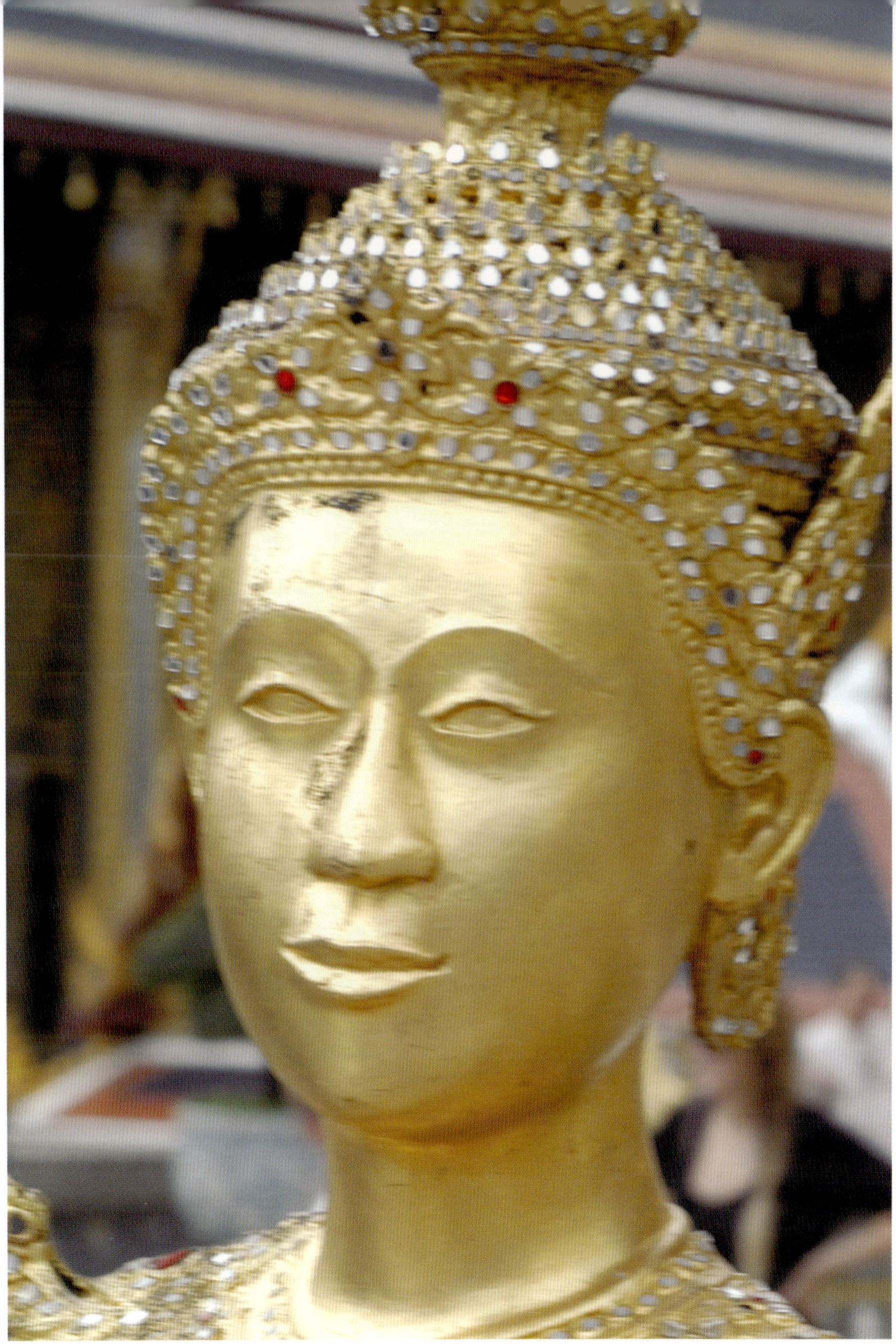

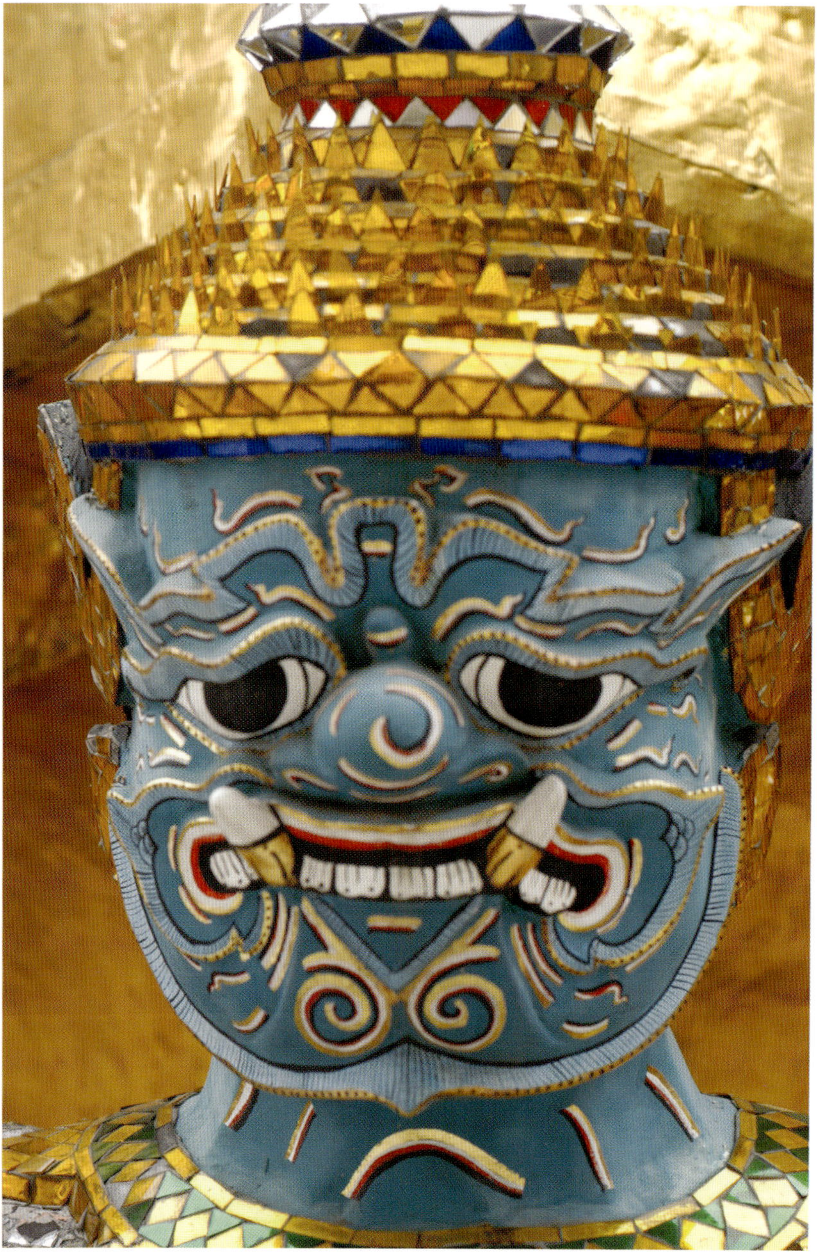

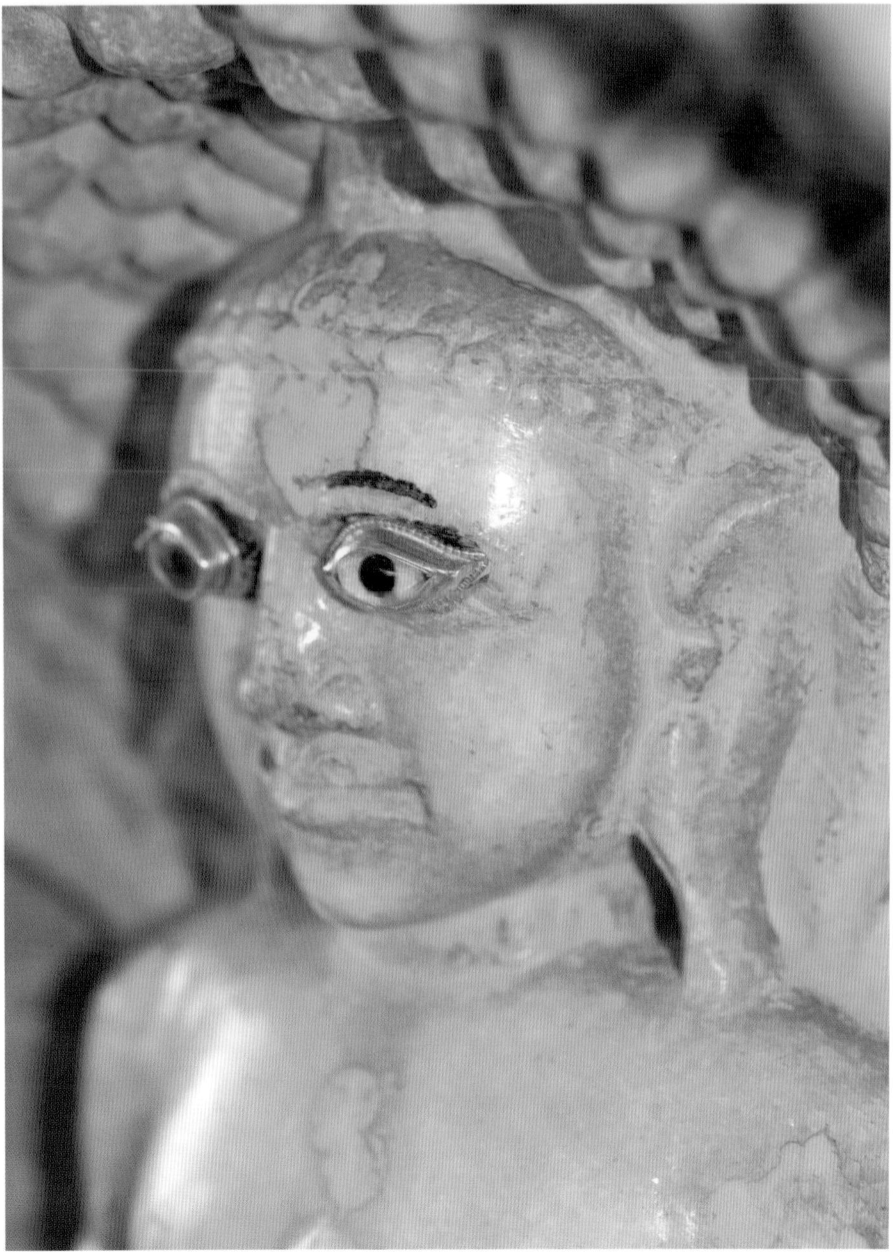

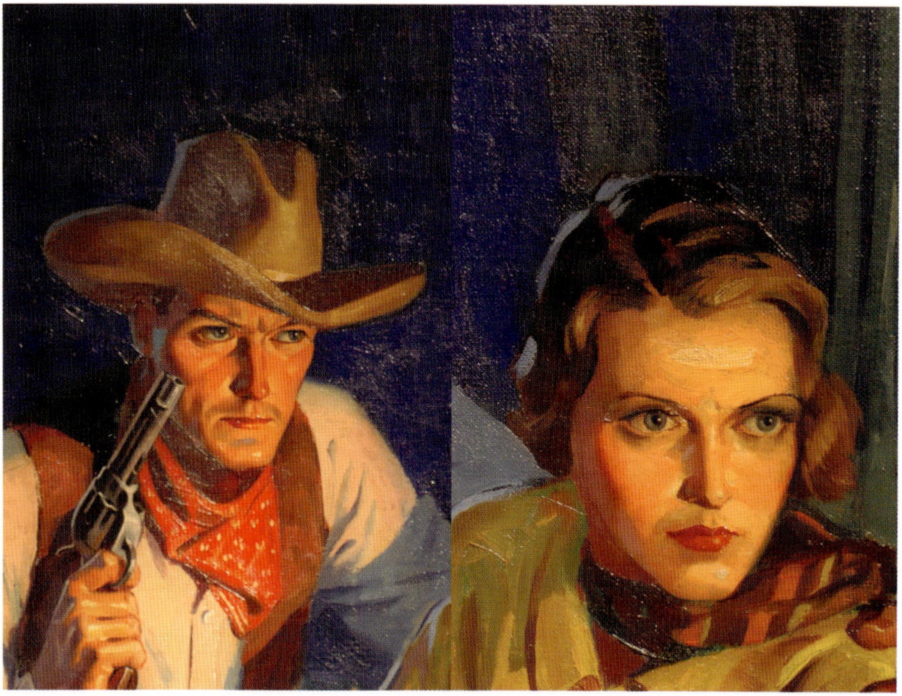

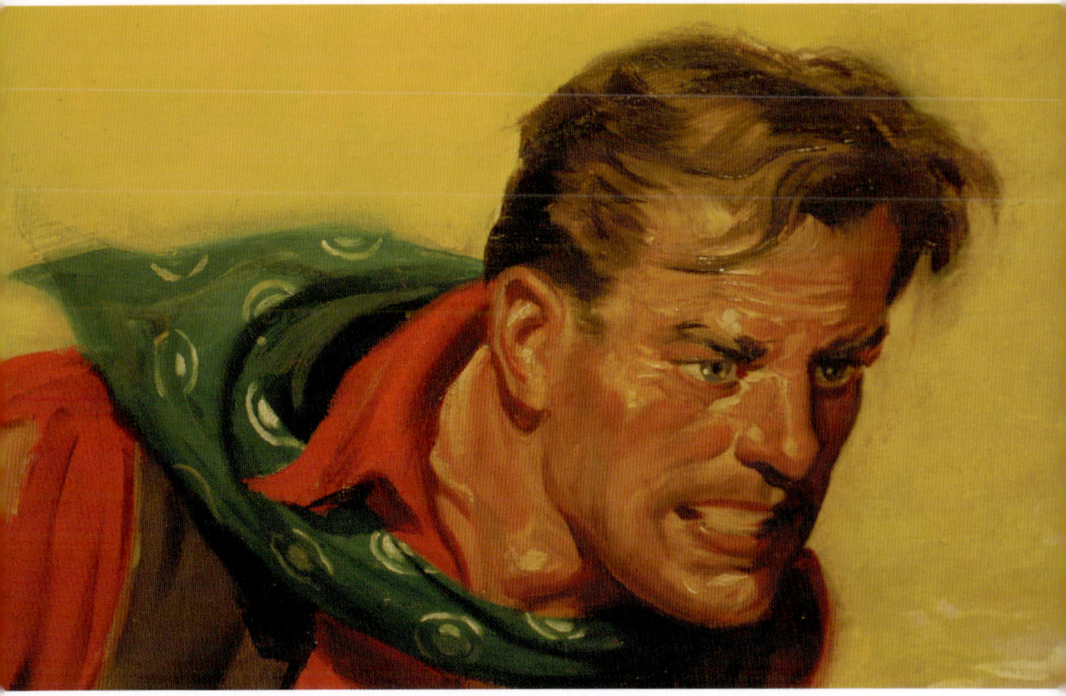

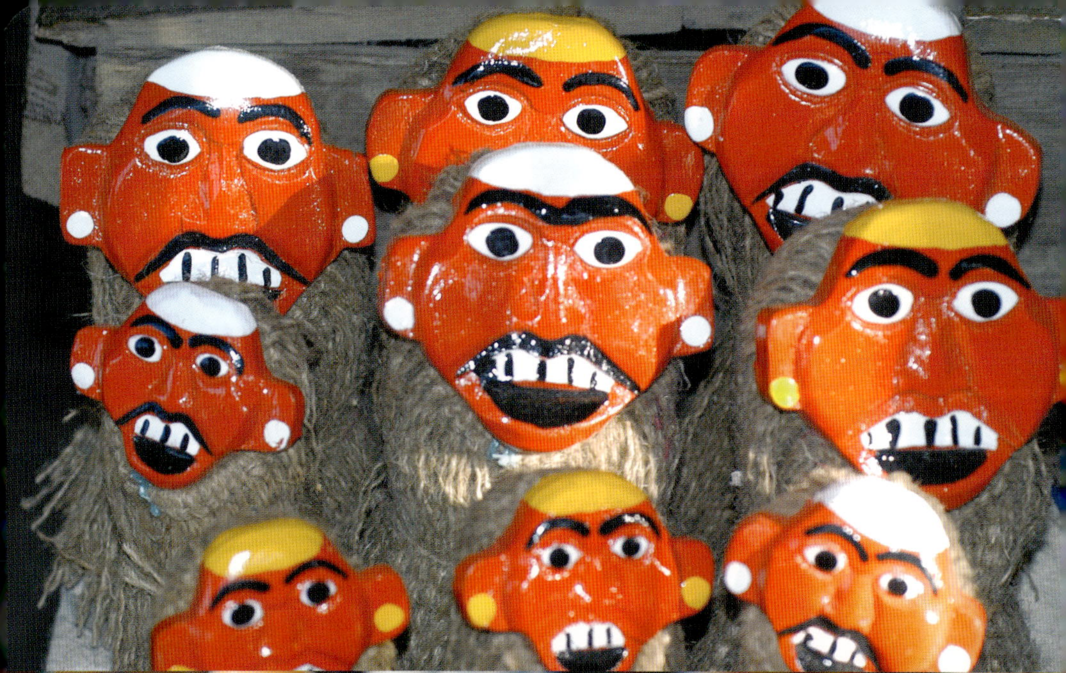

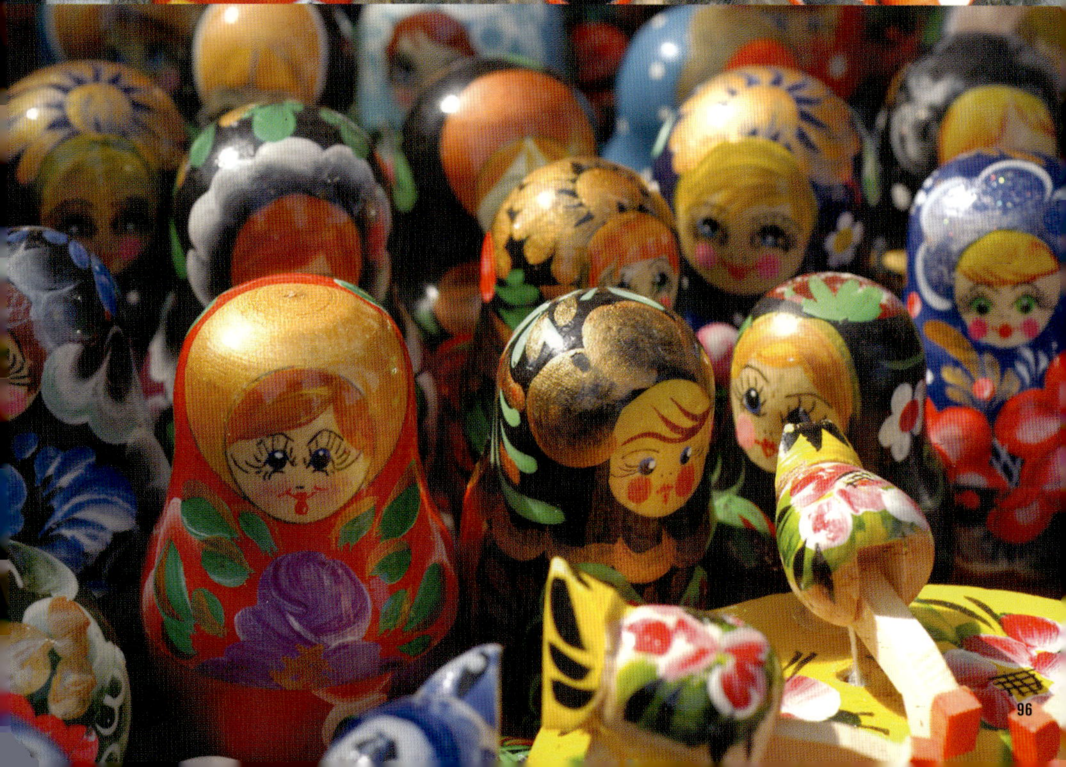

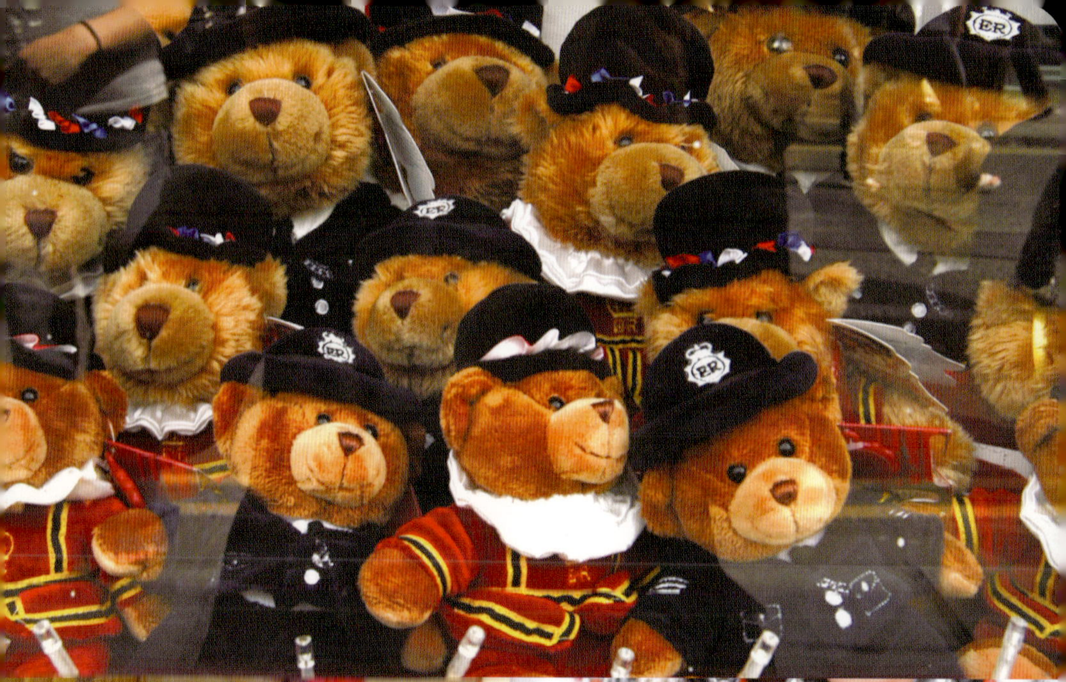
ER

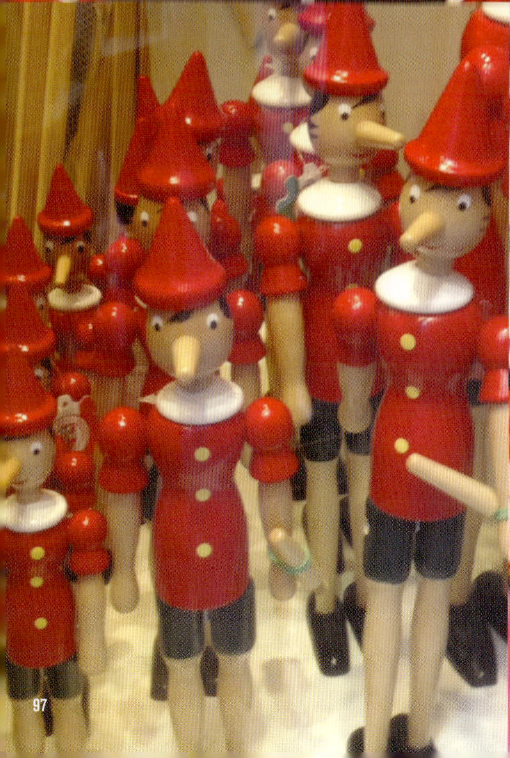

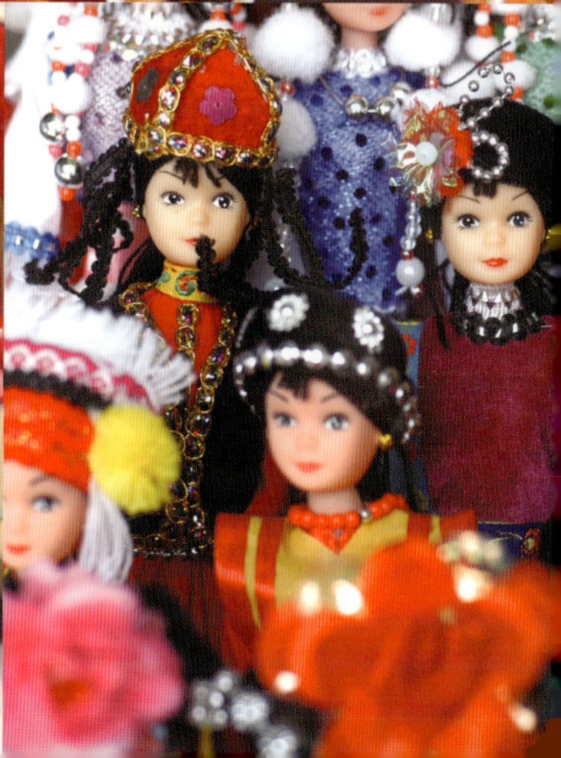

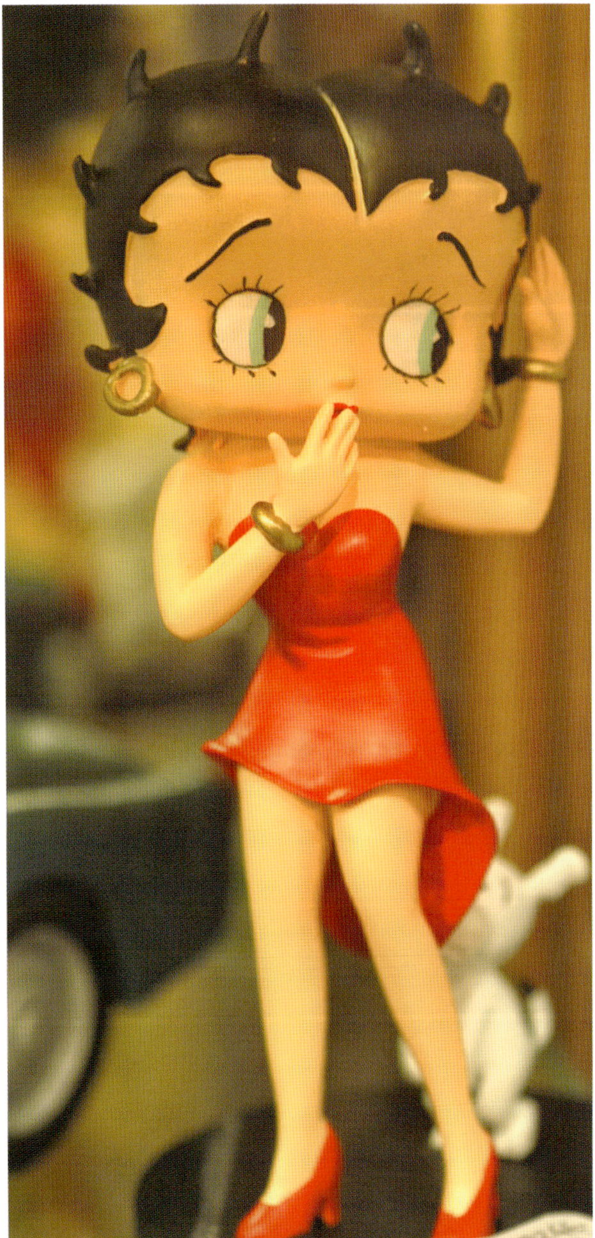

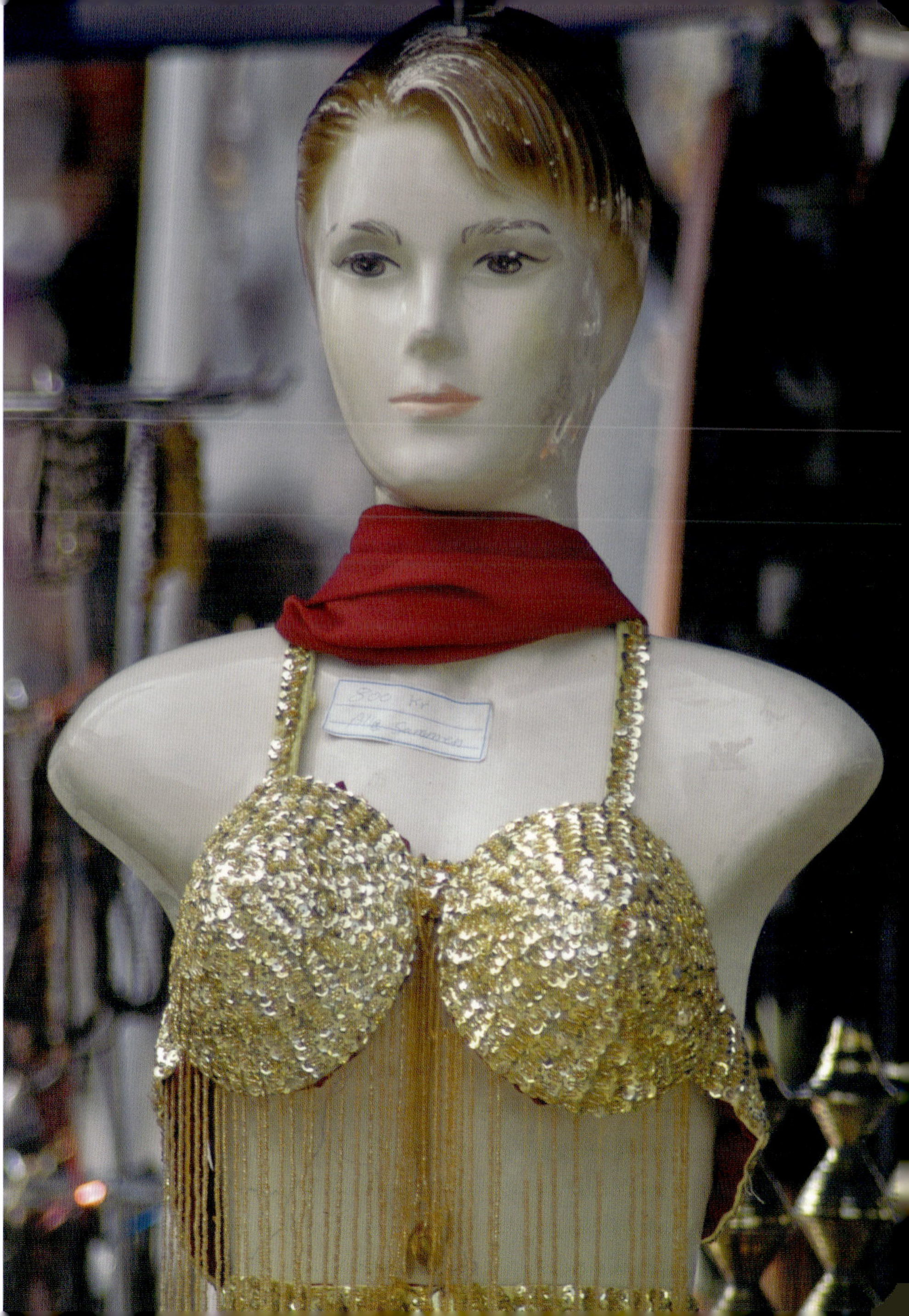
300 kr

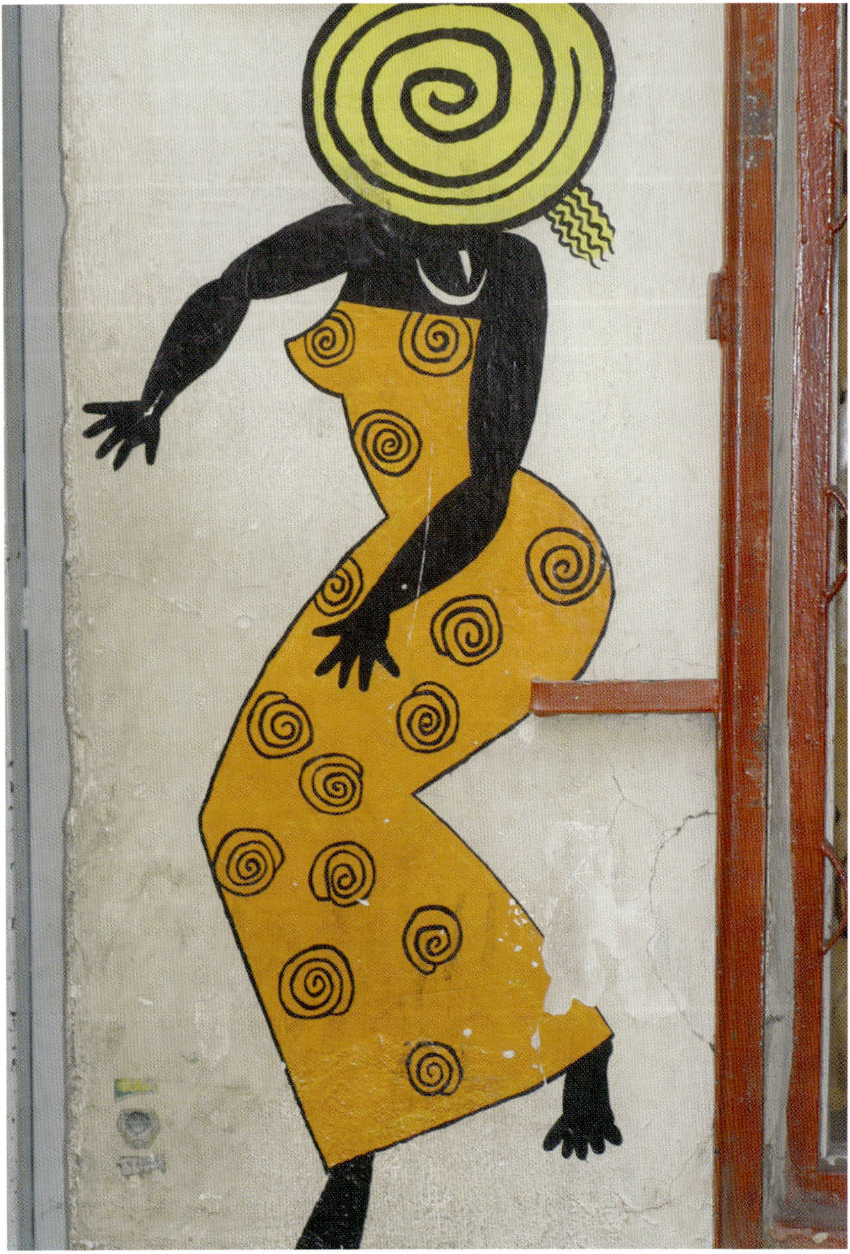

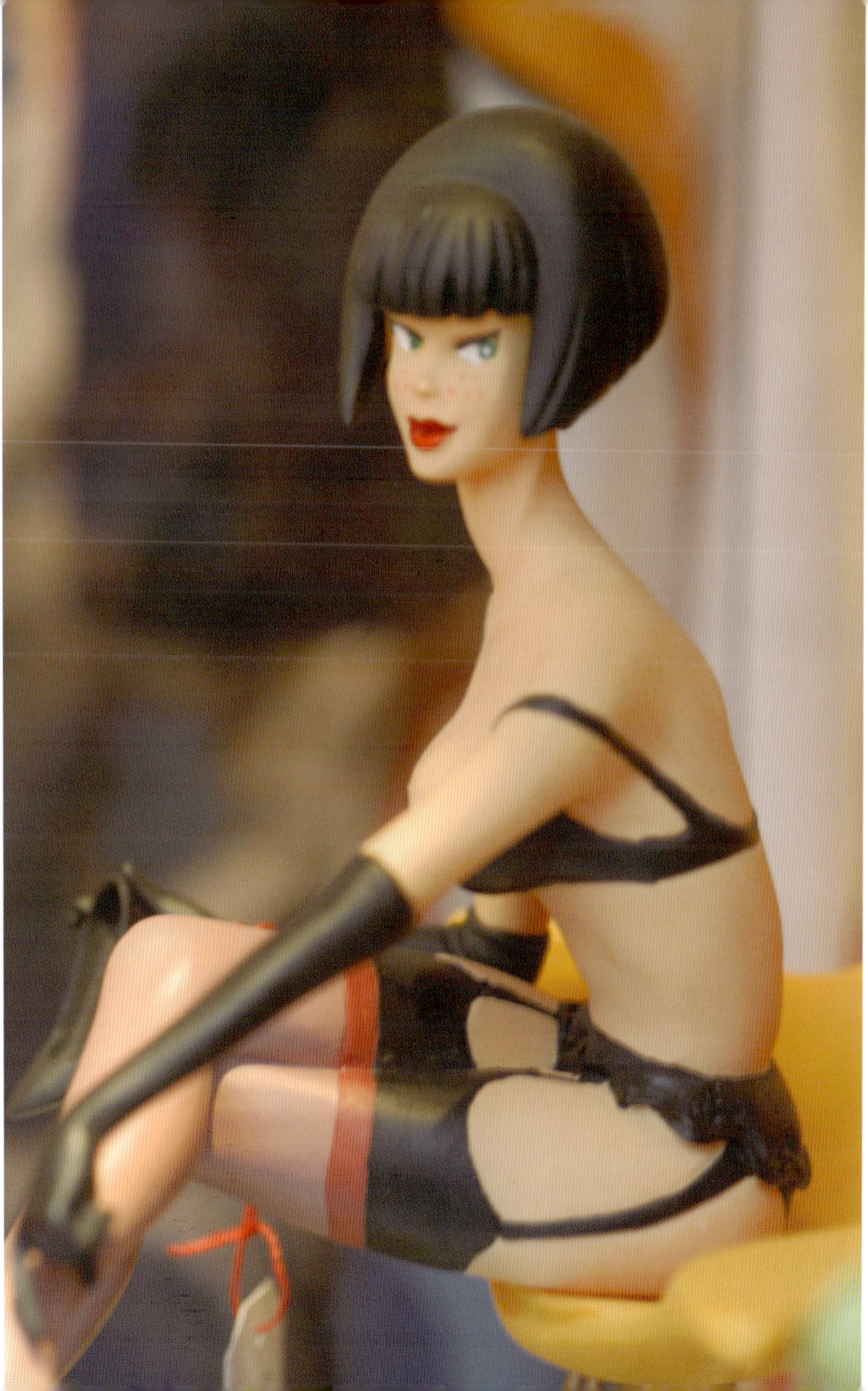

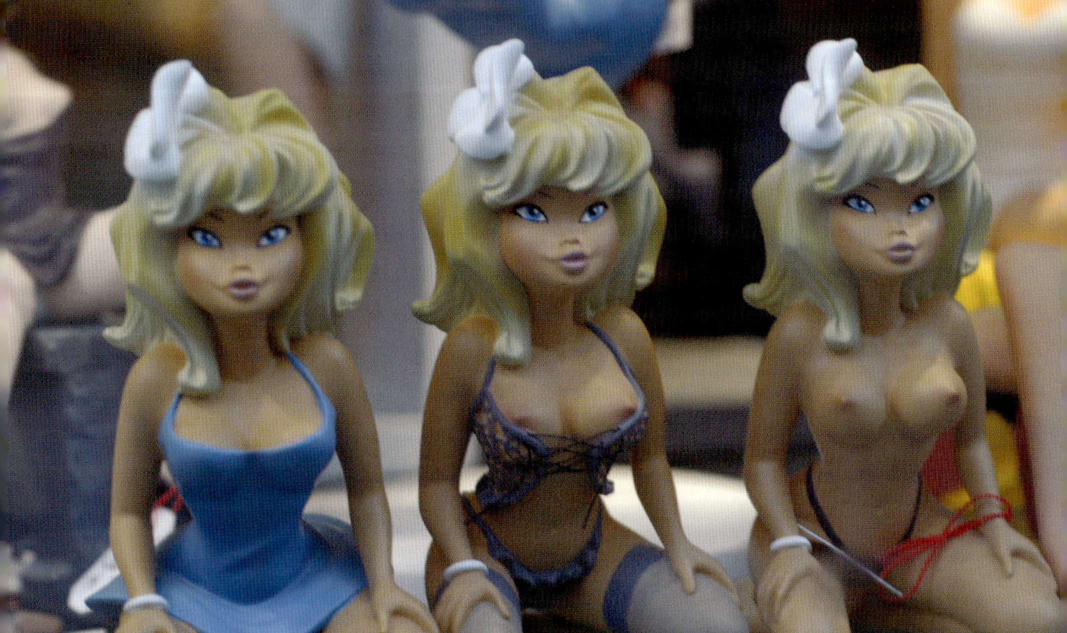

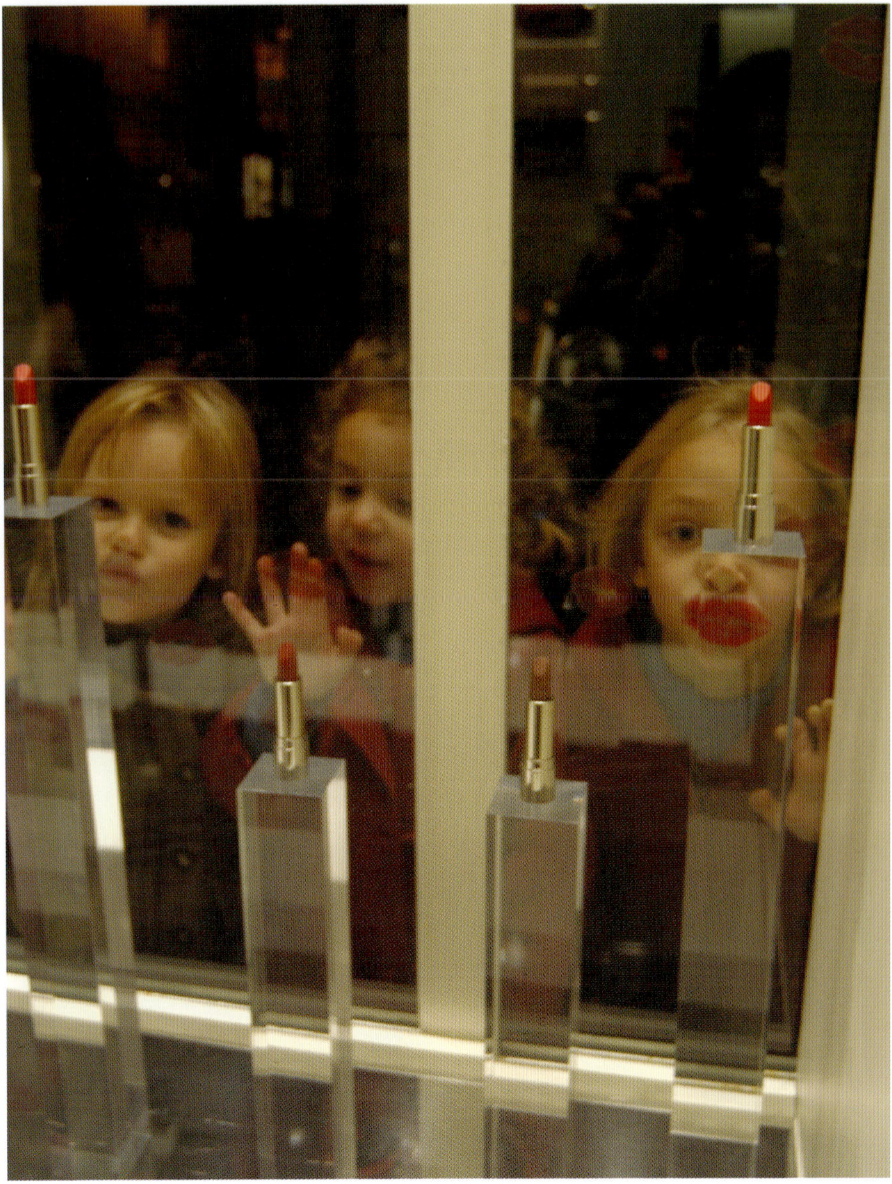

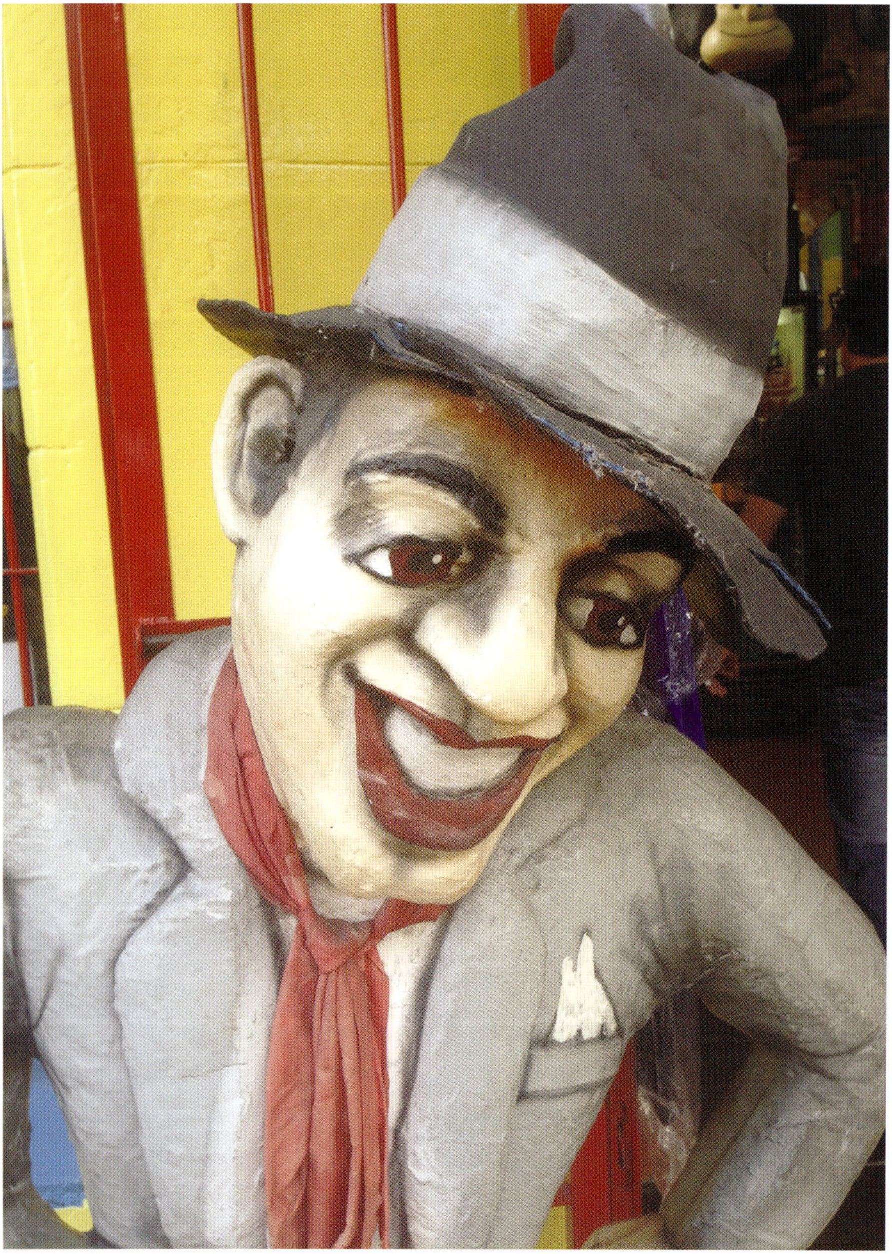

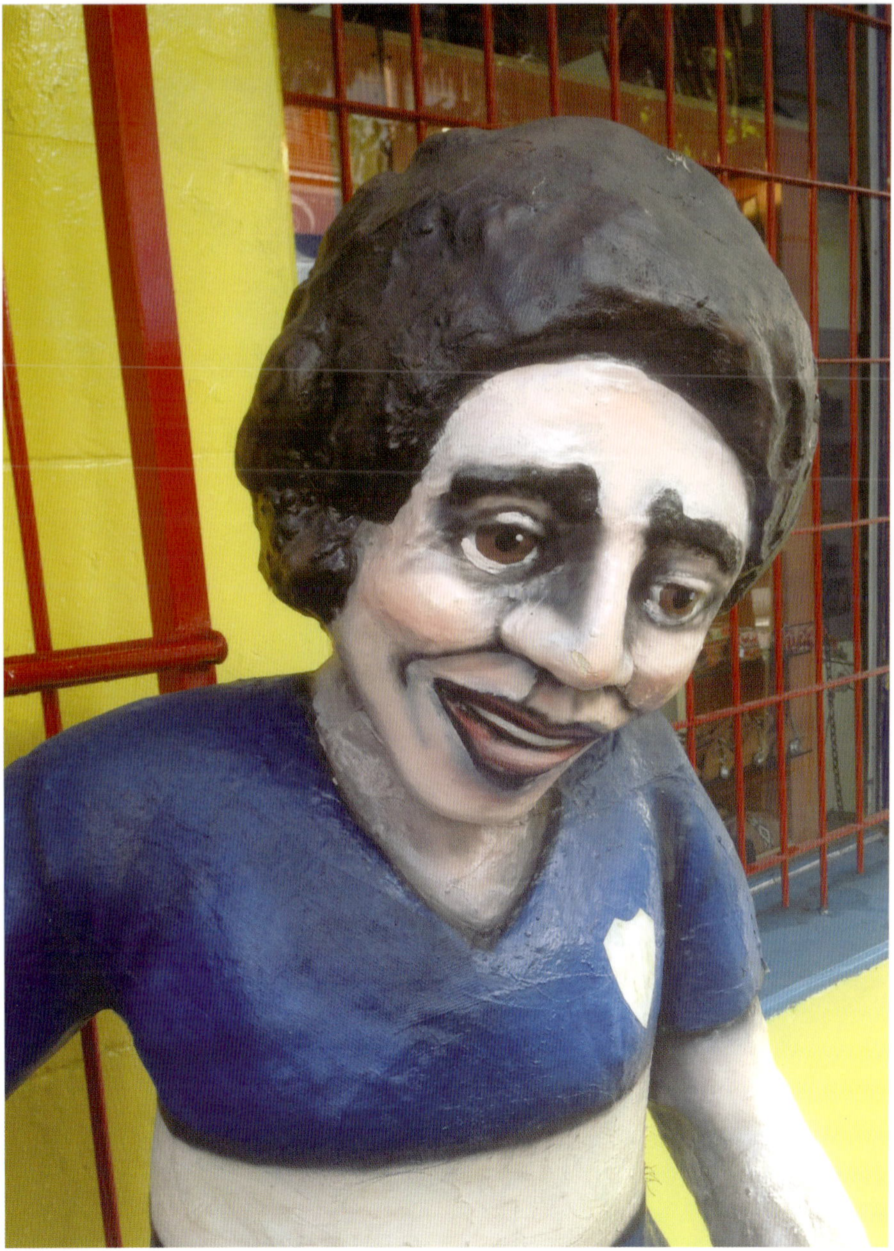

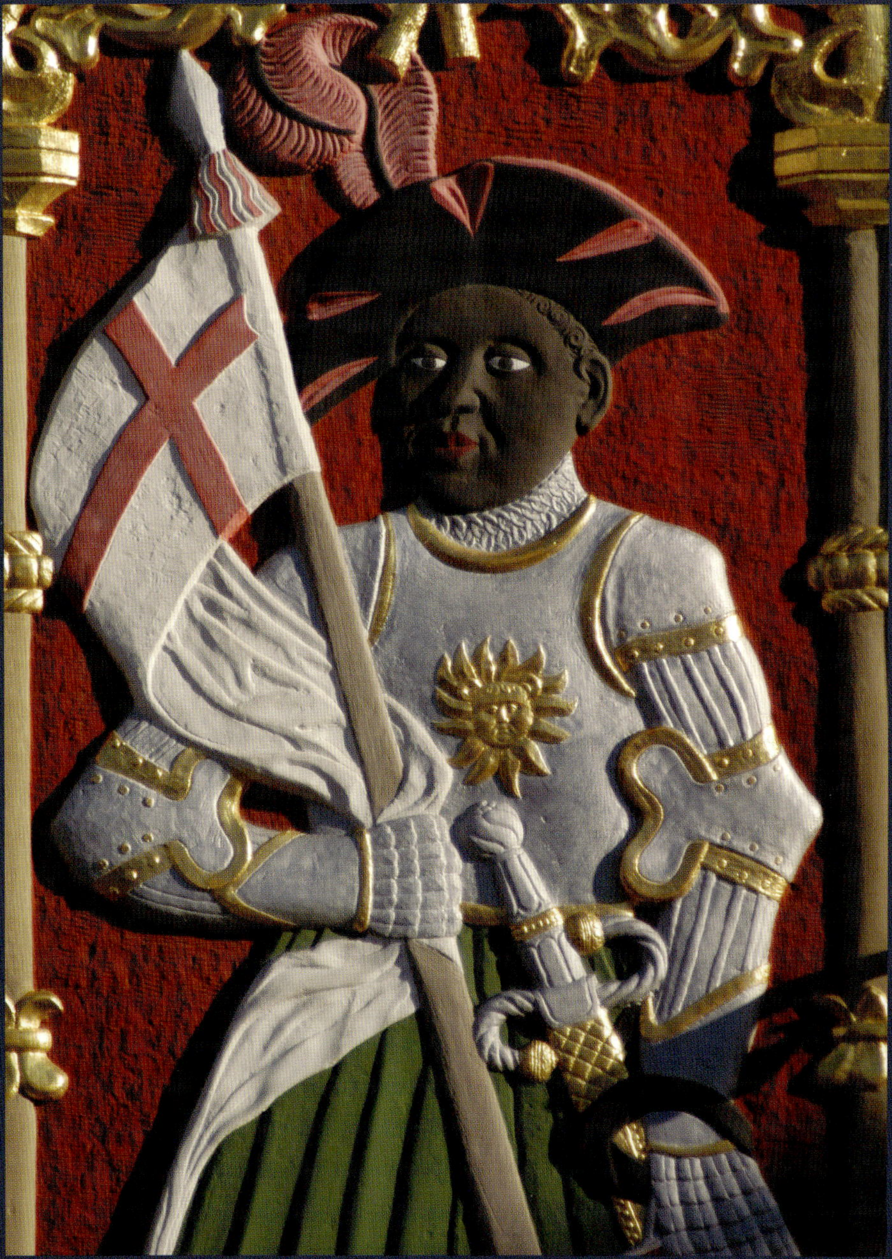

SEEING

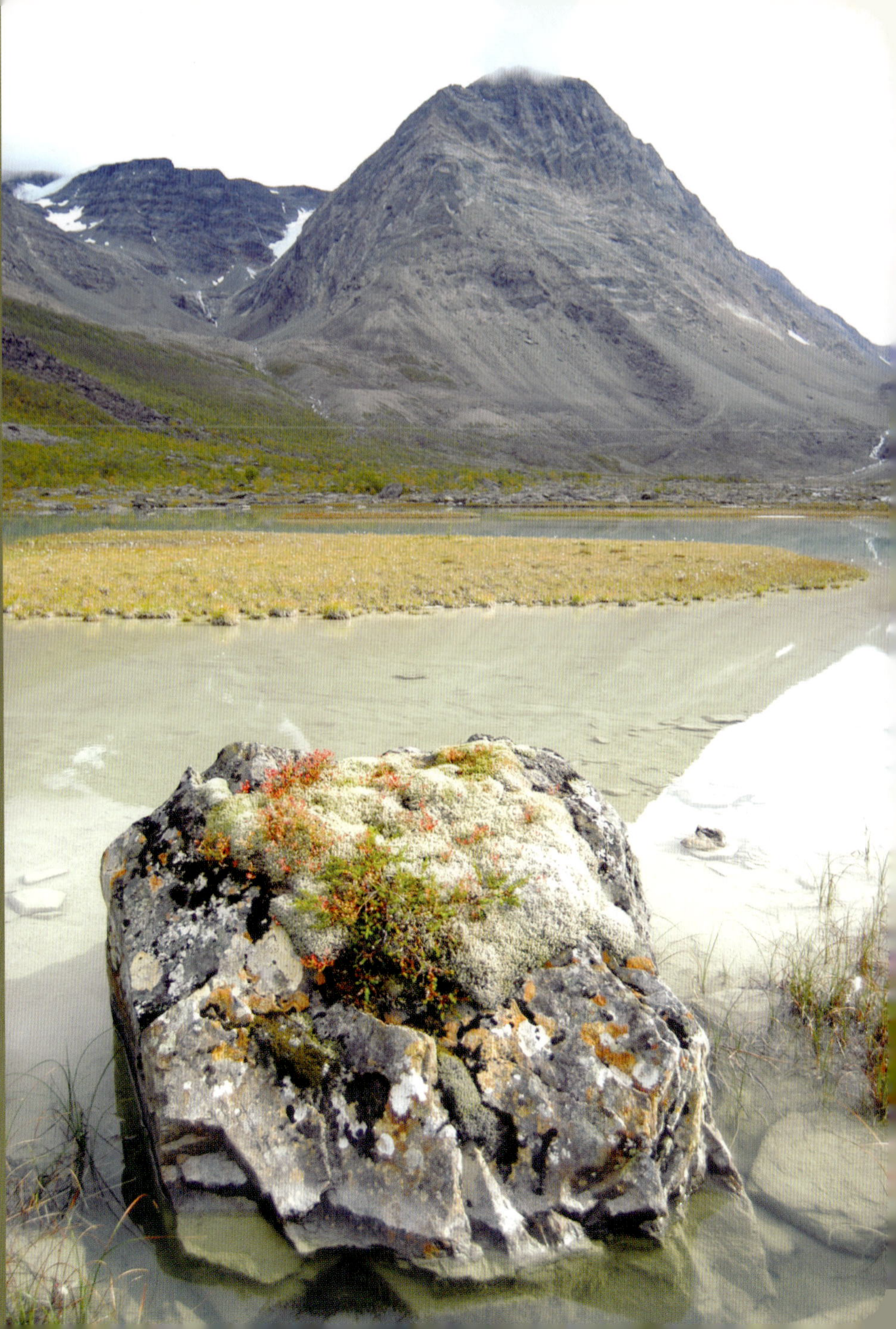

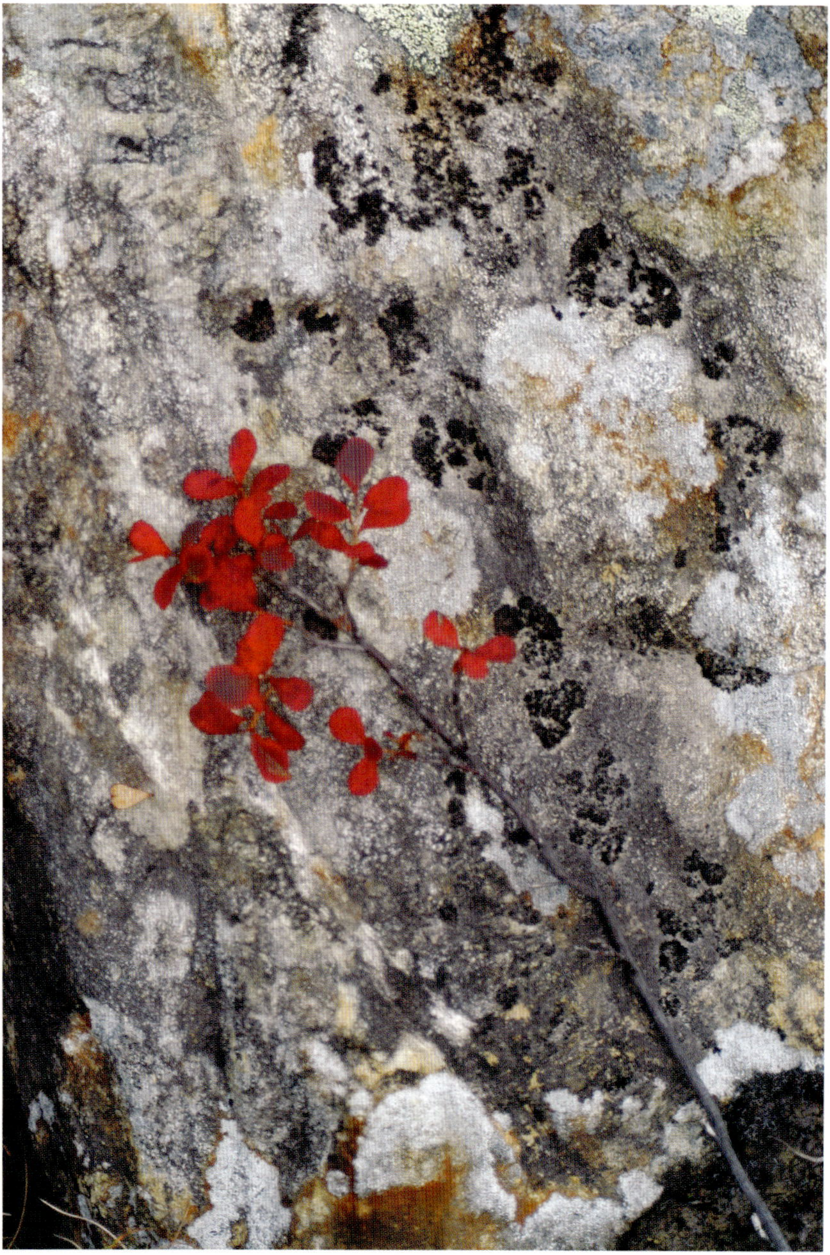

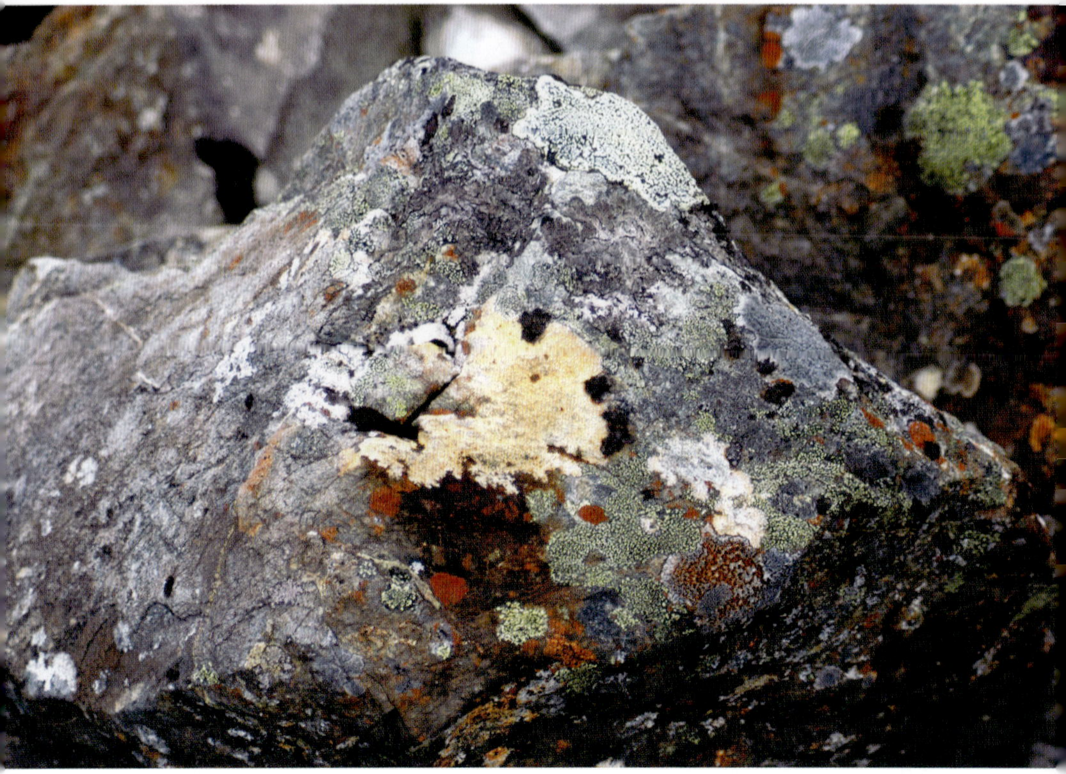

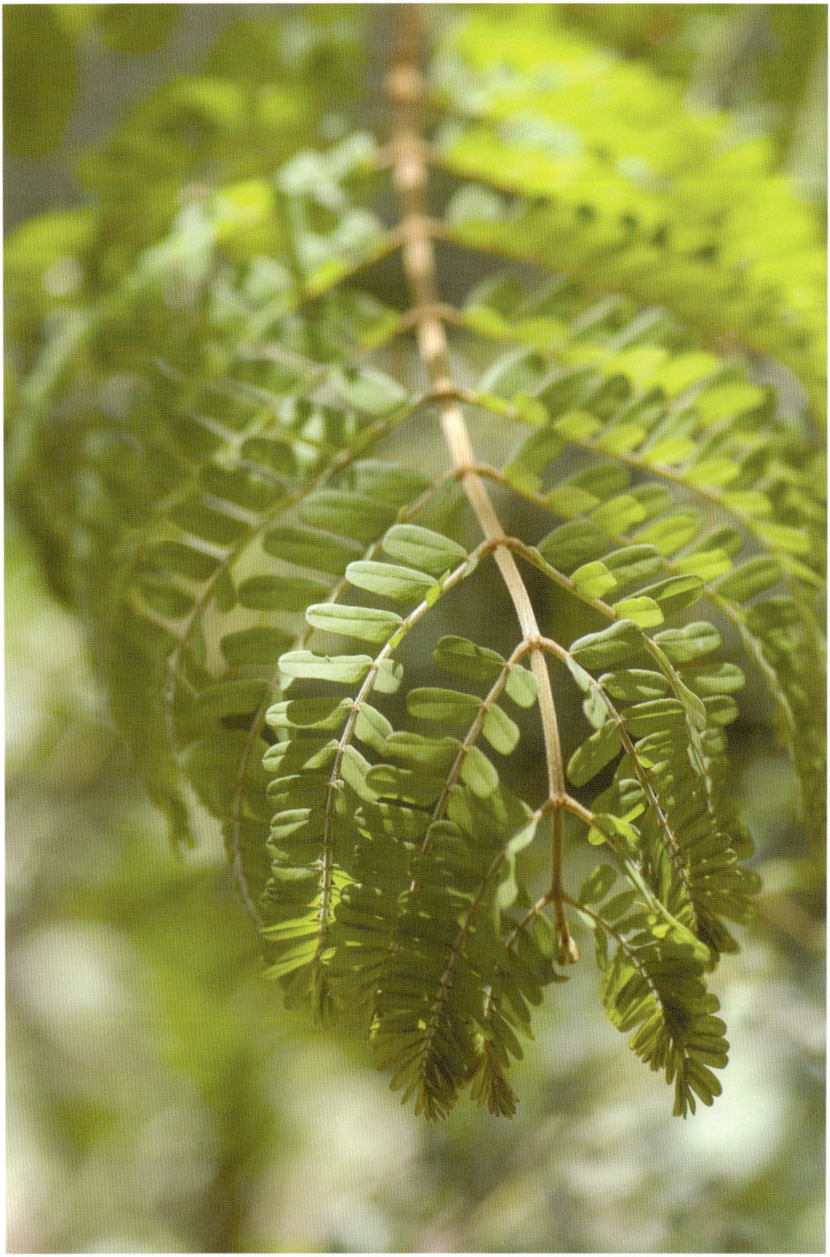

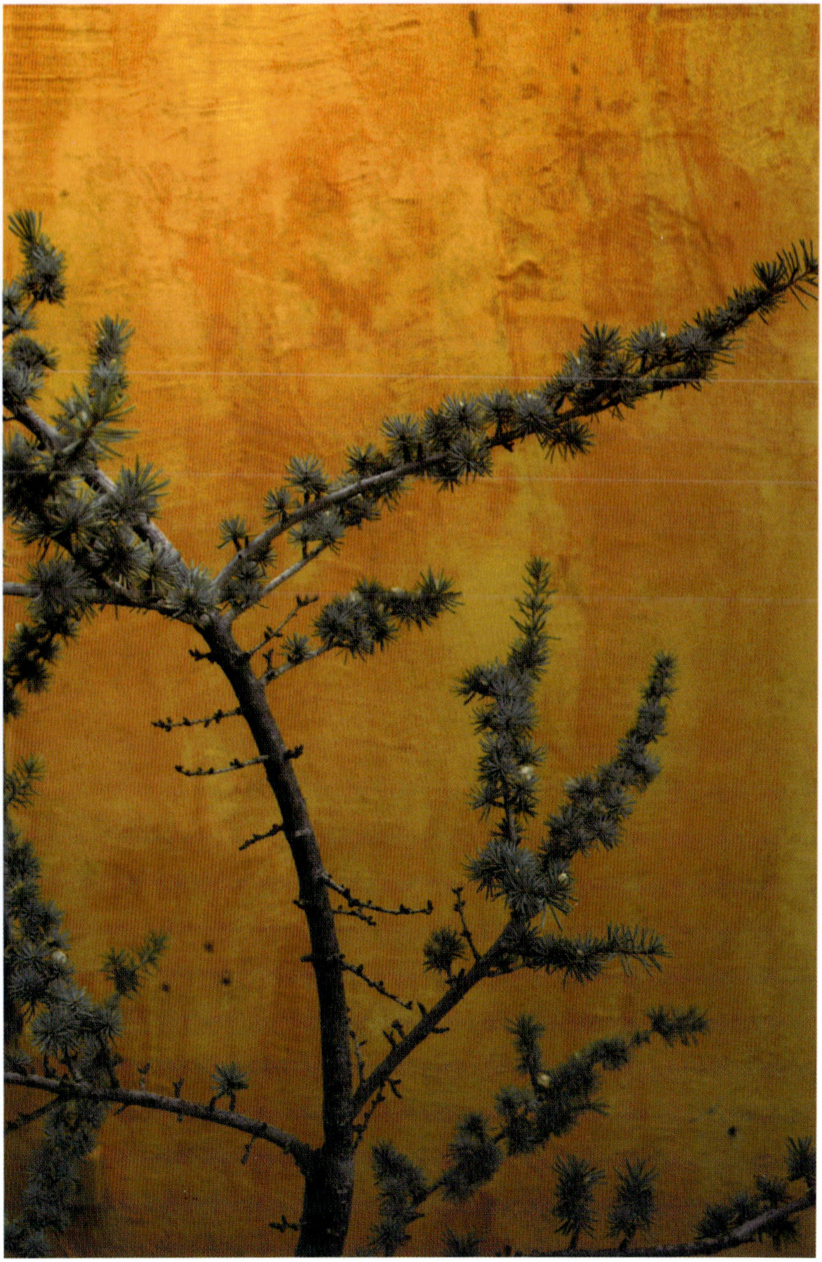

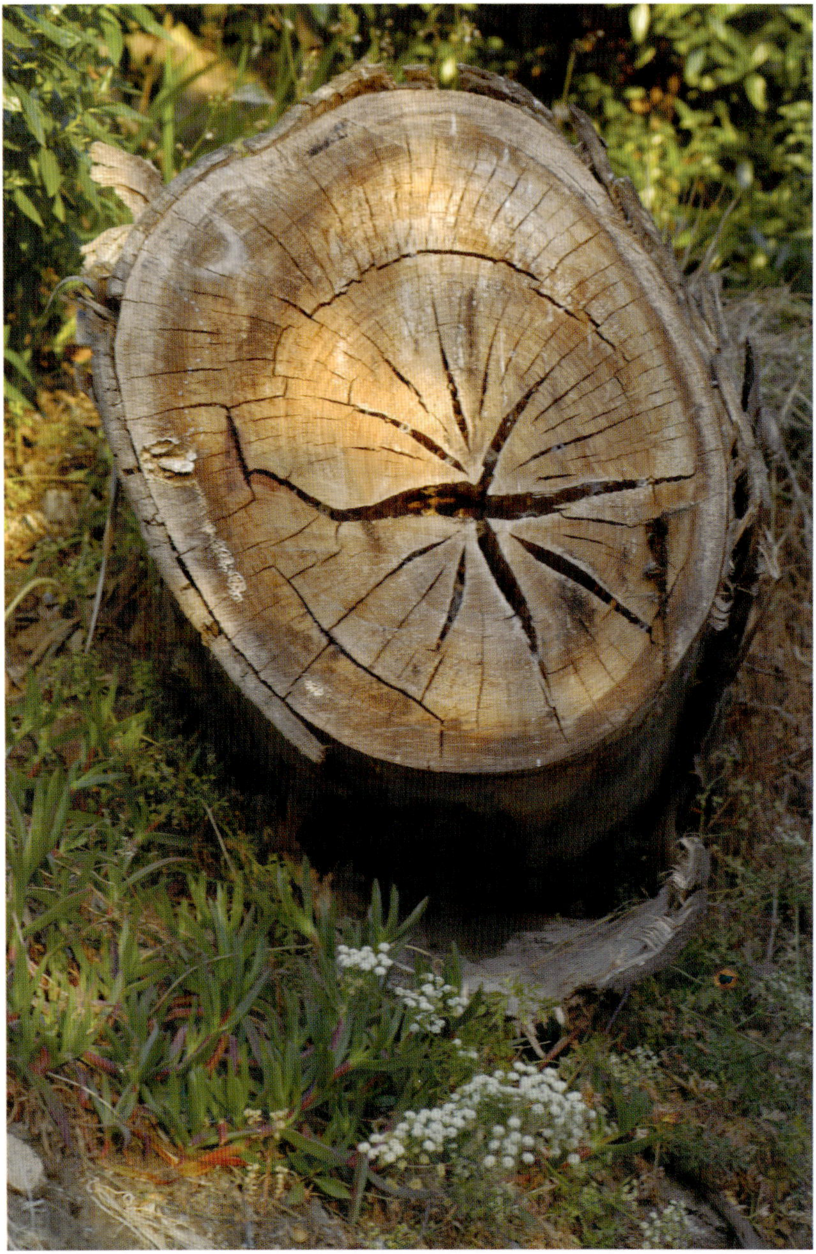

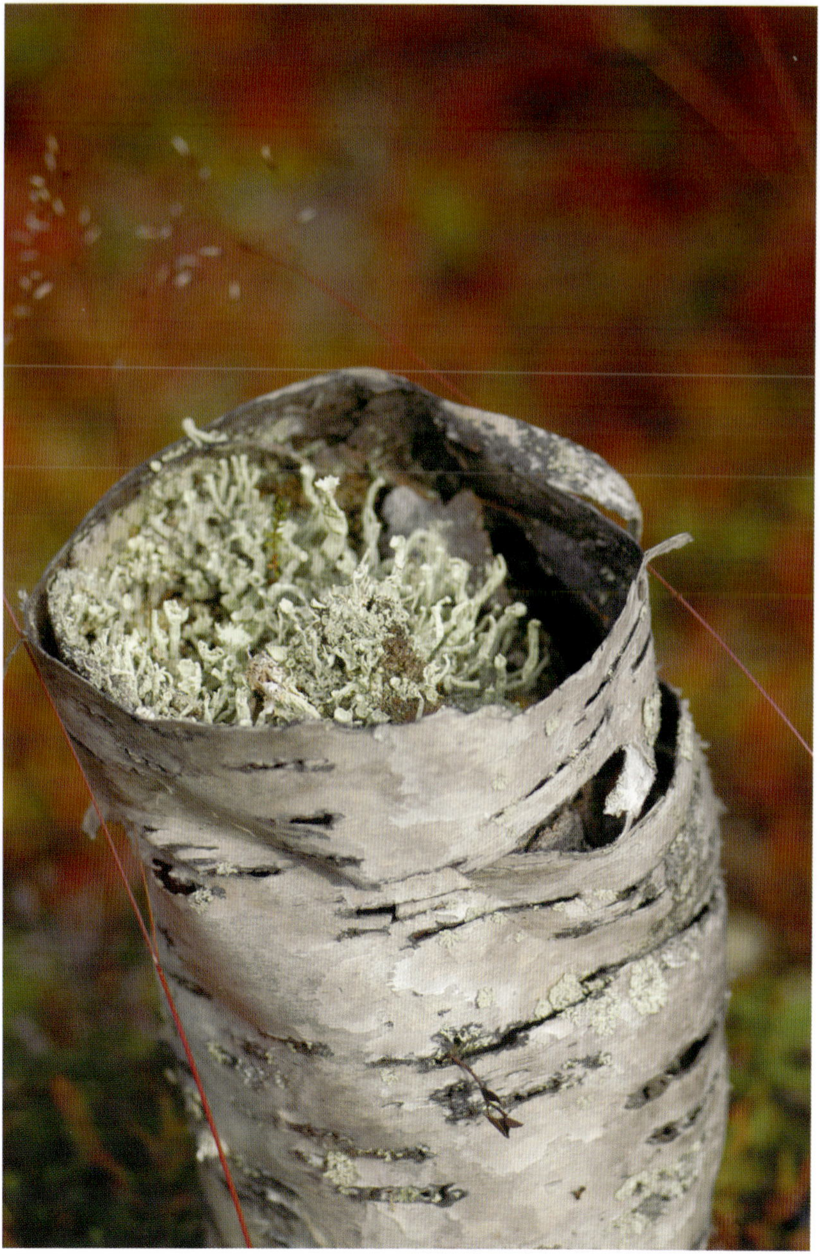

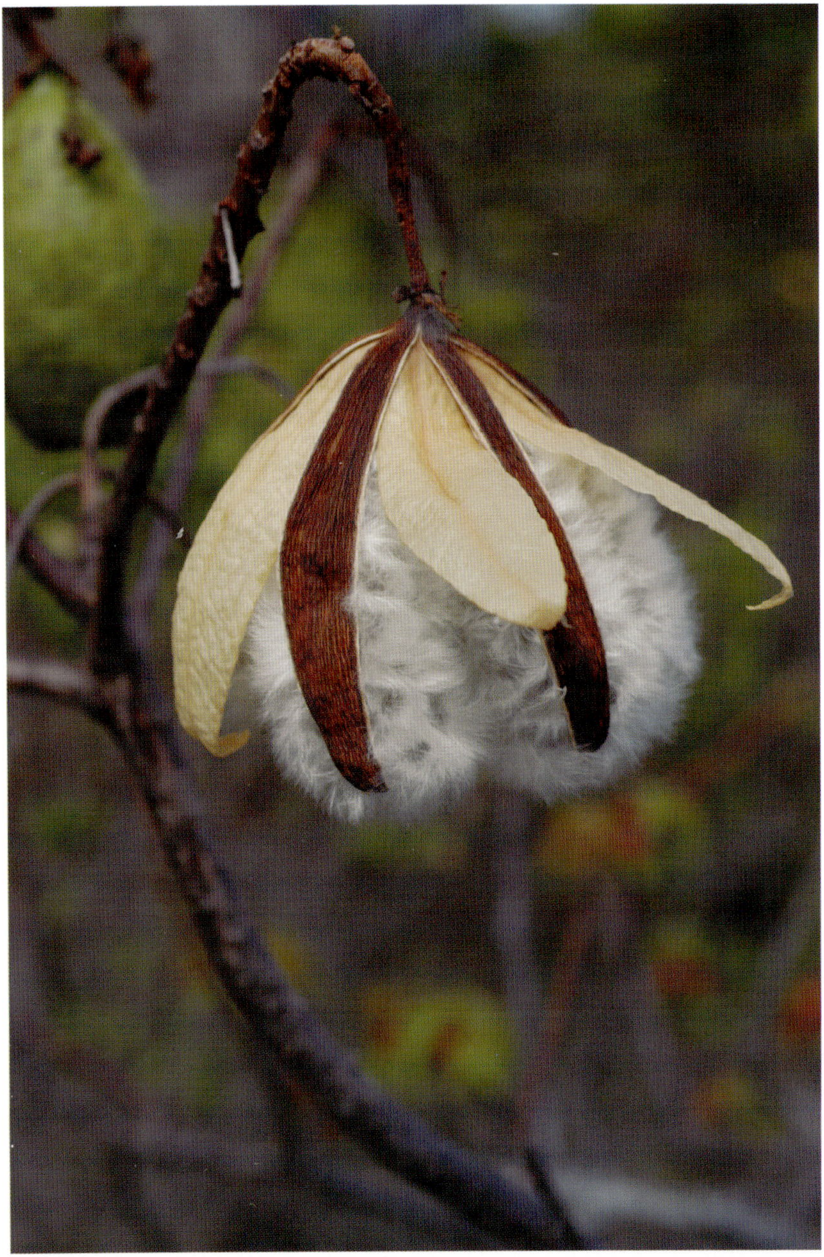

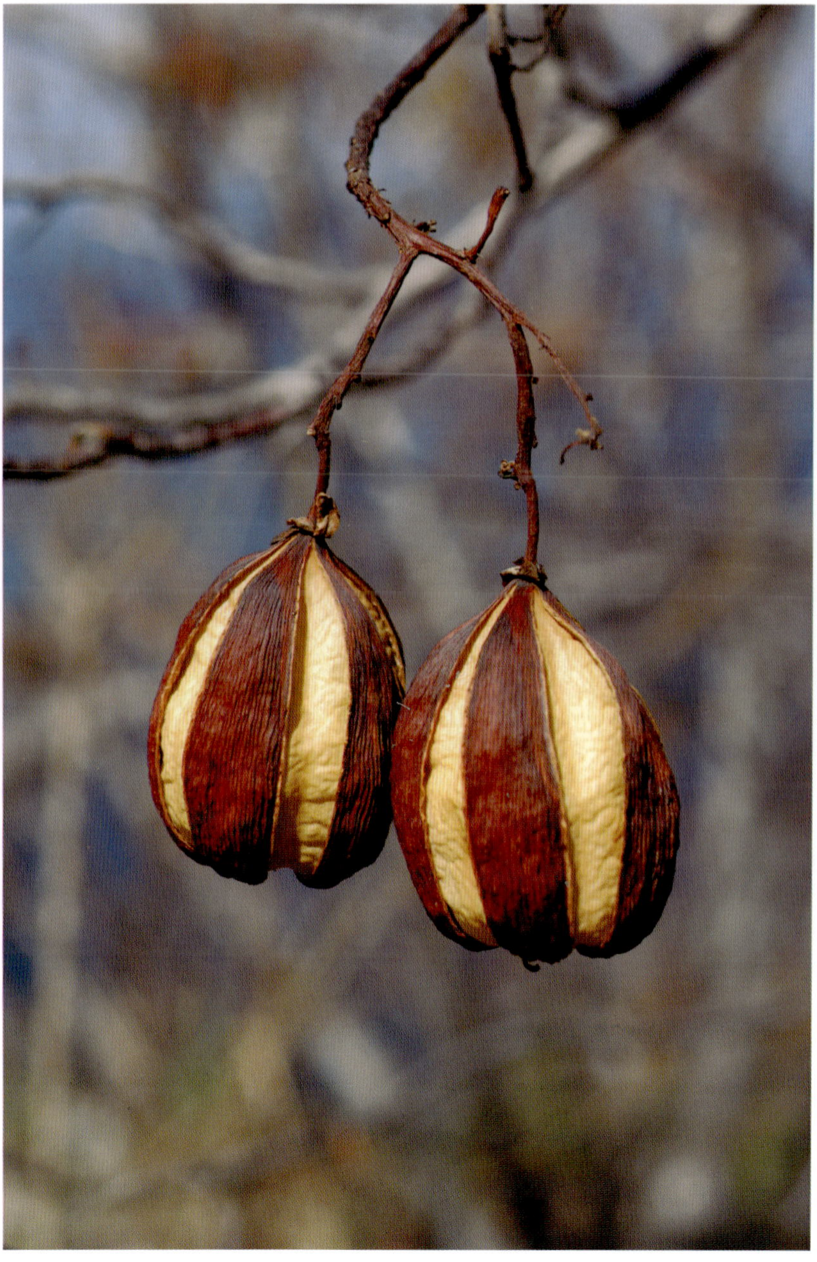

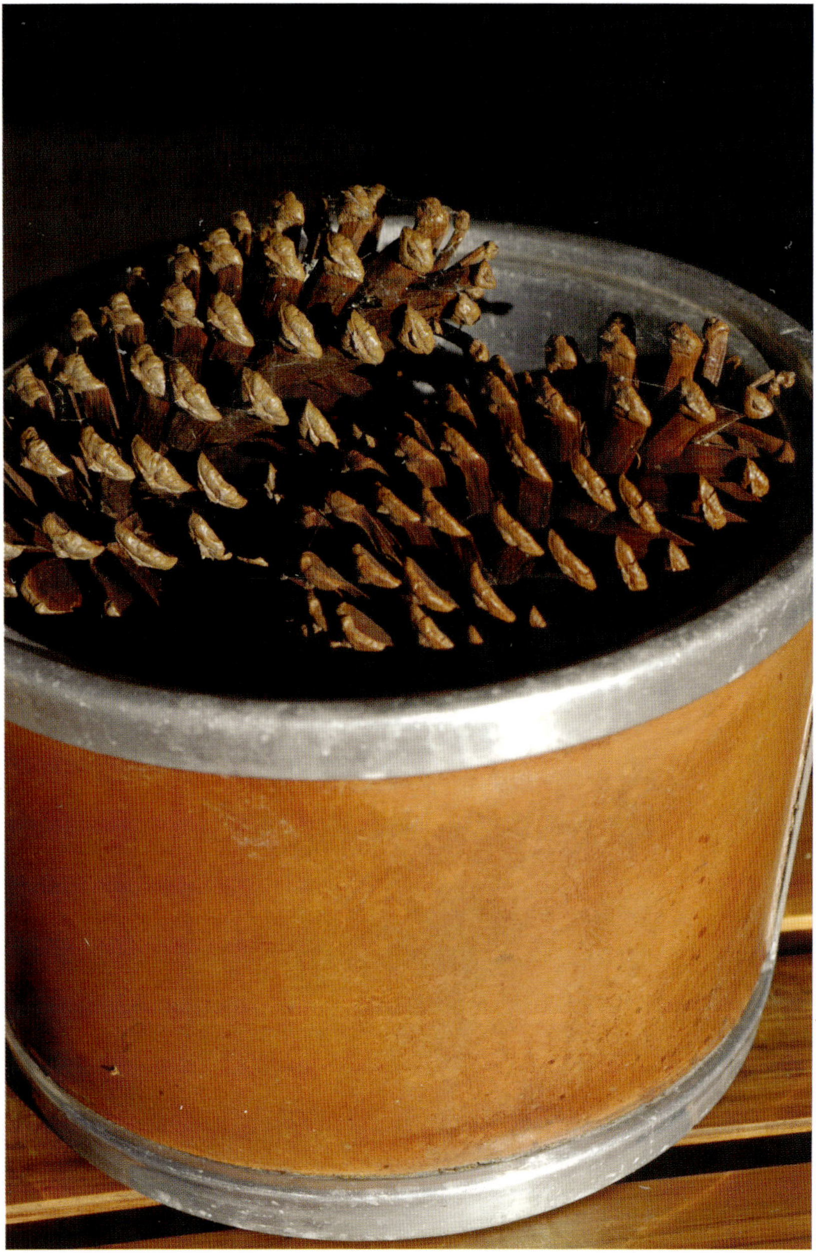

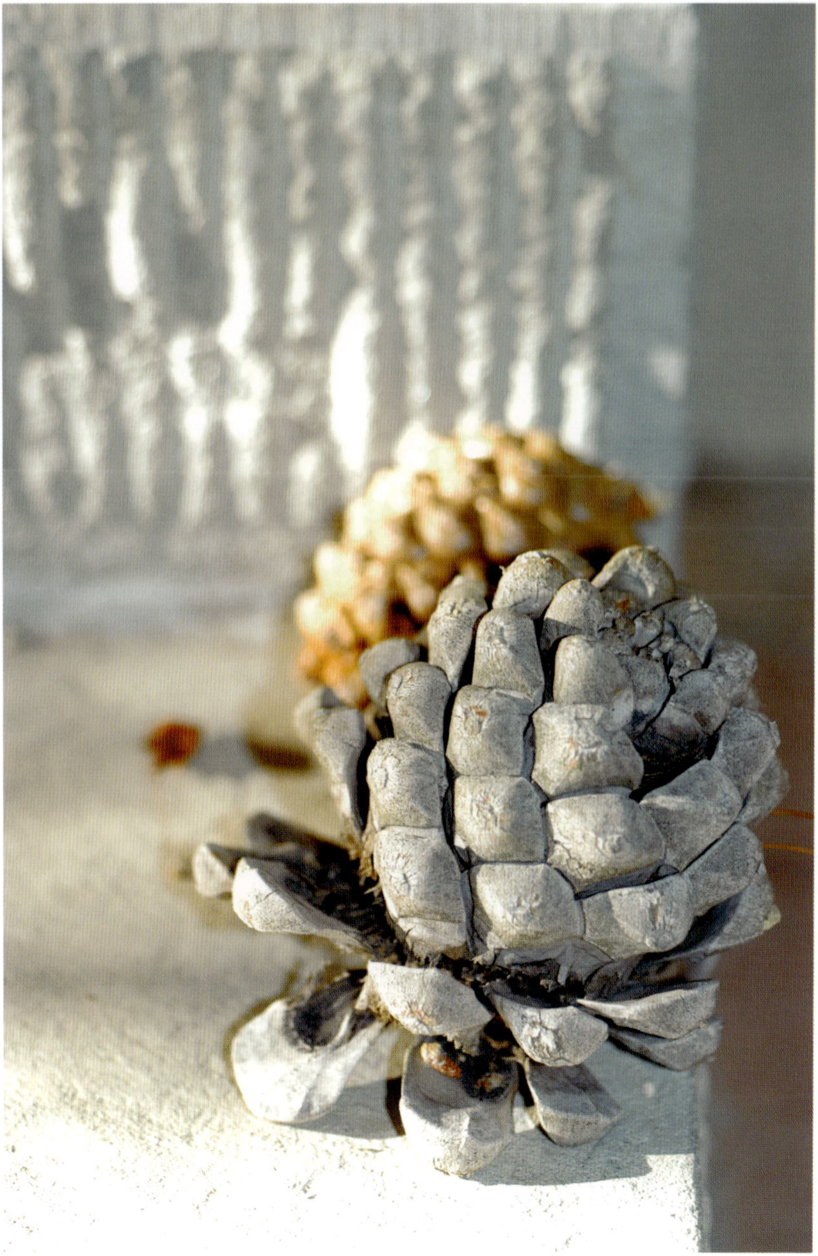

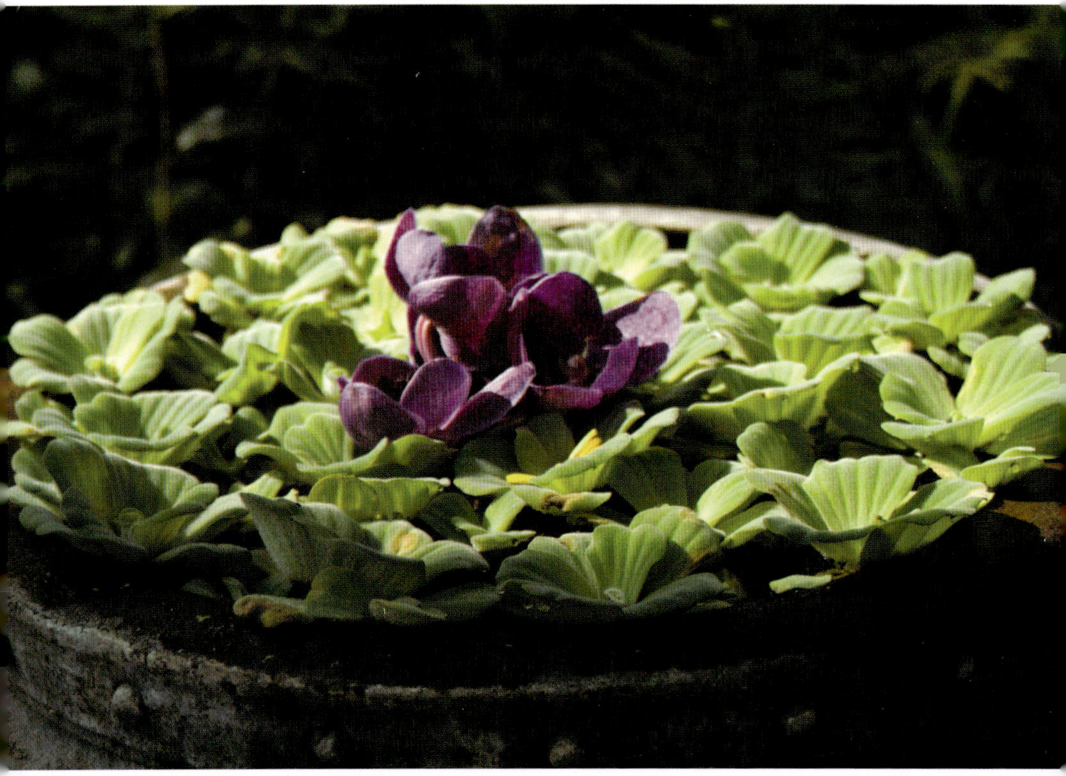

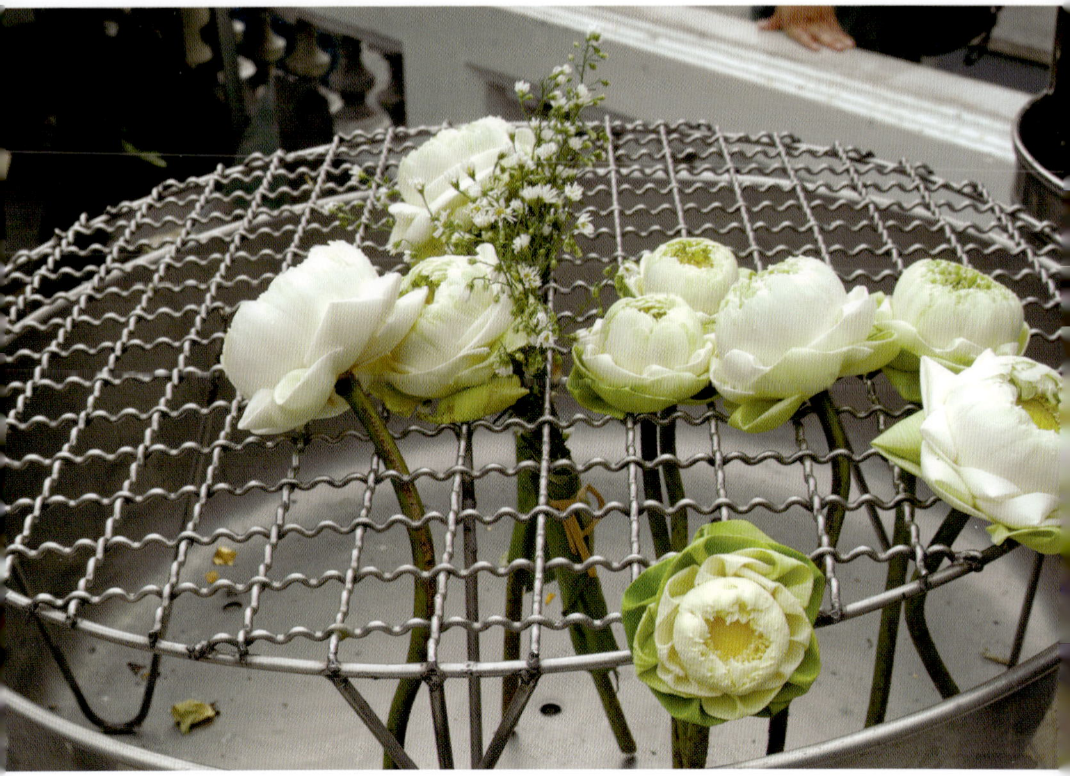

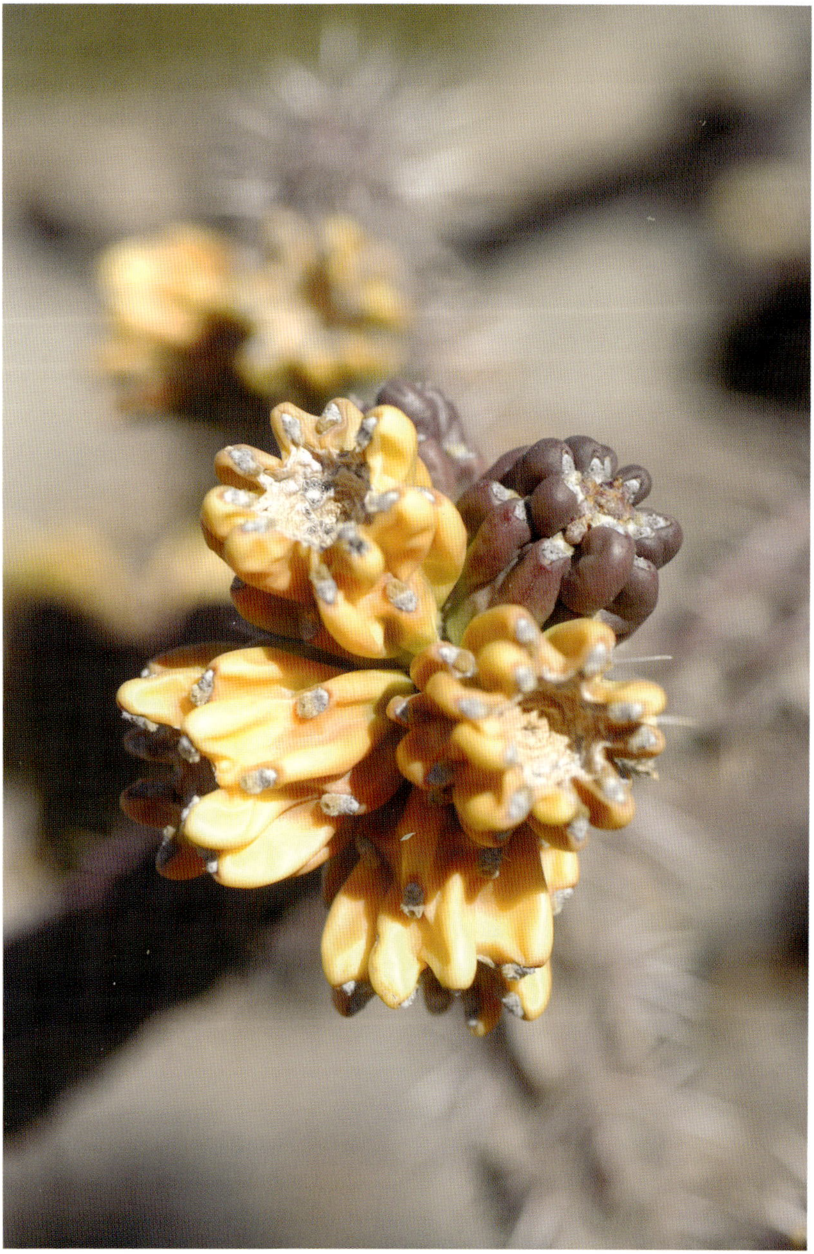

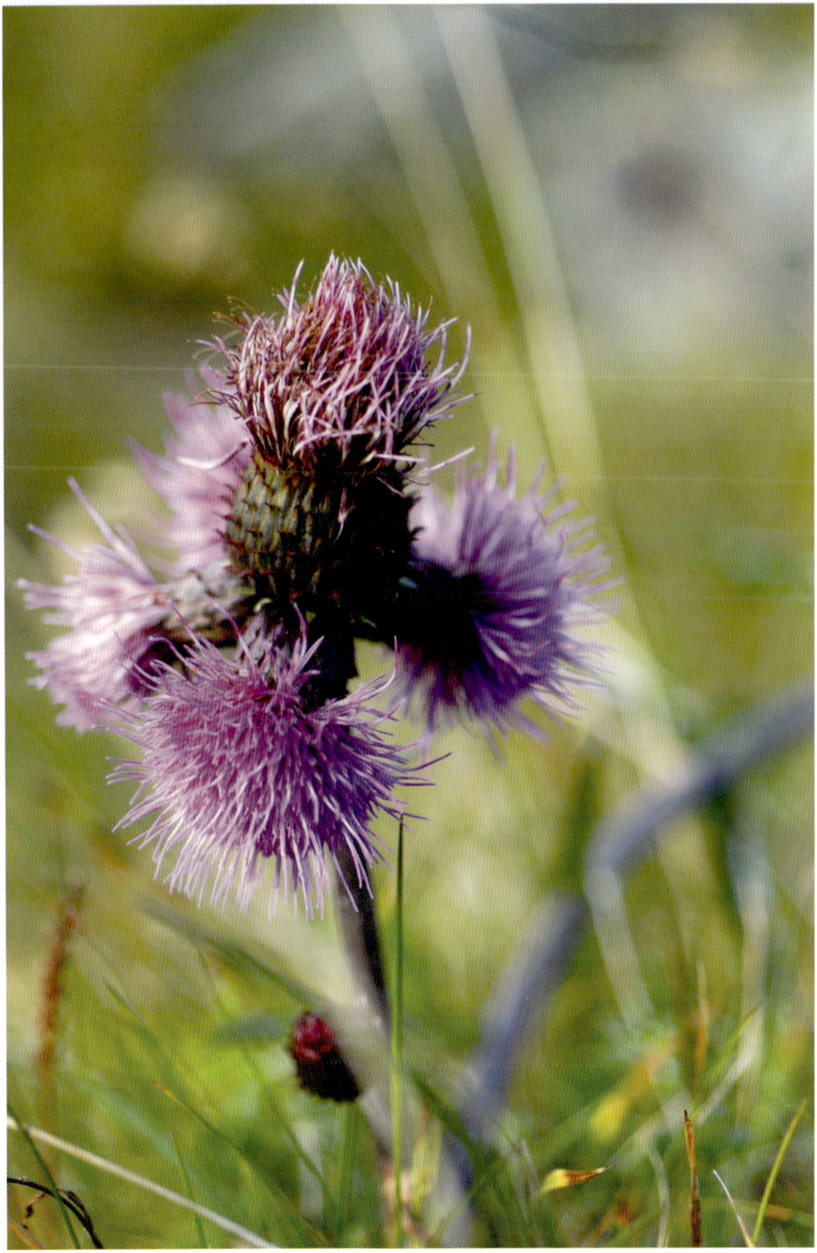

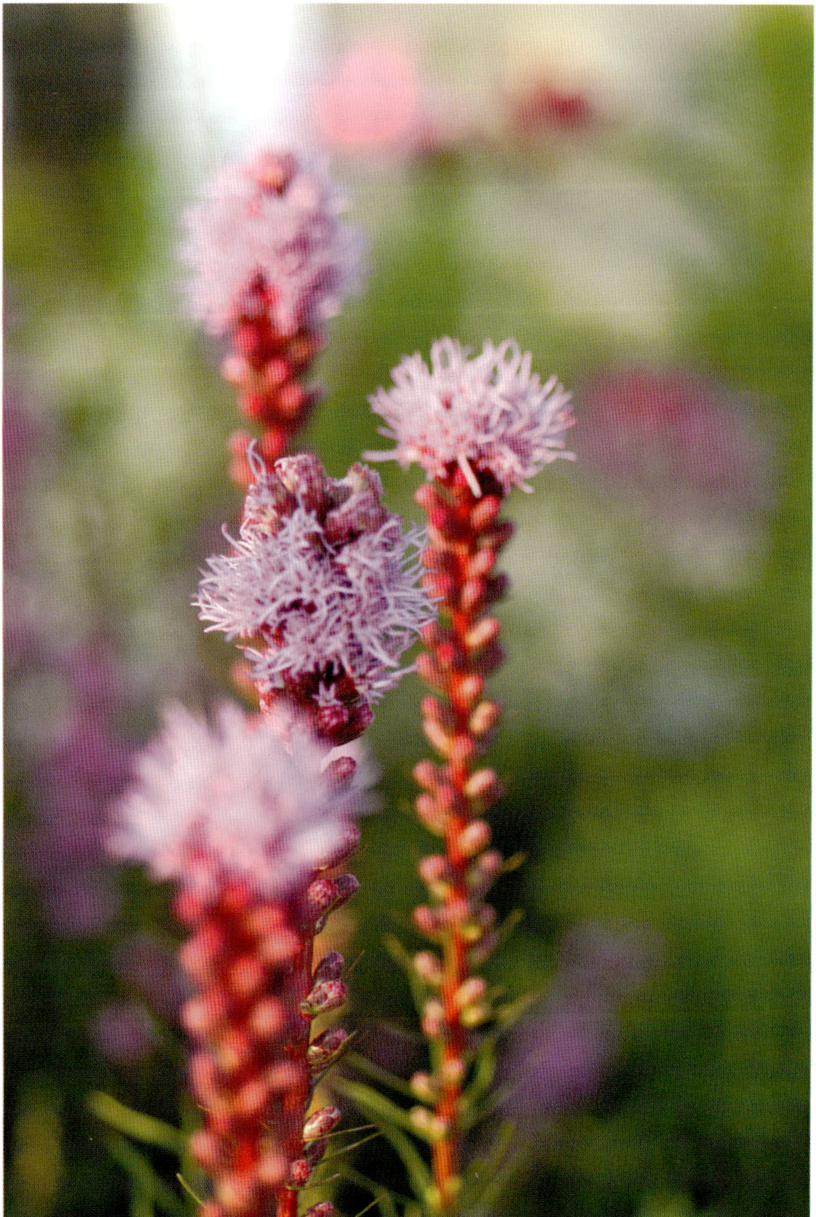

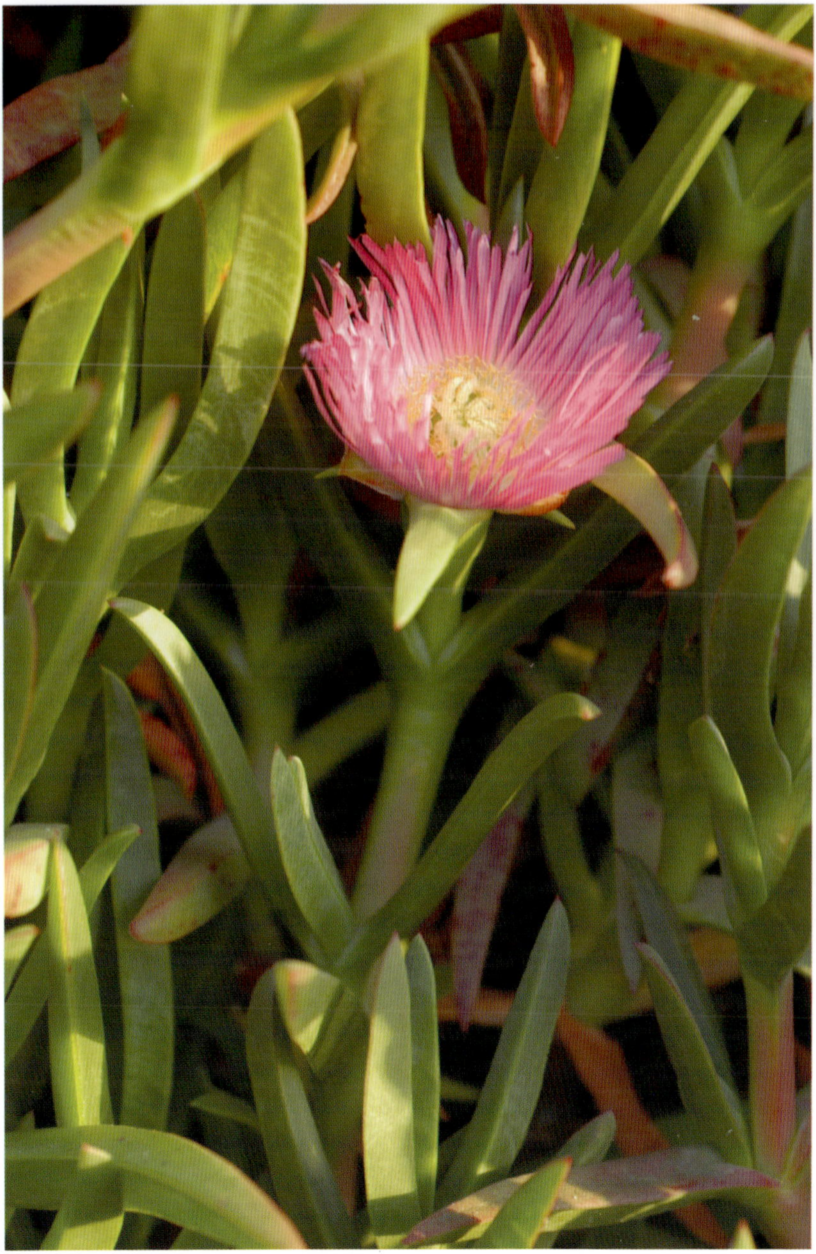

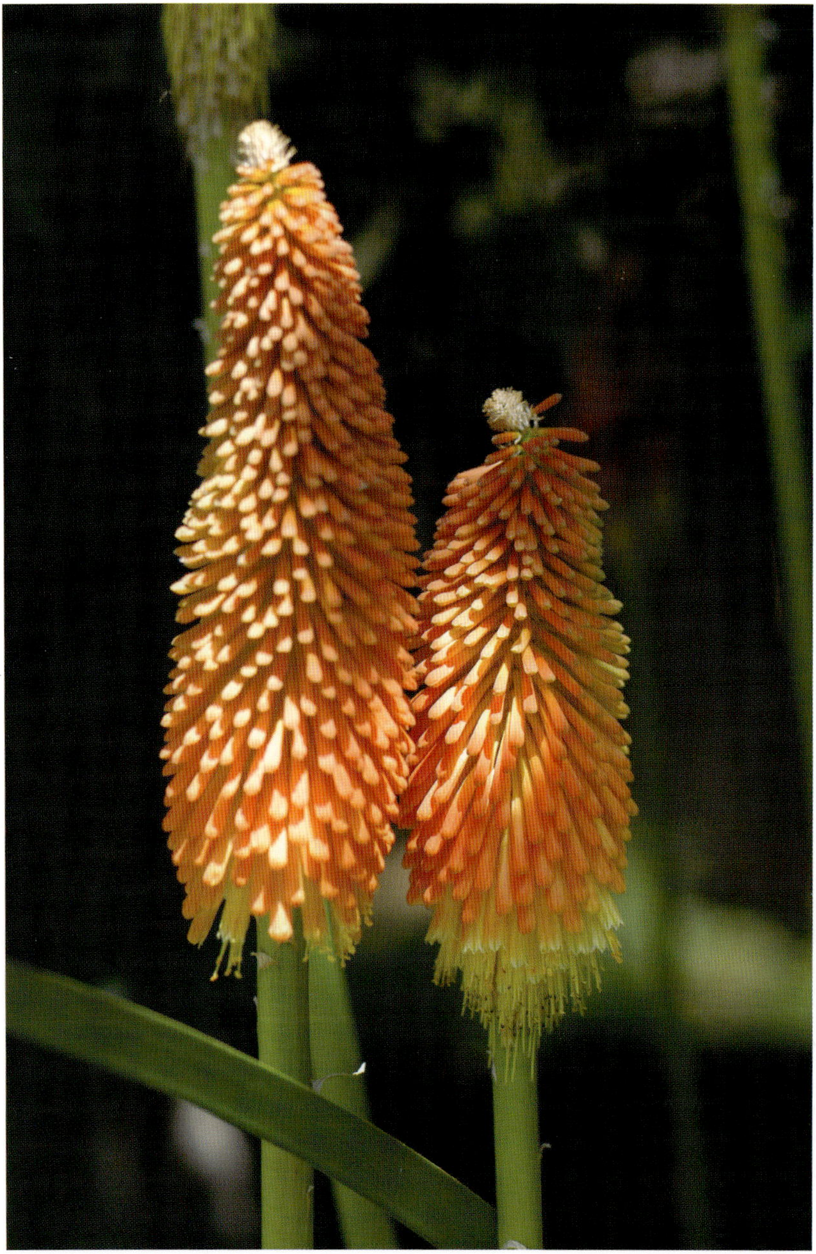

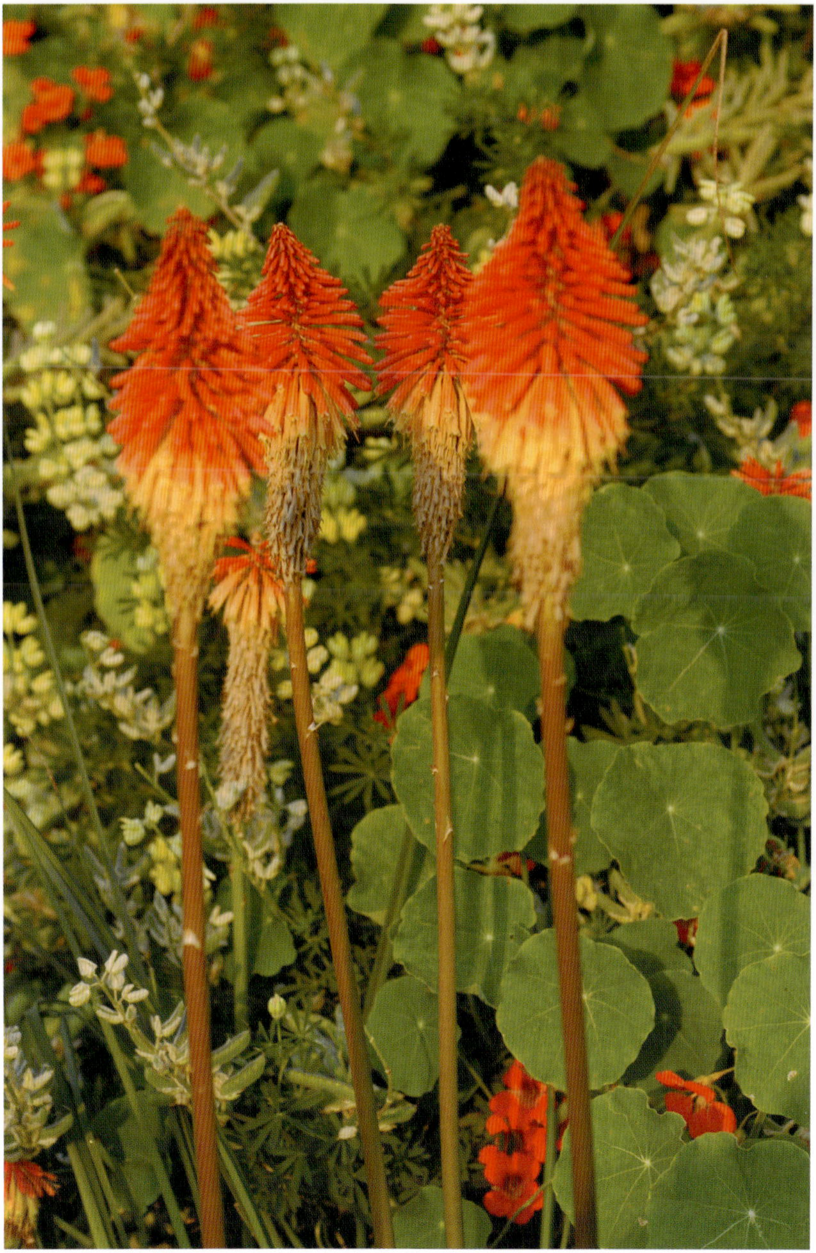

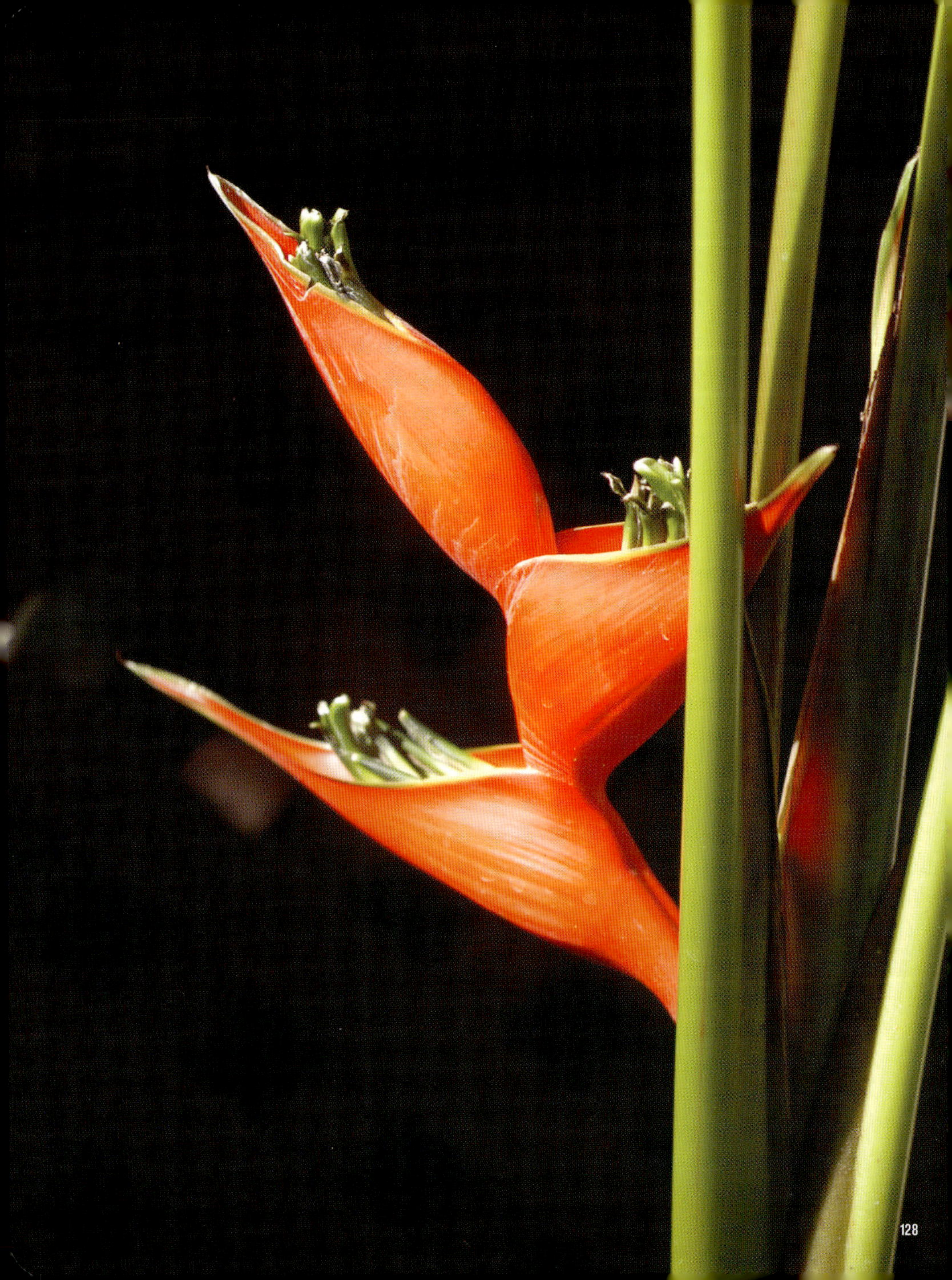

REFLECTING

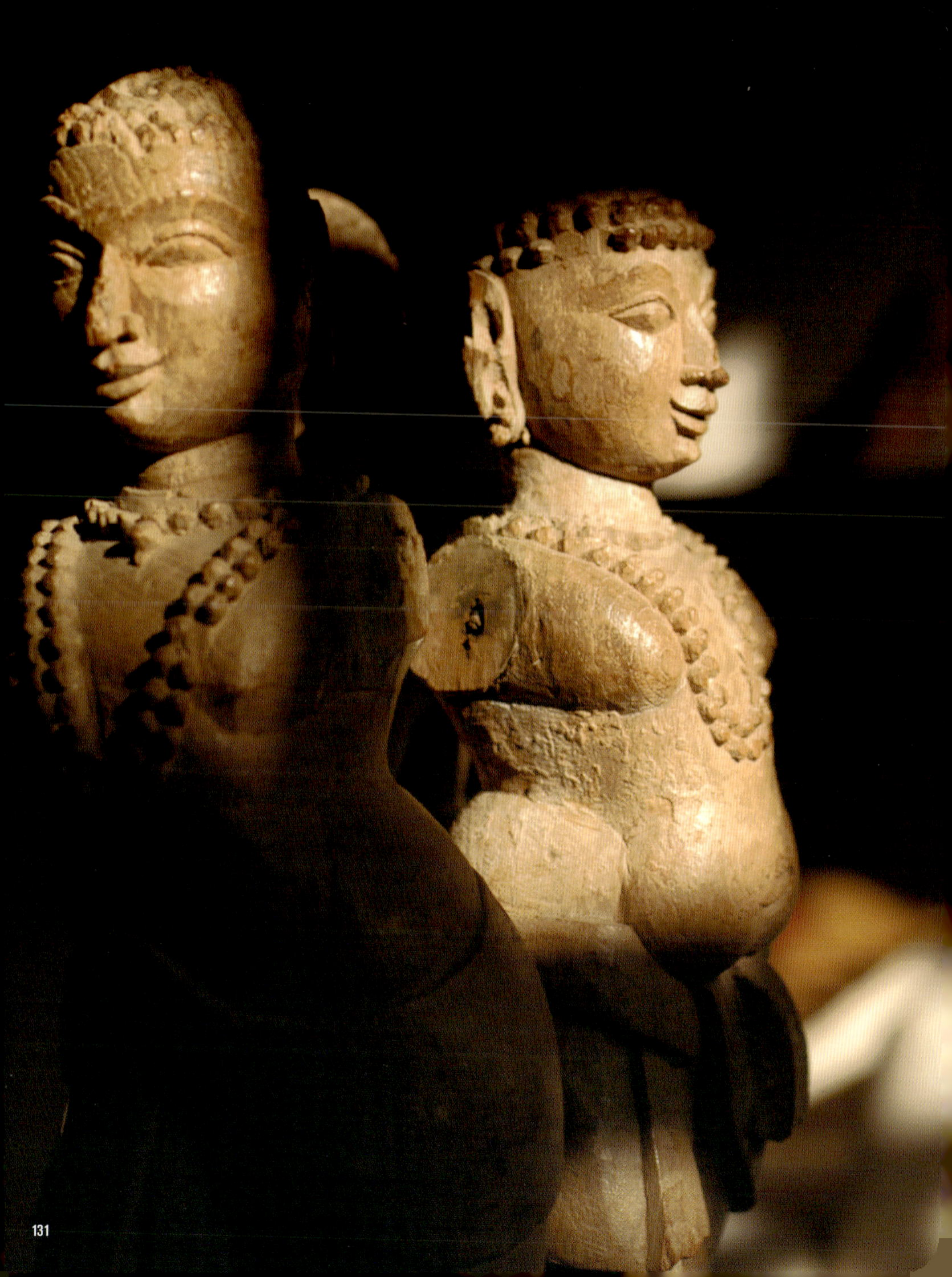

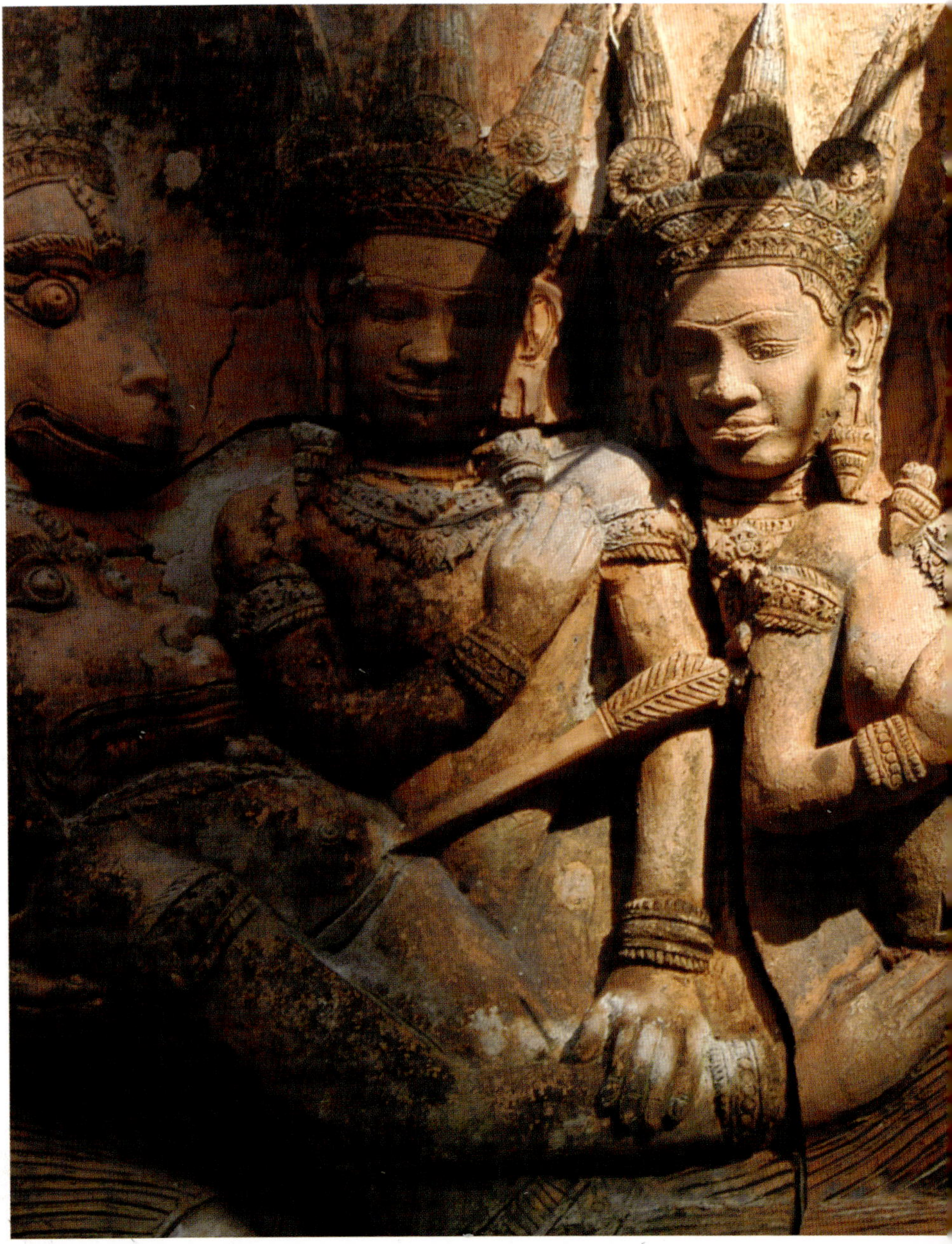

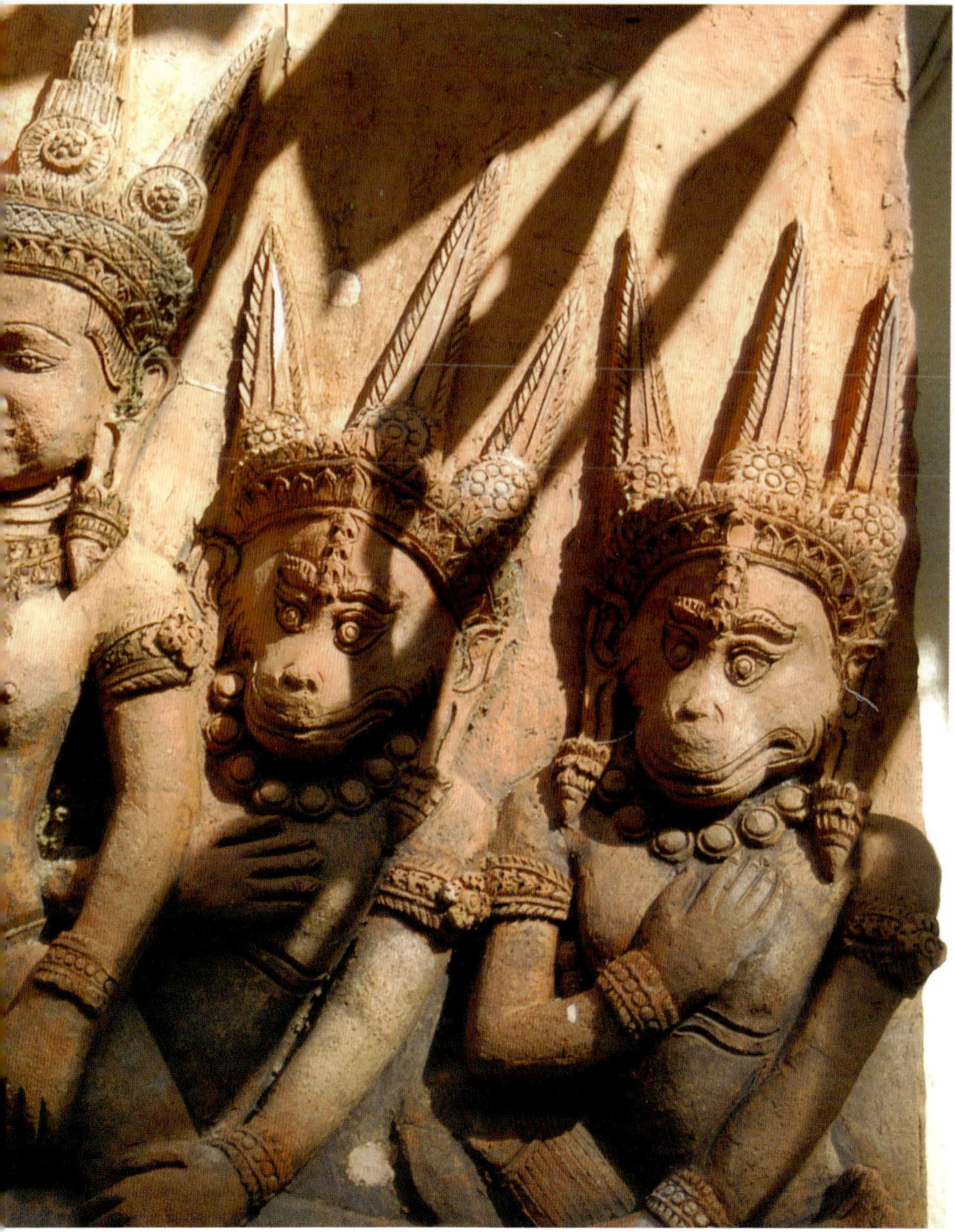

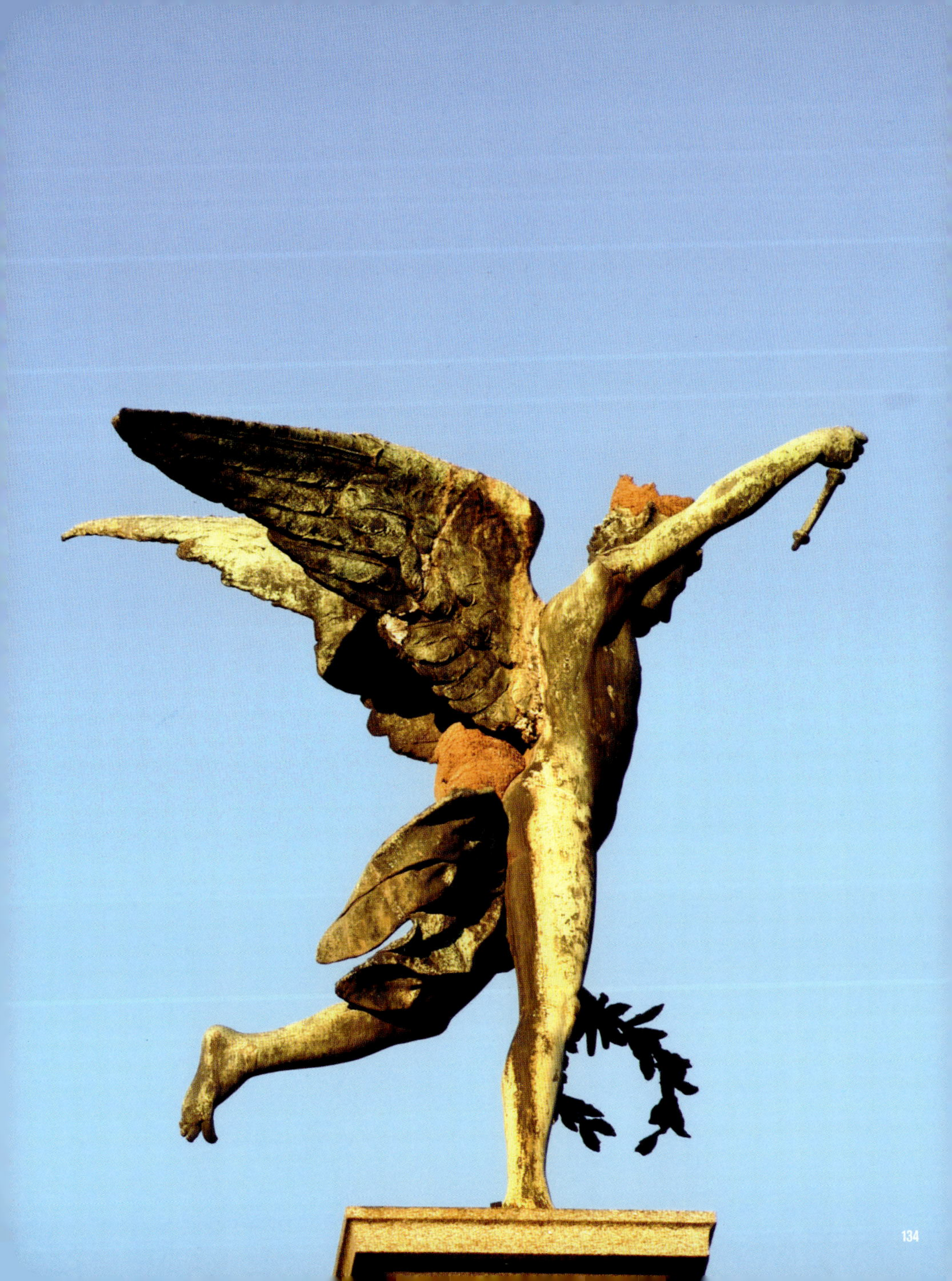

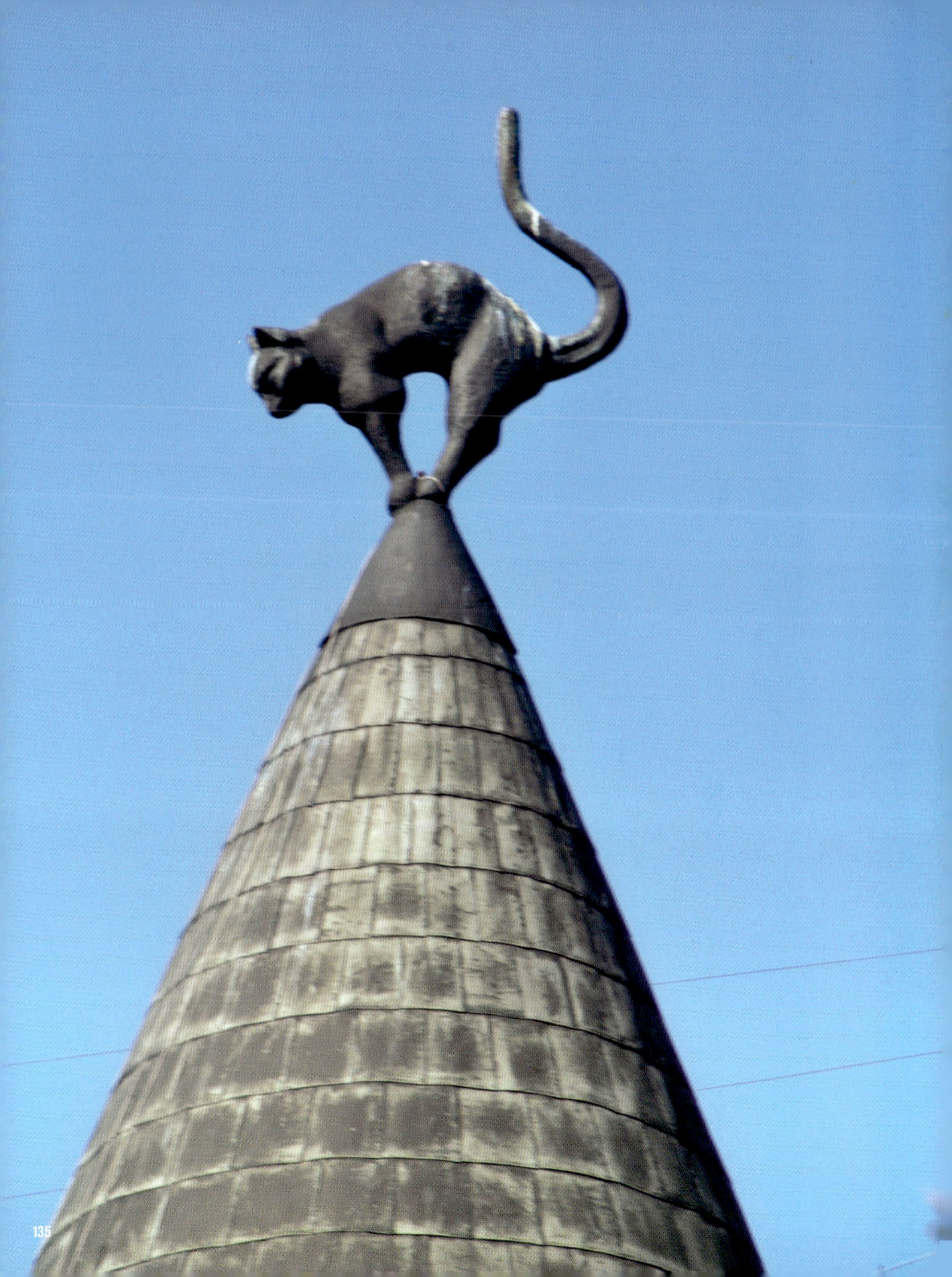

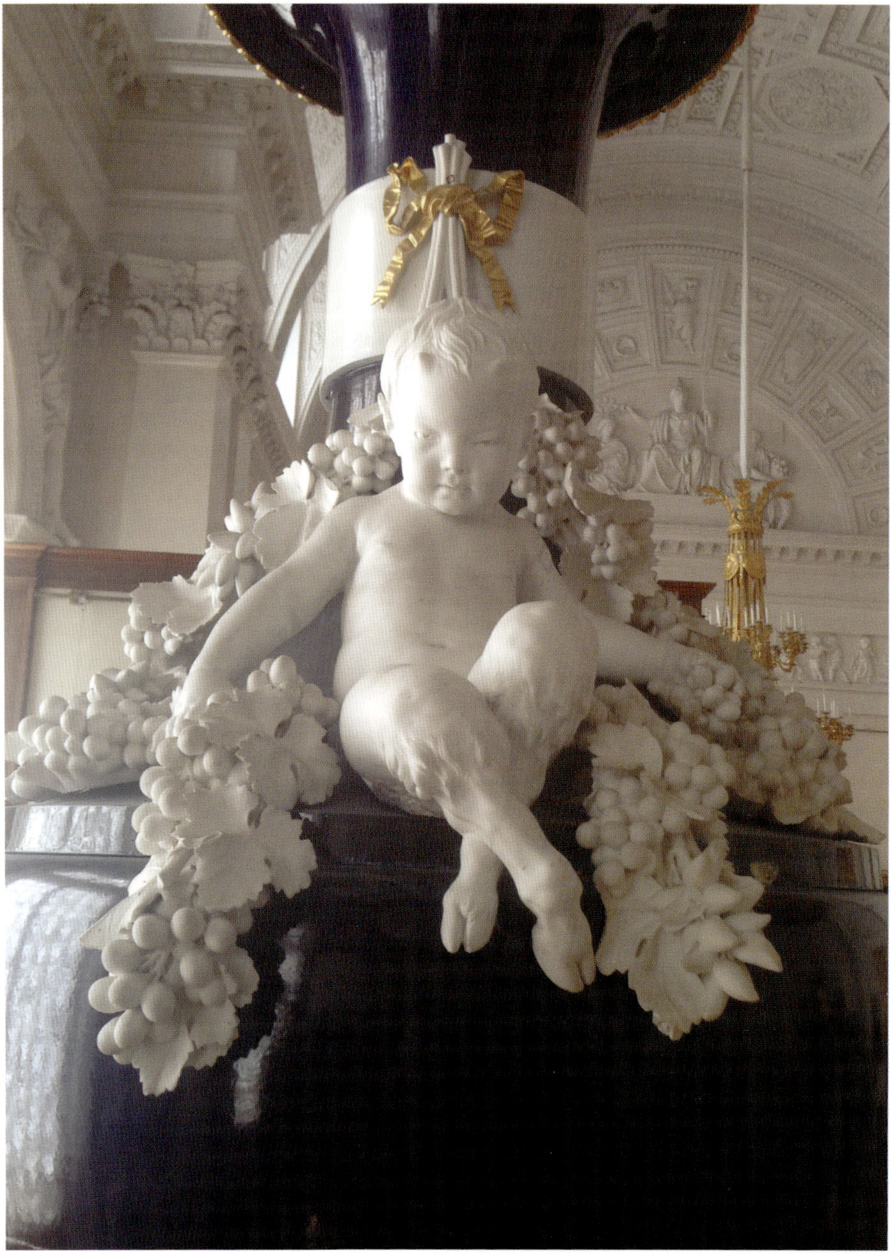

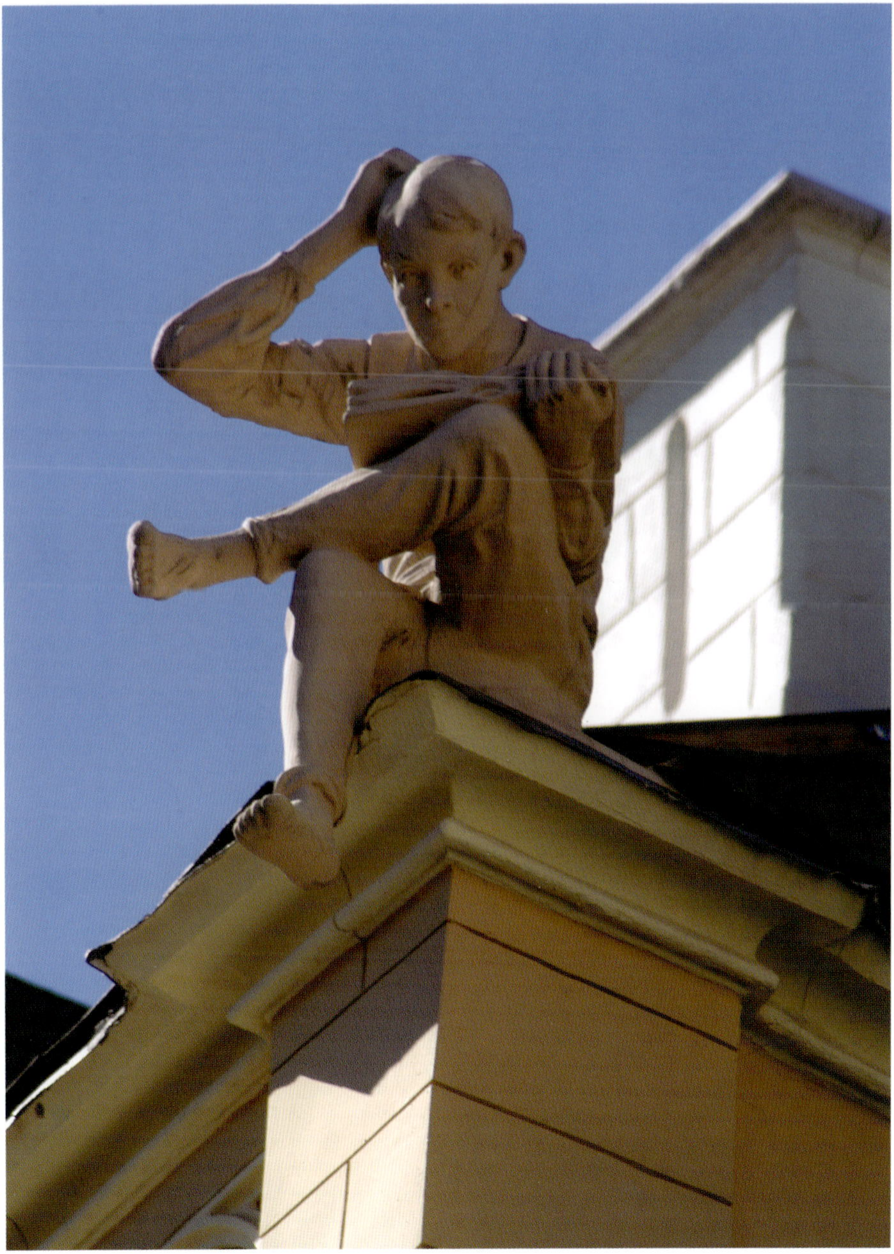

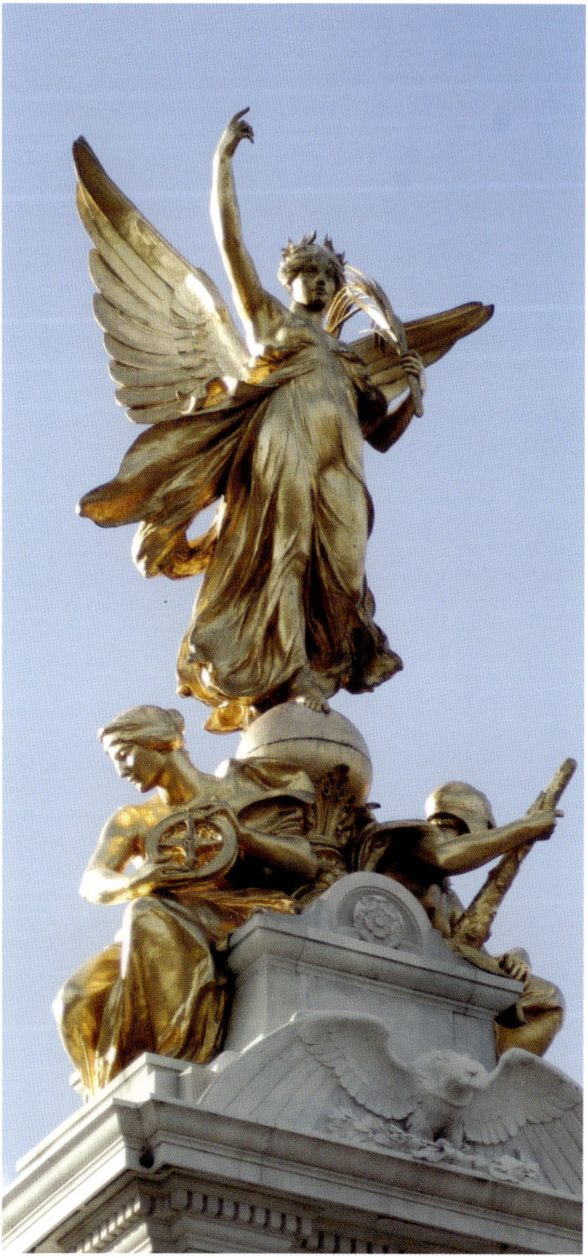

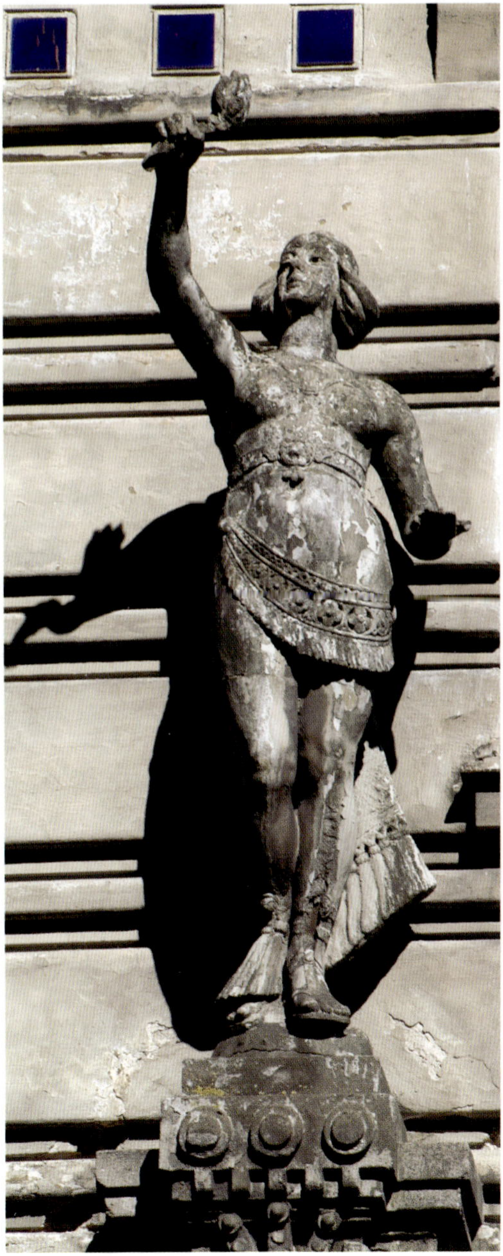

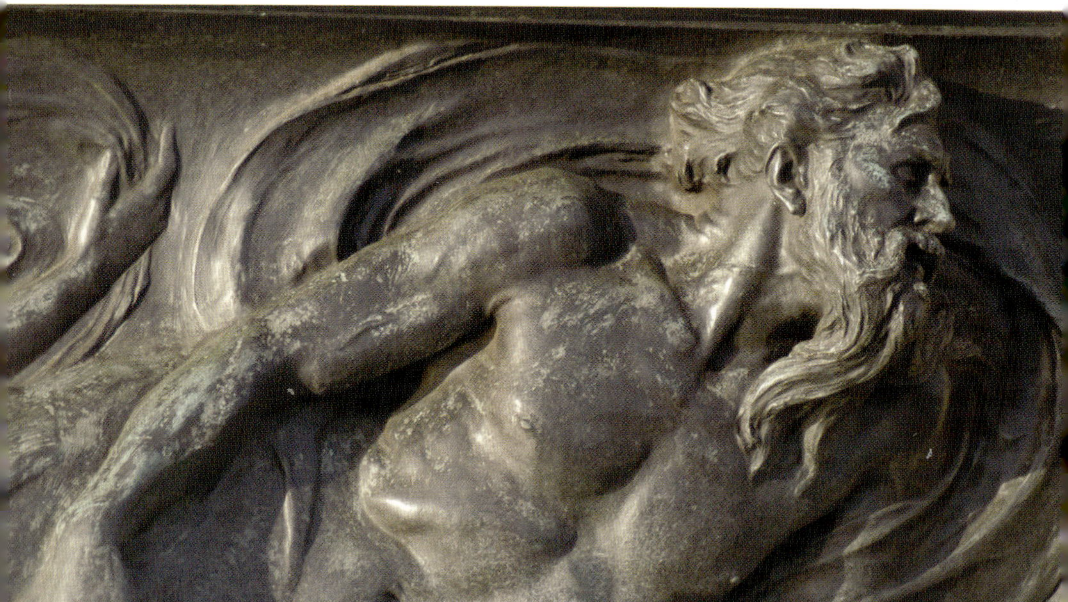

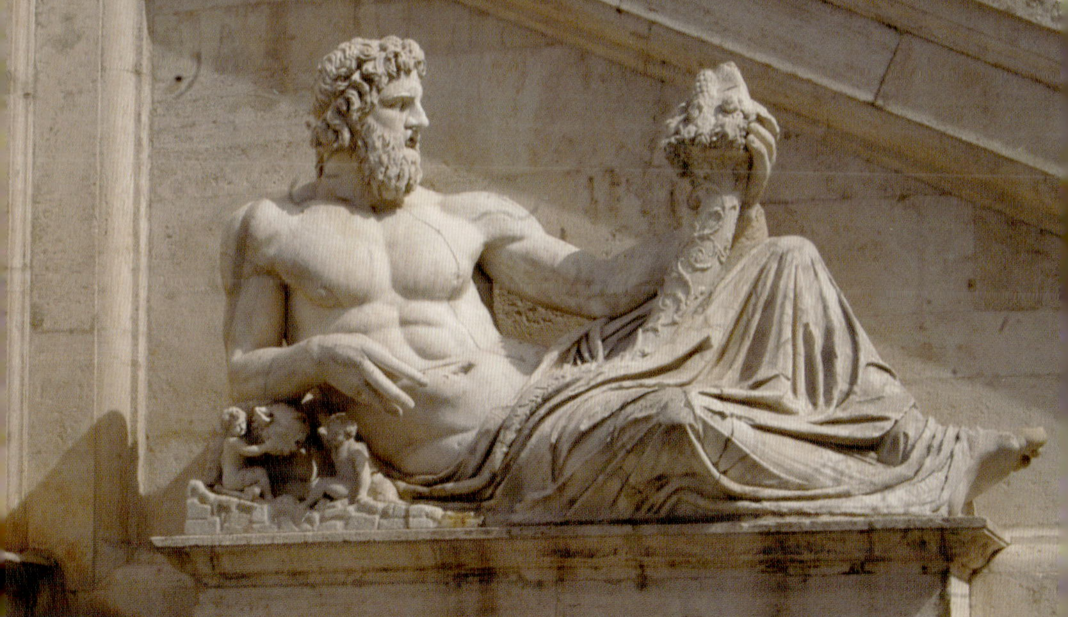

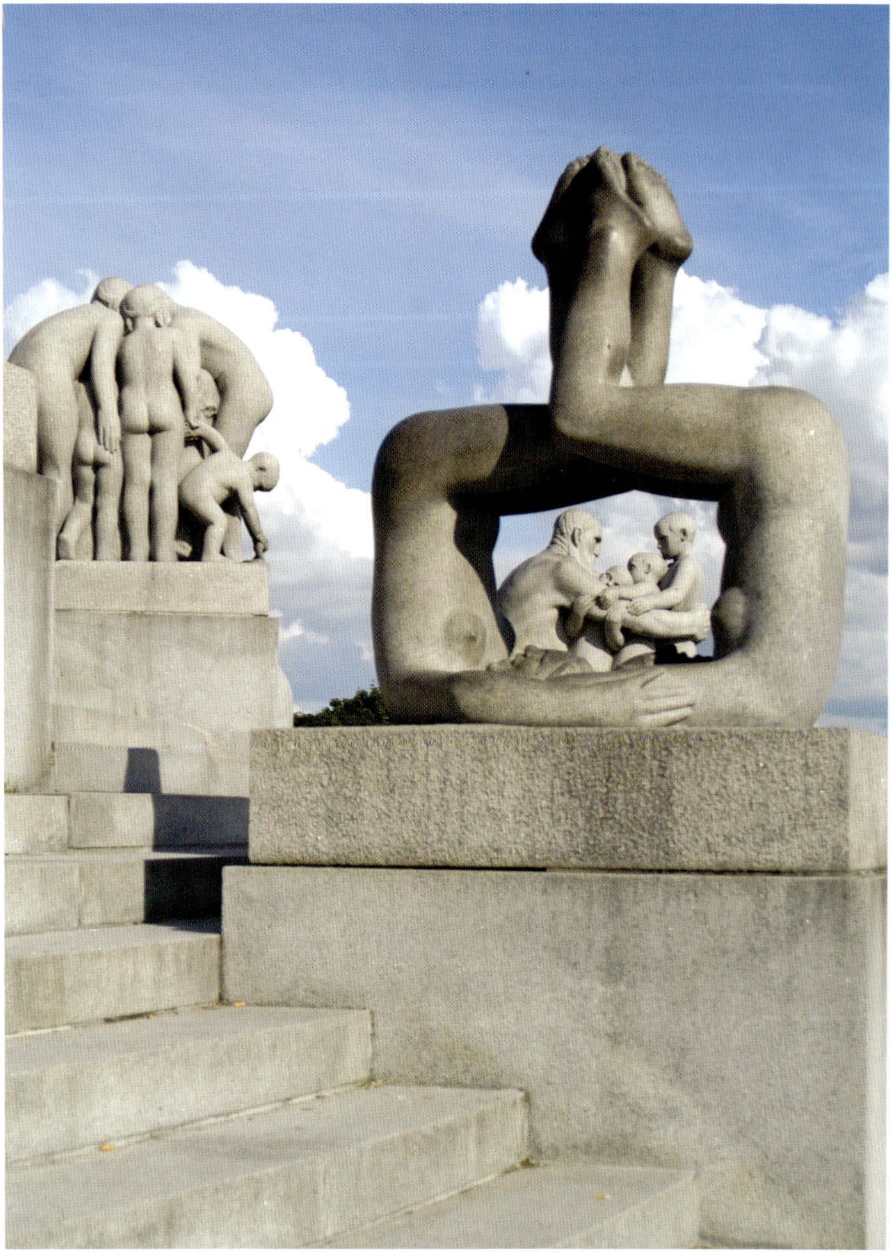

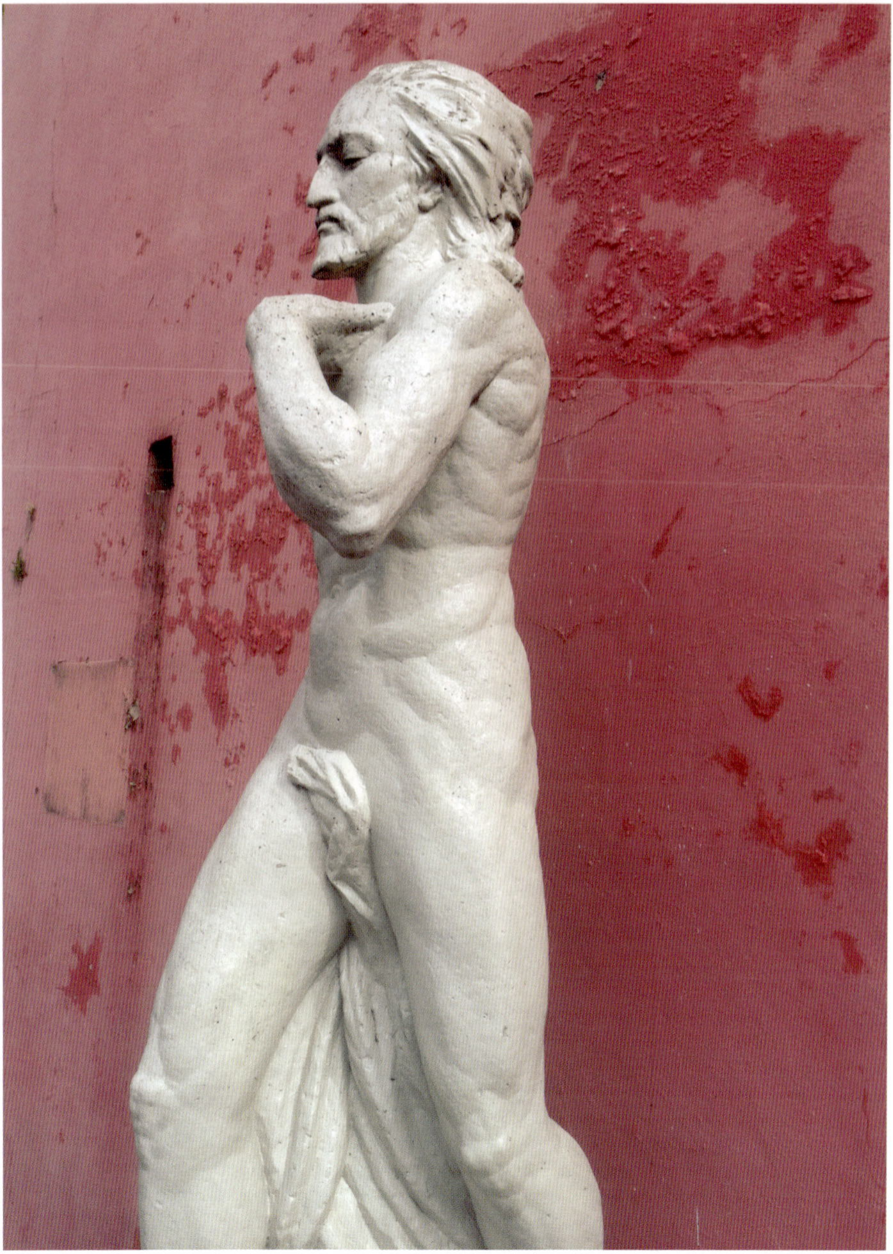

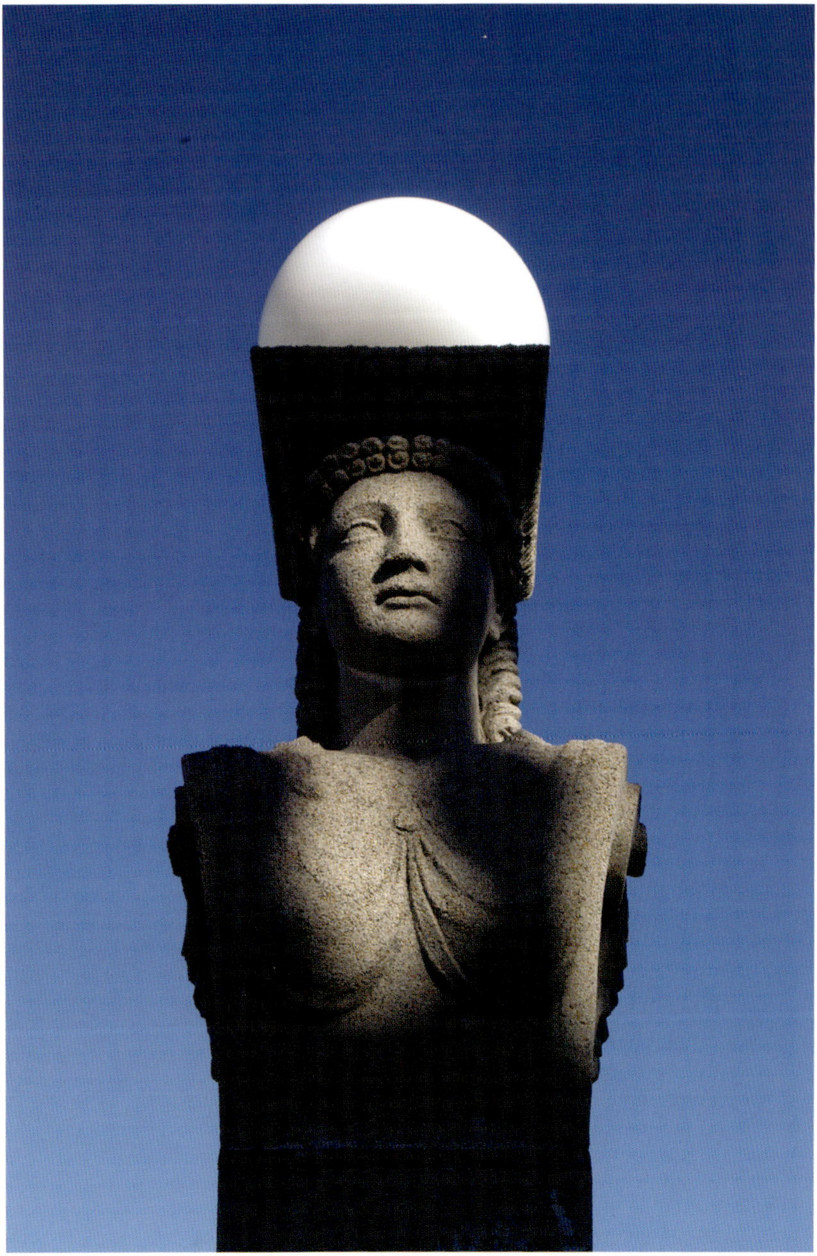

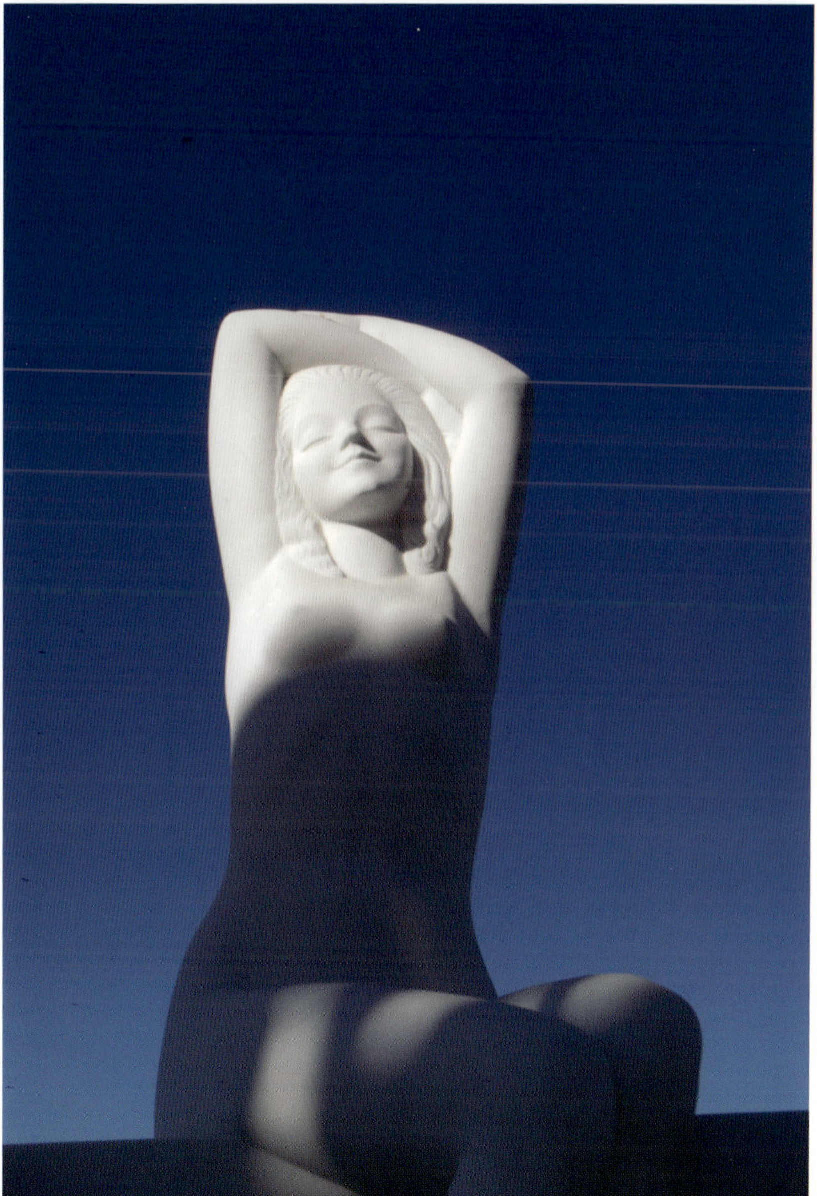

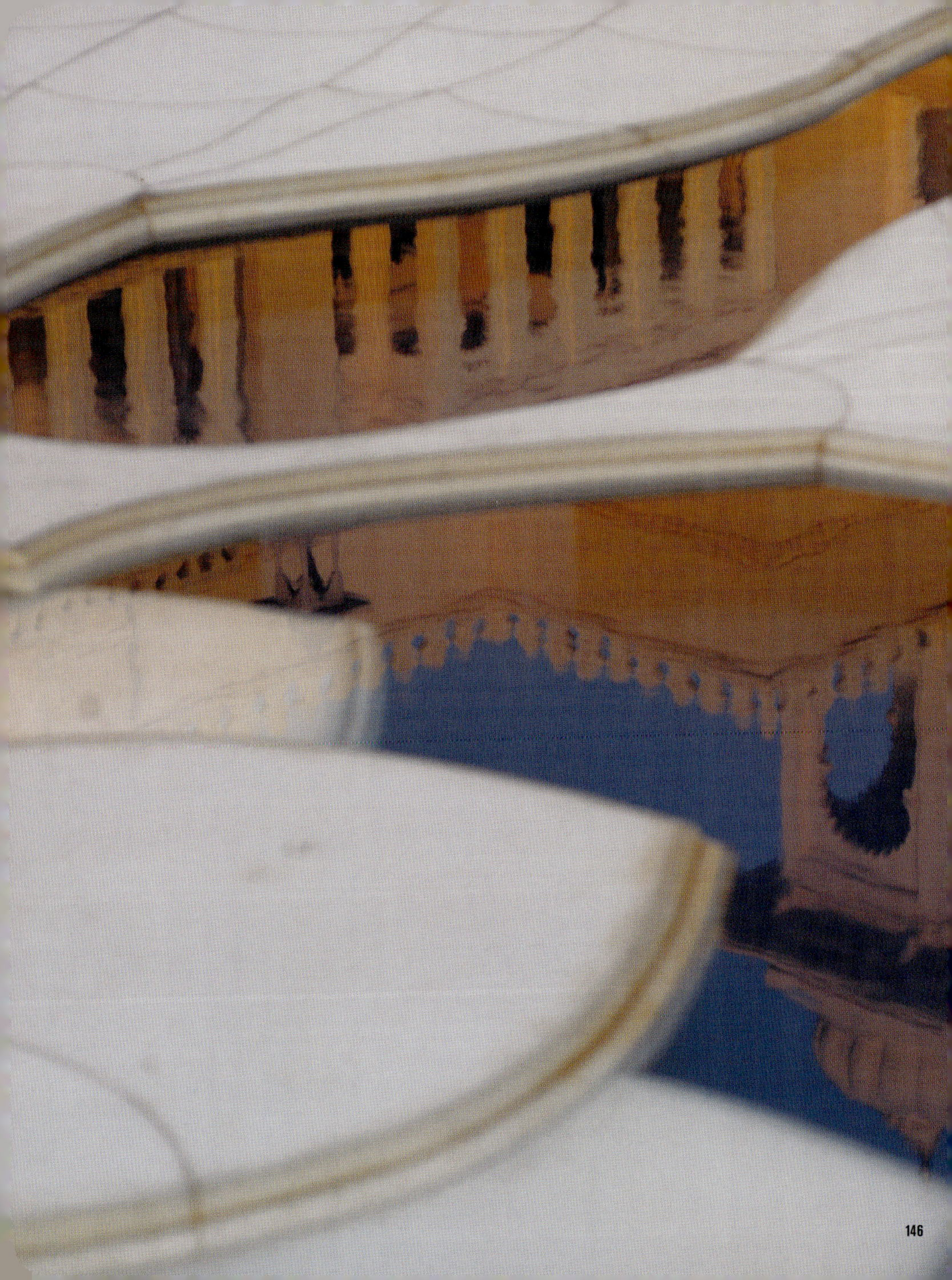

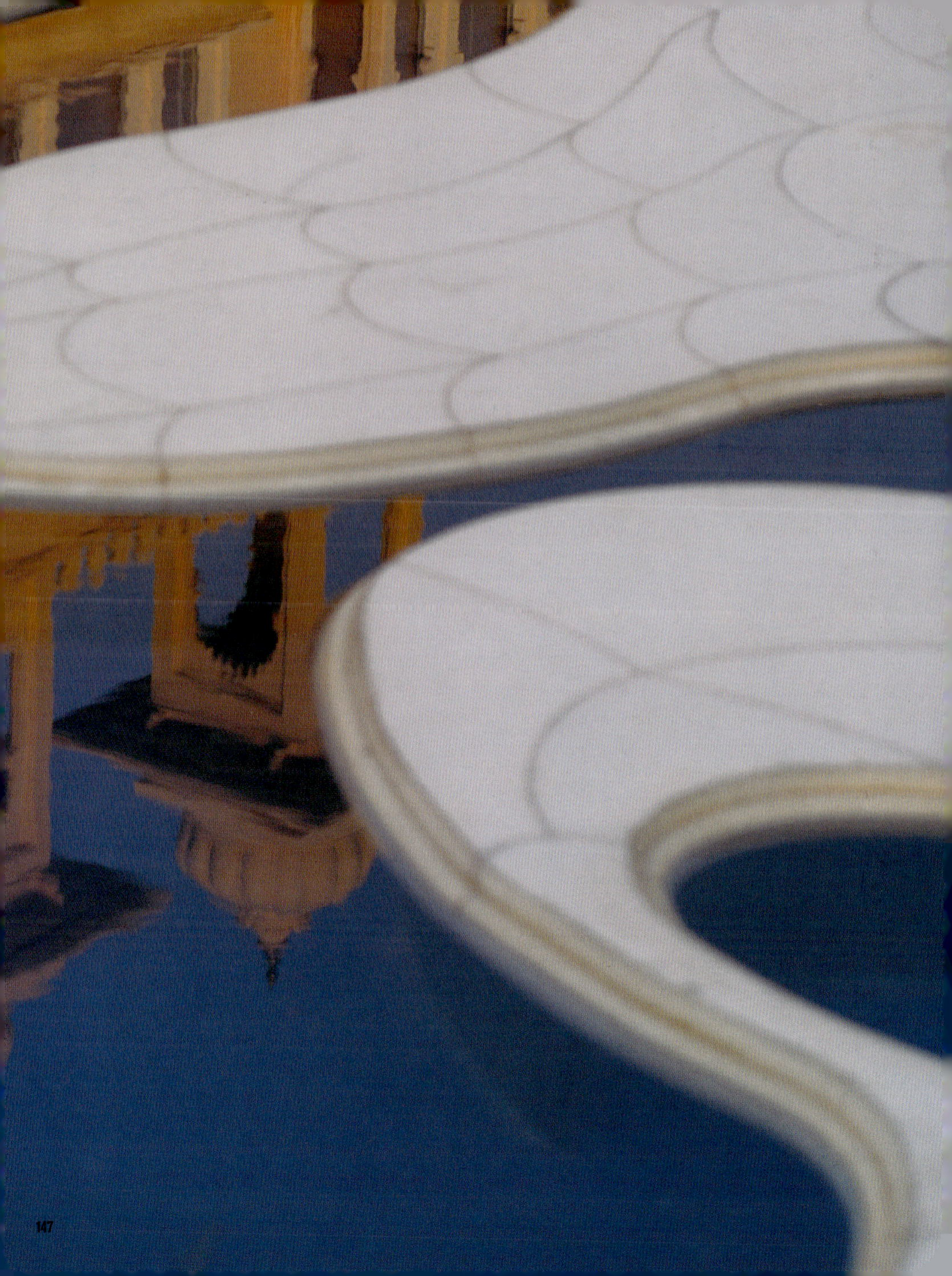

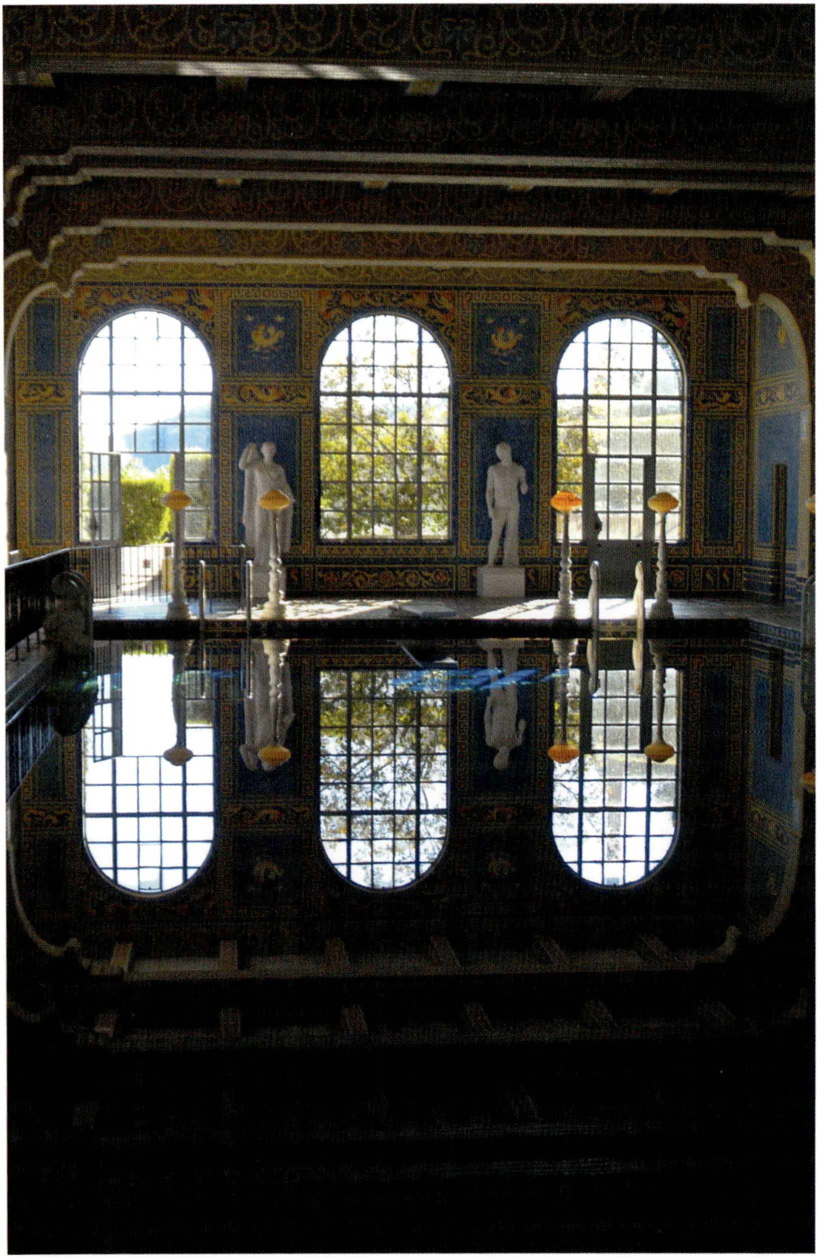

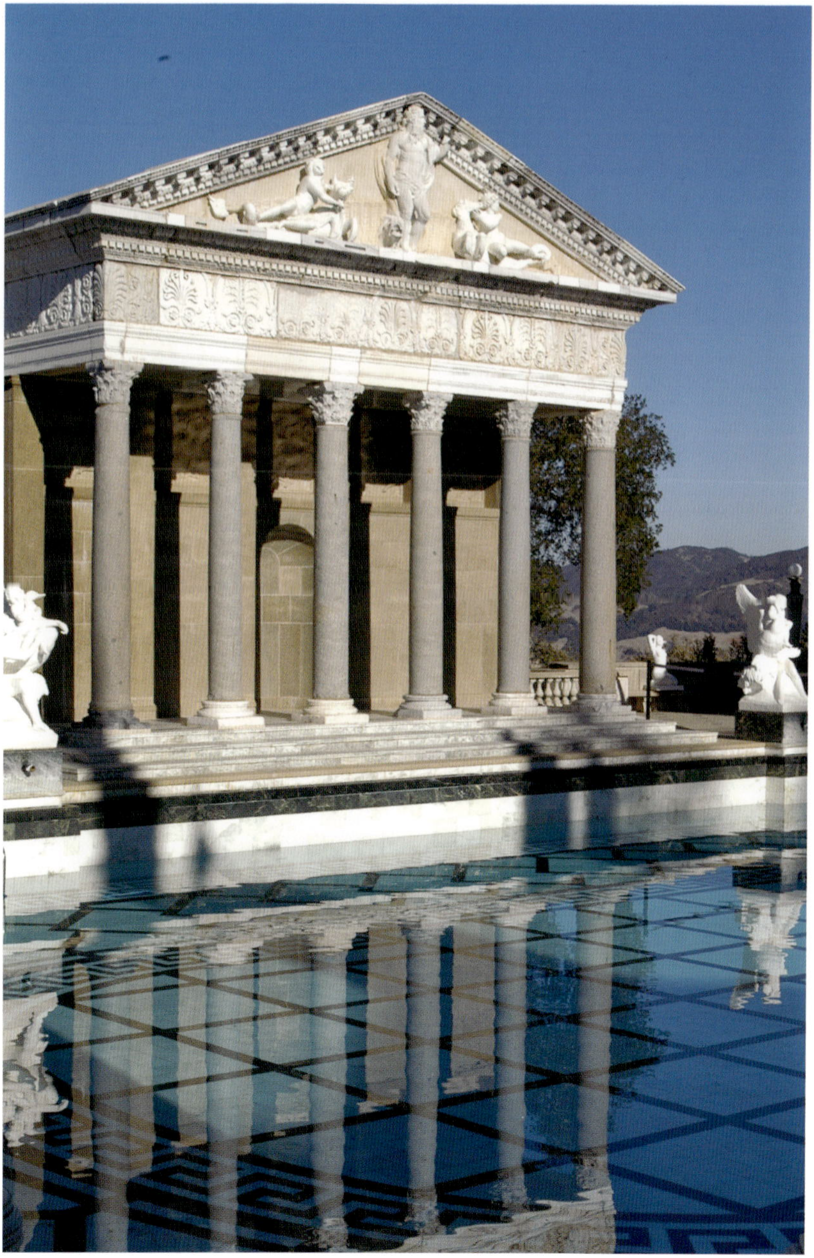

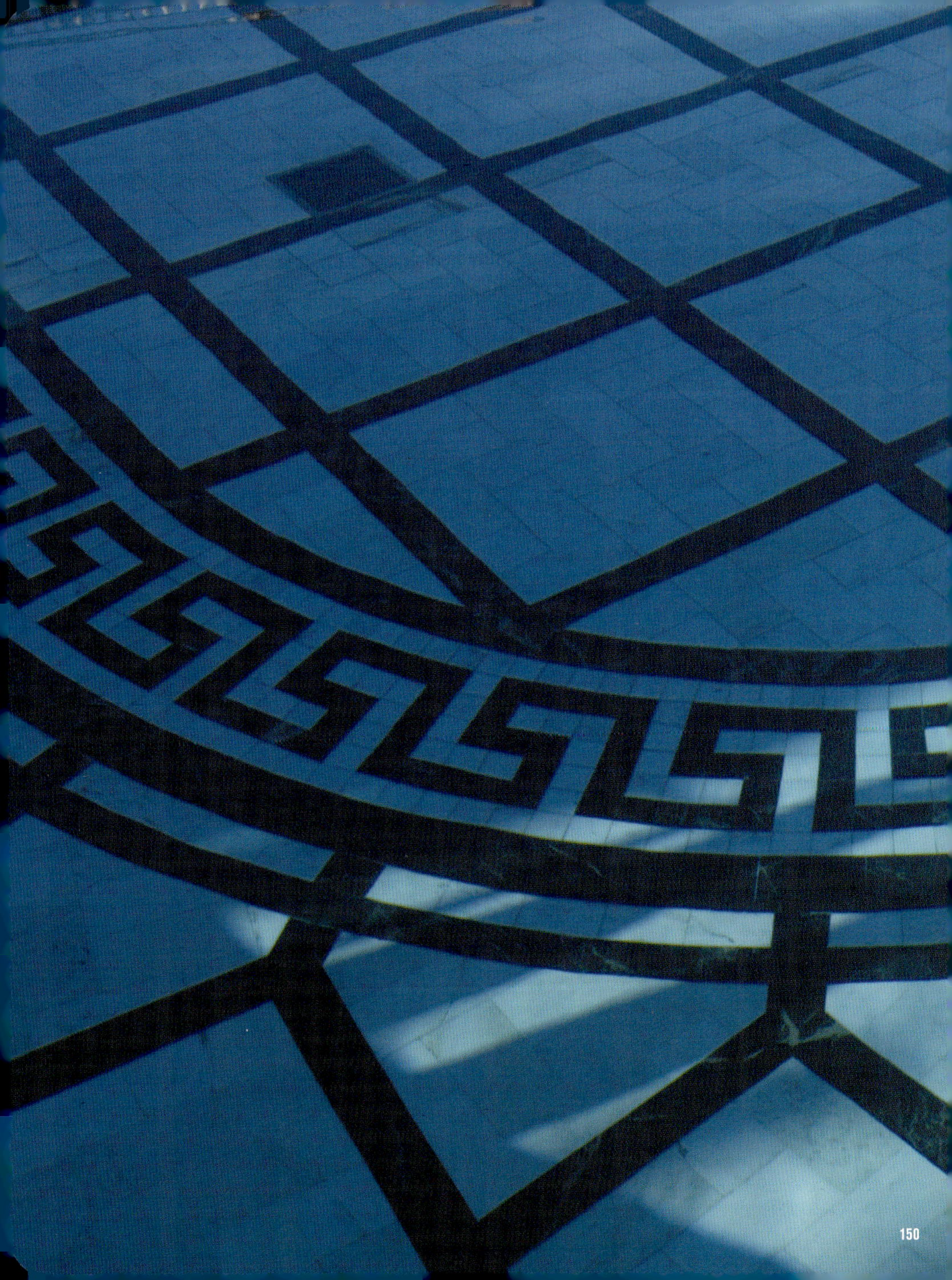

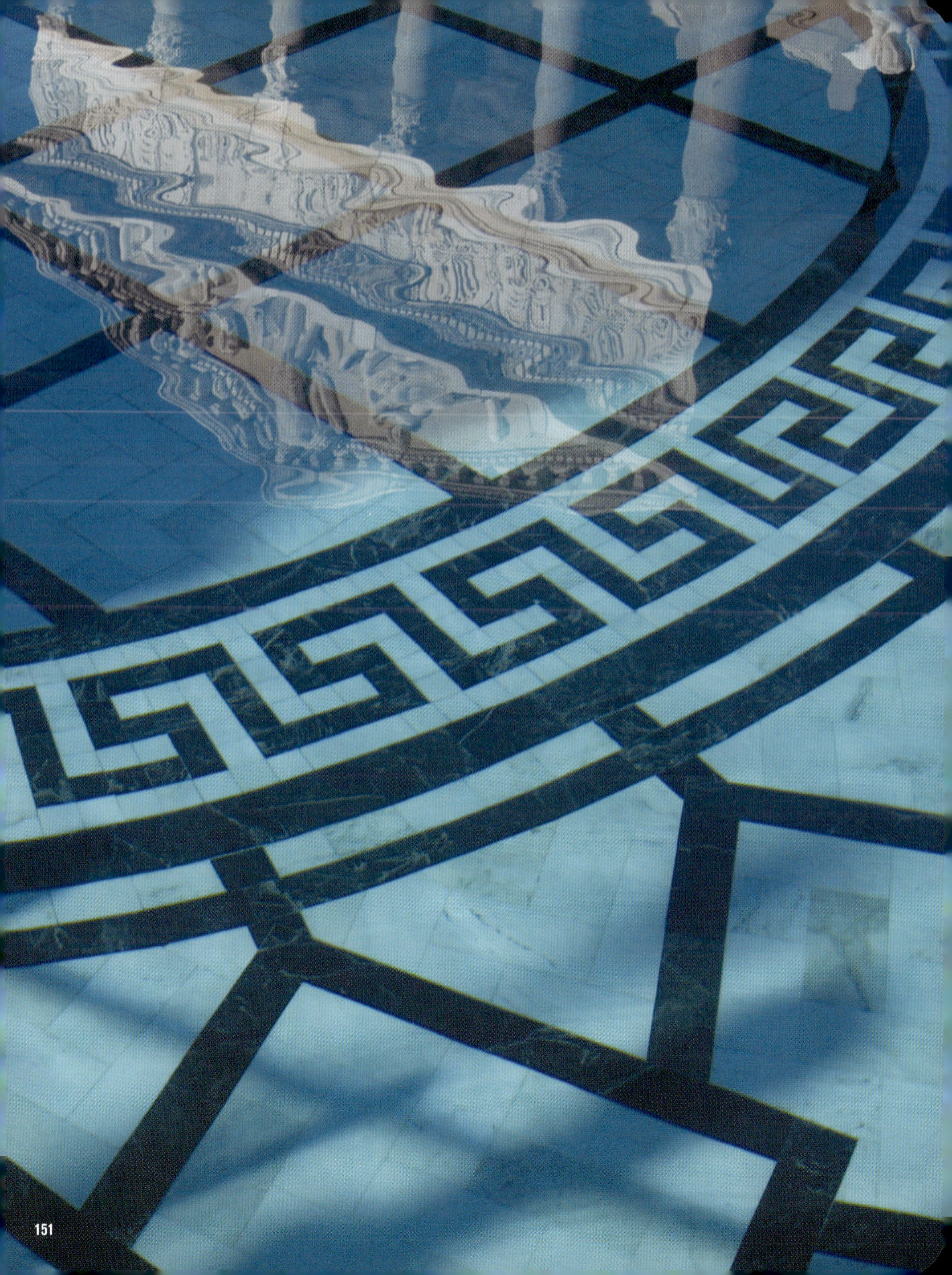

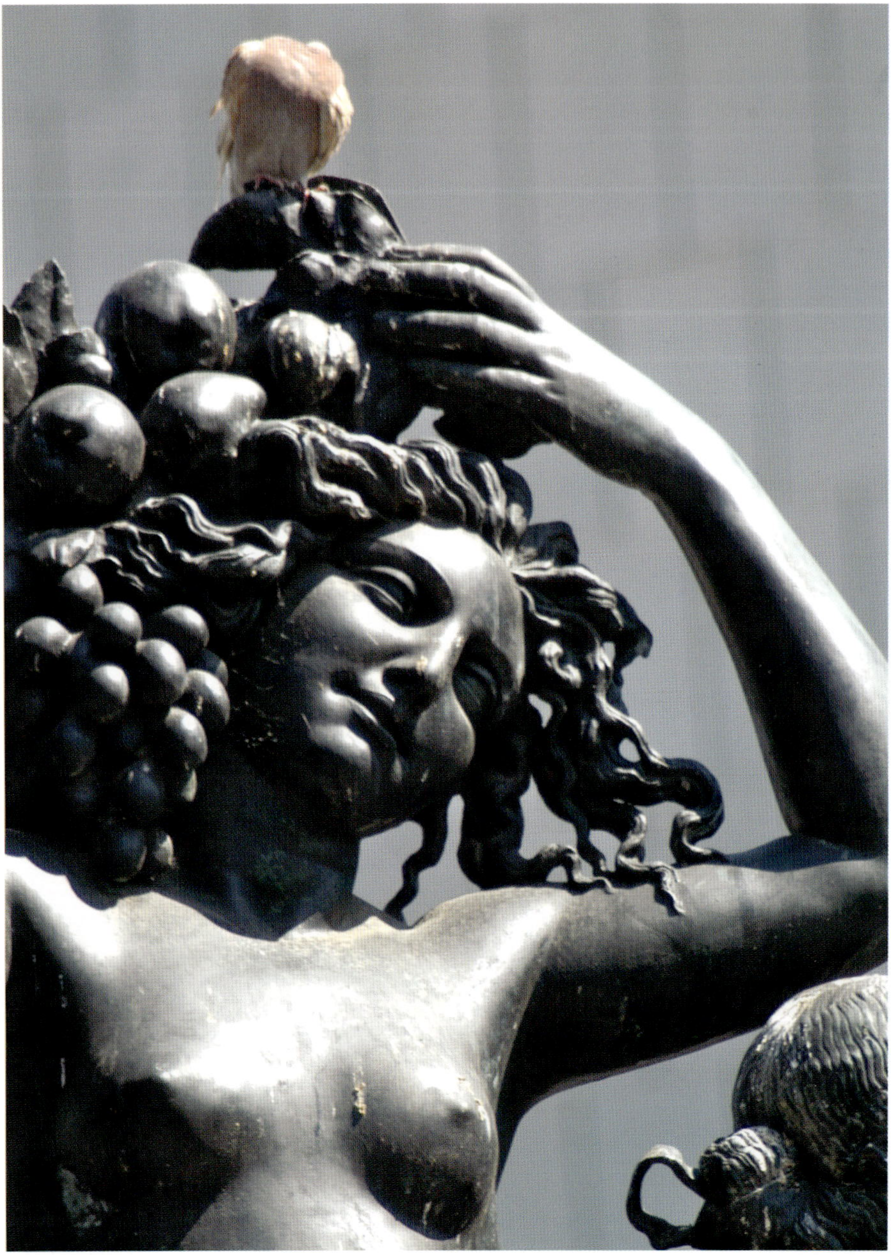

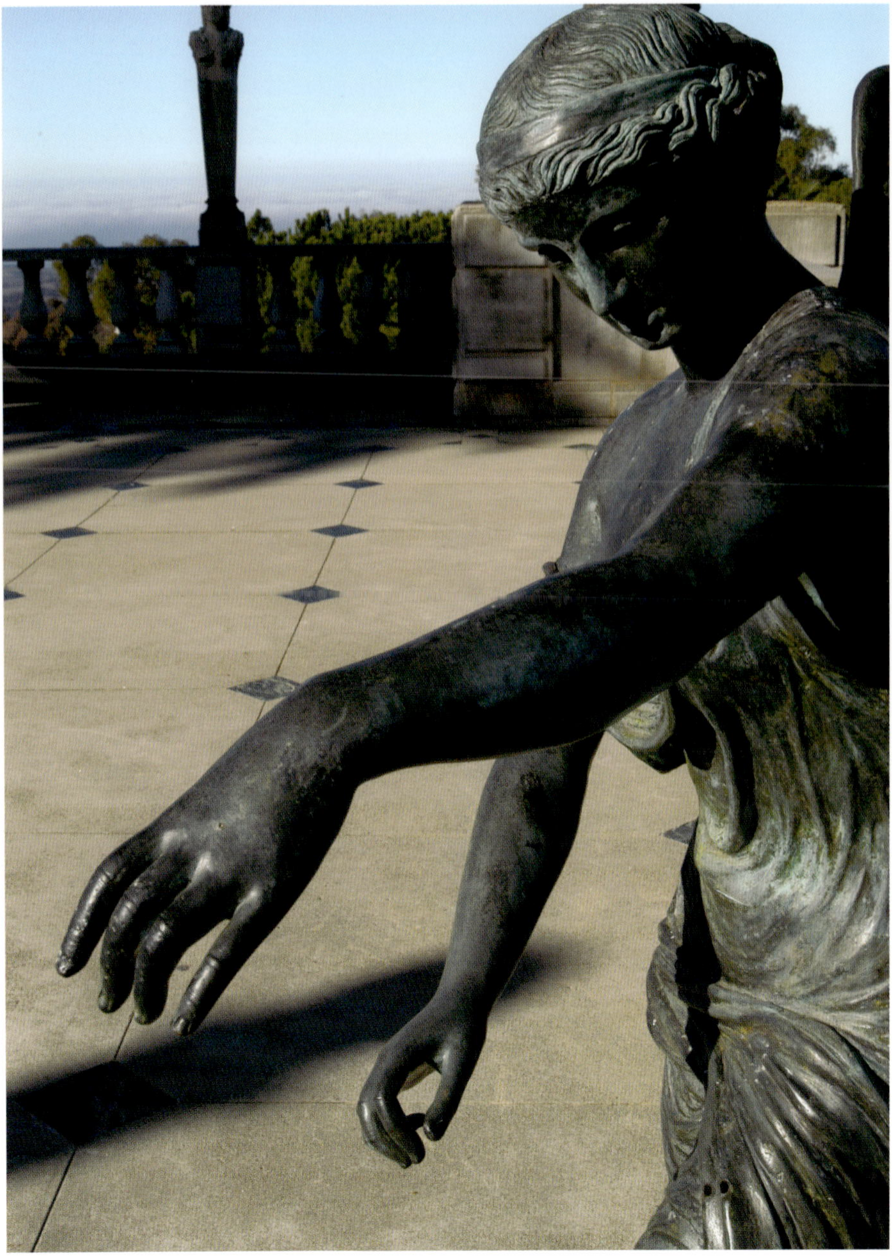

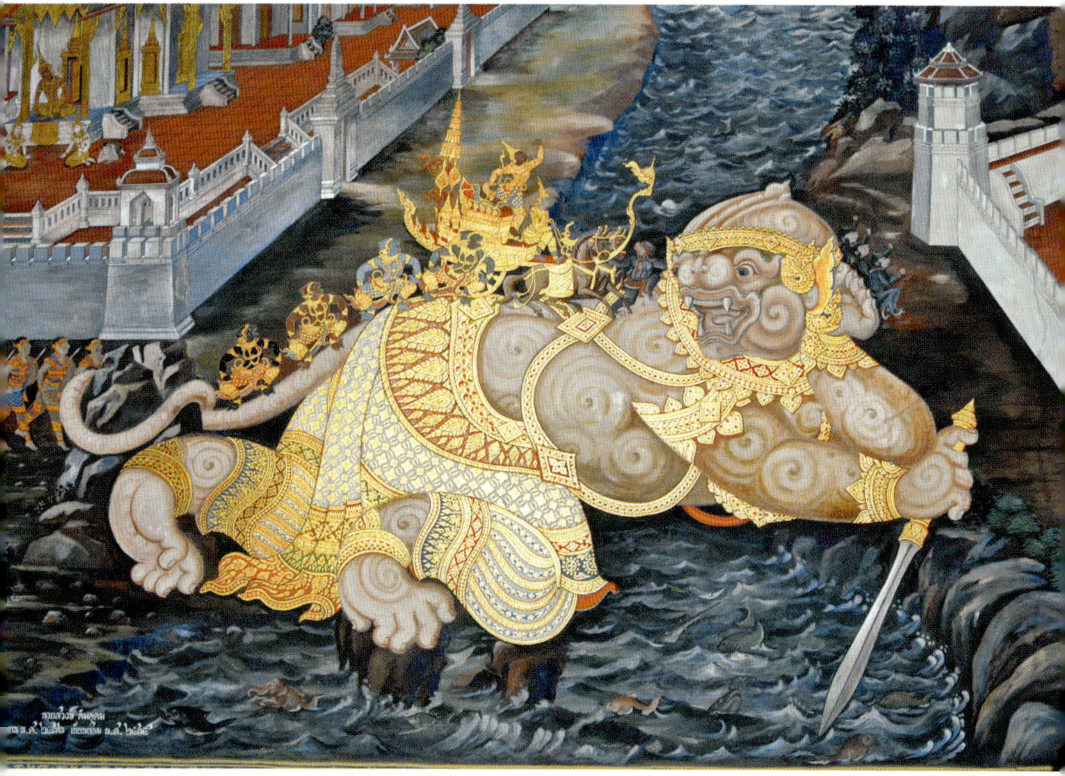

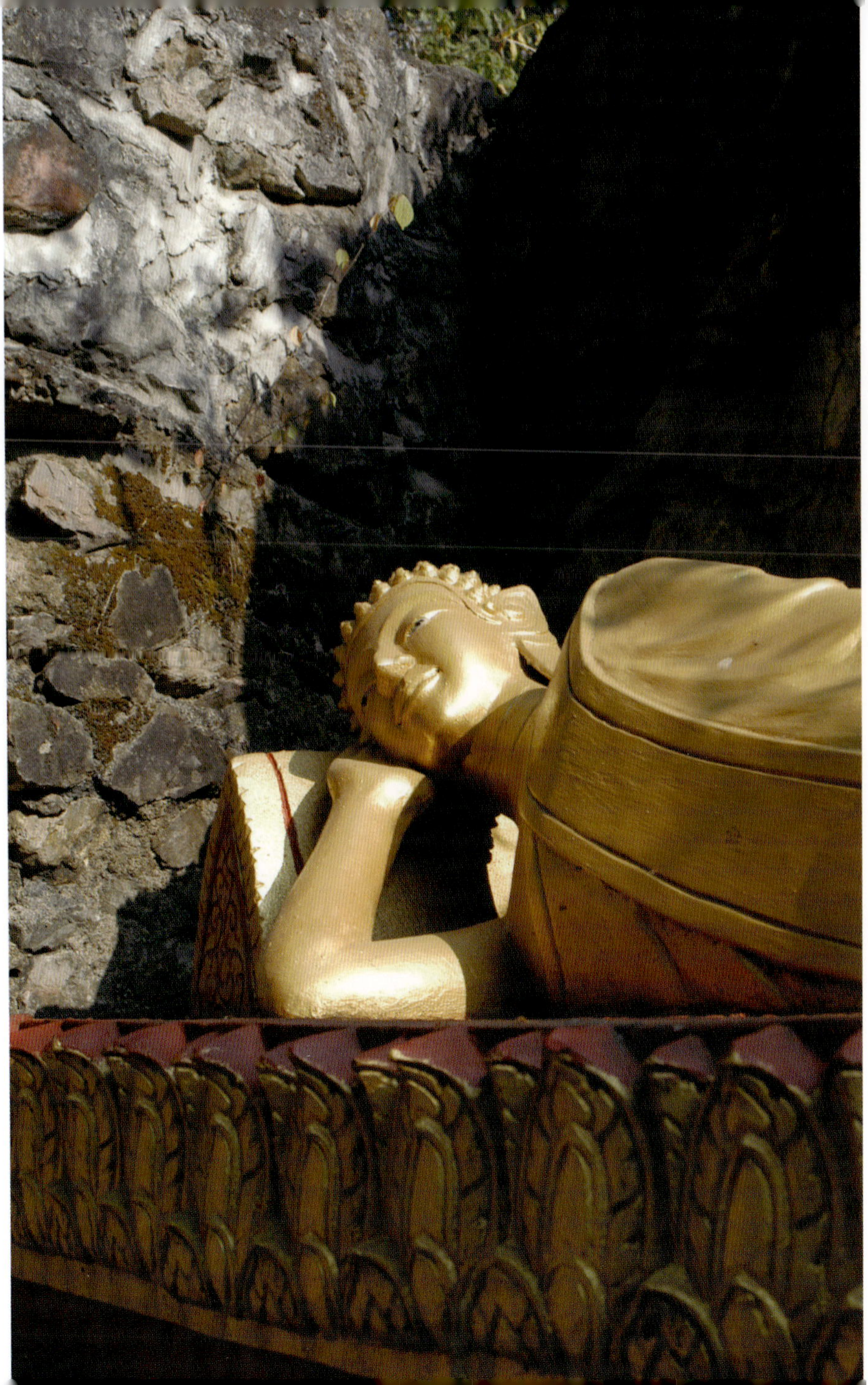

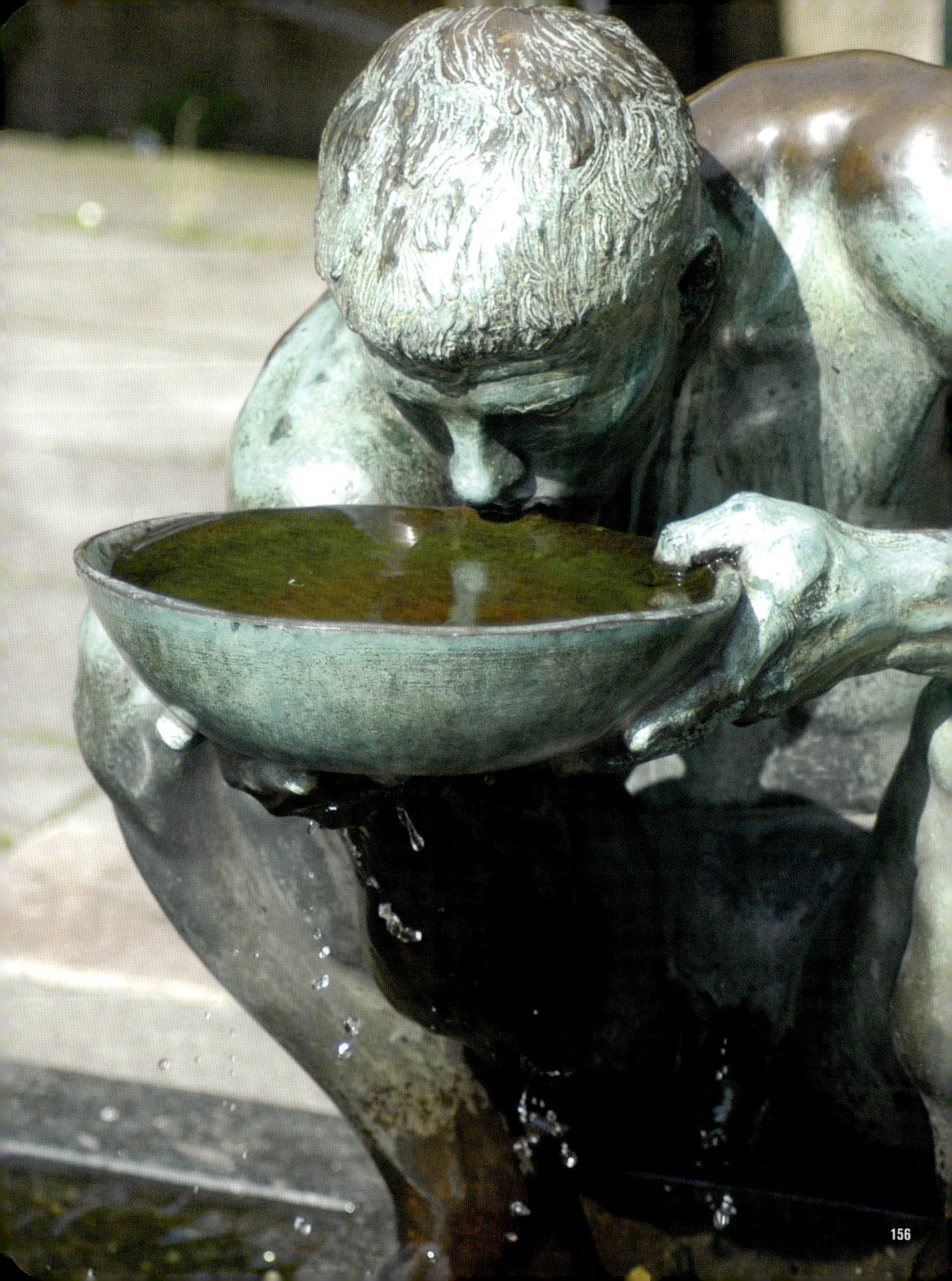

VIEWING

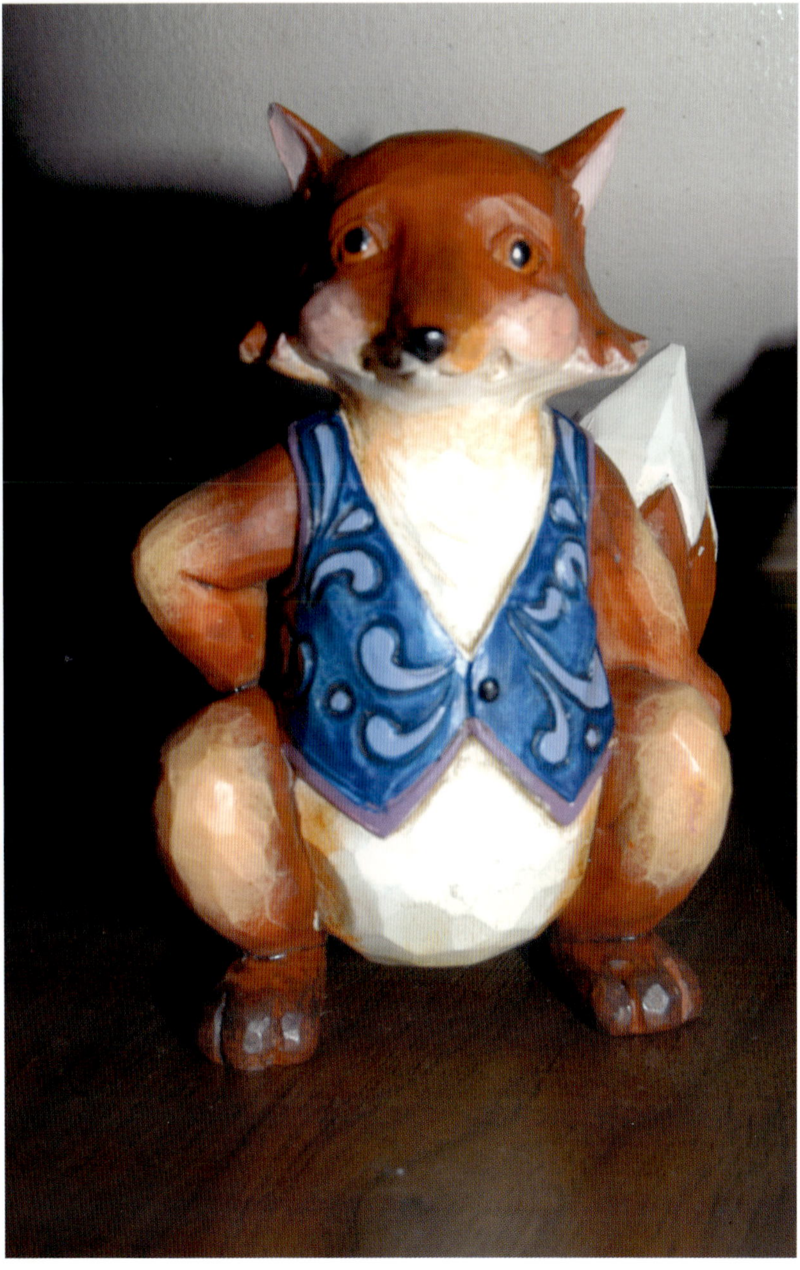

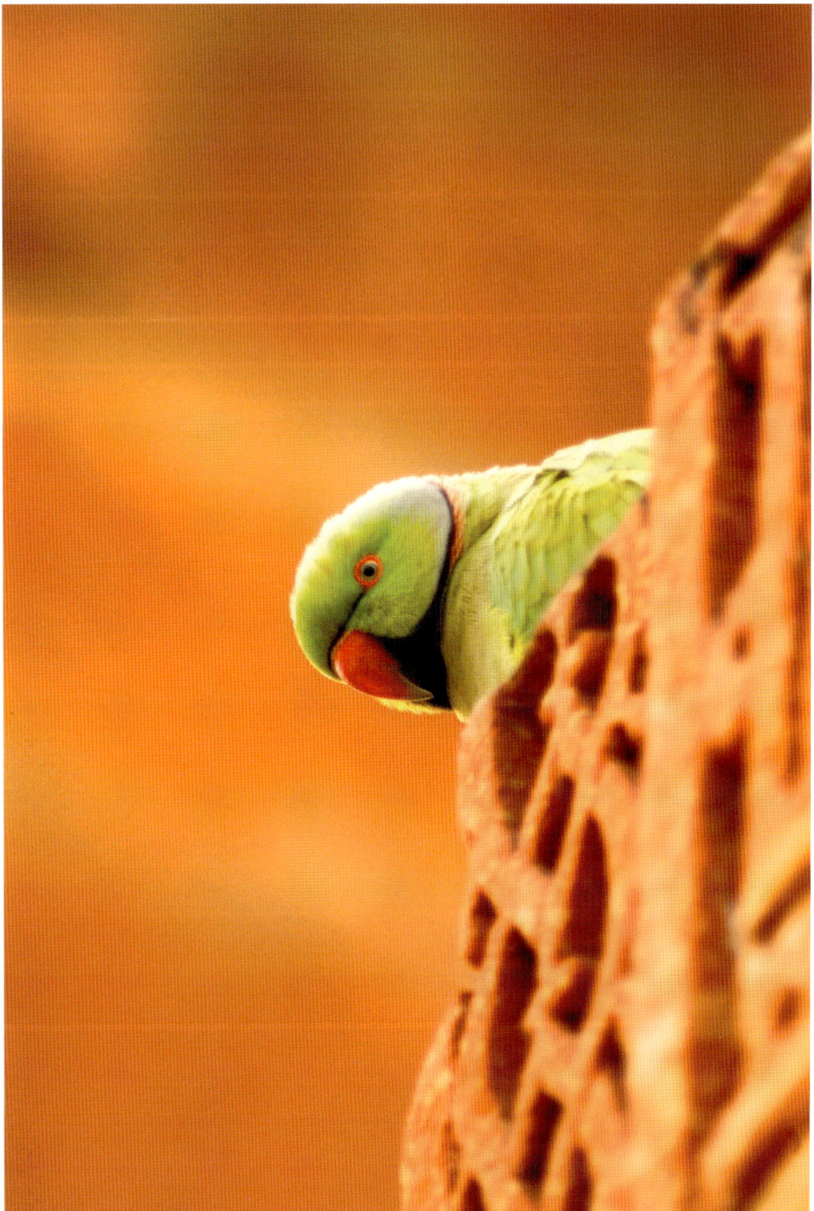

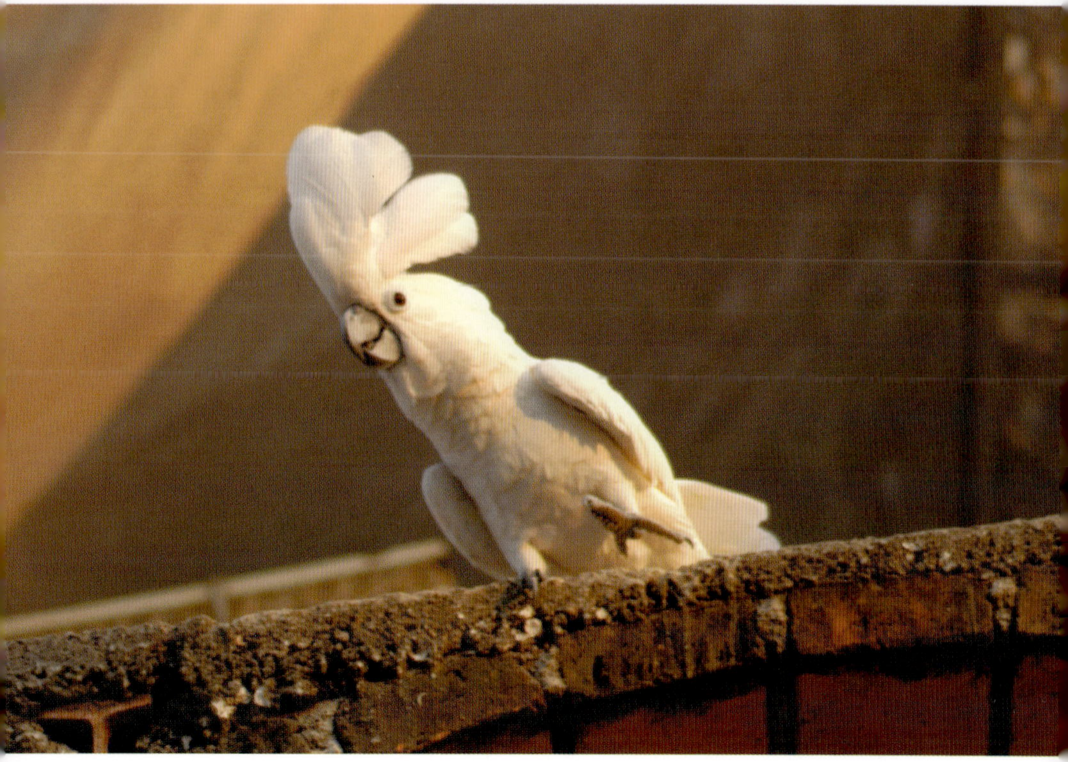

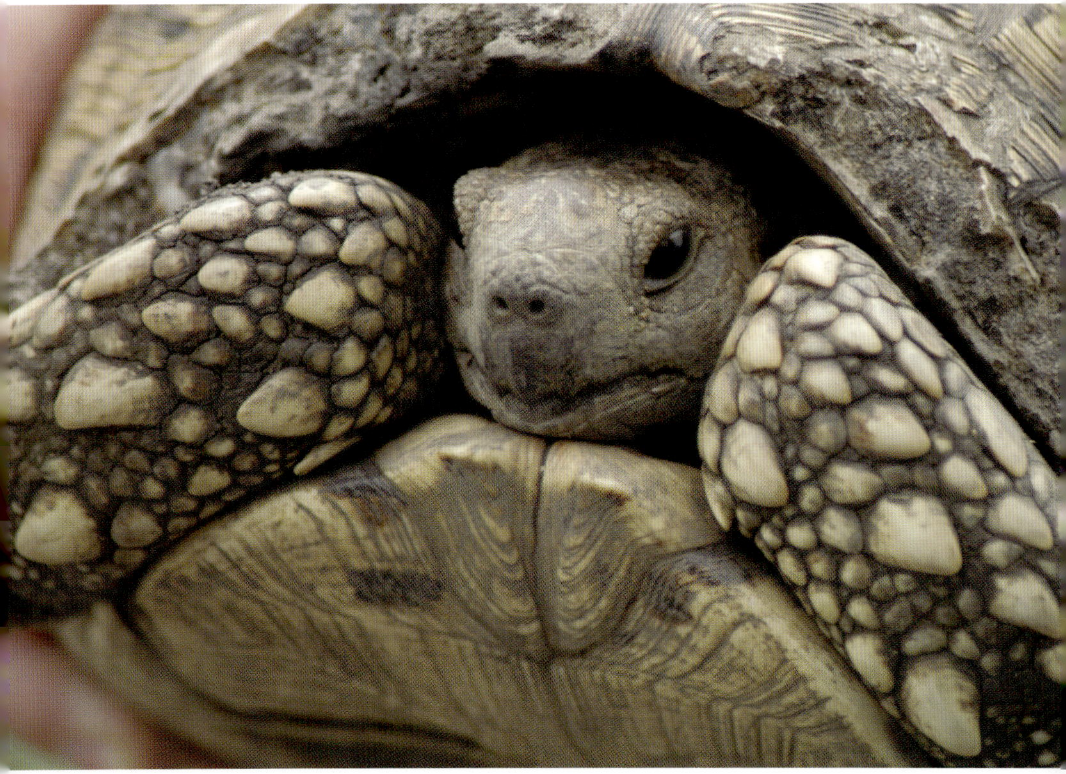

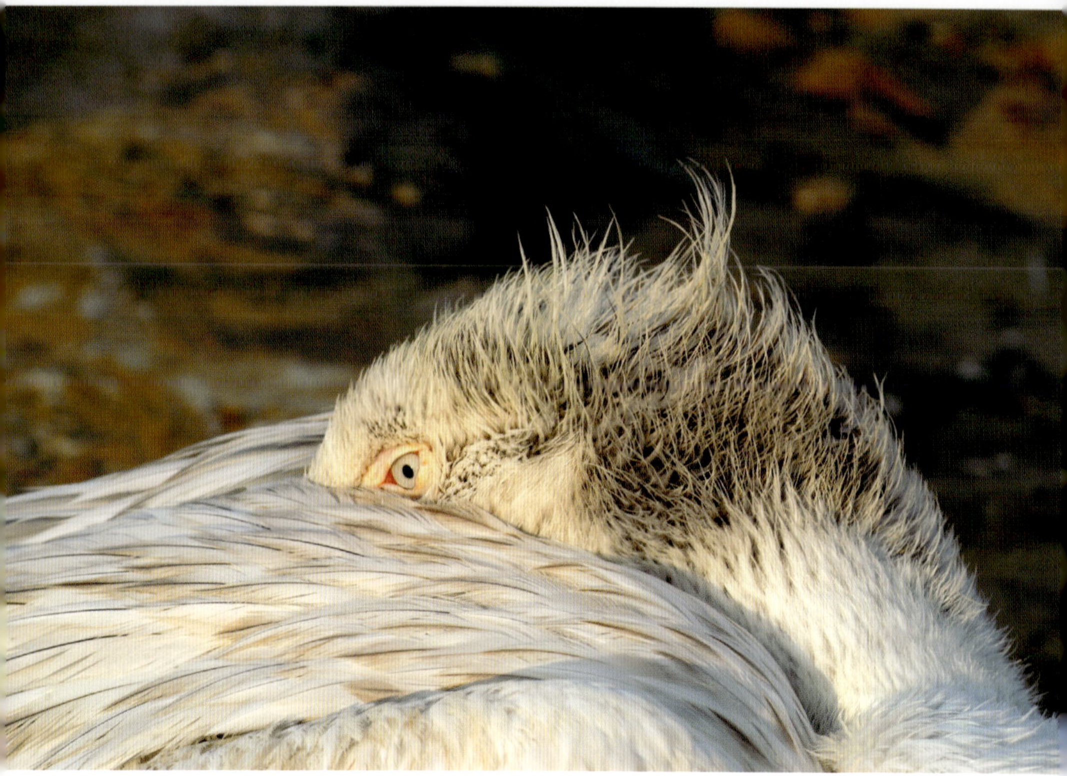

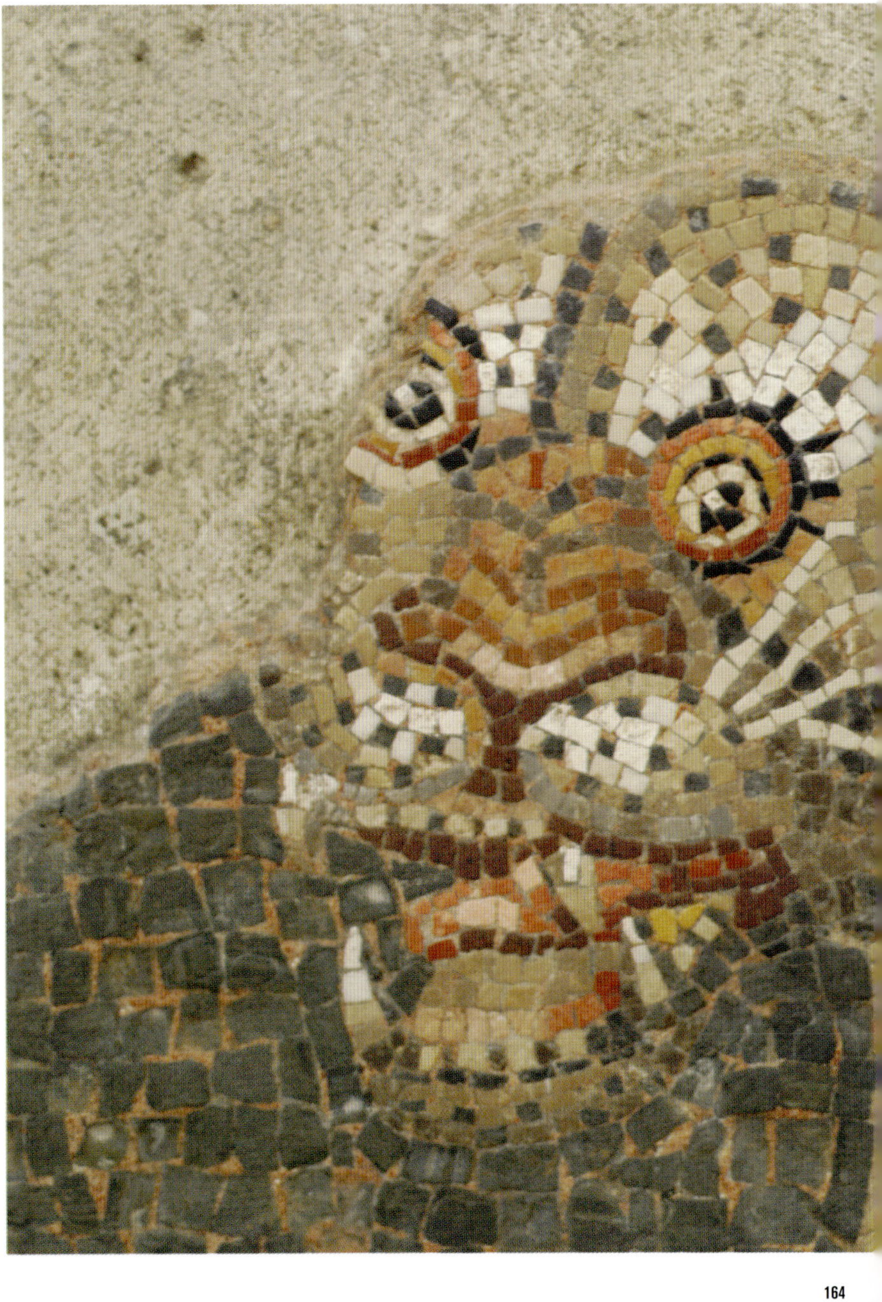

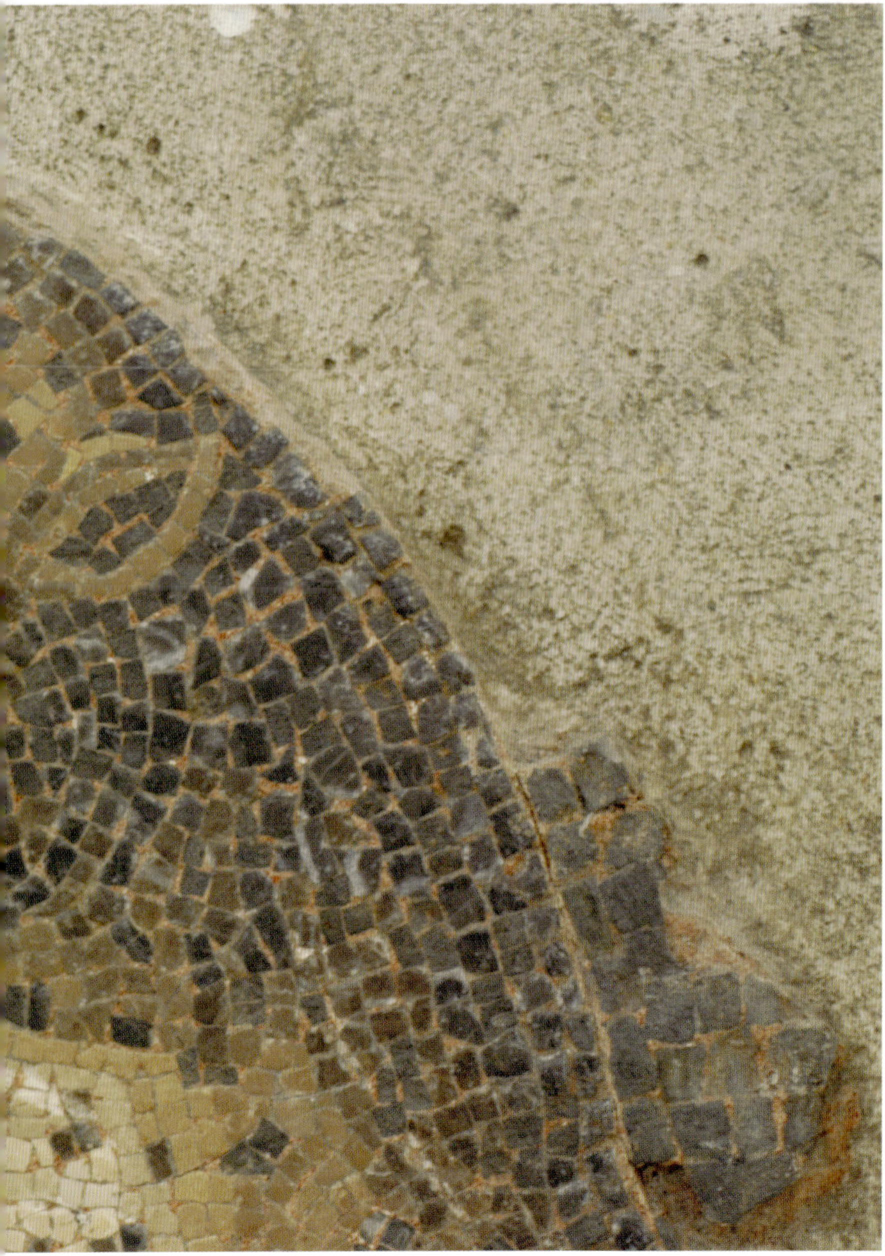

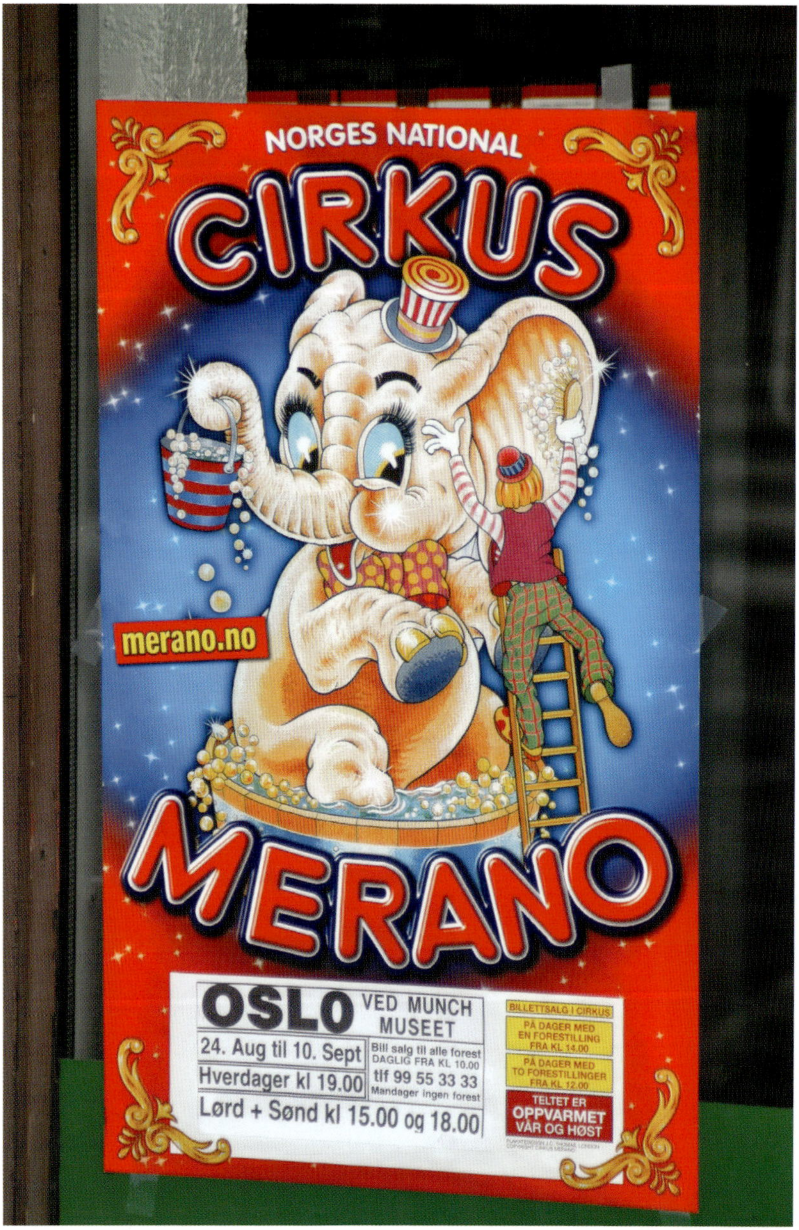

NORGES NATIONAL
CIRKUS
MERANO
merano.no
OSLO
VED MUNCH MUSEET
24. Aug til 10. Sept
Hverdager kl 19.00
Lørd + Sønd kl 15.00 og 18.00
Bill salg til alle forest DAGLIG FRA KL 10.00
tlf 99 55 33 33
Mandager ingen forest
BILLETTSALG I CIRKUS
PÅ DAGER MED EN FORESTILLING FRA KL 14.00
PÅ DAGER MED TO FORESTILLINGER FRA KL 12.00
TELTET ER OPPVARMET VÅR OG HØST

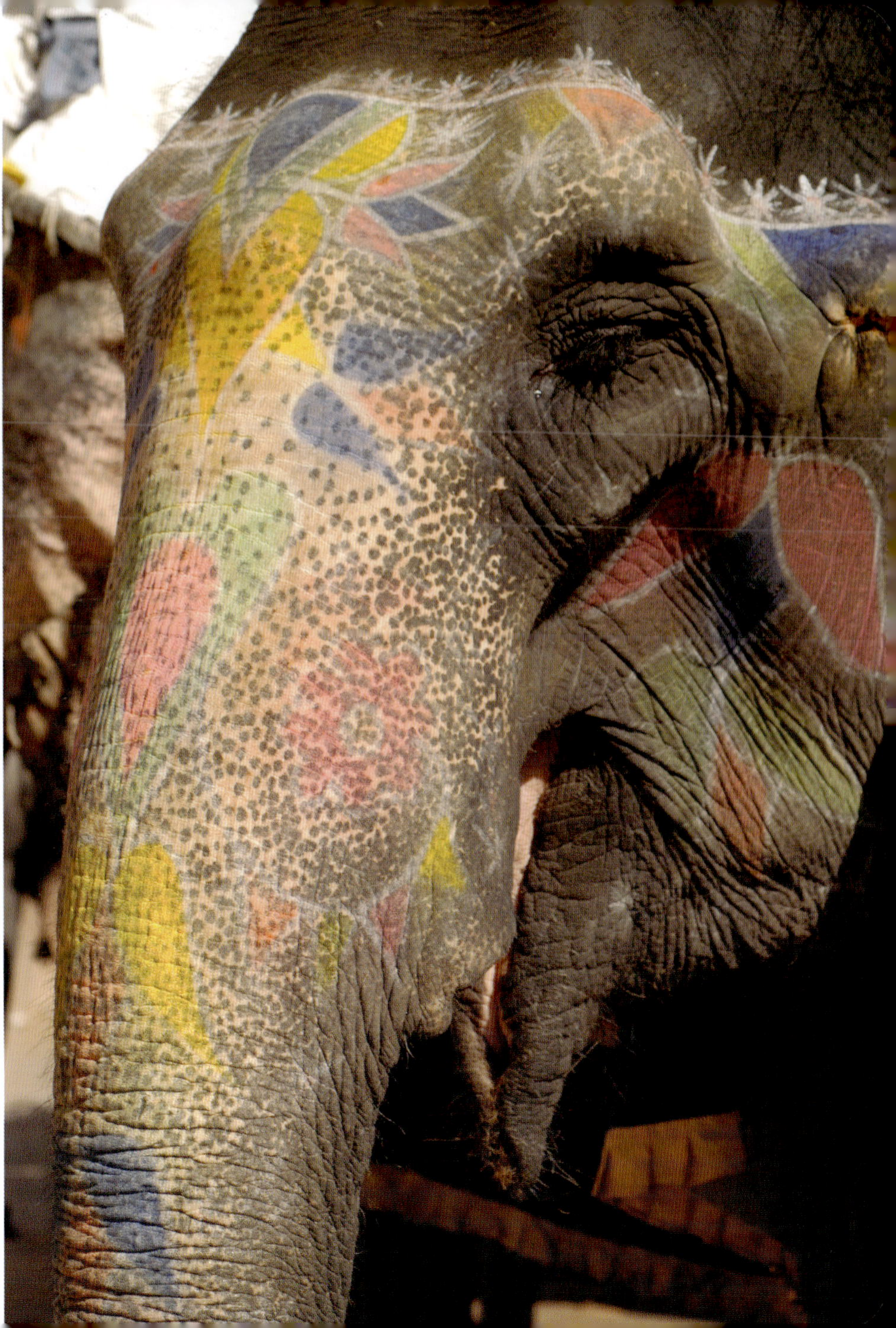

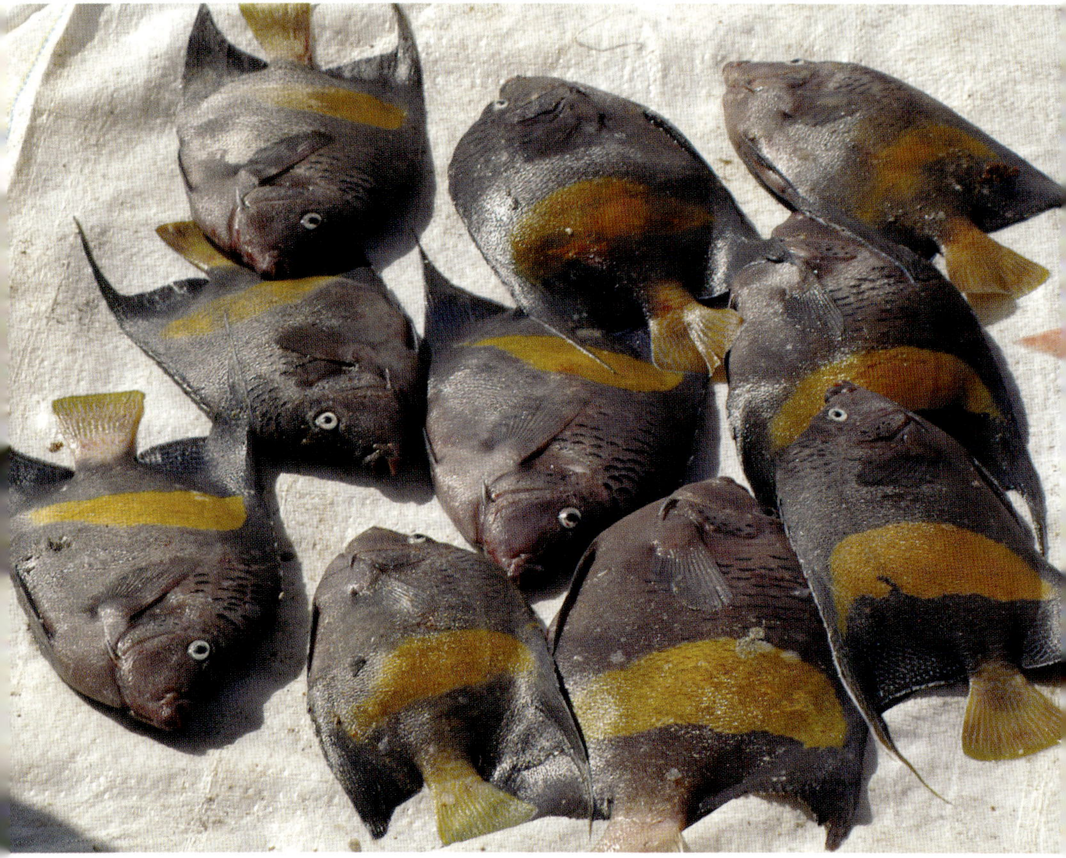

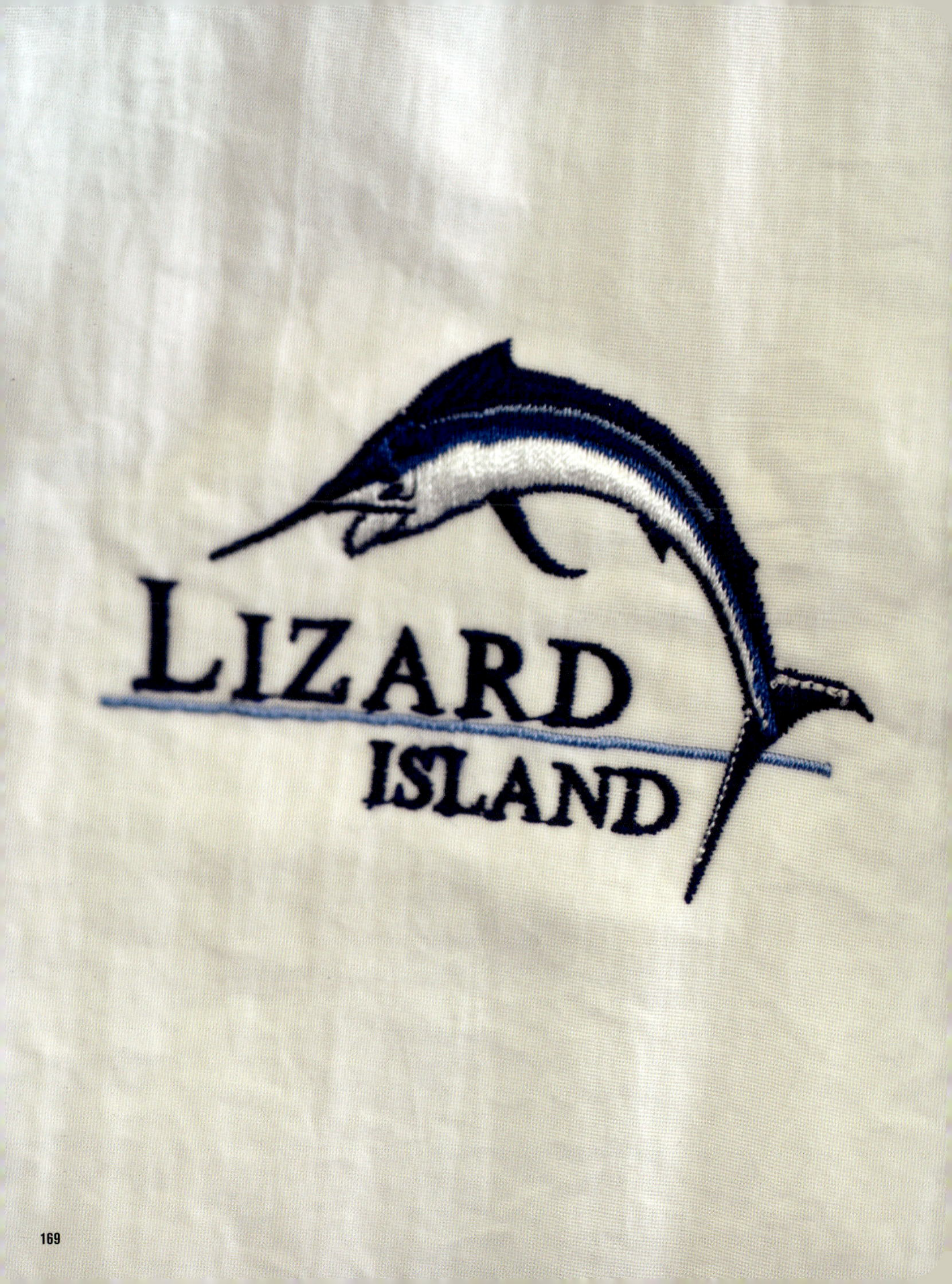
LIZARD
ISLAND

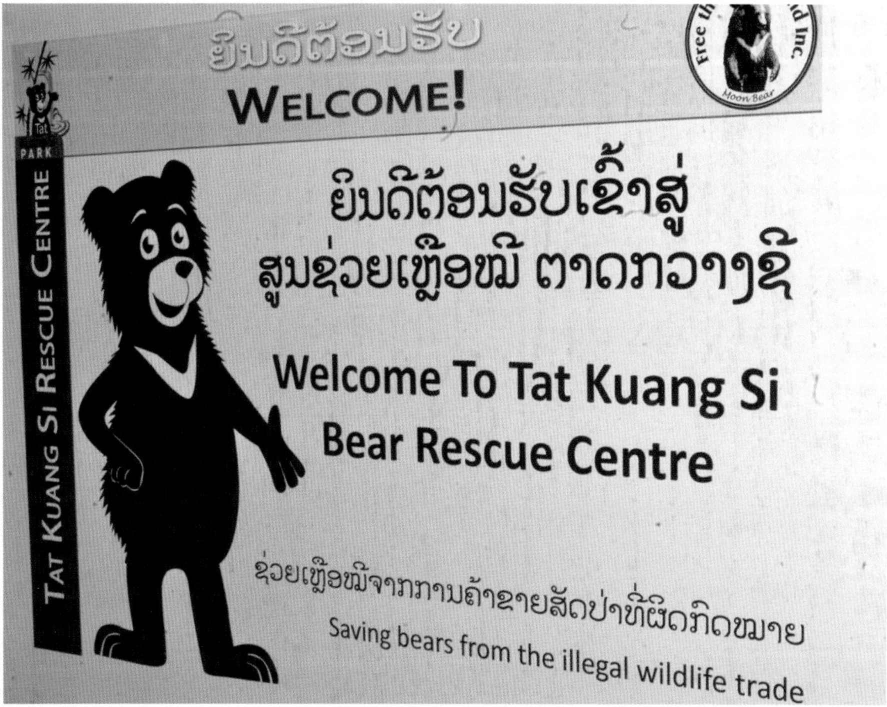
ຍິນດີຕ້ອນຮັບ
WELCOME!
PARK
TAT KUANG SI RESCUE CENTRE
ຍິນດີຕ້ອນຮັບເຂົ້າສູ່
ສູນຊ່ວຍເຫຼືອໝີ ຕາດກວາງຊີ
Welcome To Tat Kuang Si
Bear Rescue Centre
ຊ່ວຍເຫຼືອໝີຈາກການຄ້າຂາຍສັດປ່າທີ່ຜິດກົດໝາຍ
Saving bears from the illegal wildlife trade

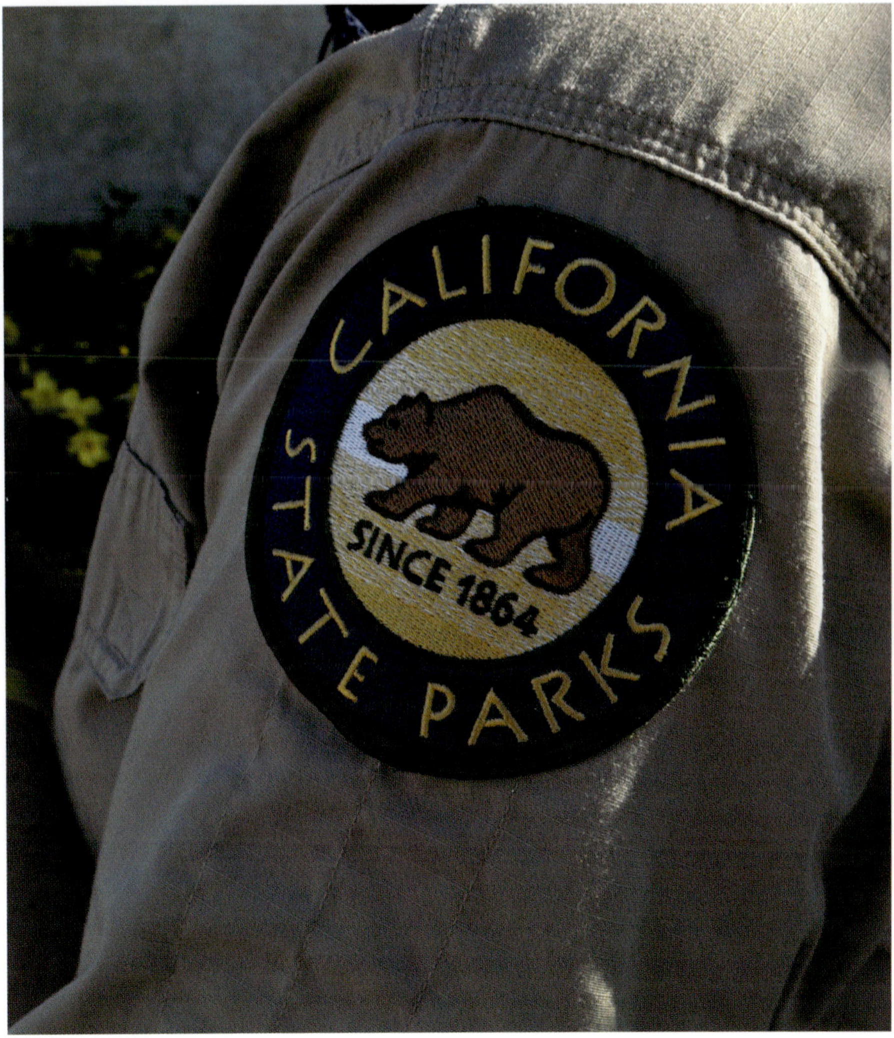
CALIFORNIA
SINCE 1864
STATE PARKS

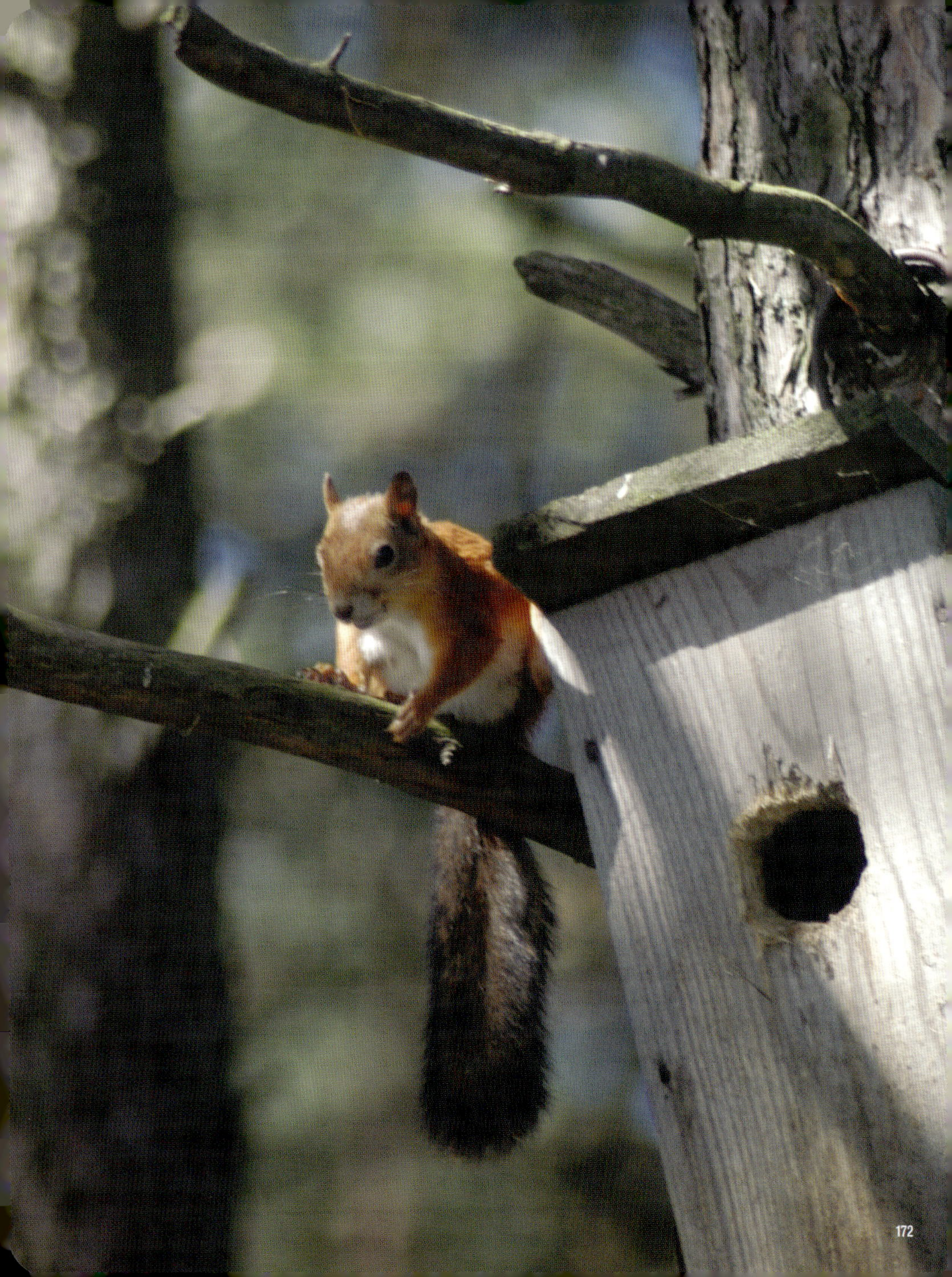

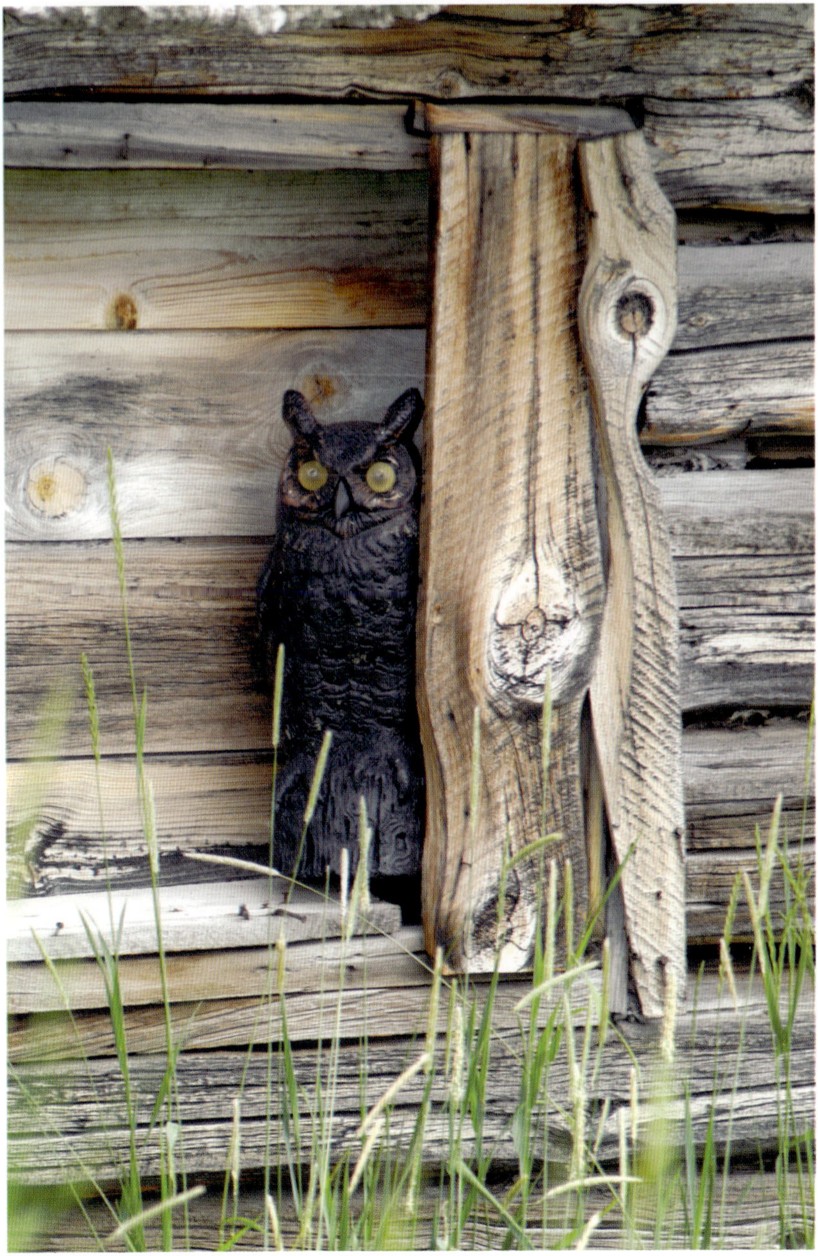

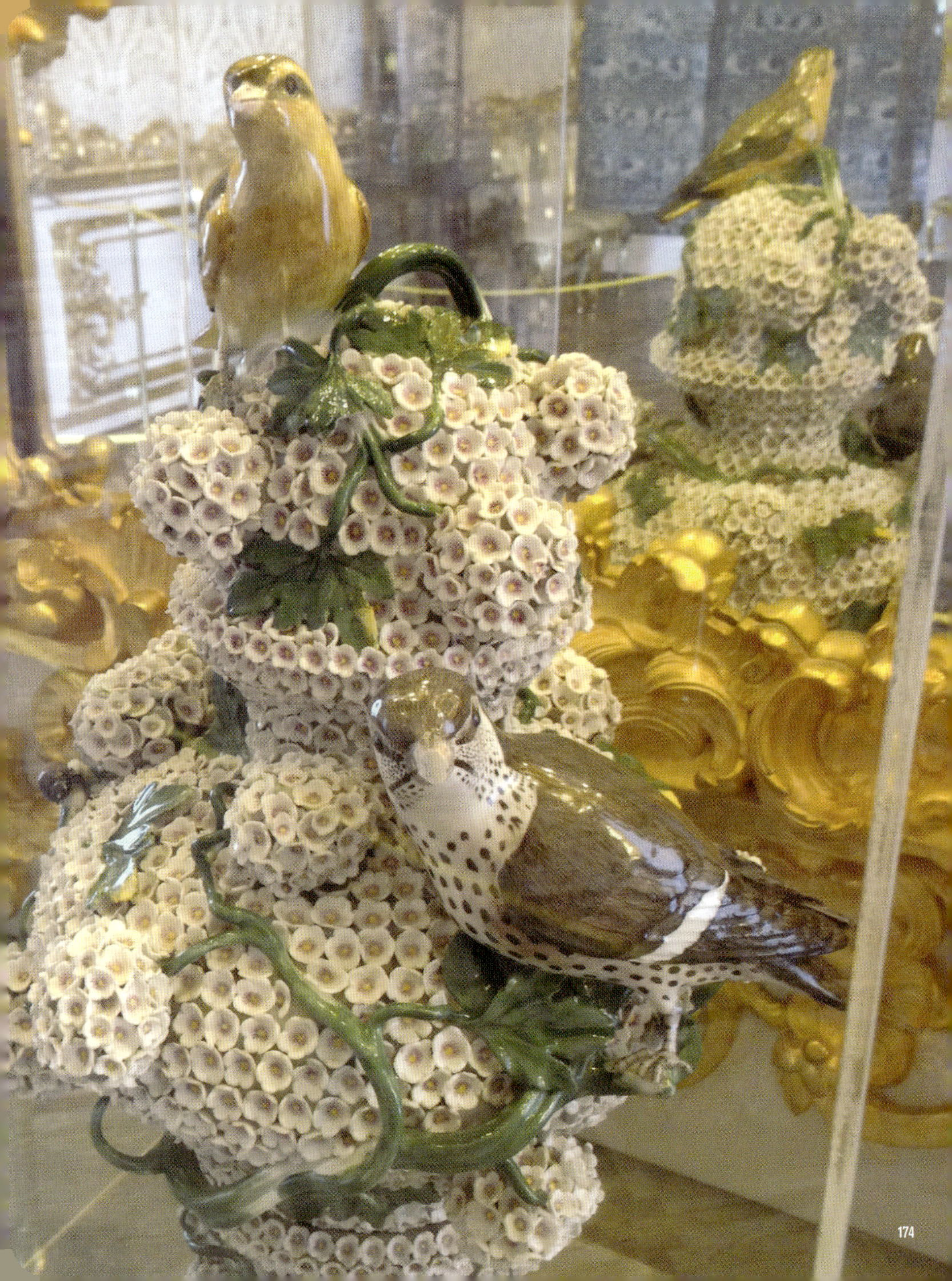

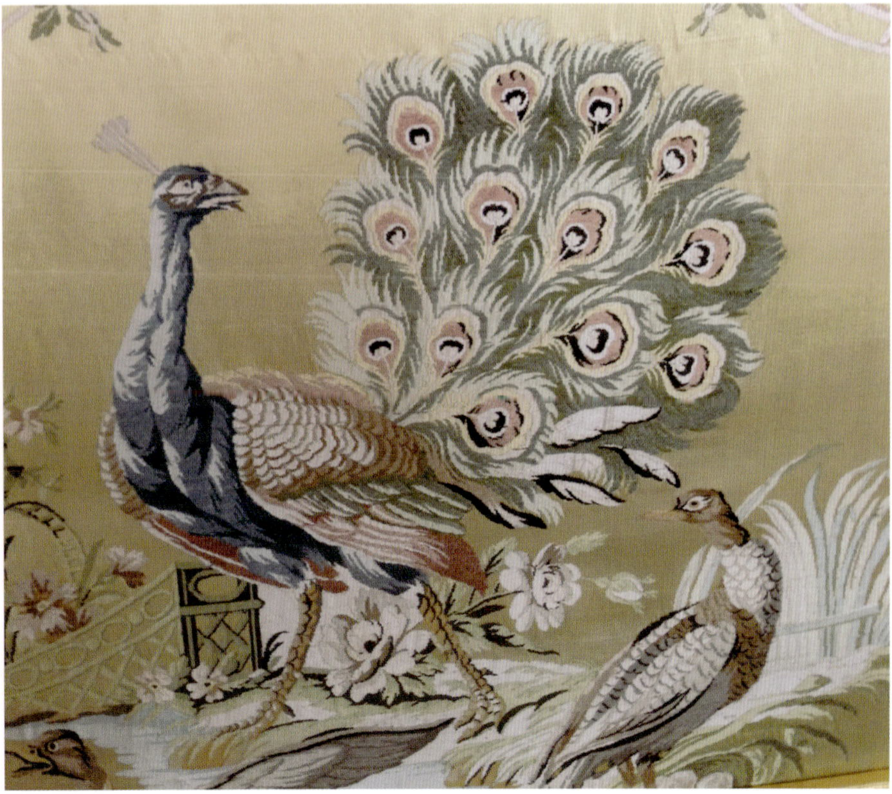

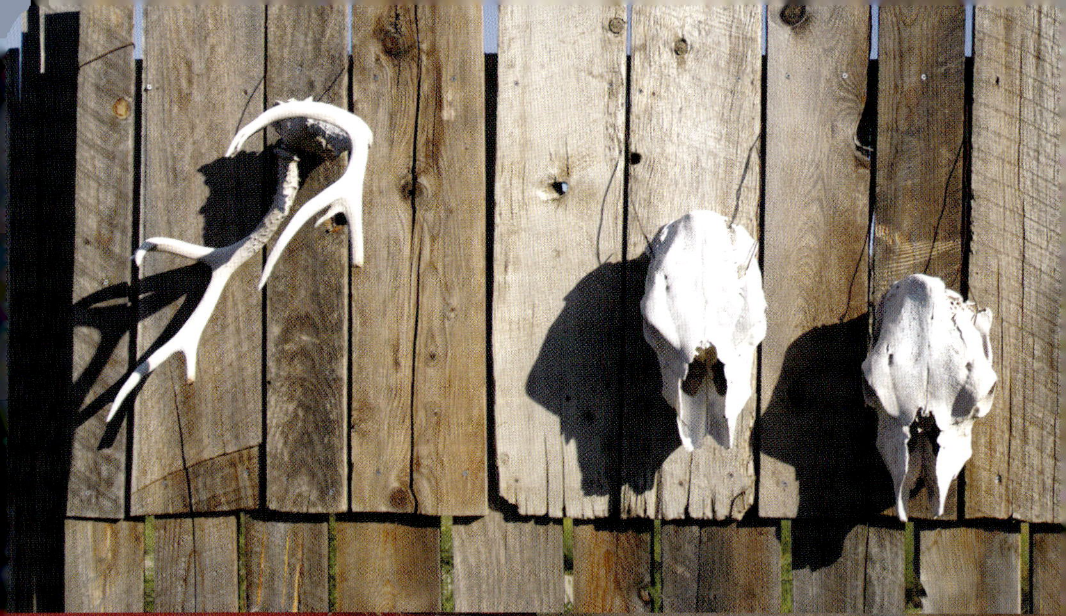
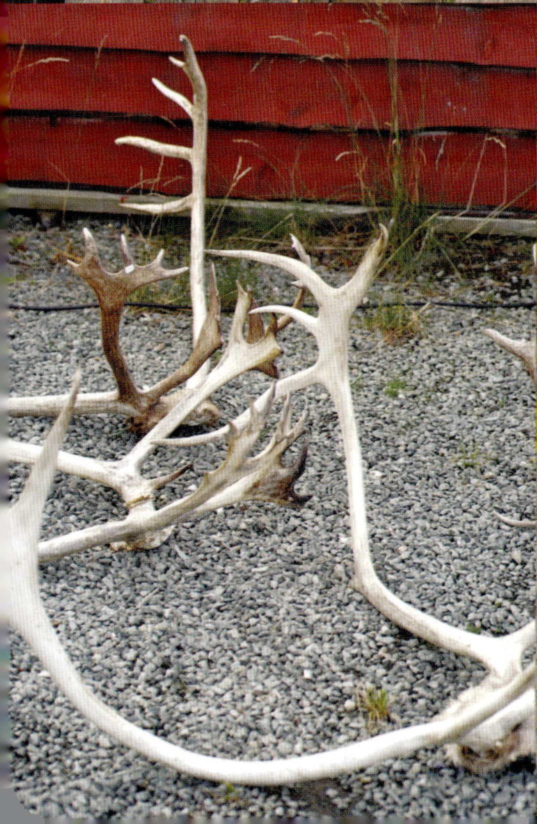
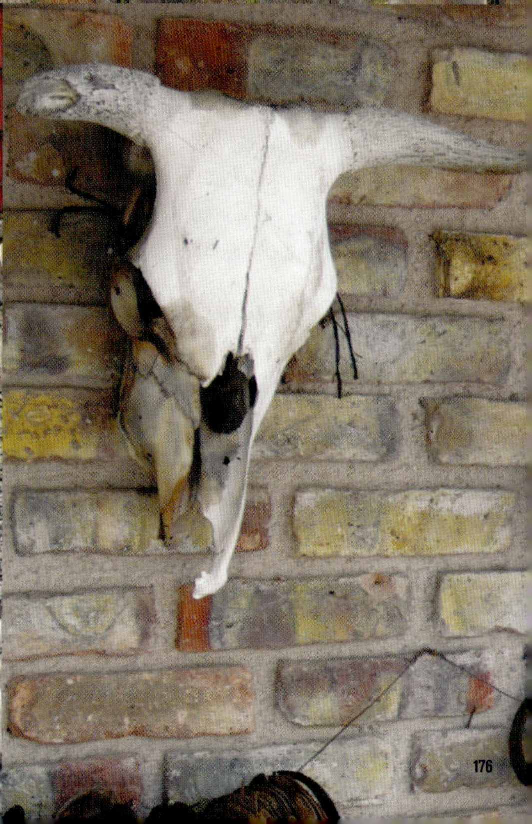

FOCUSING

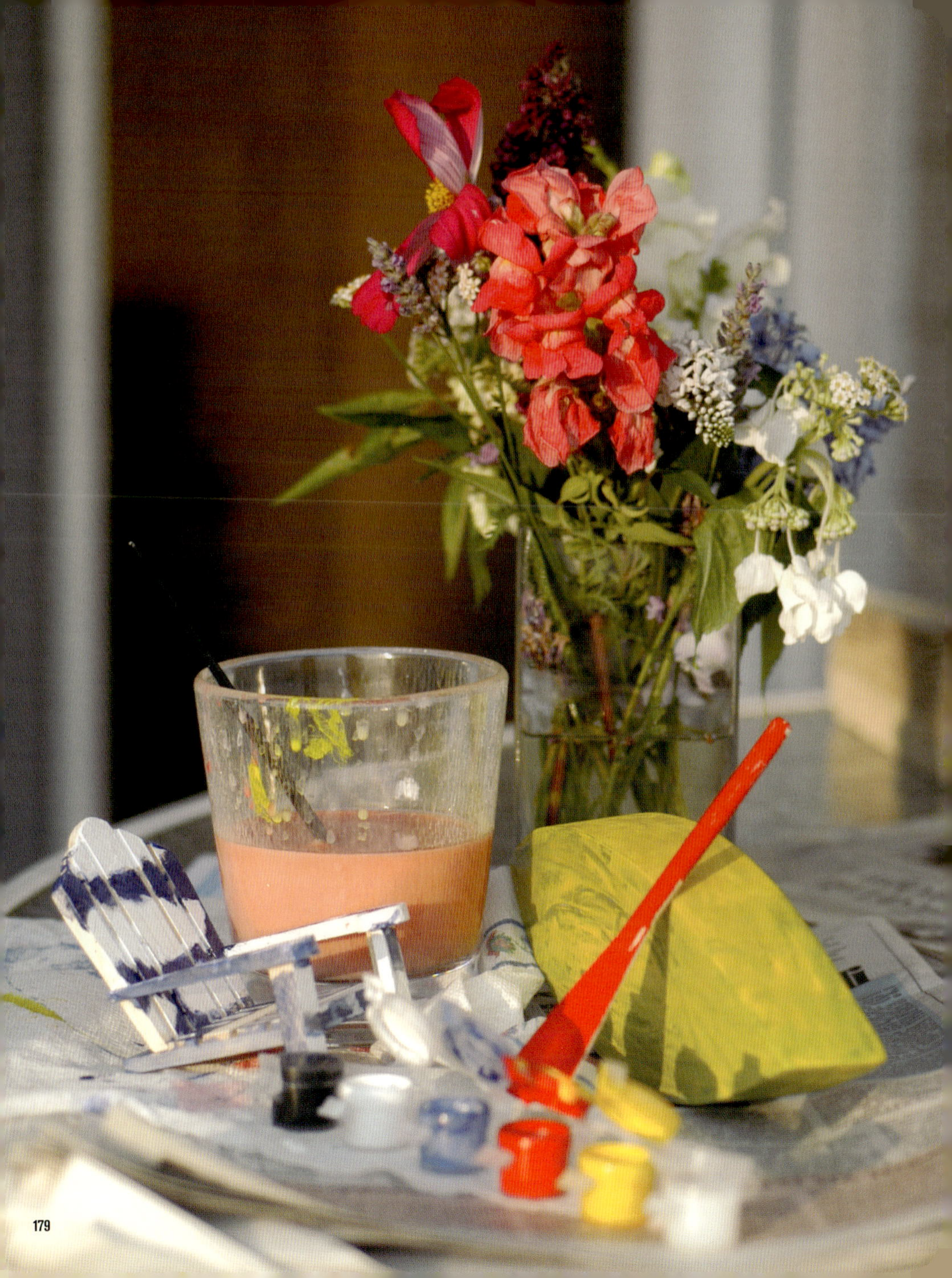

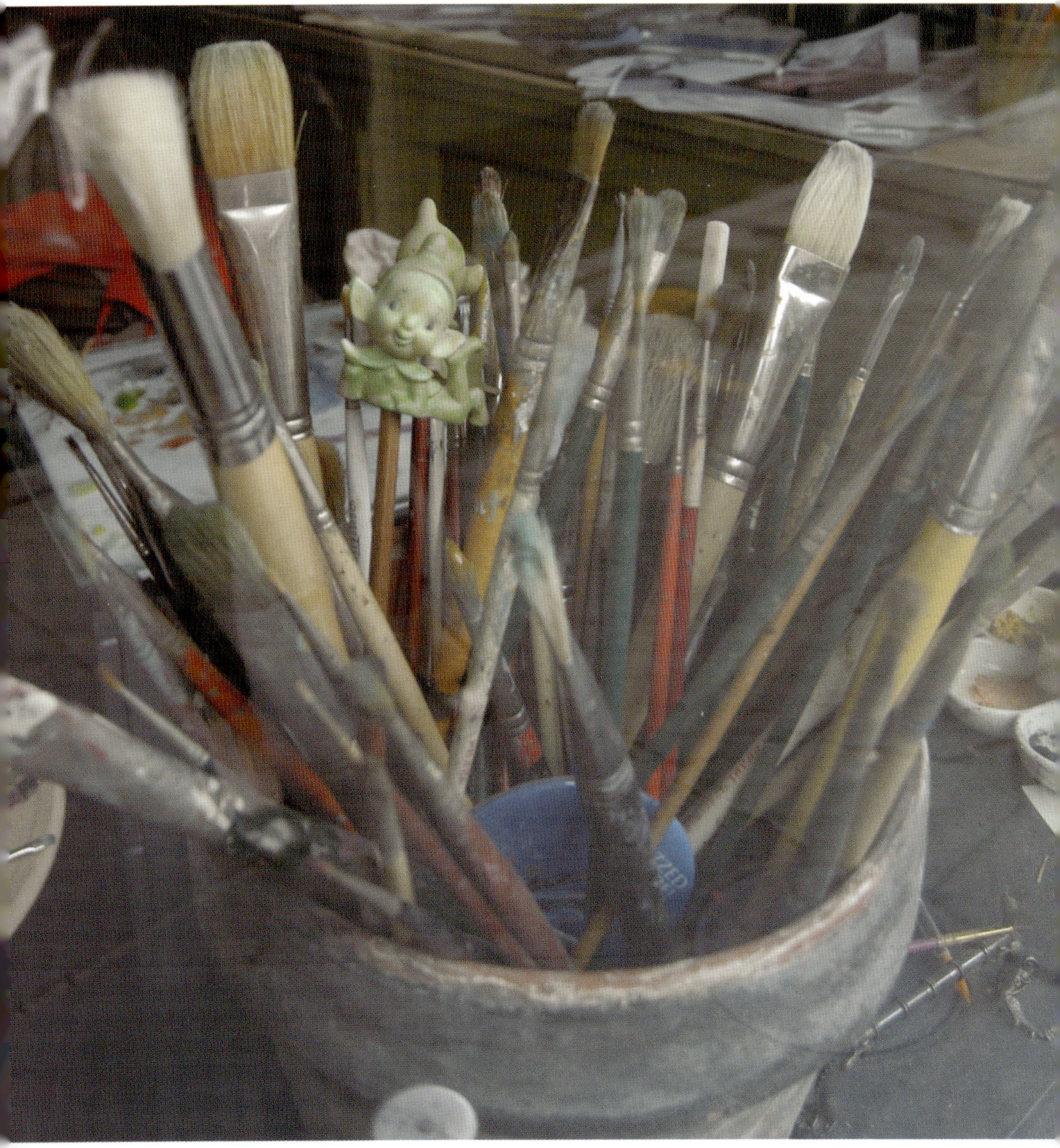

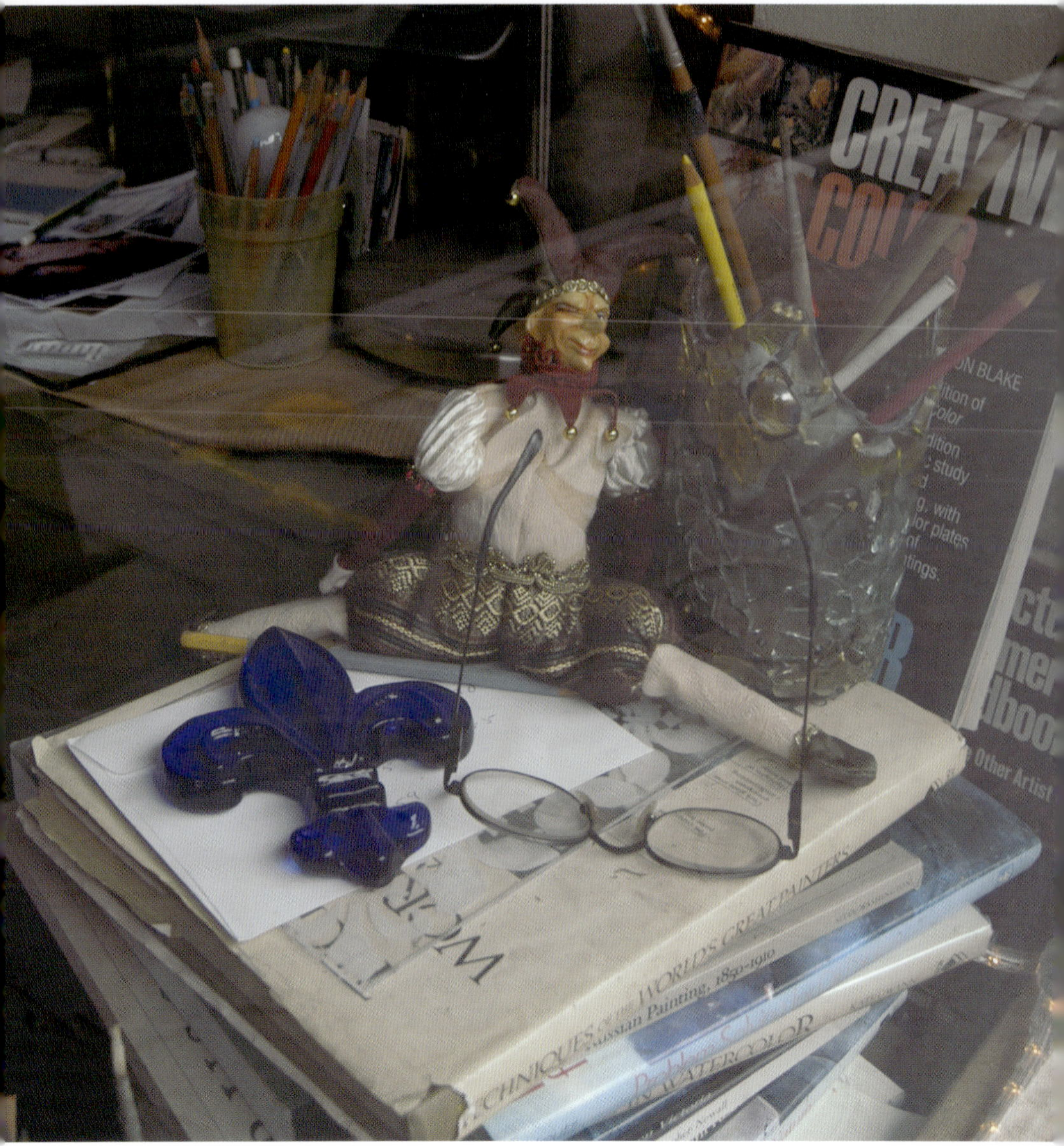
WORLD'S GREAT PAINTERS
WATERCOLOR
Other Artist

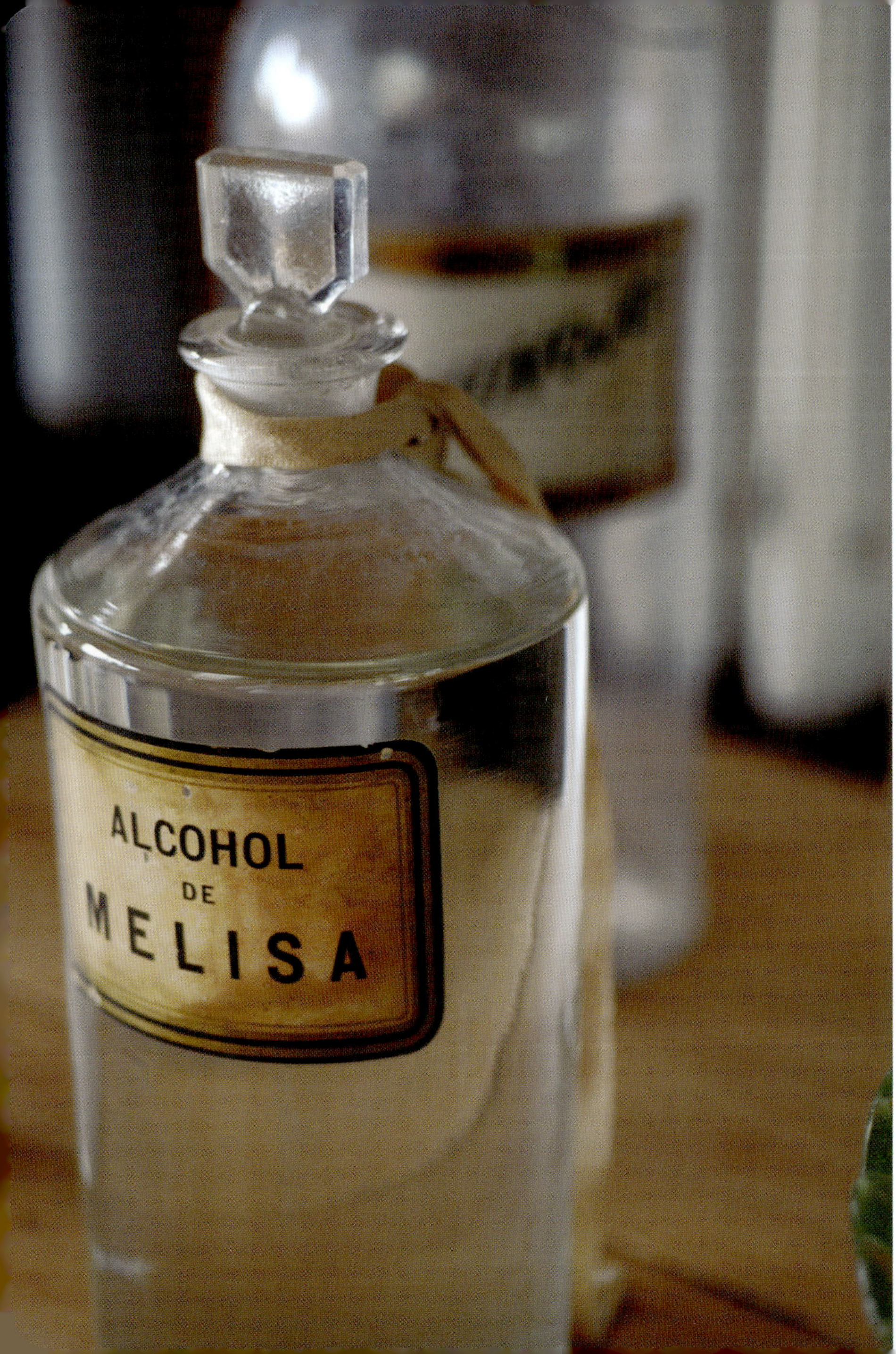
ALCOHOL
DE
MELISA

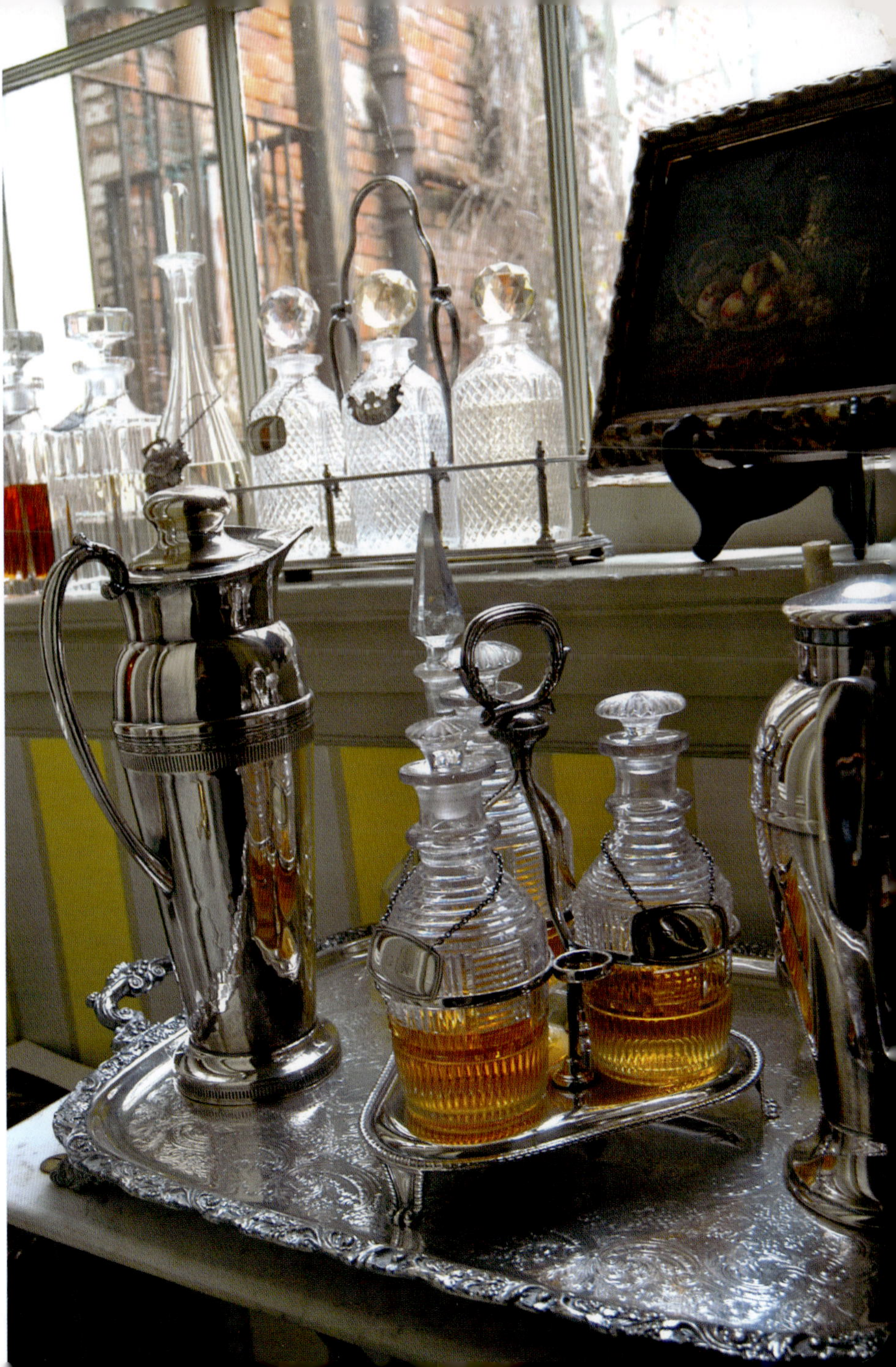

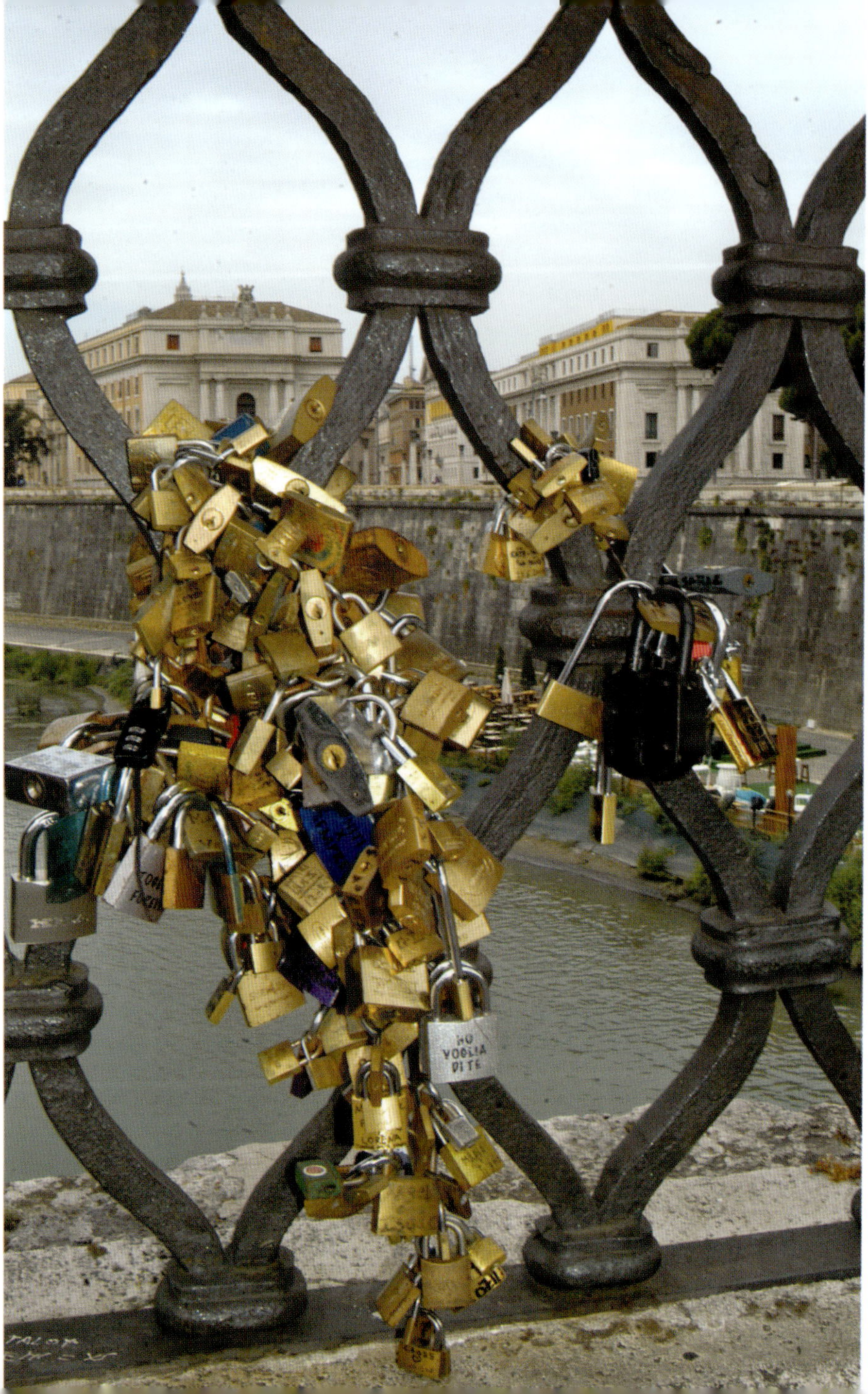
HO
VOGLIA
DI TE

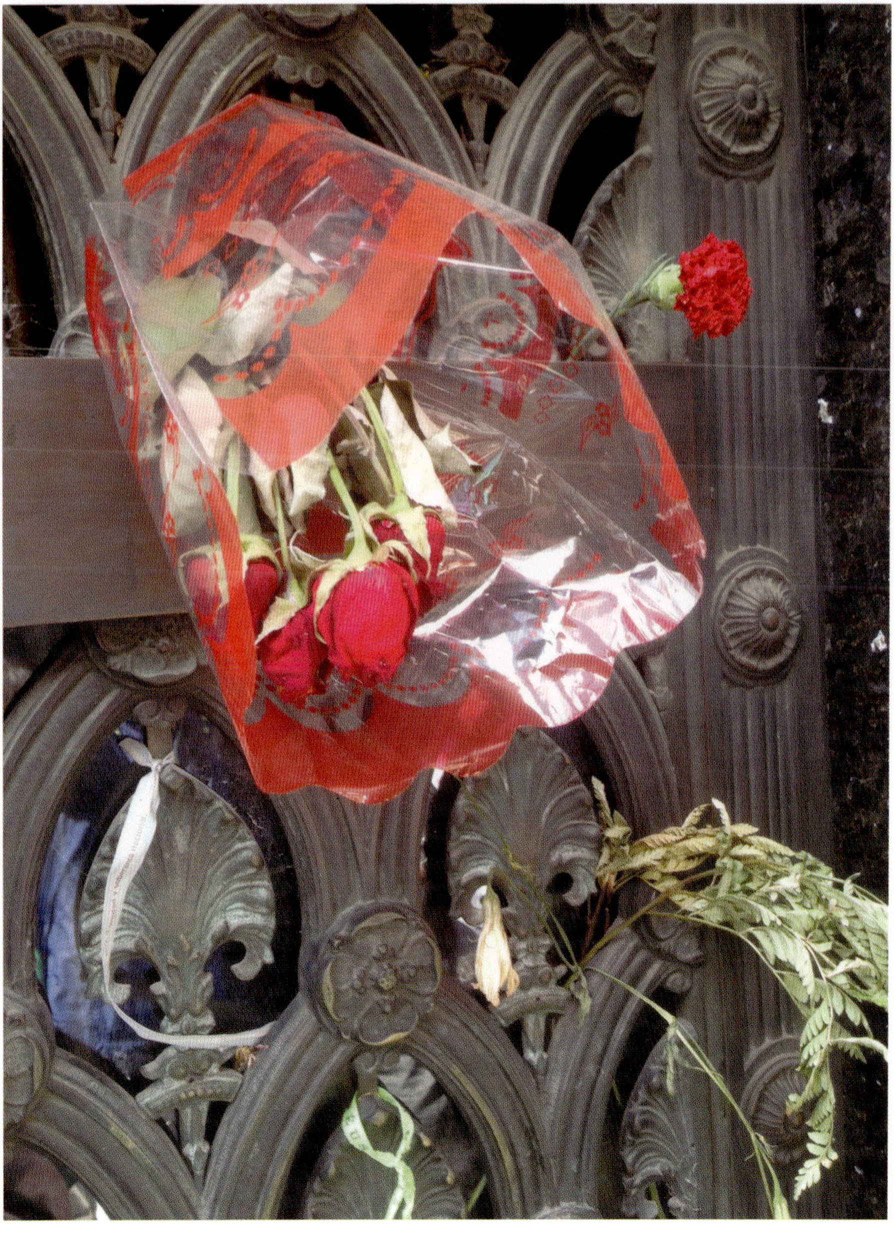

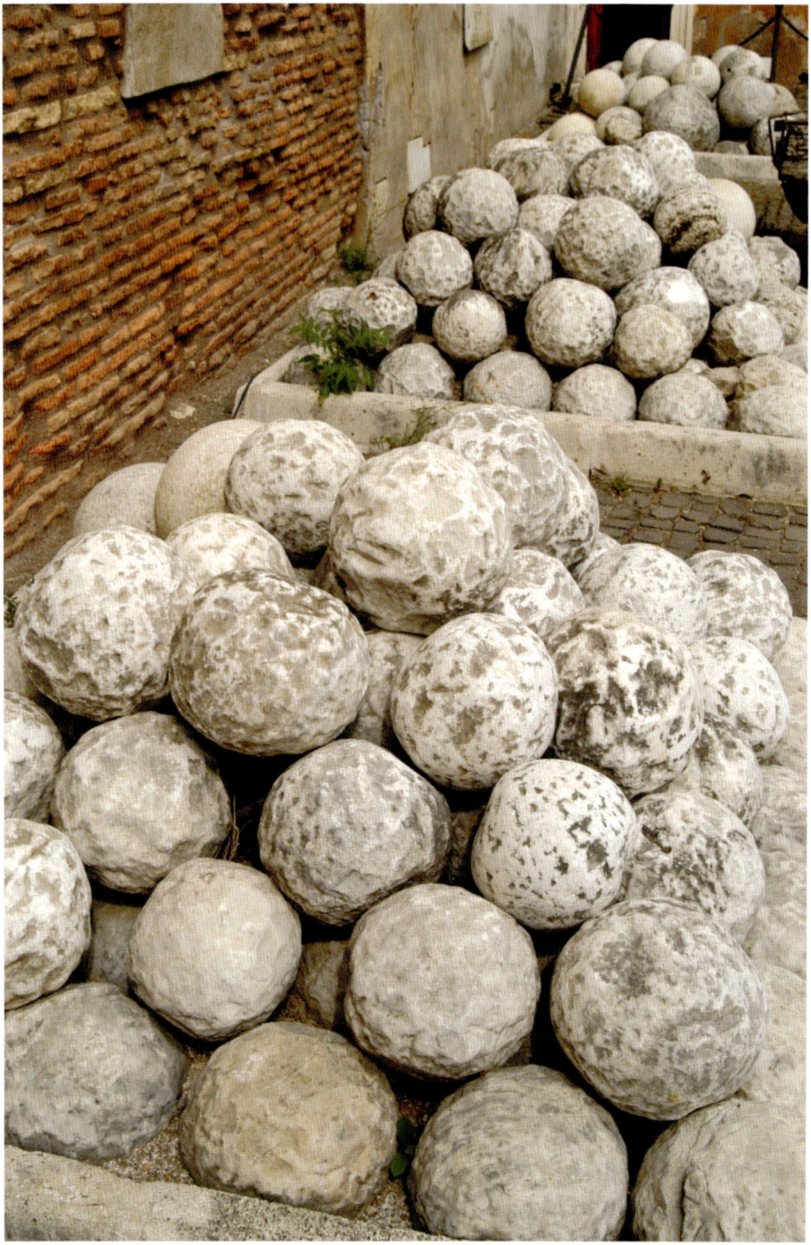

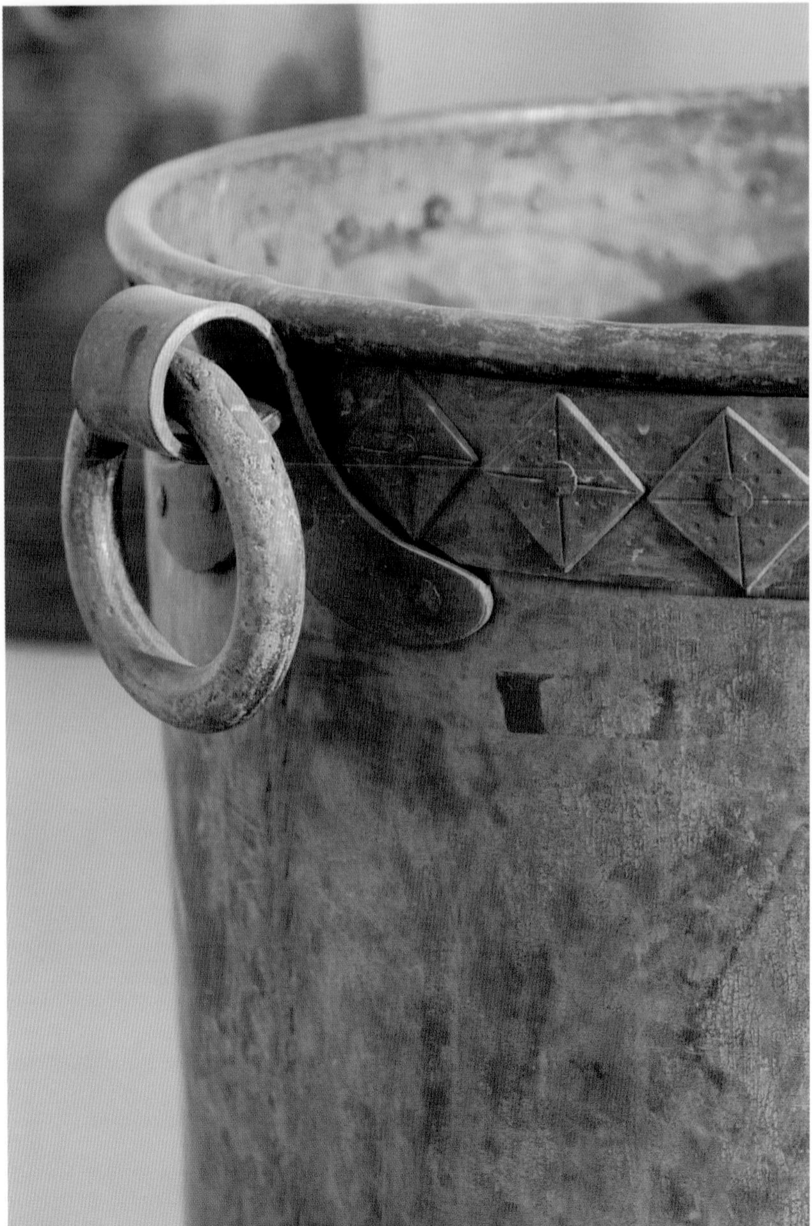

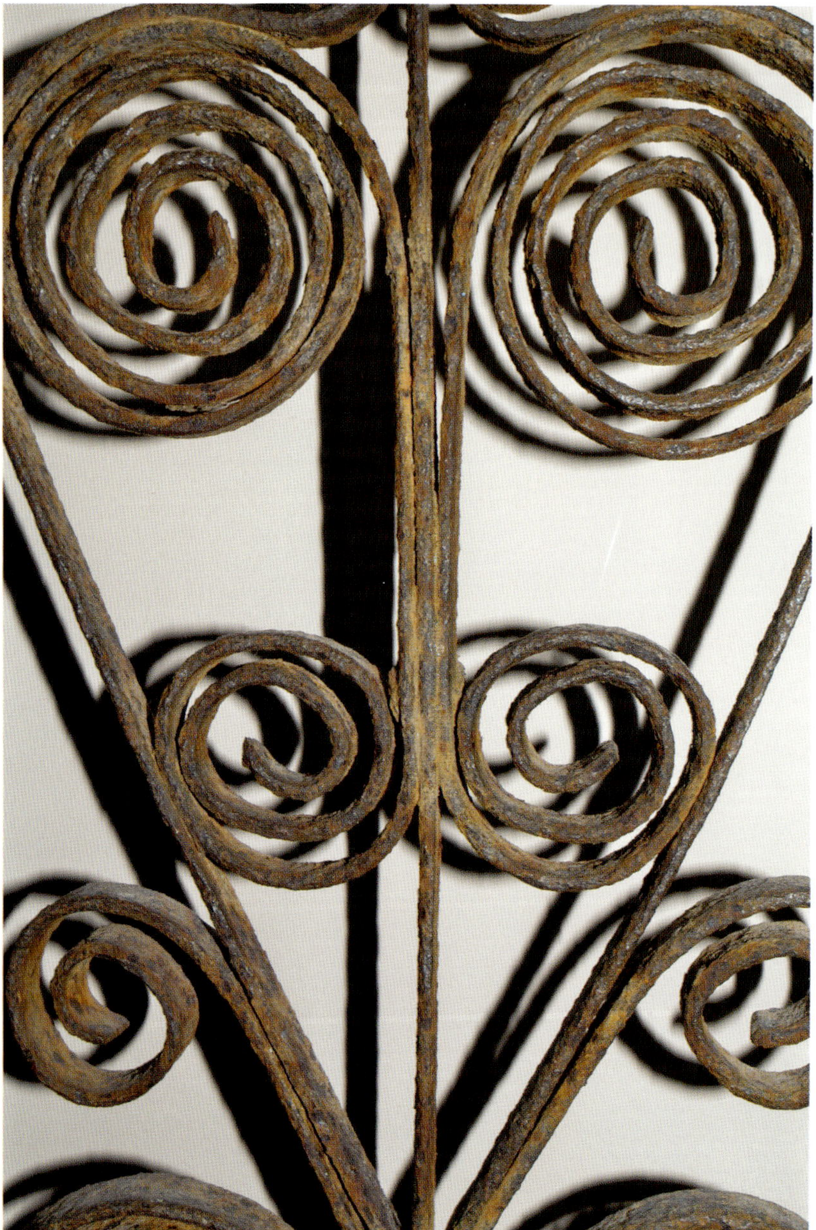

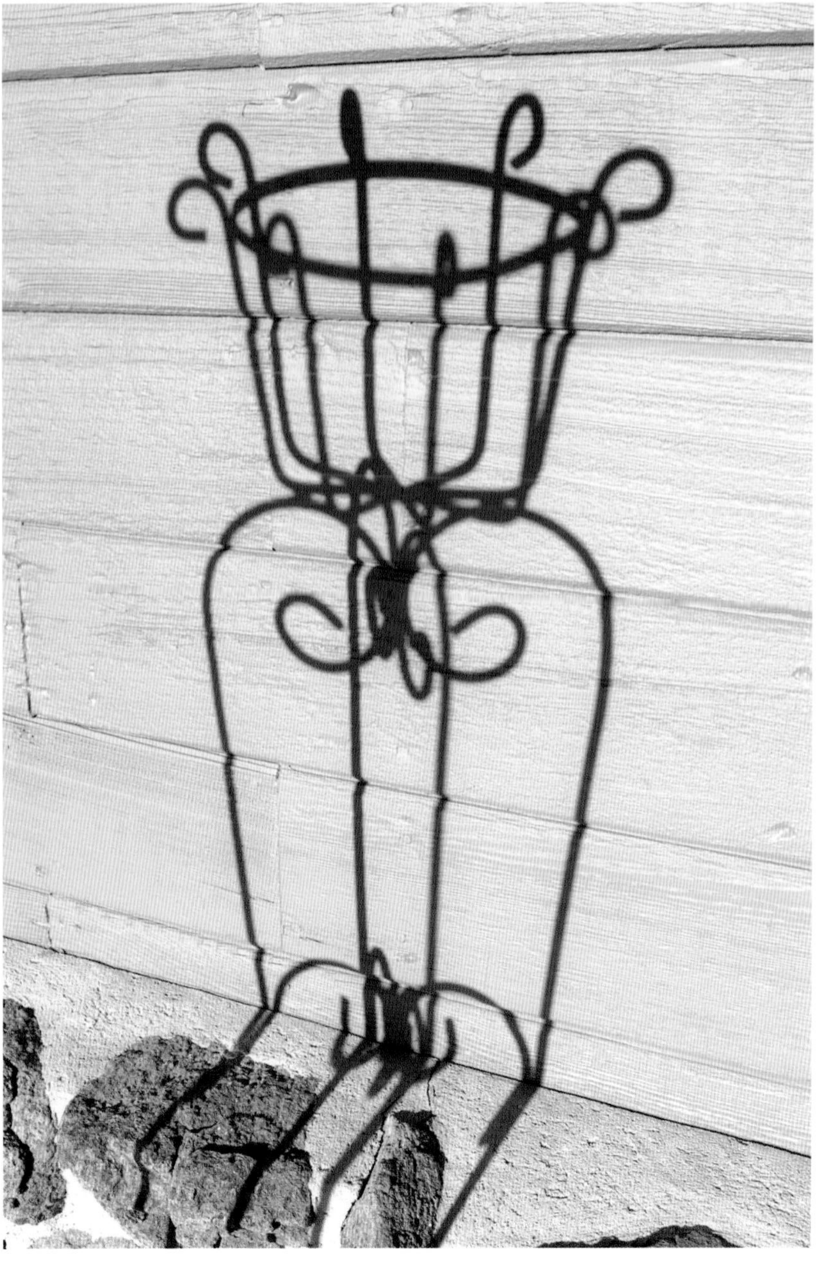

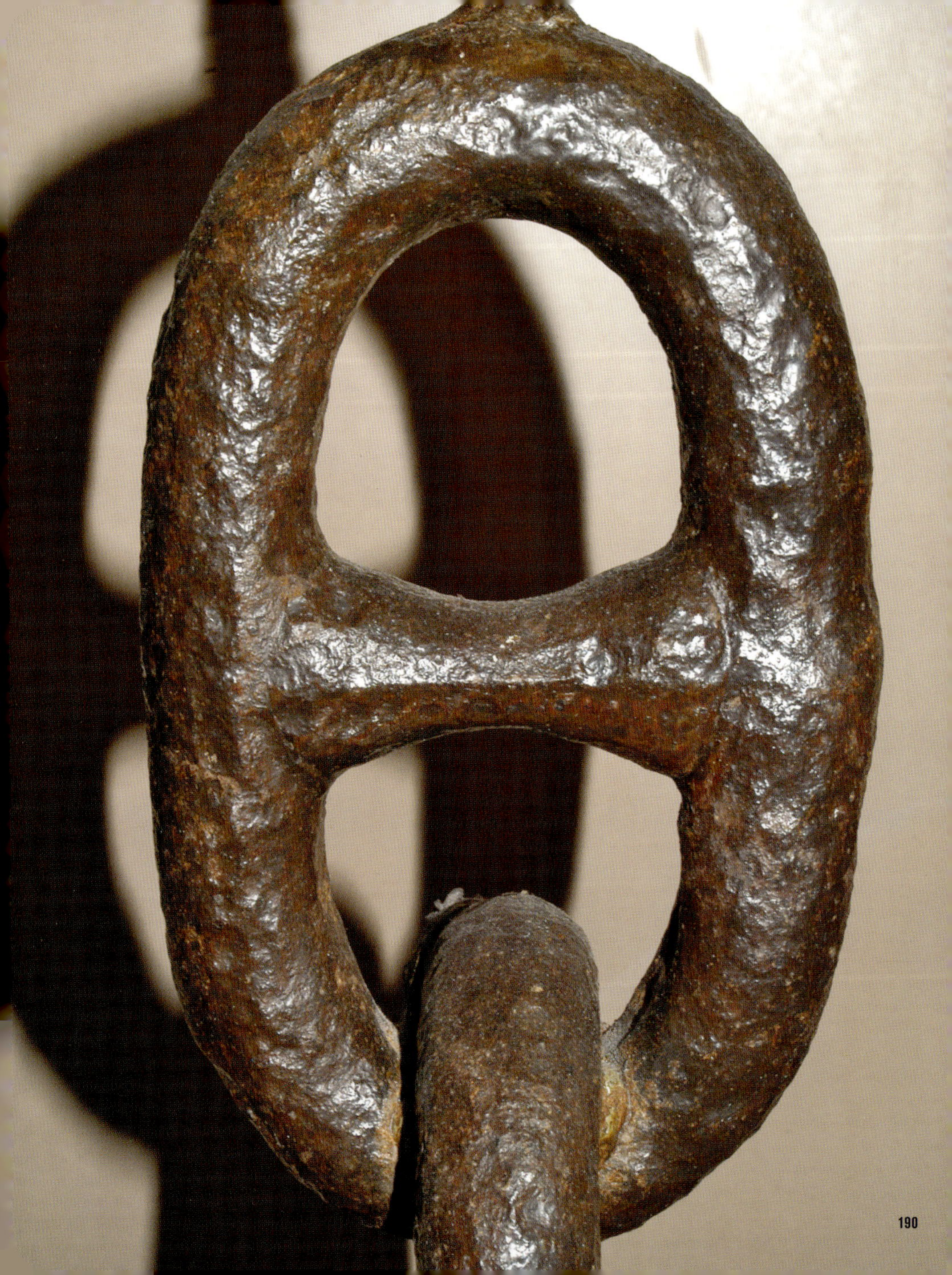

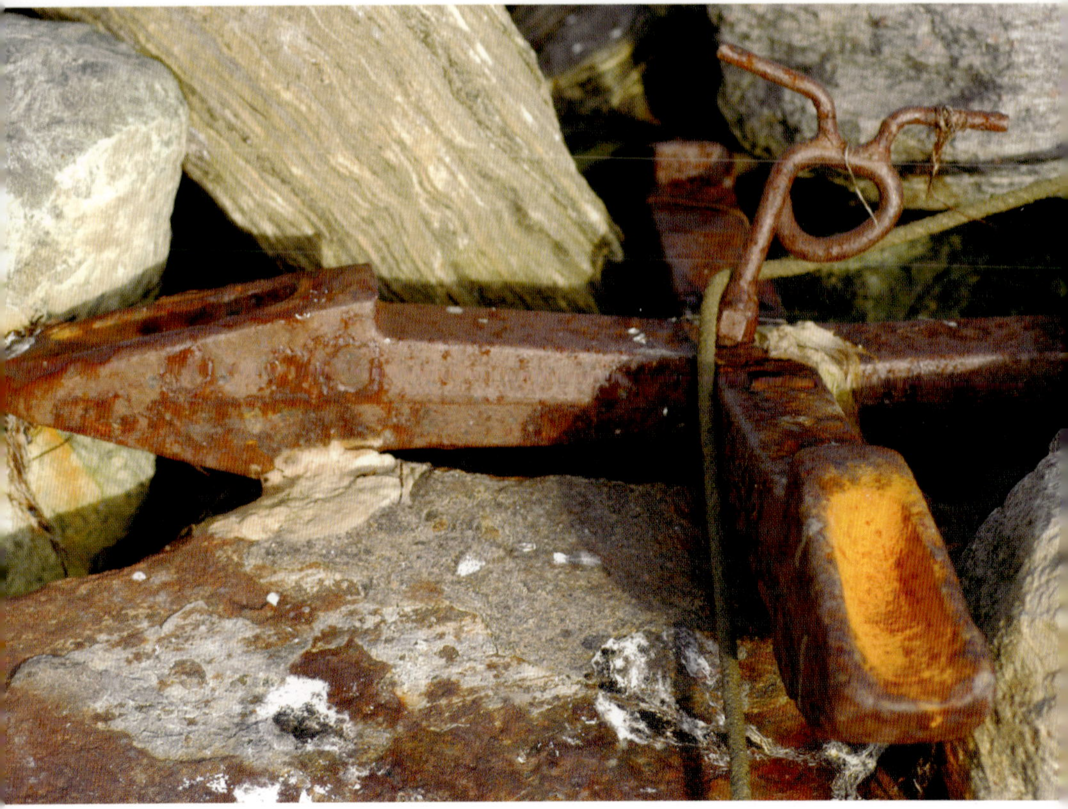

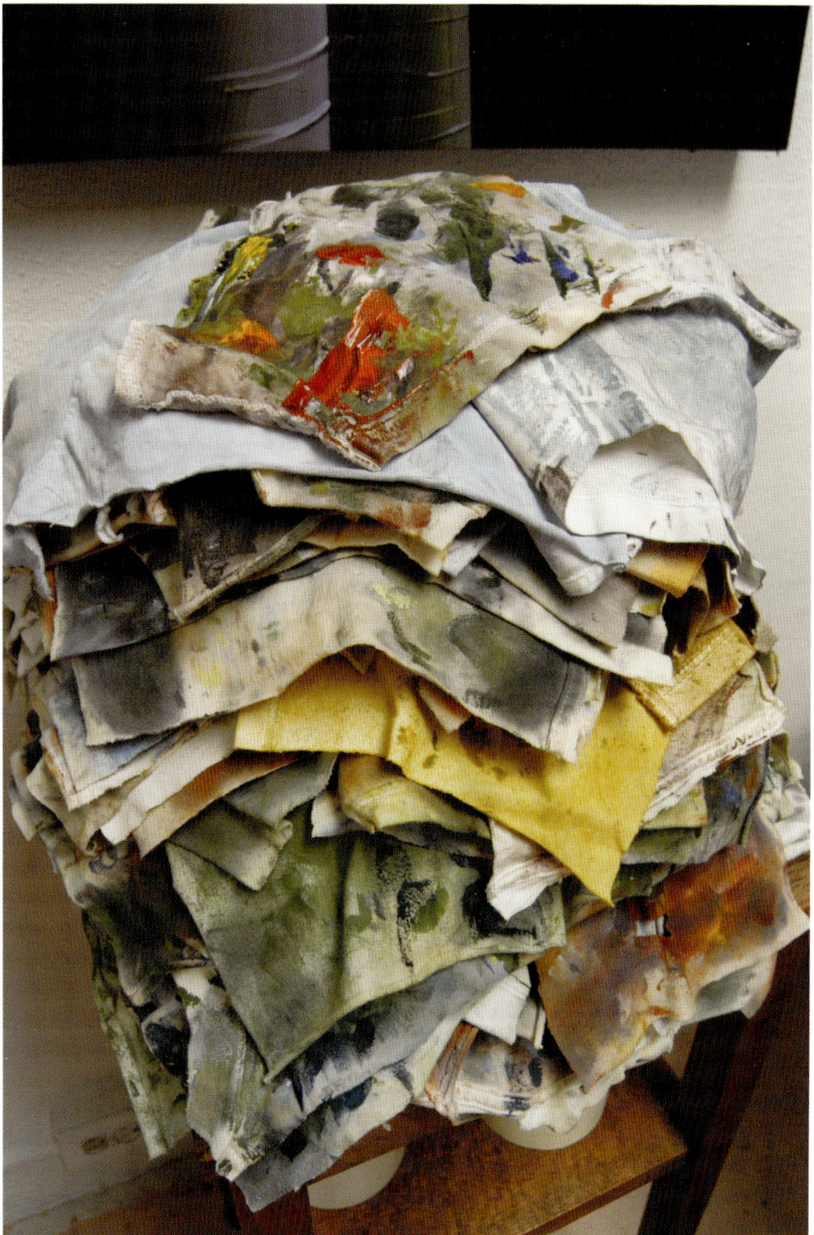

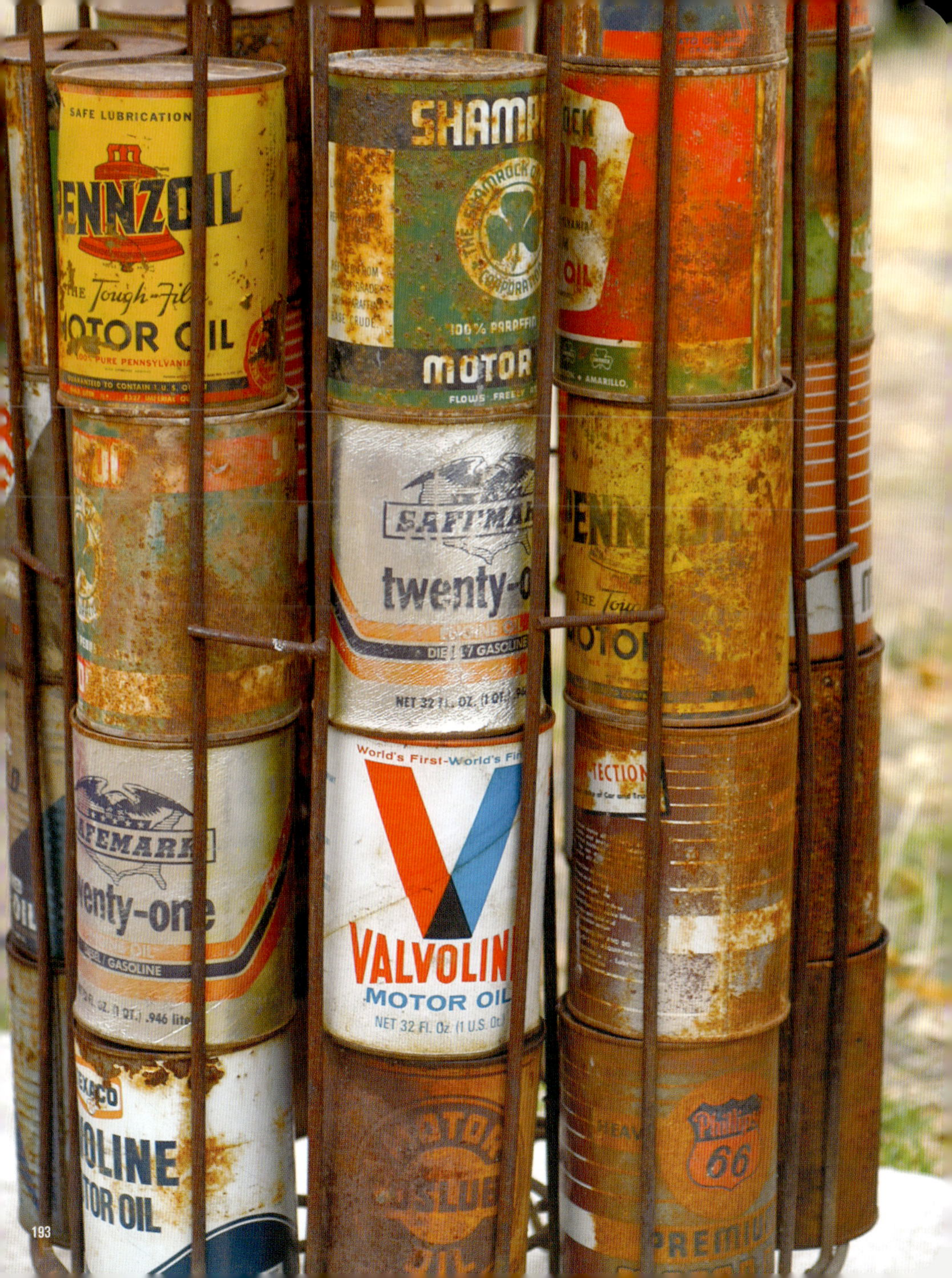
SAFE LUBRICATION
PENNZOIL
MOTOR OIL
100% PARAFFIN
MOTOR
FLOWS FREELY
MOTOR OIL
NET 32 Fl. Oz (1 U.S. Qt.)
66

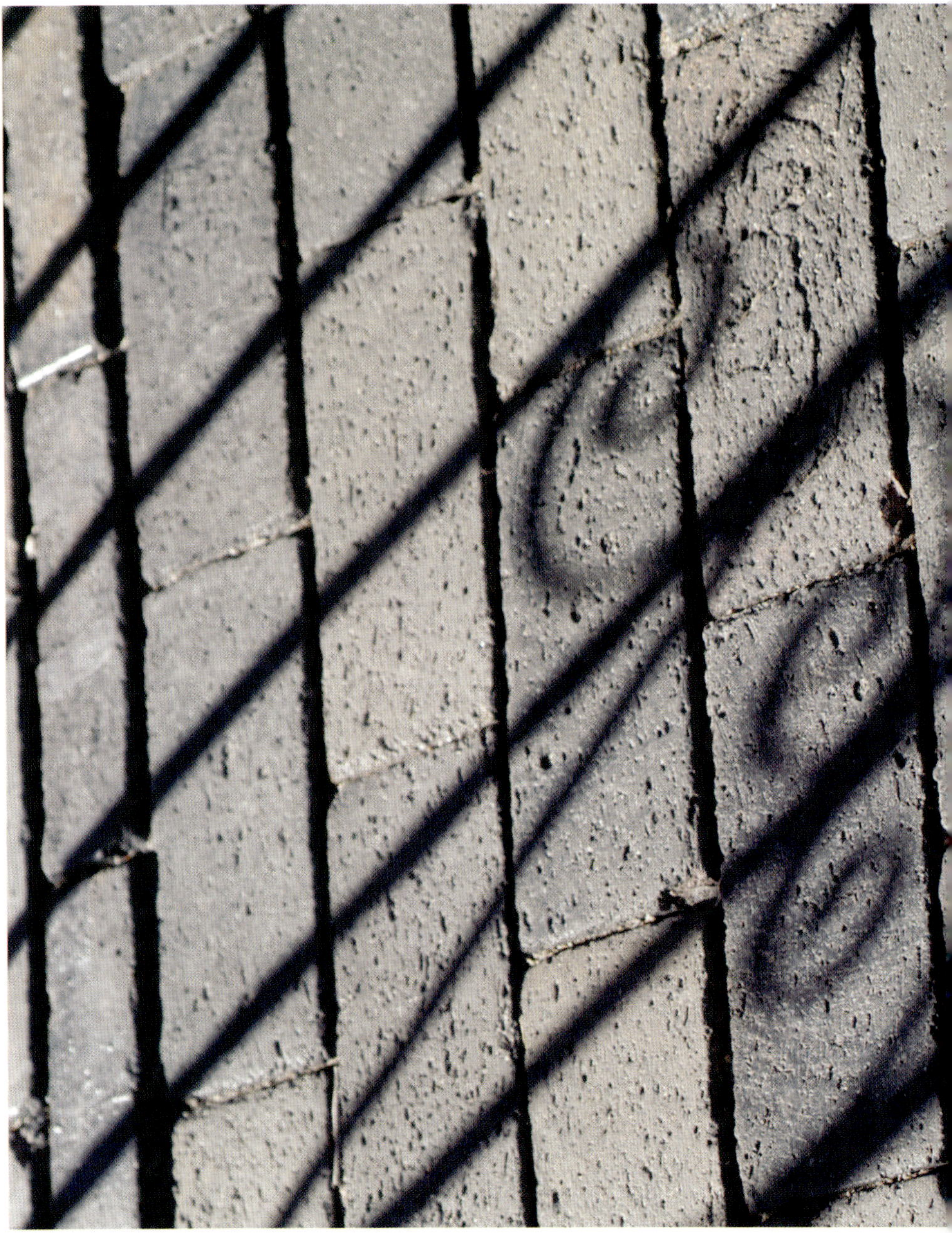

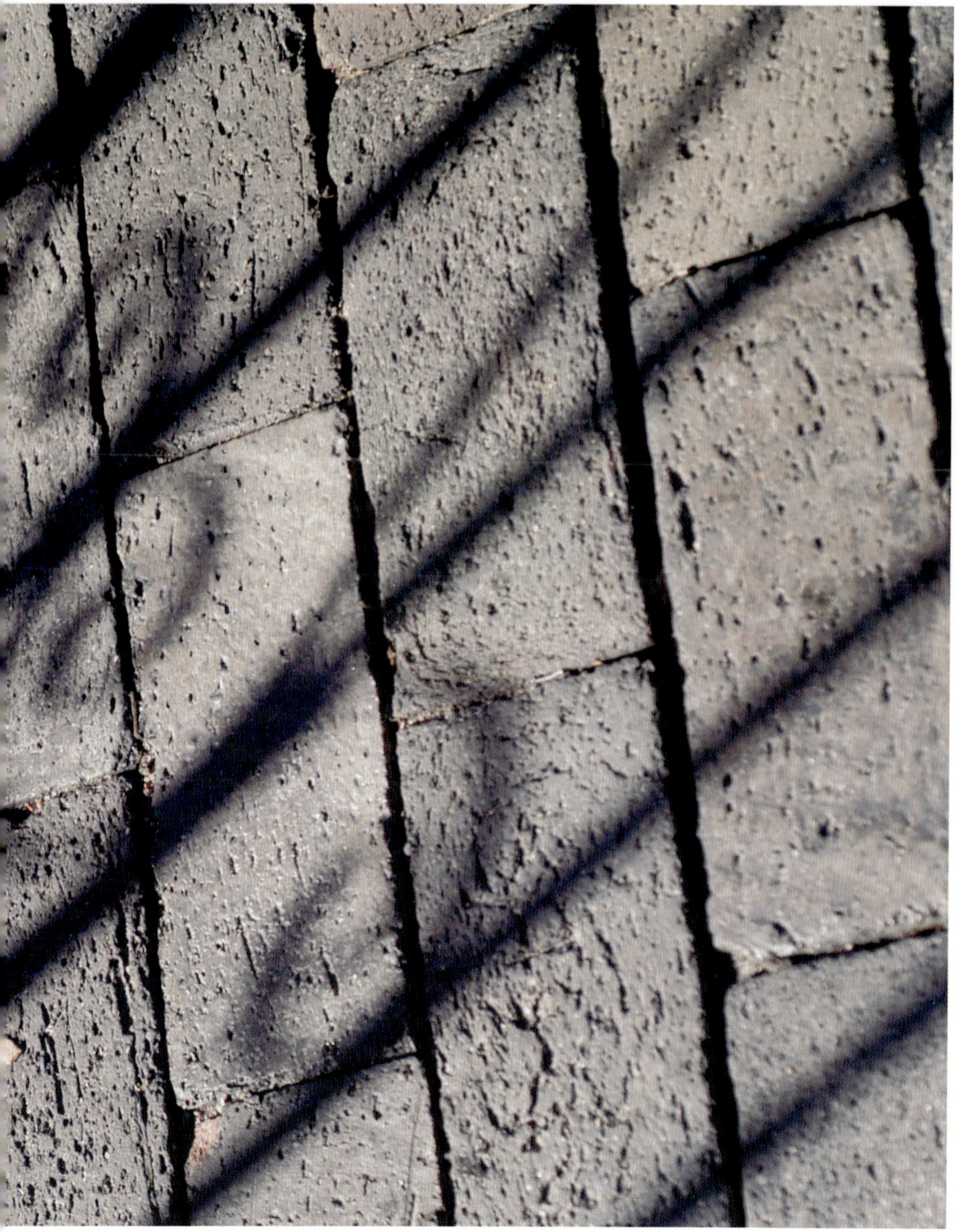

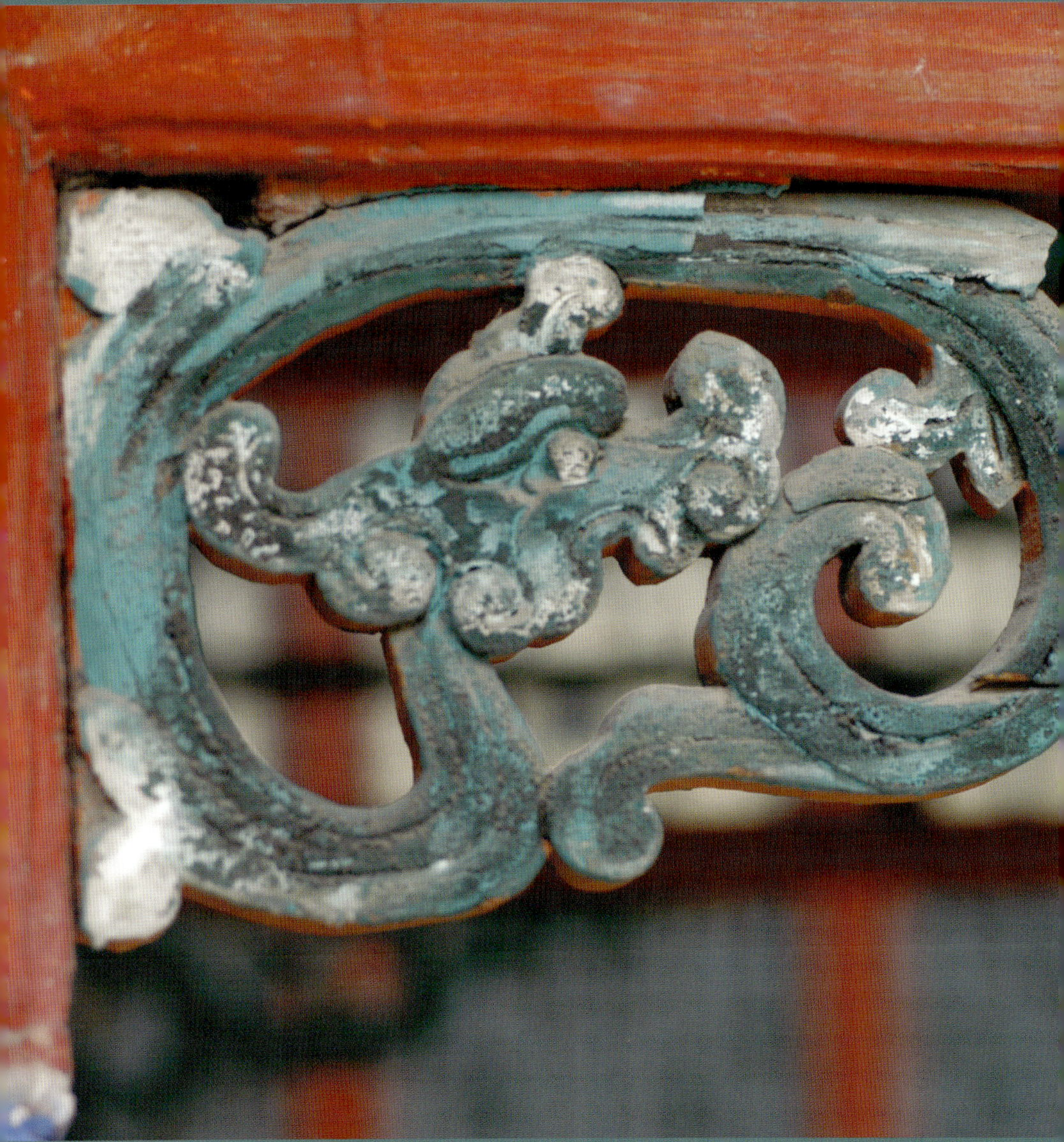

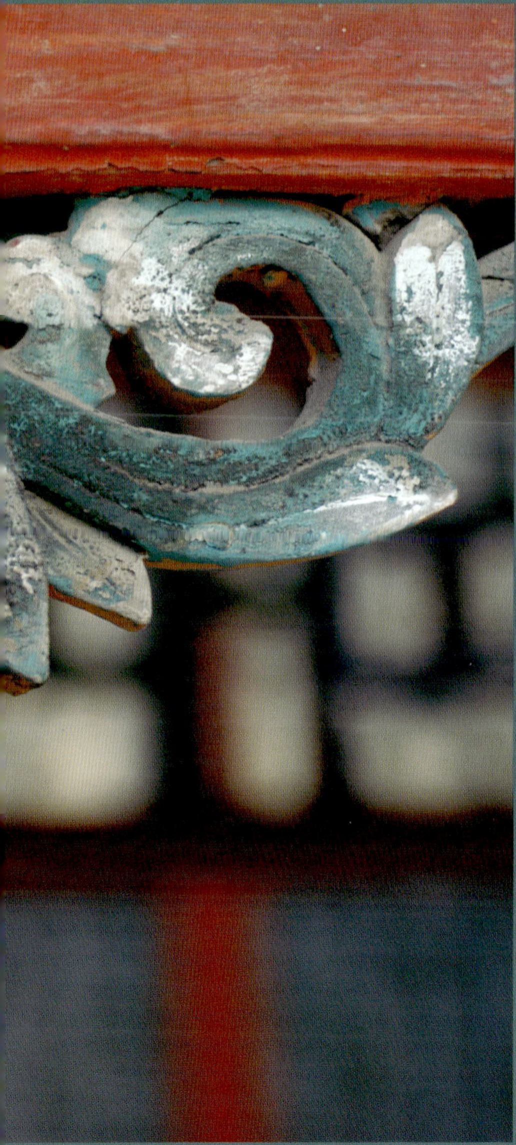

ENJOYING

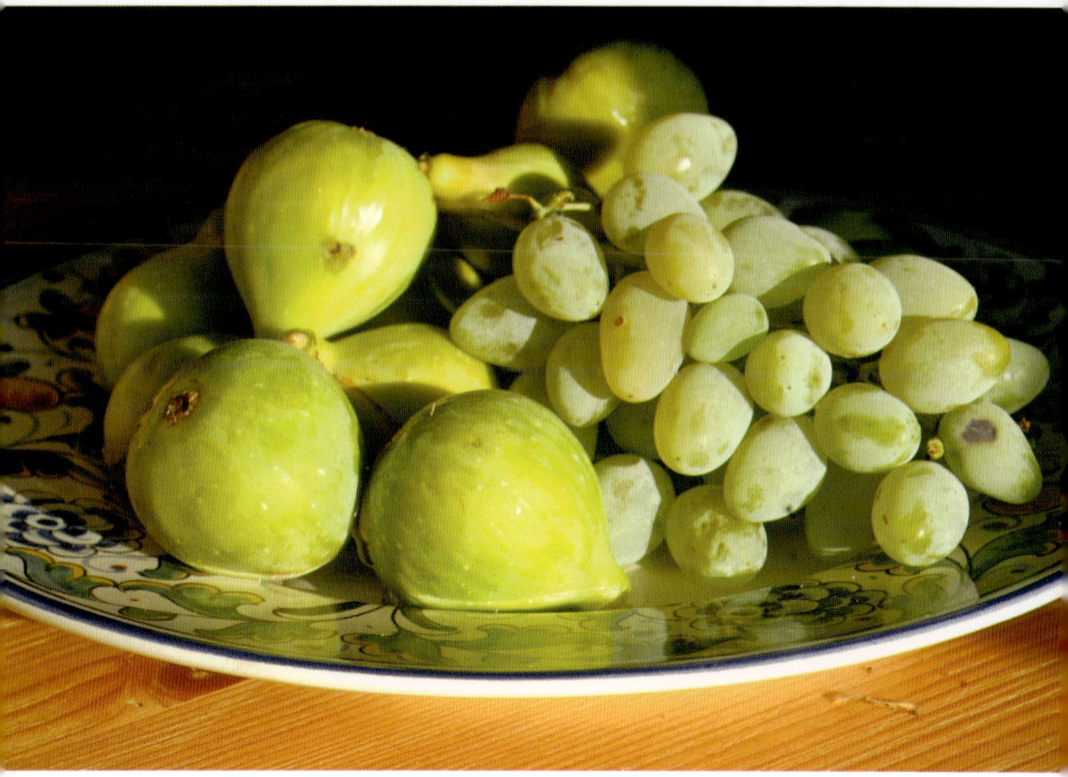

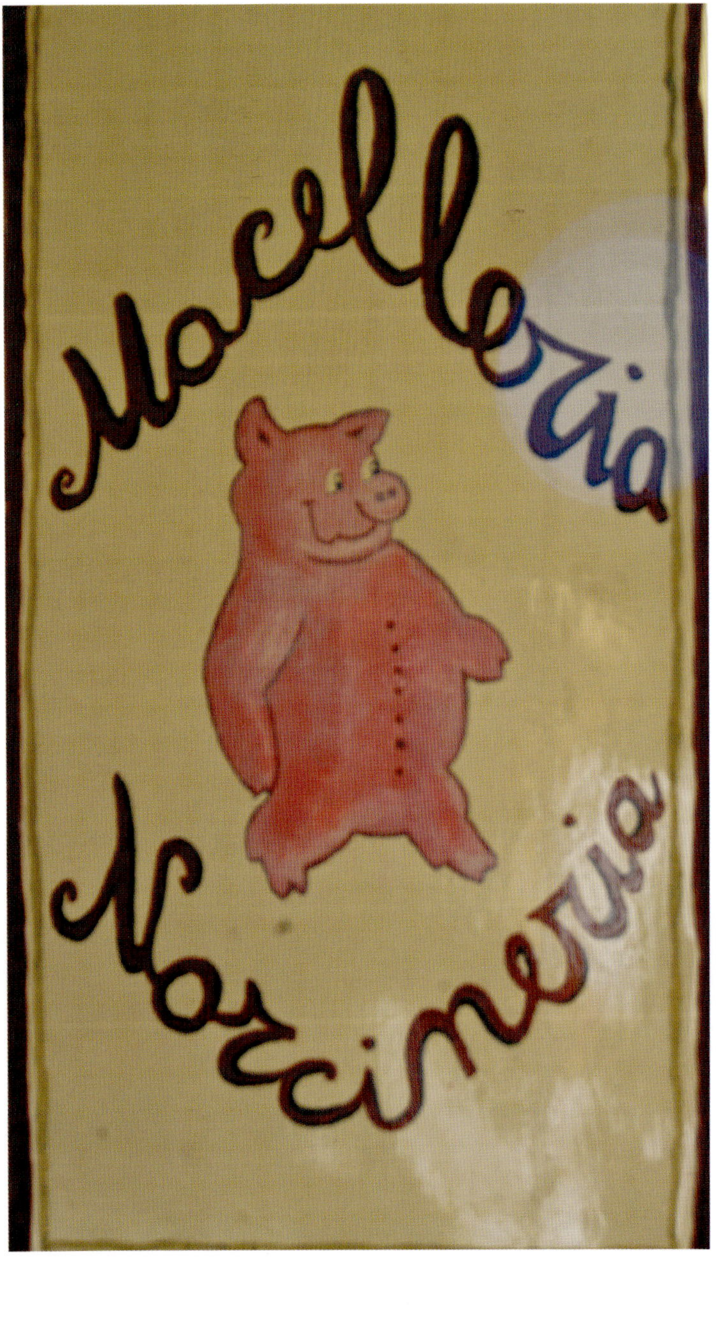
Macelleria
Norcineria

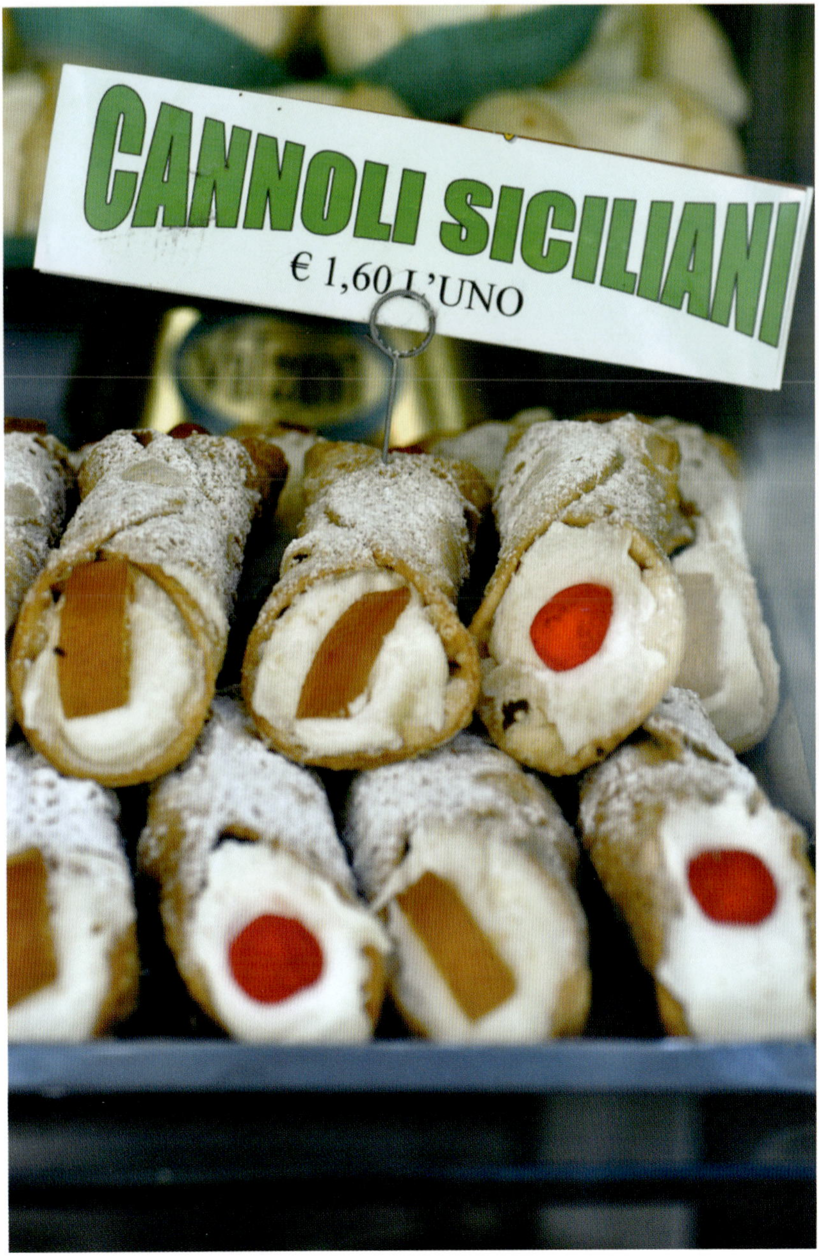
CANNOLI SICILIANI
€ 1,60 L'UNO

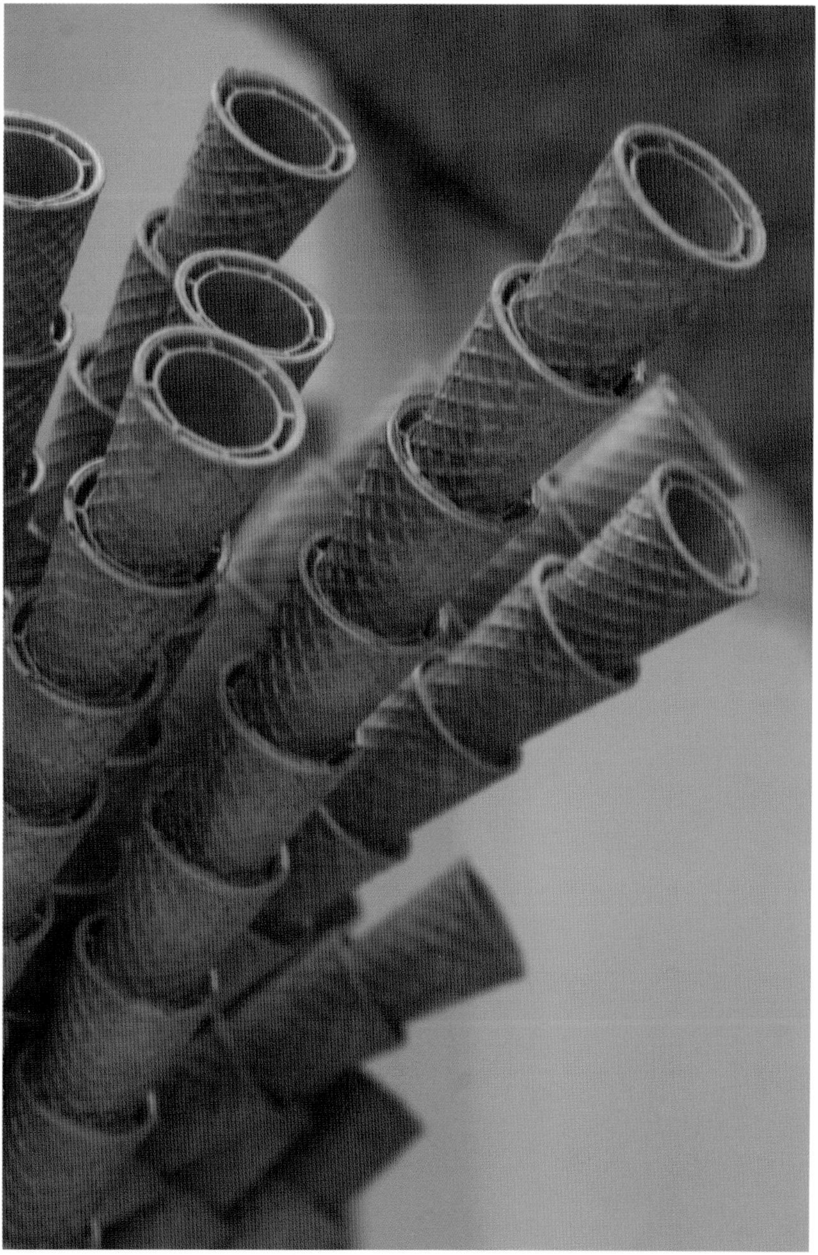

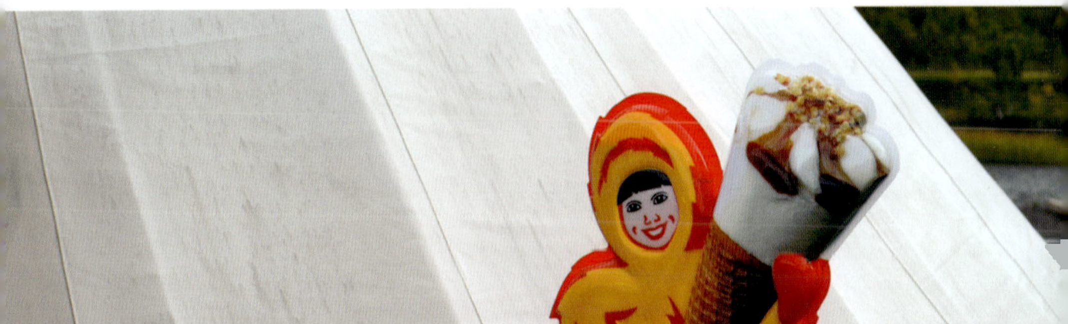
REINSDYRSUPPE
DIPLOM-IS

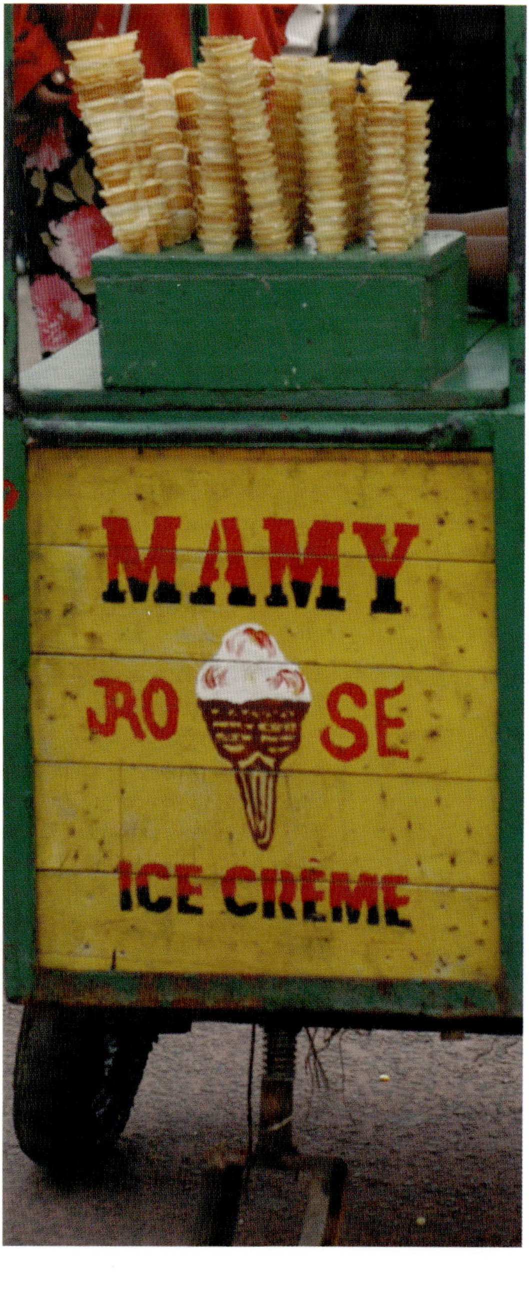
MAMY
ROSE
ICE CRÈME

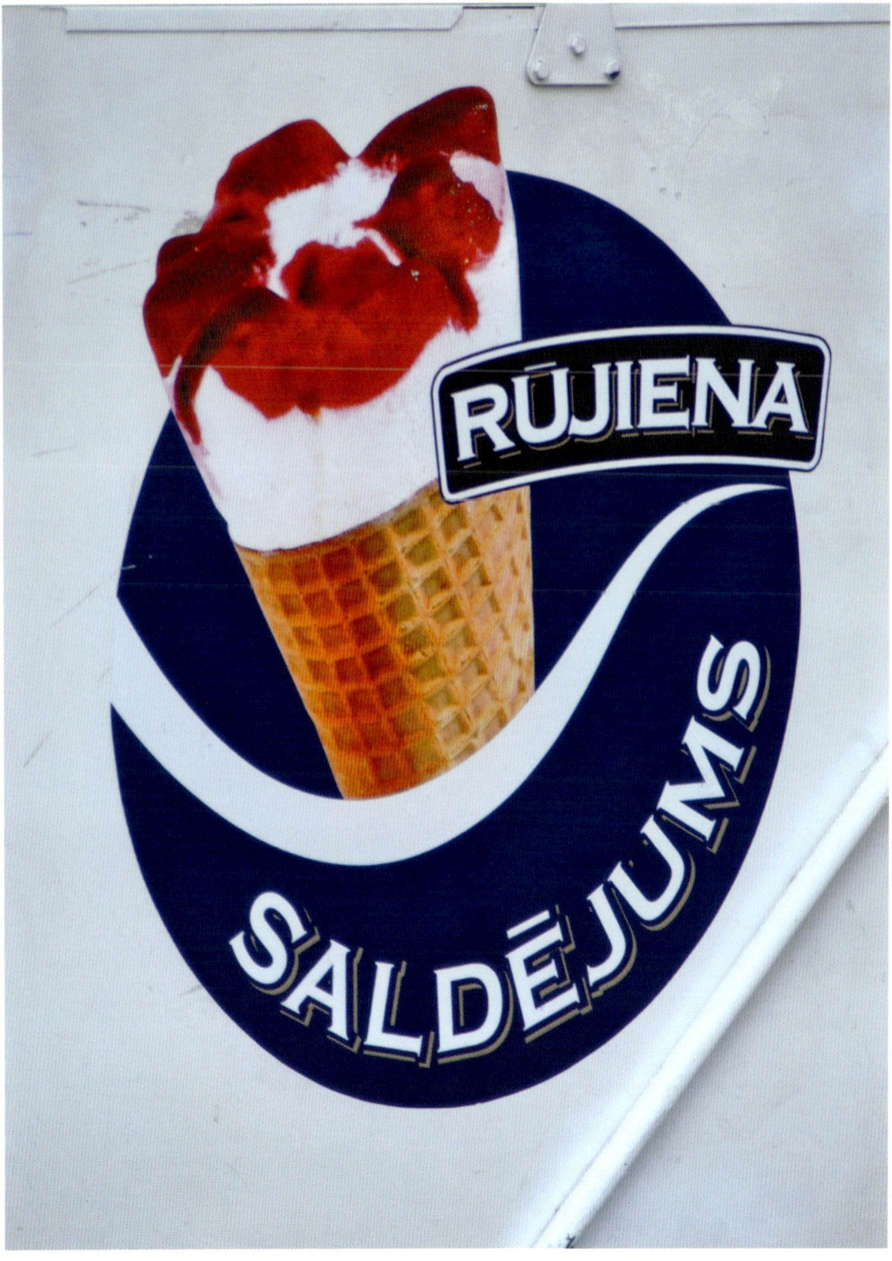
RŪJIENA
SALDĒJUMS

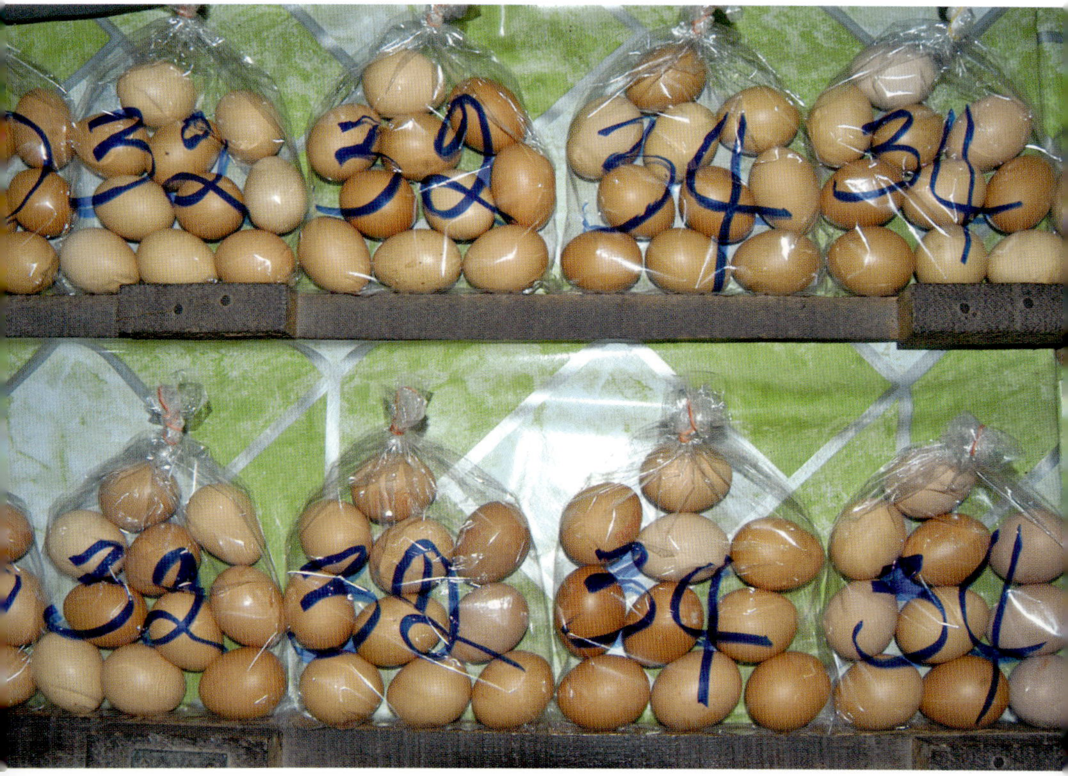
32
30
34
34
32
30
34
34

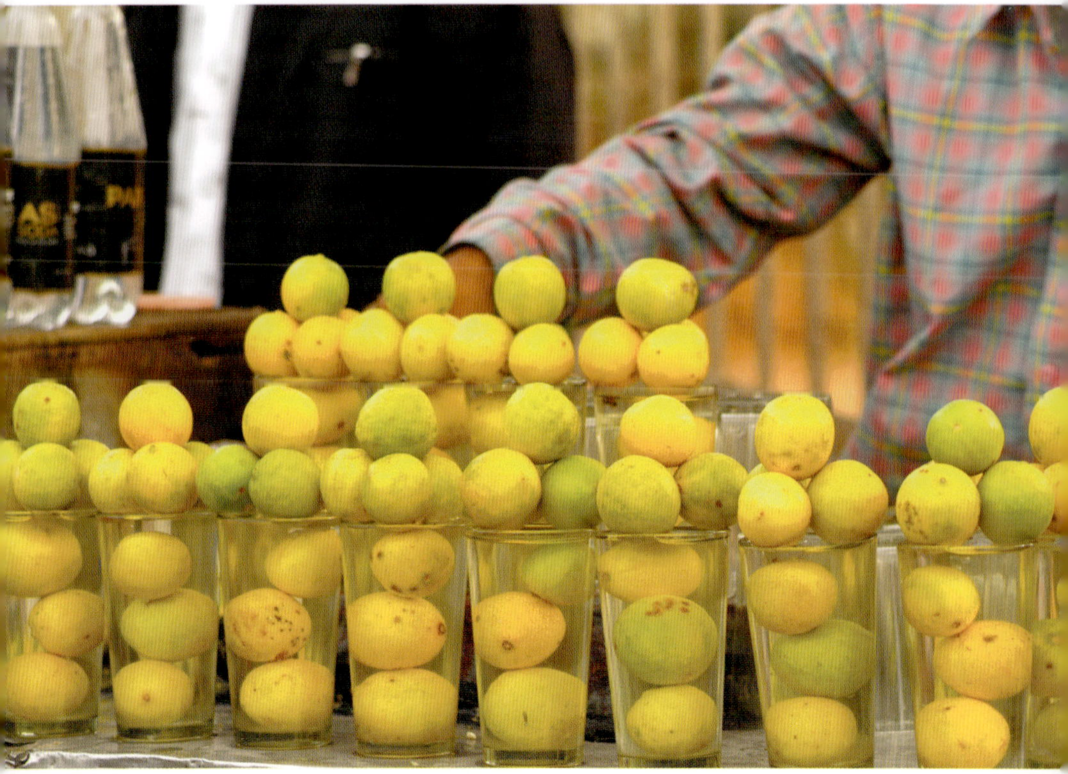

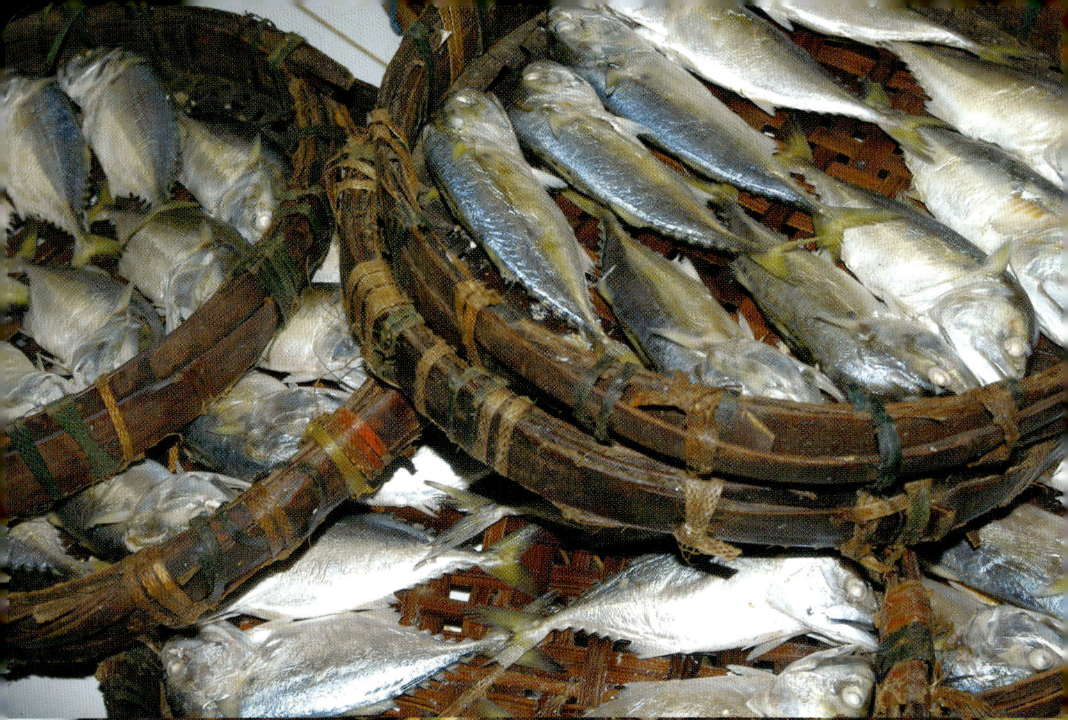

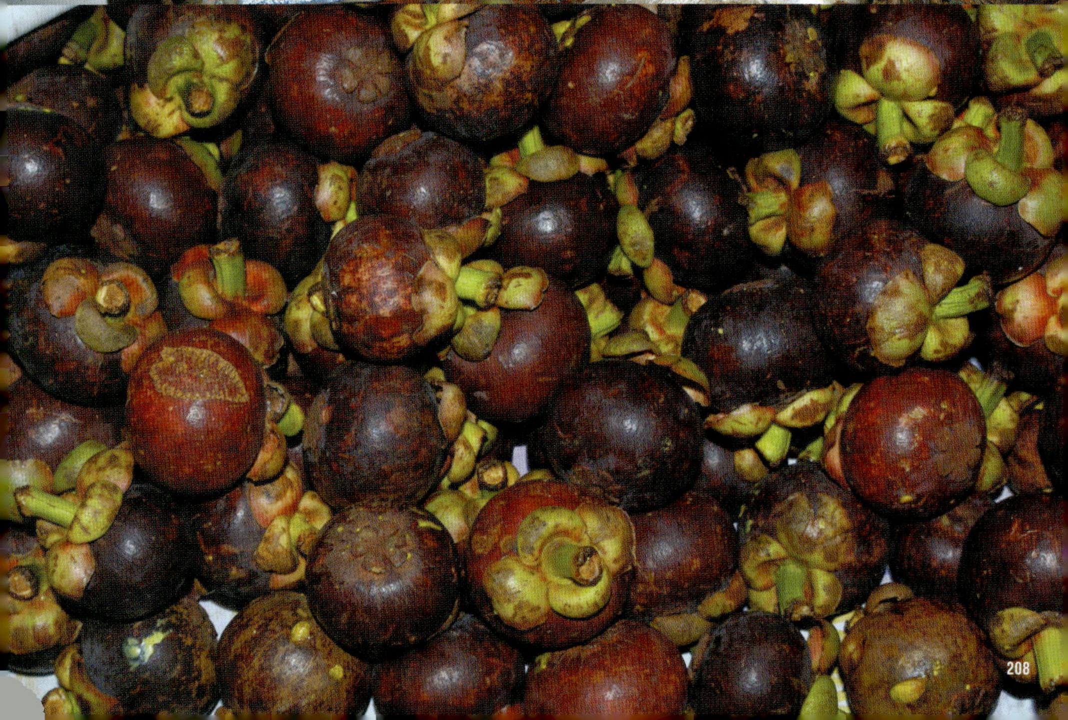

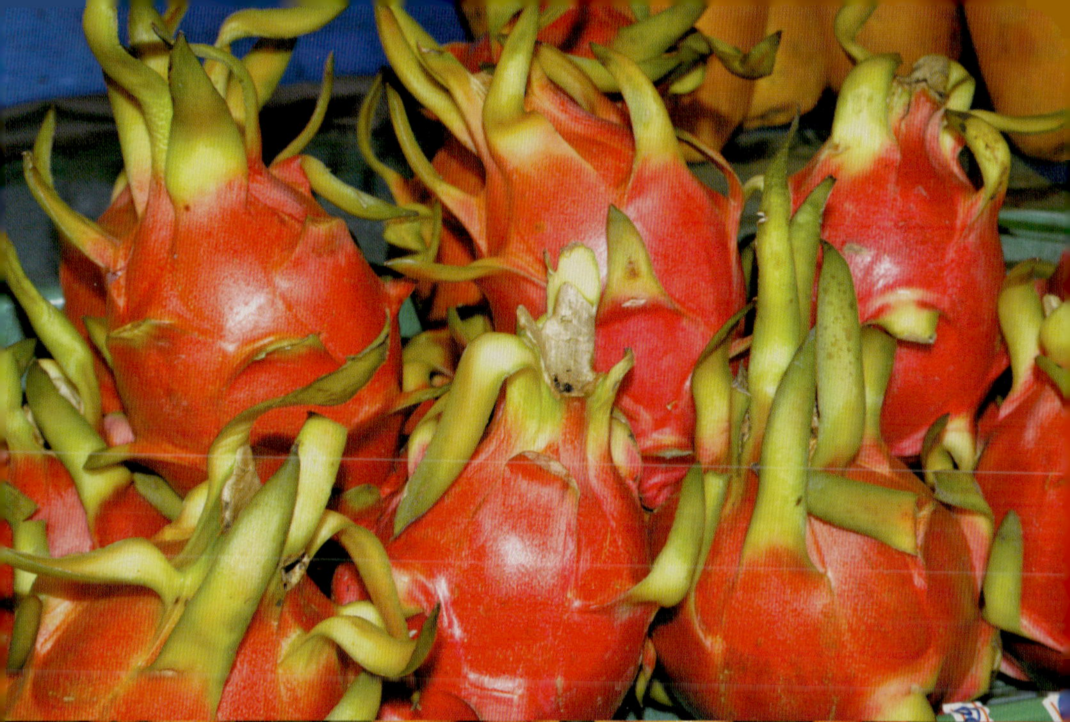

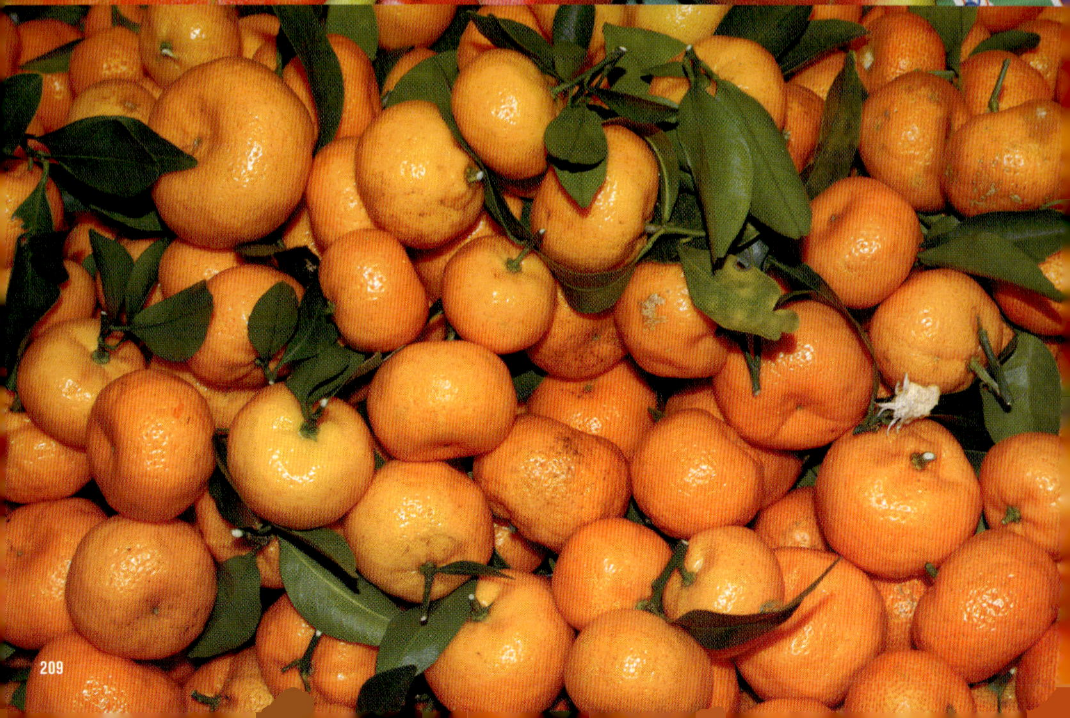

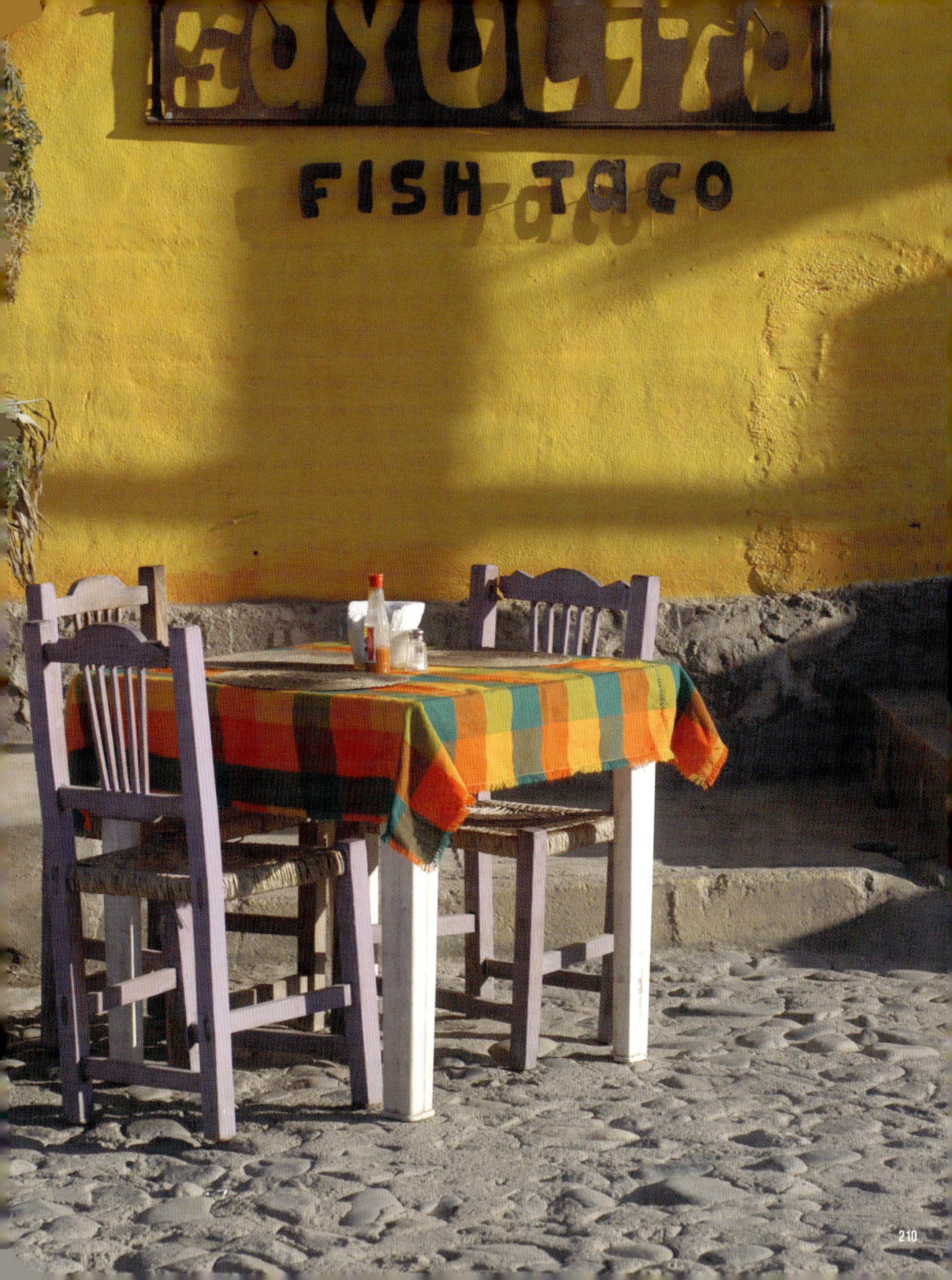
FISH TACO

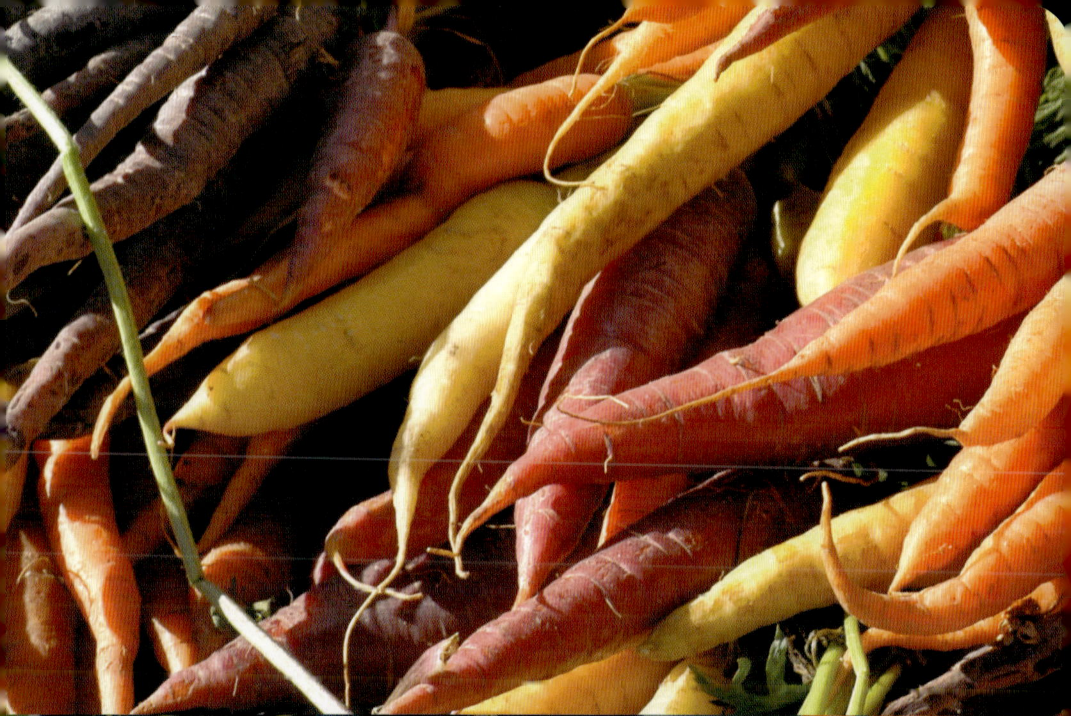

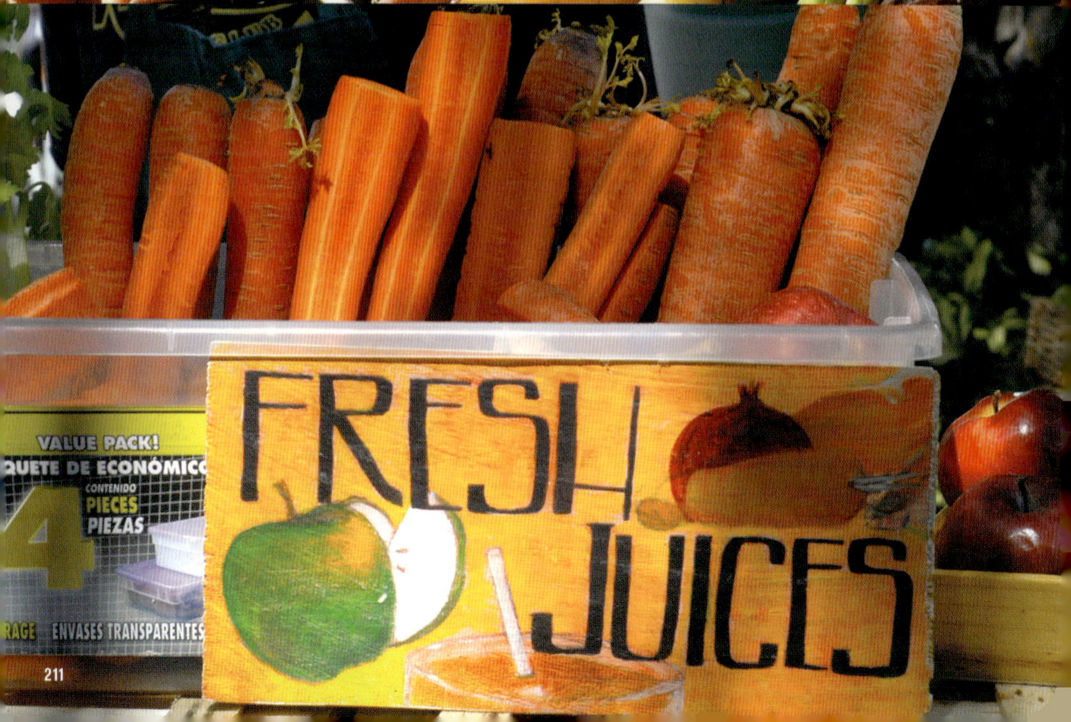
VALUE PACK!
CONTENIDO
4
PIECES
PIEZAS
ENVASES TRANSPARENTES
FRESH JUICES

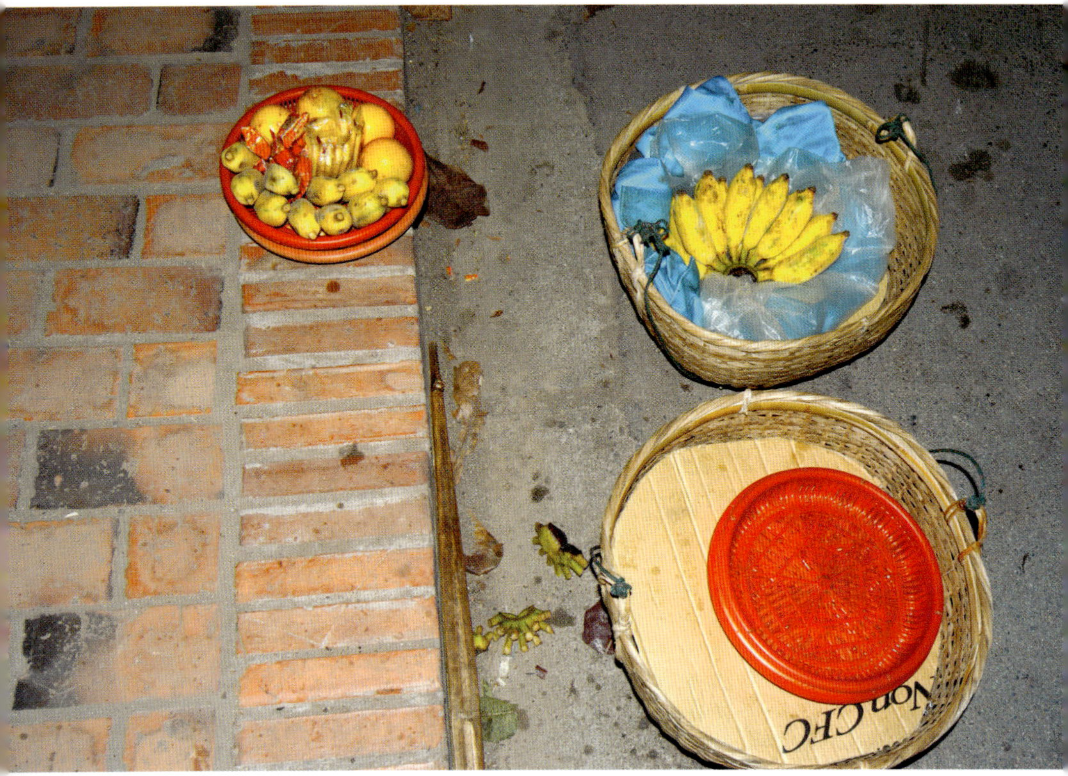
Non CFC

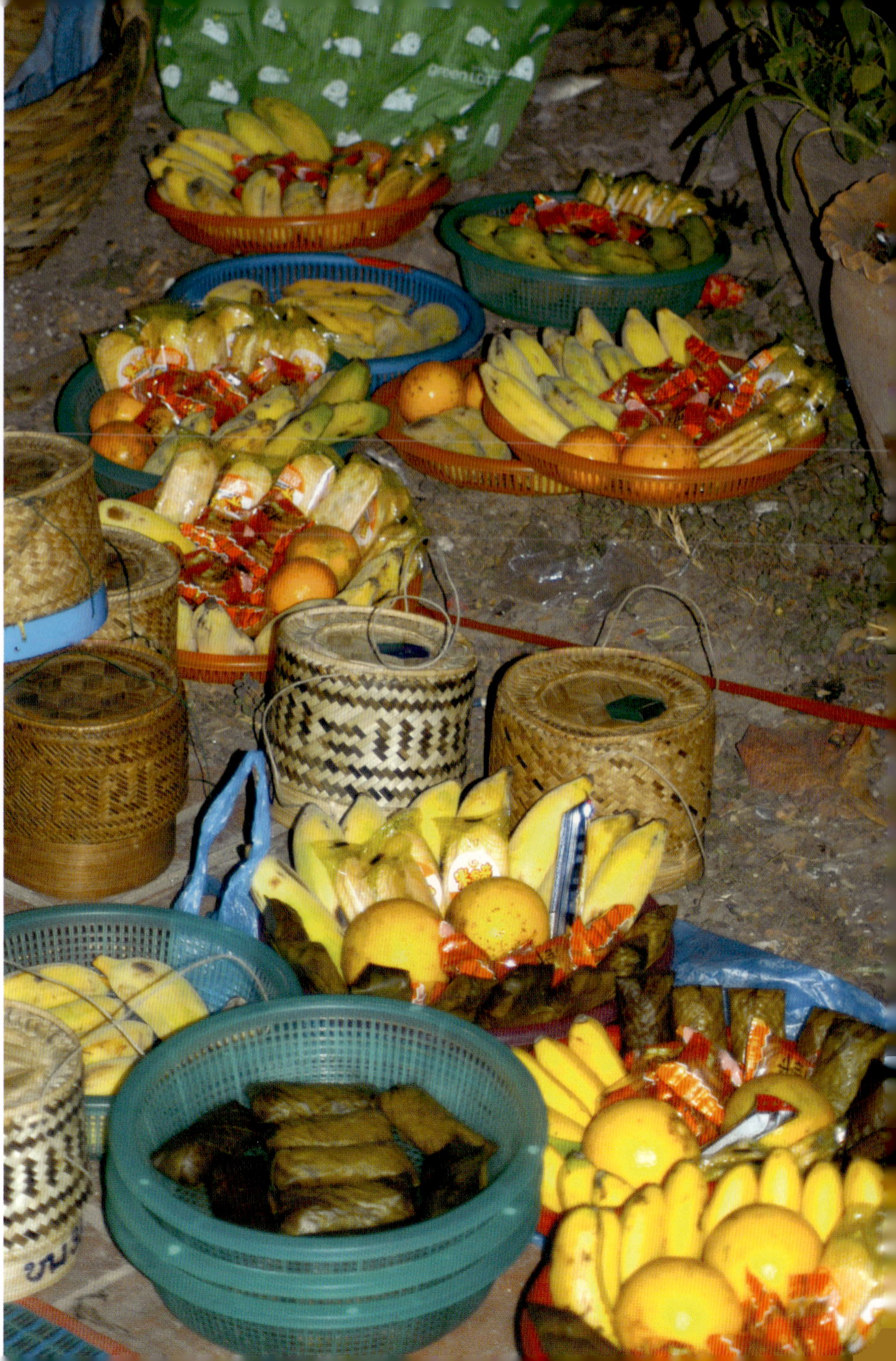

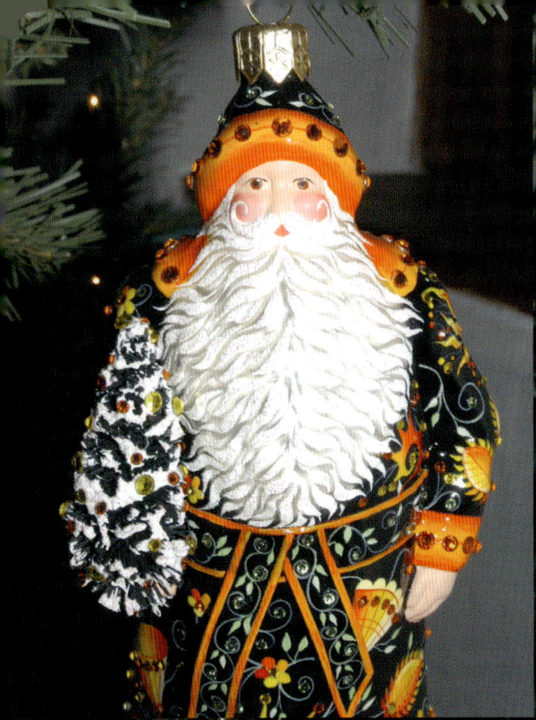
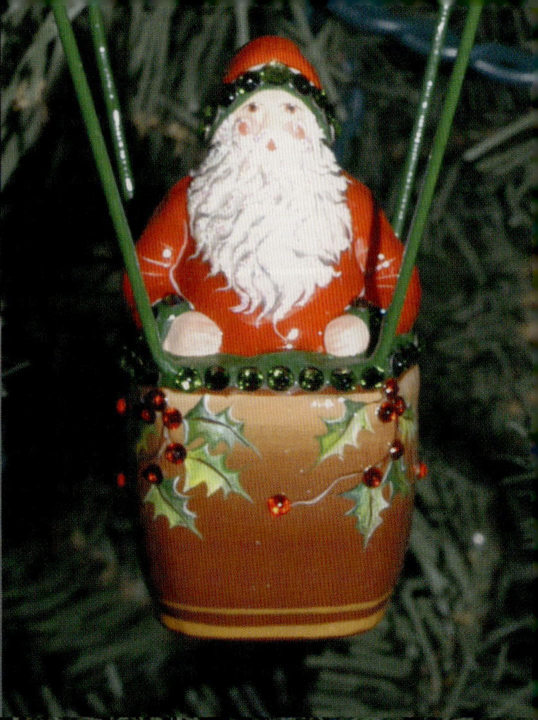
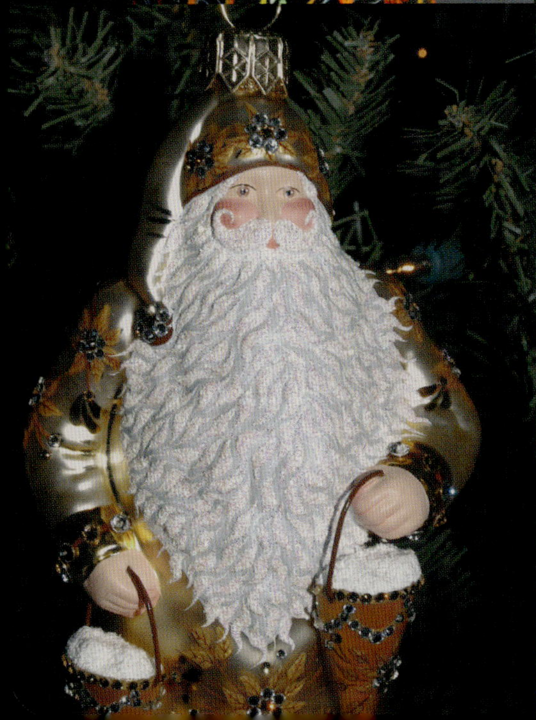
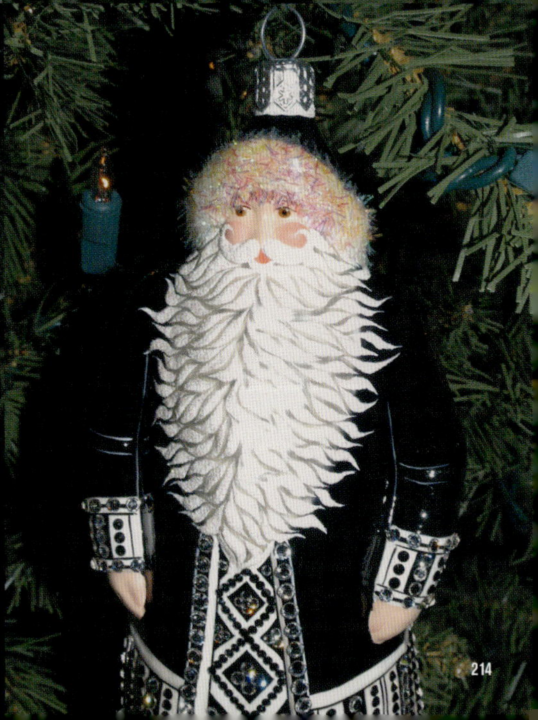

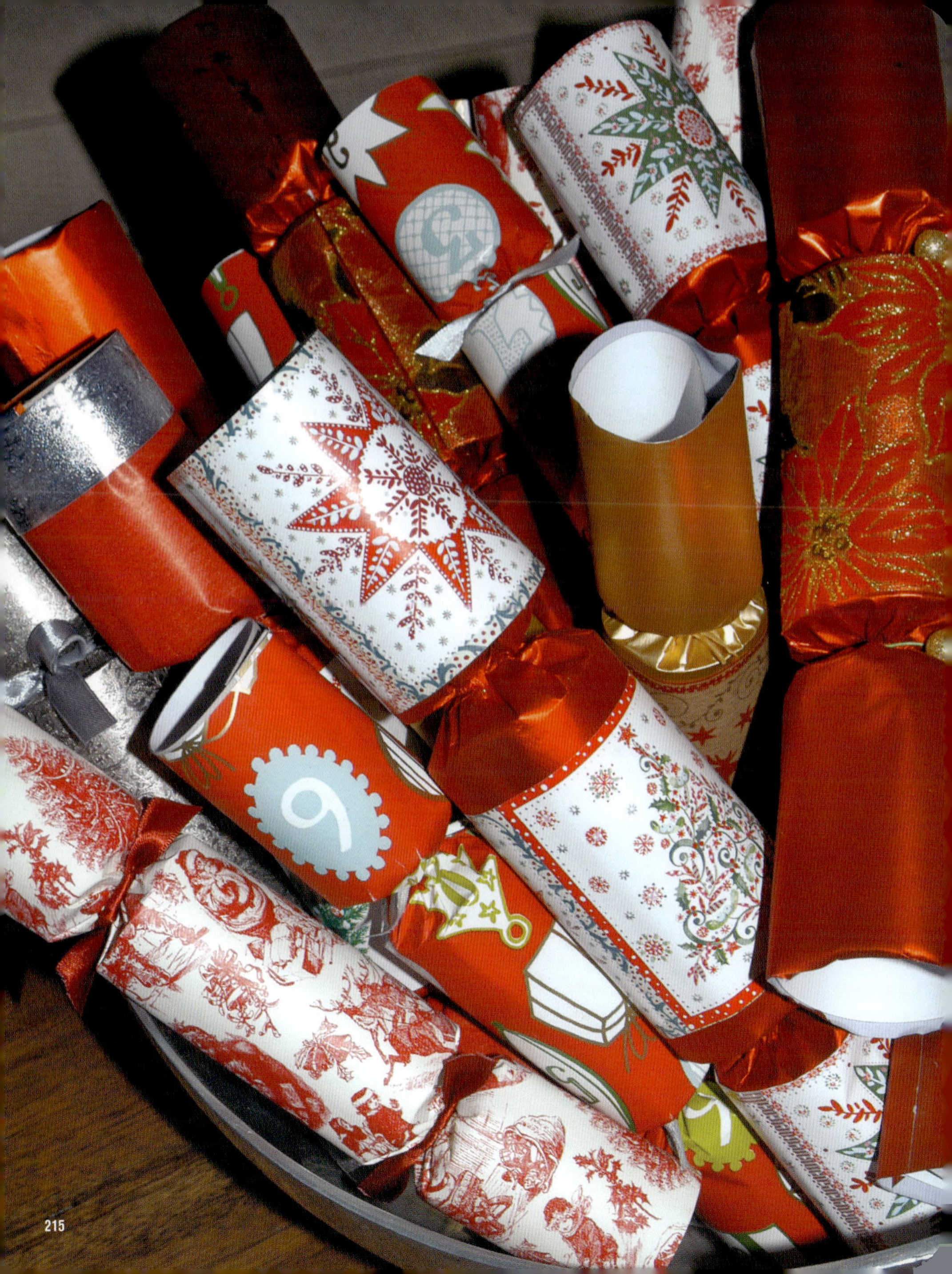

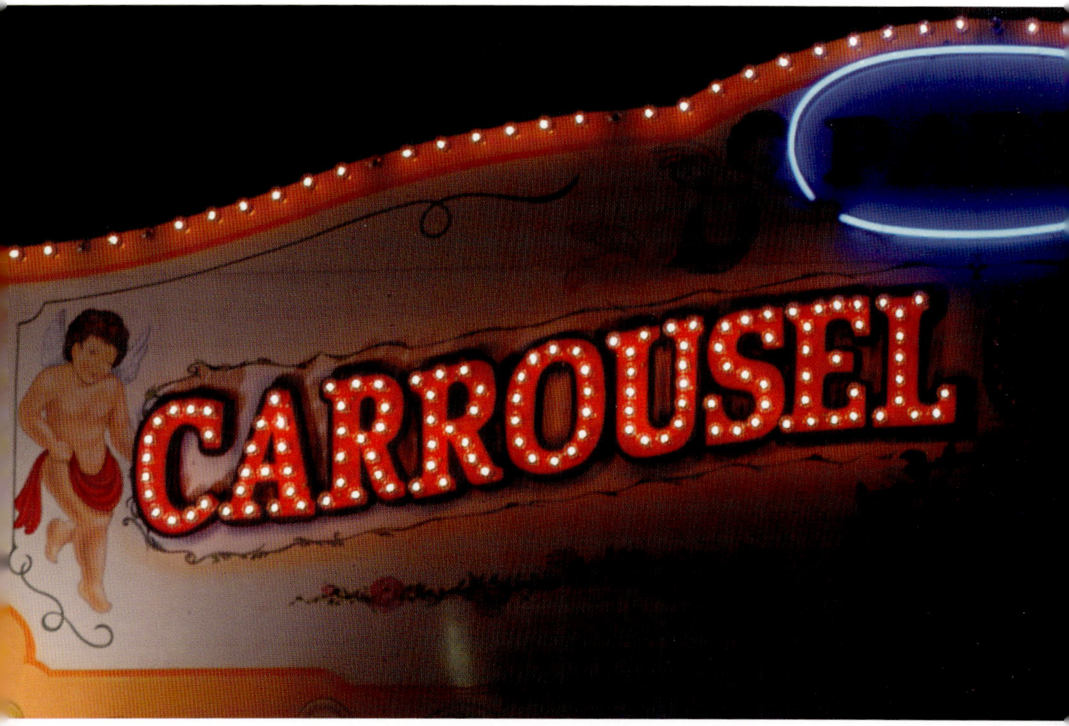
CARROUSEL

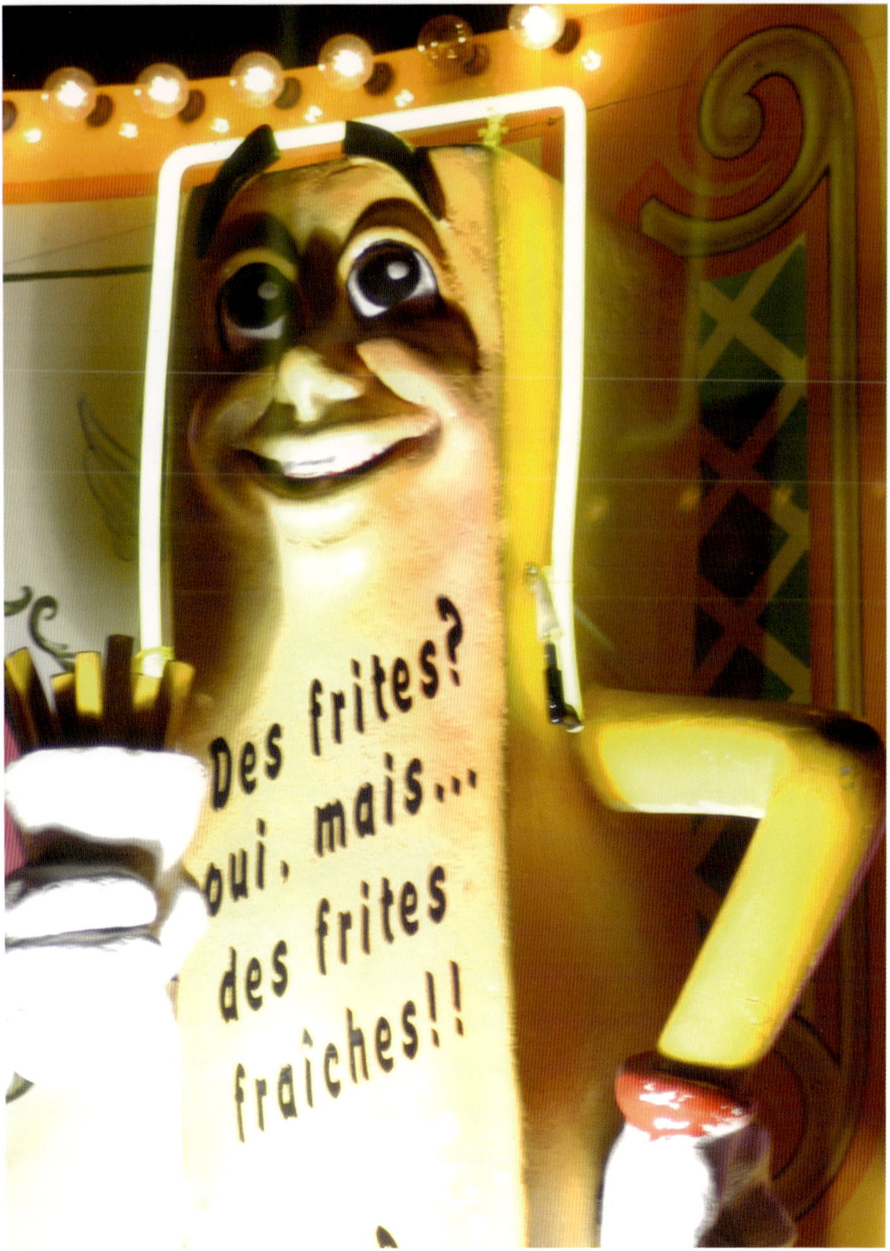
Des frites?
oui, mais...
des frites
fraîches!!

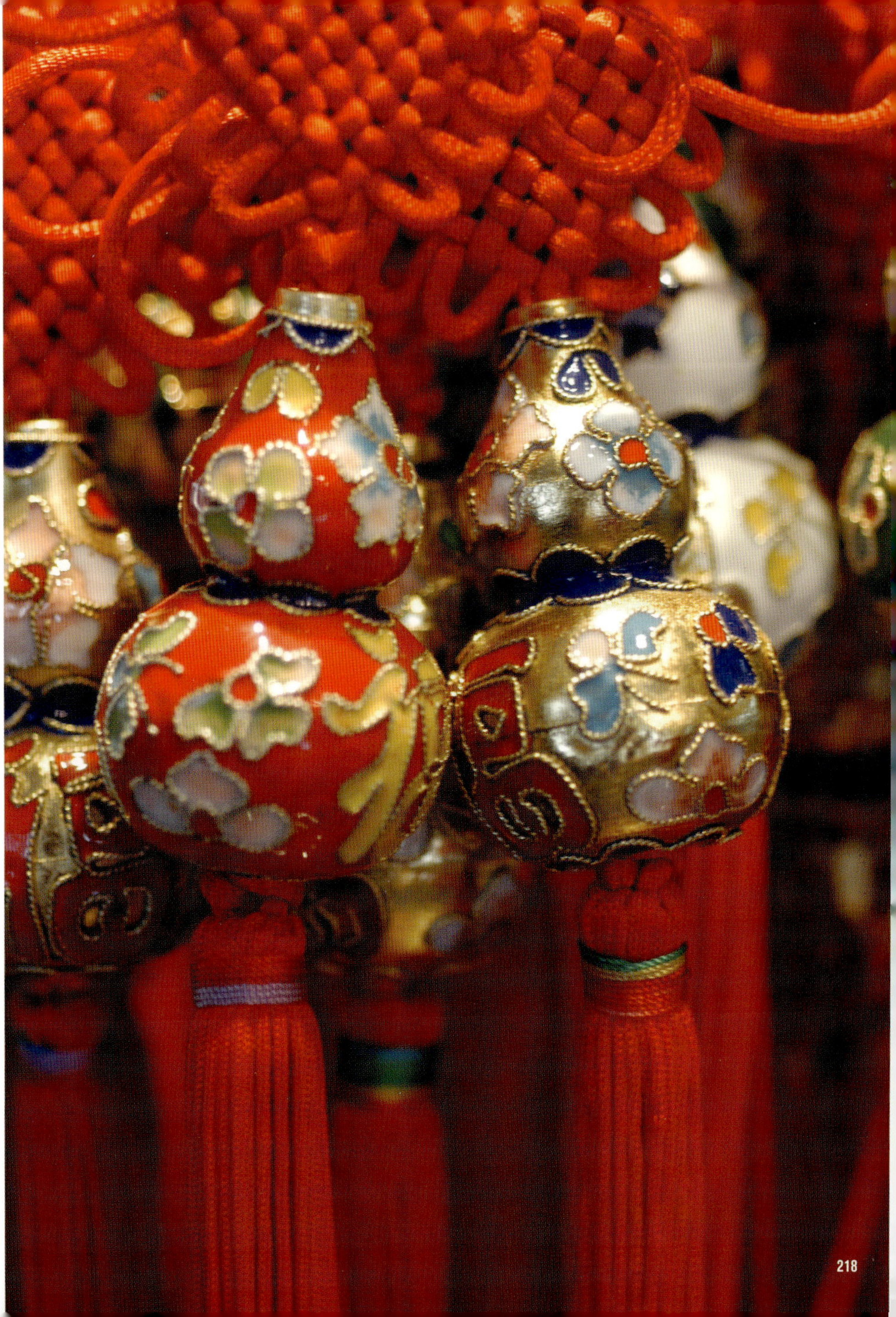

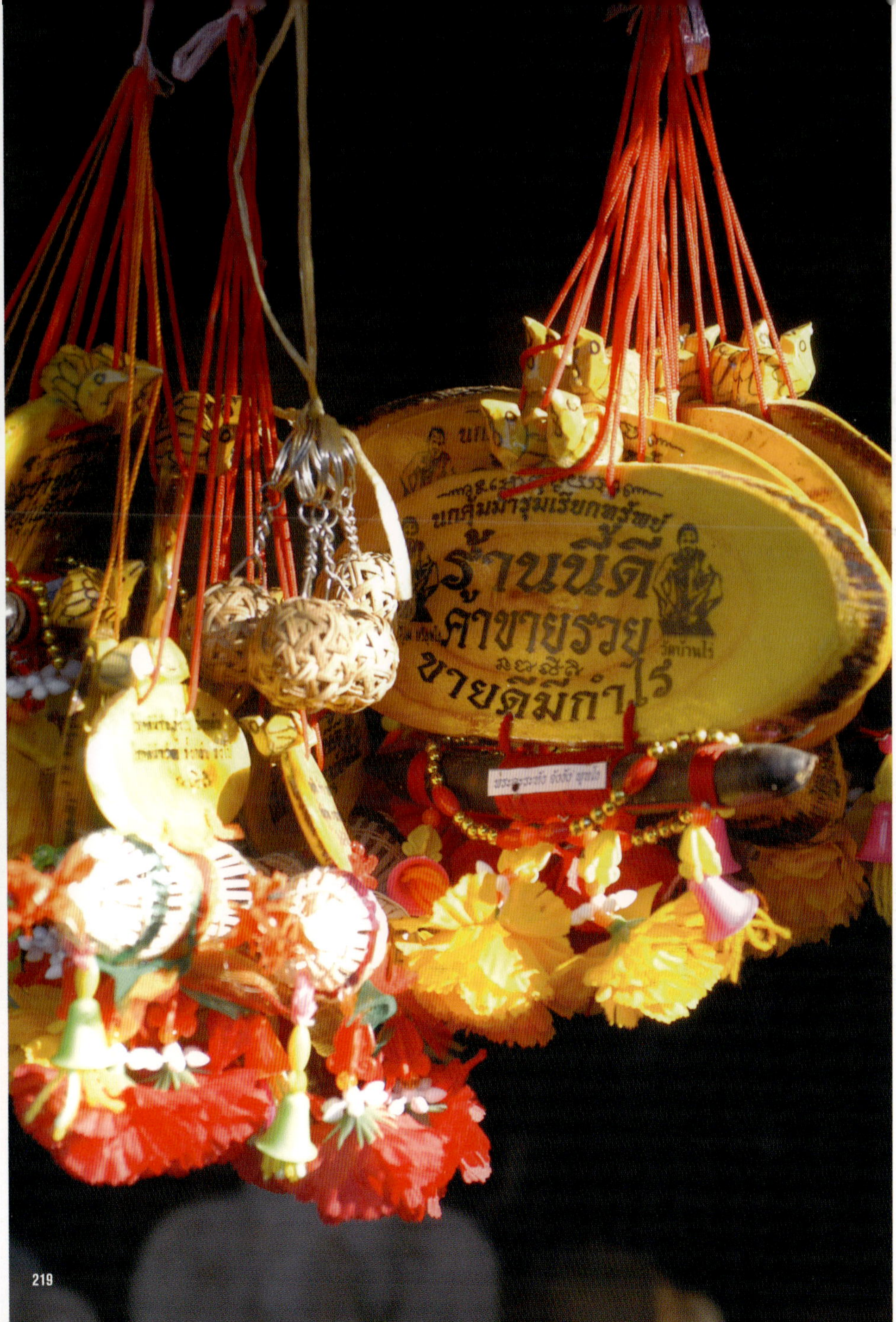

นกคุ้มมารุมเรียกทรัพย์
ร้านนี้ดี
ค้าขายรวย
ขายดีมีกำไร
วัดบ้านไร่

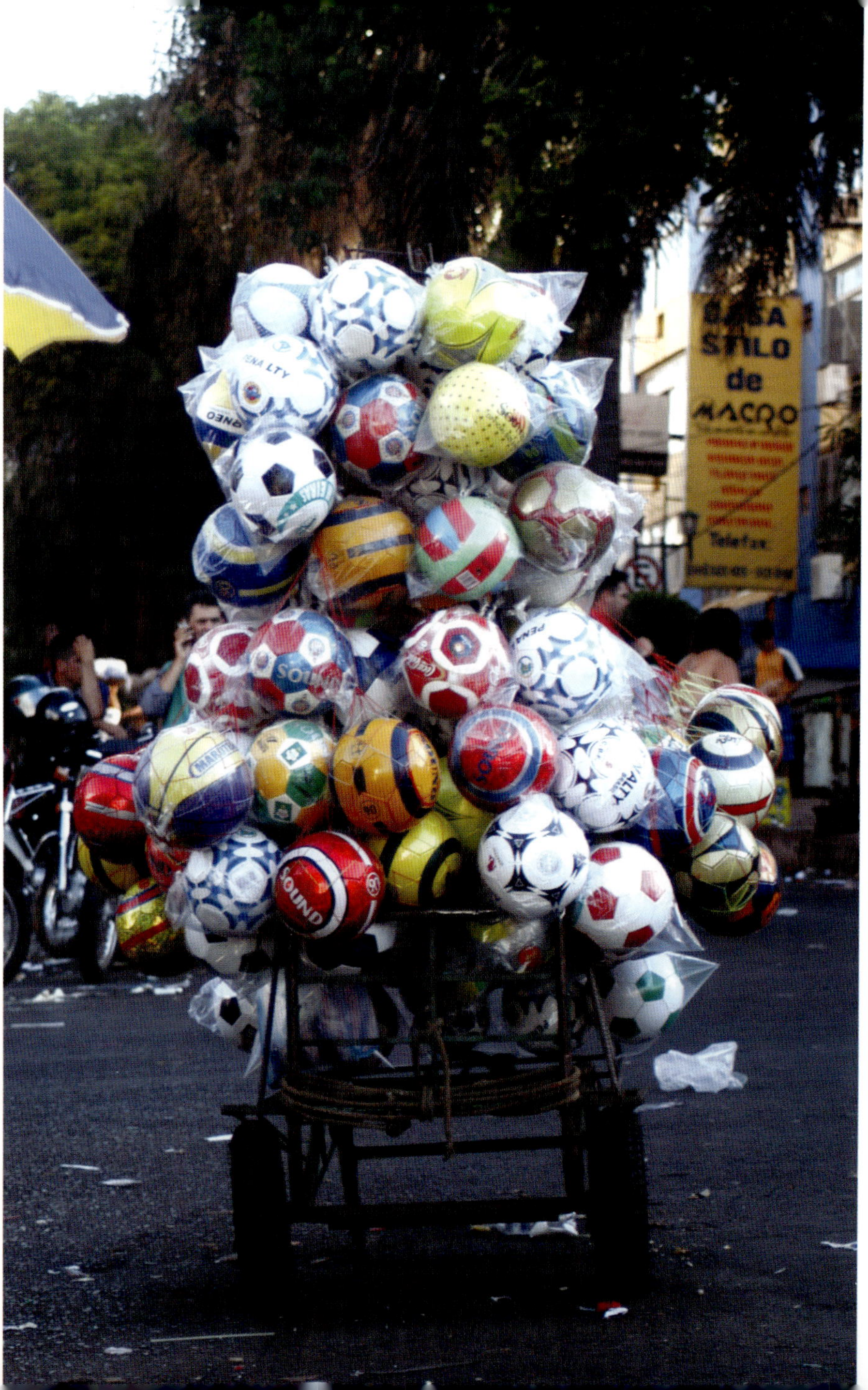
STILO
de
SOUND

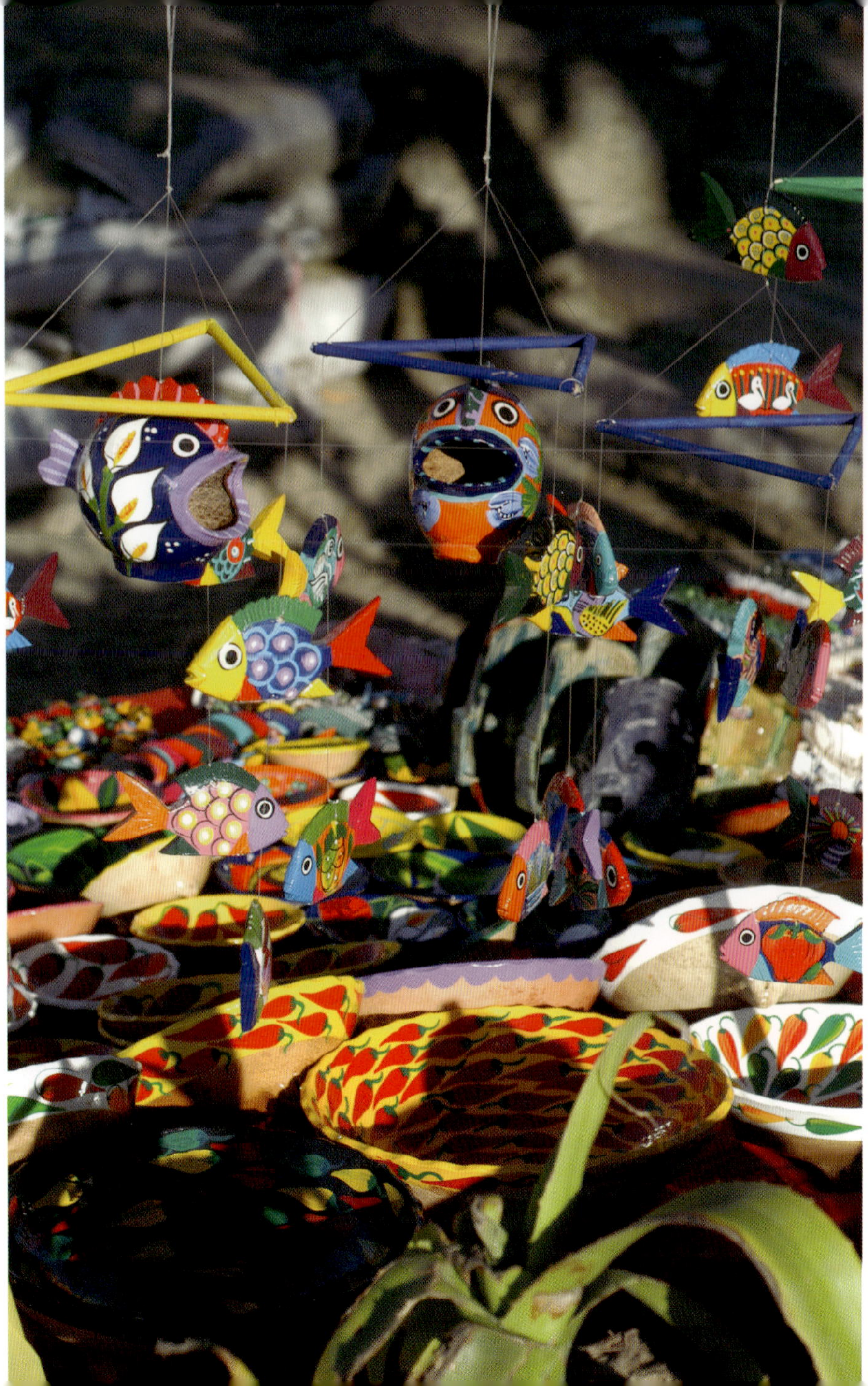

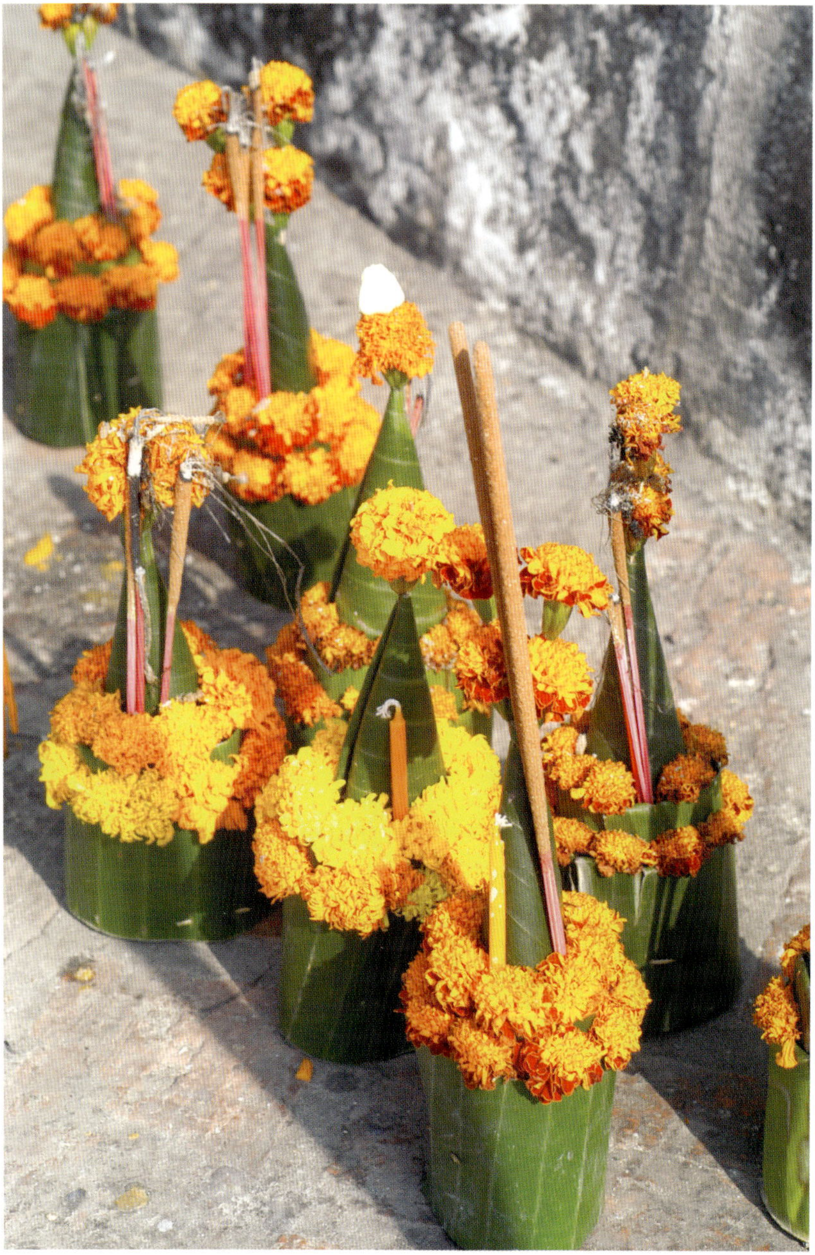

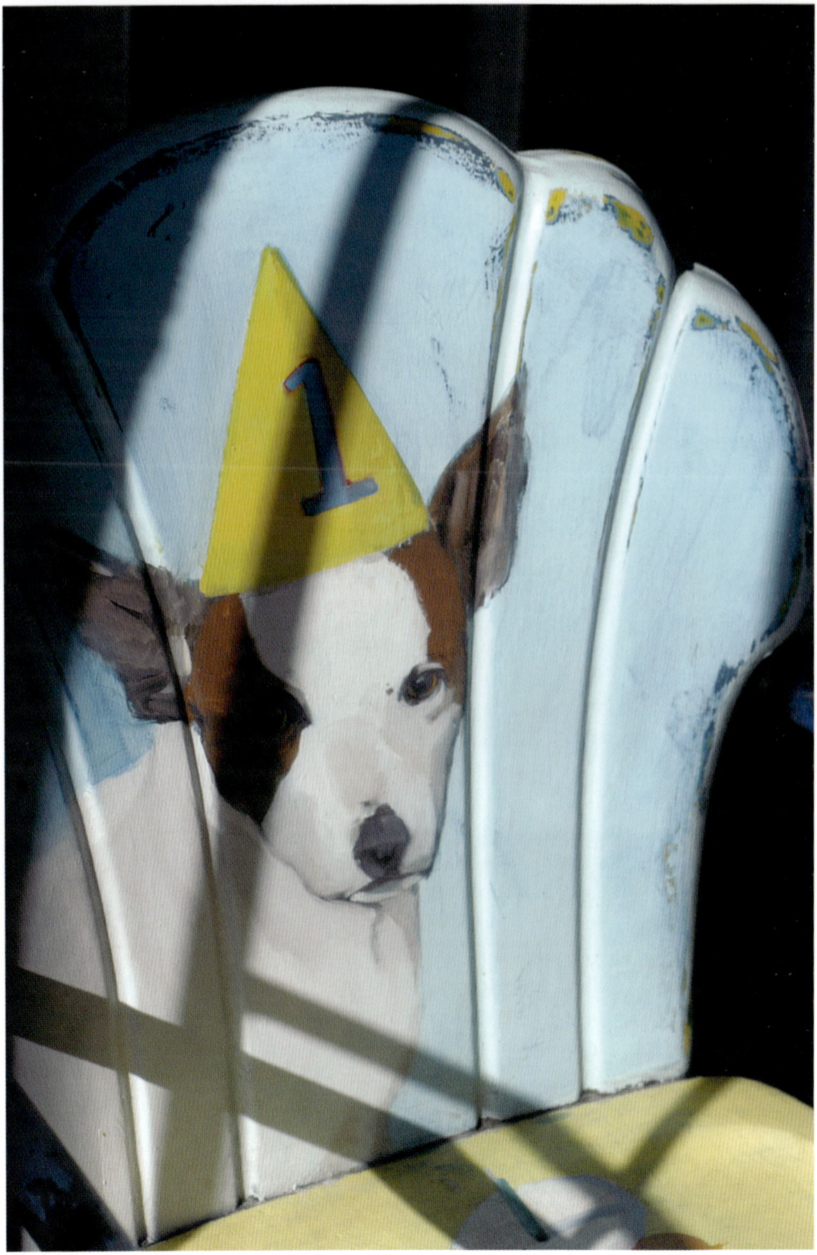
1

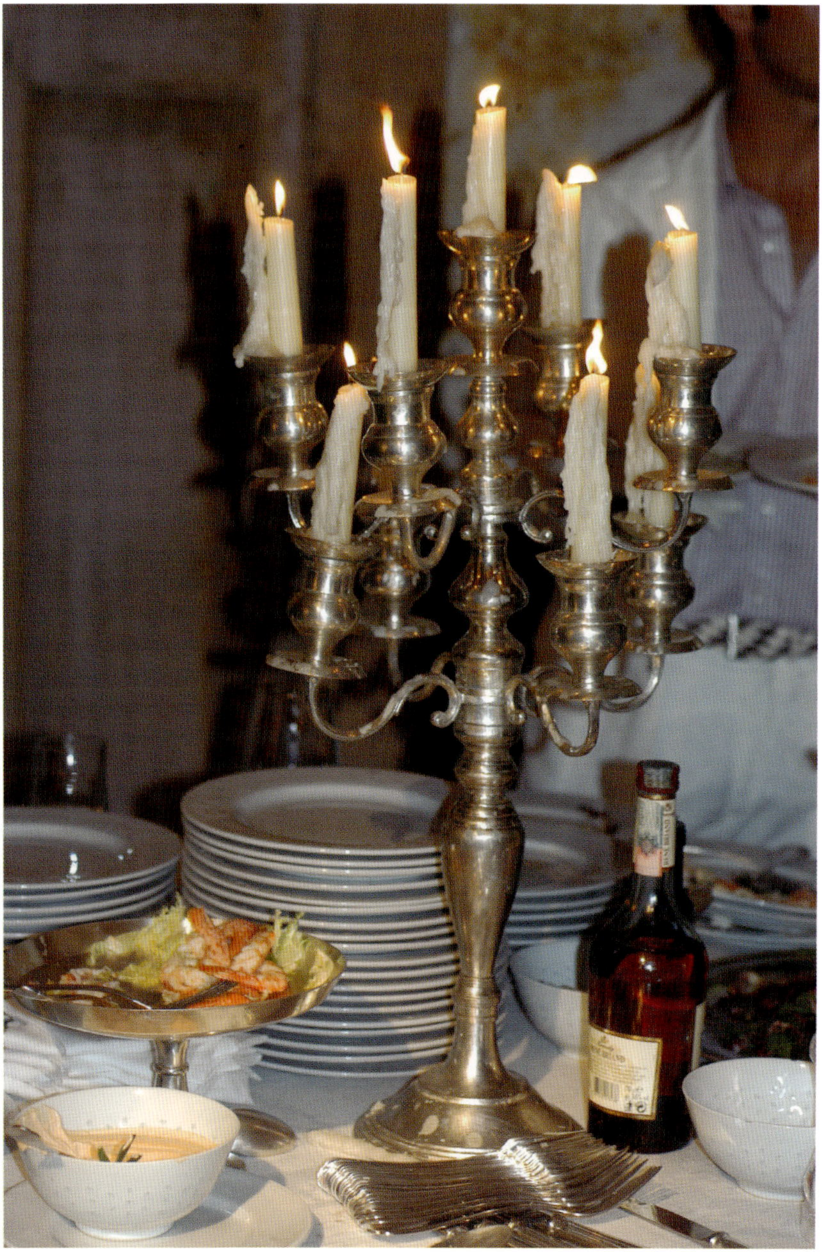

ADORING

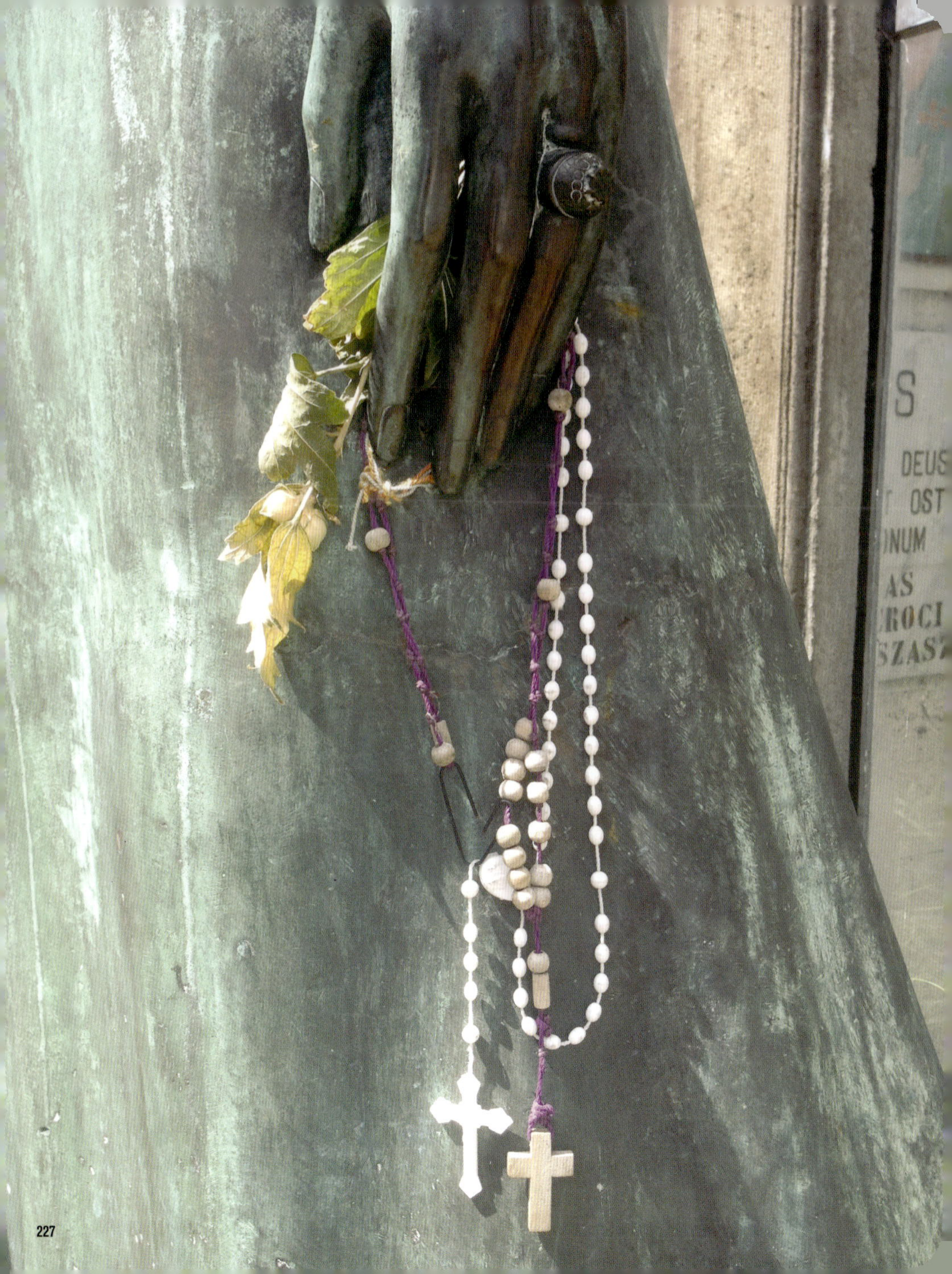
S
DEUS
T OST
NUM
AS
ROCI
SZASZ

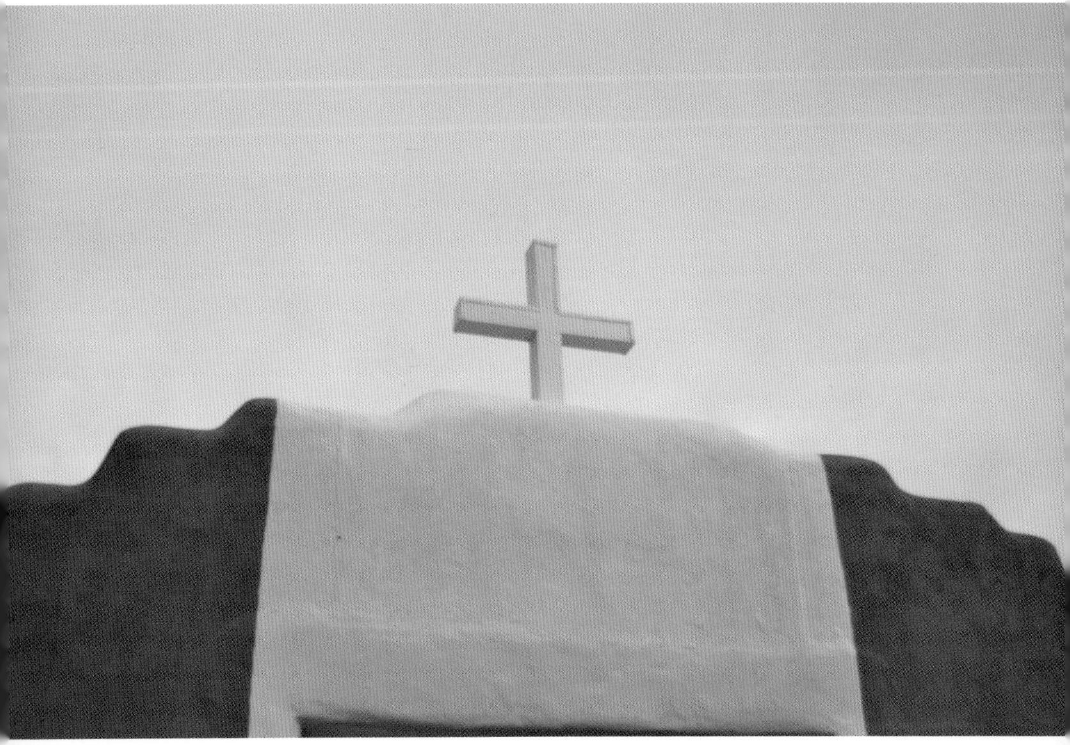

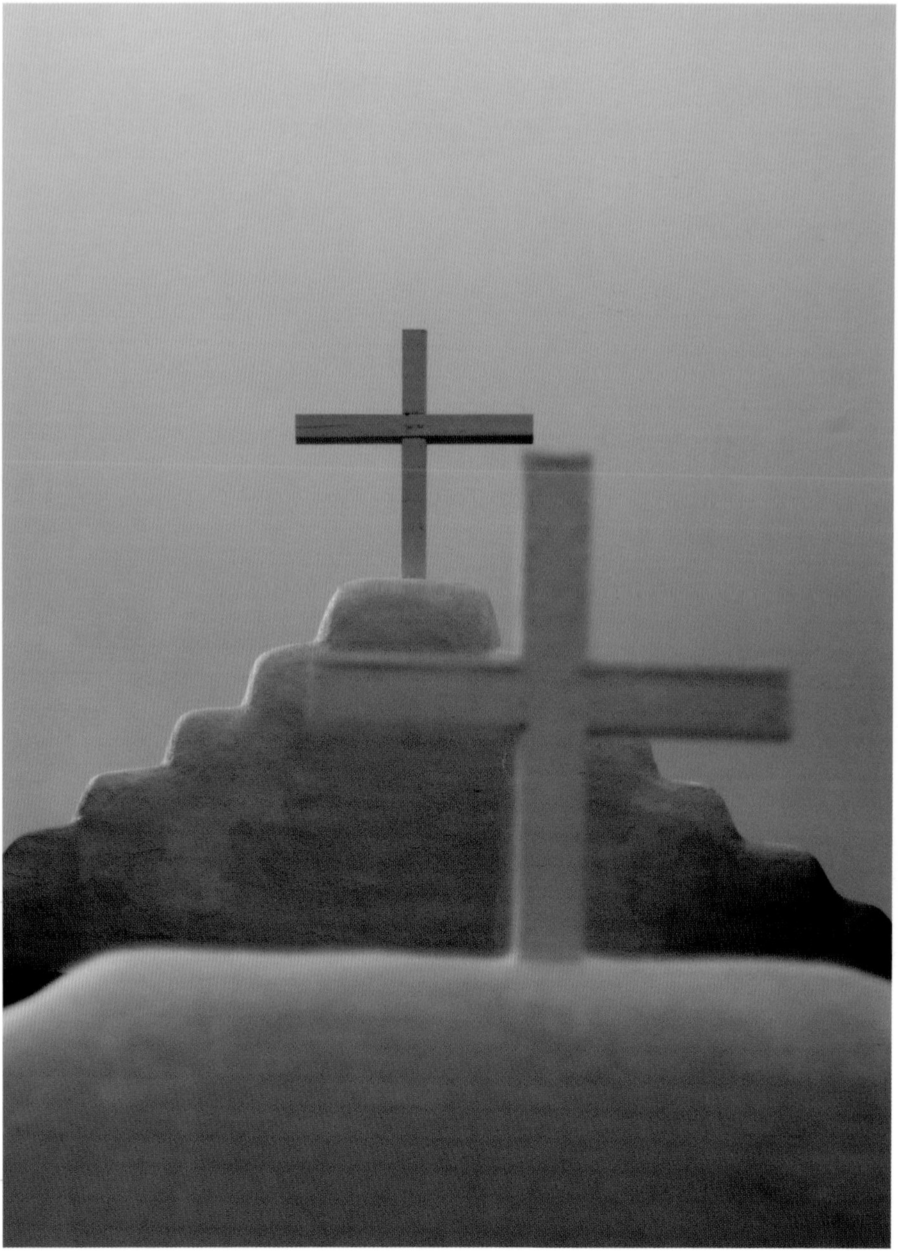

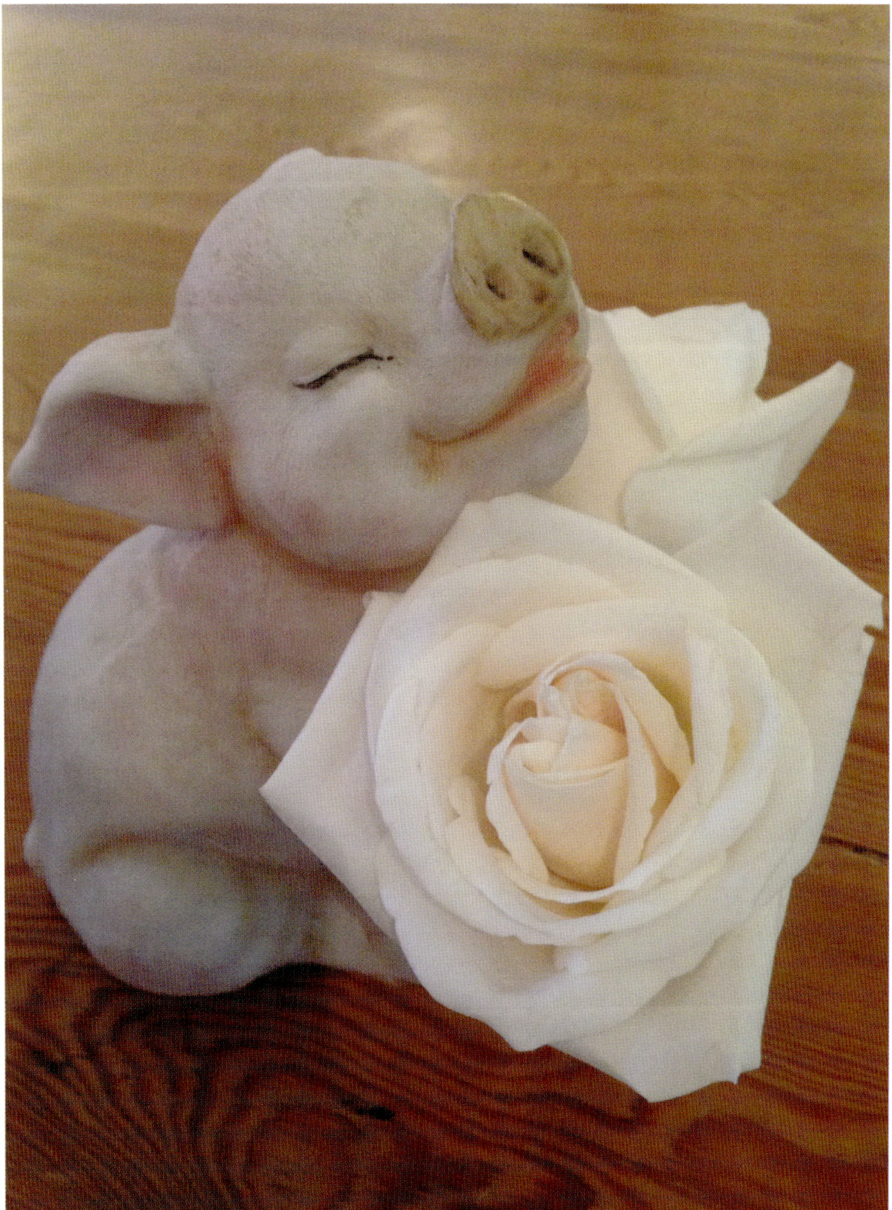

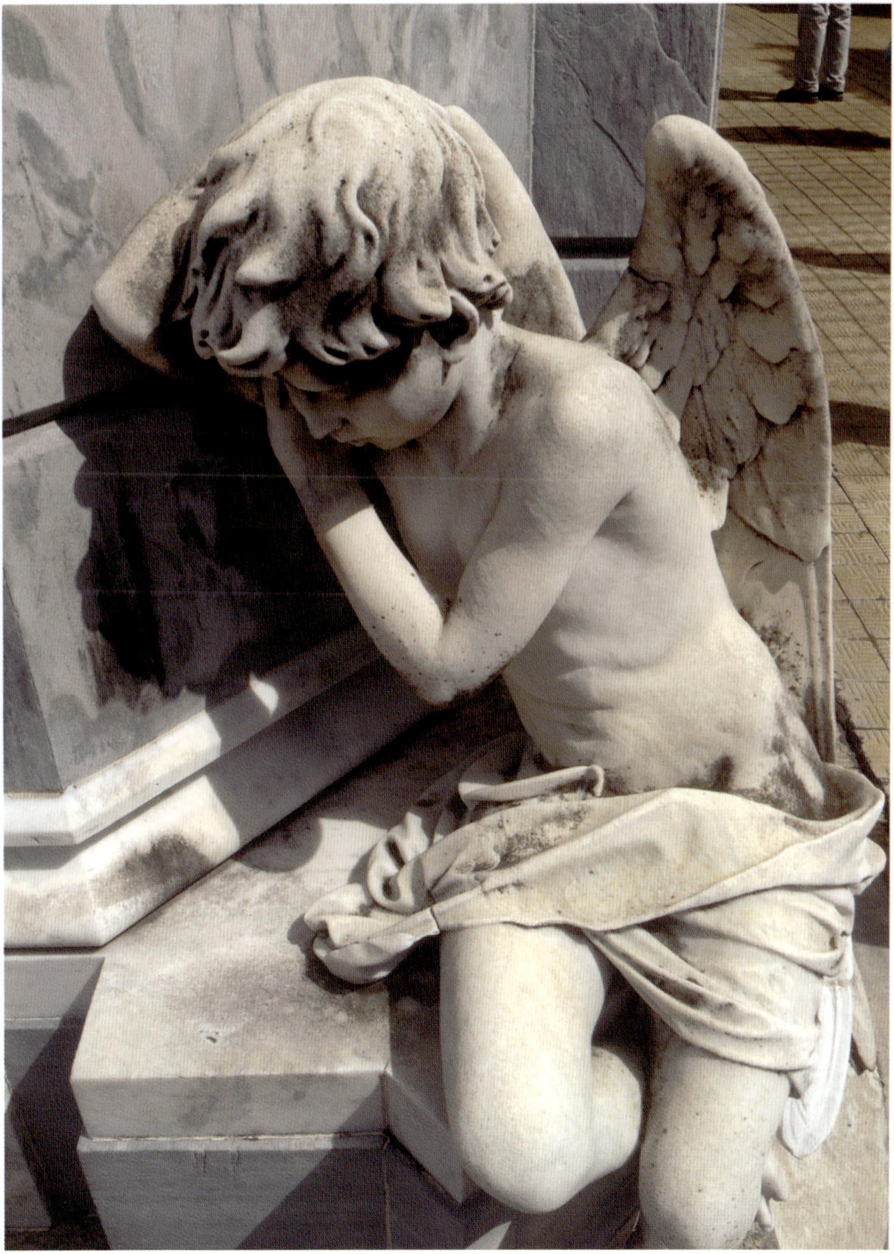

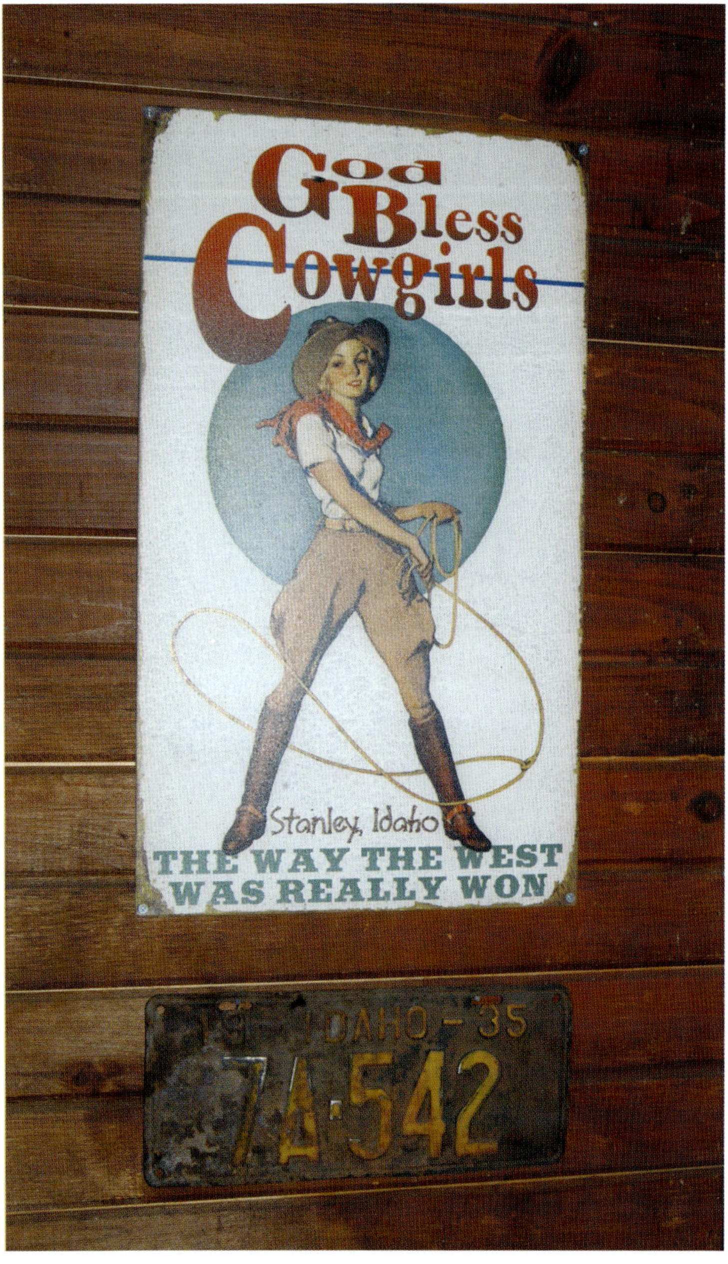
God Bless Cowgirls
Stanley, Idaho
THE WAY THE WEST WAS REALLY WON
IDAHO-35
7A-542

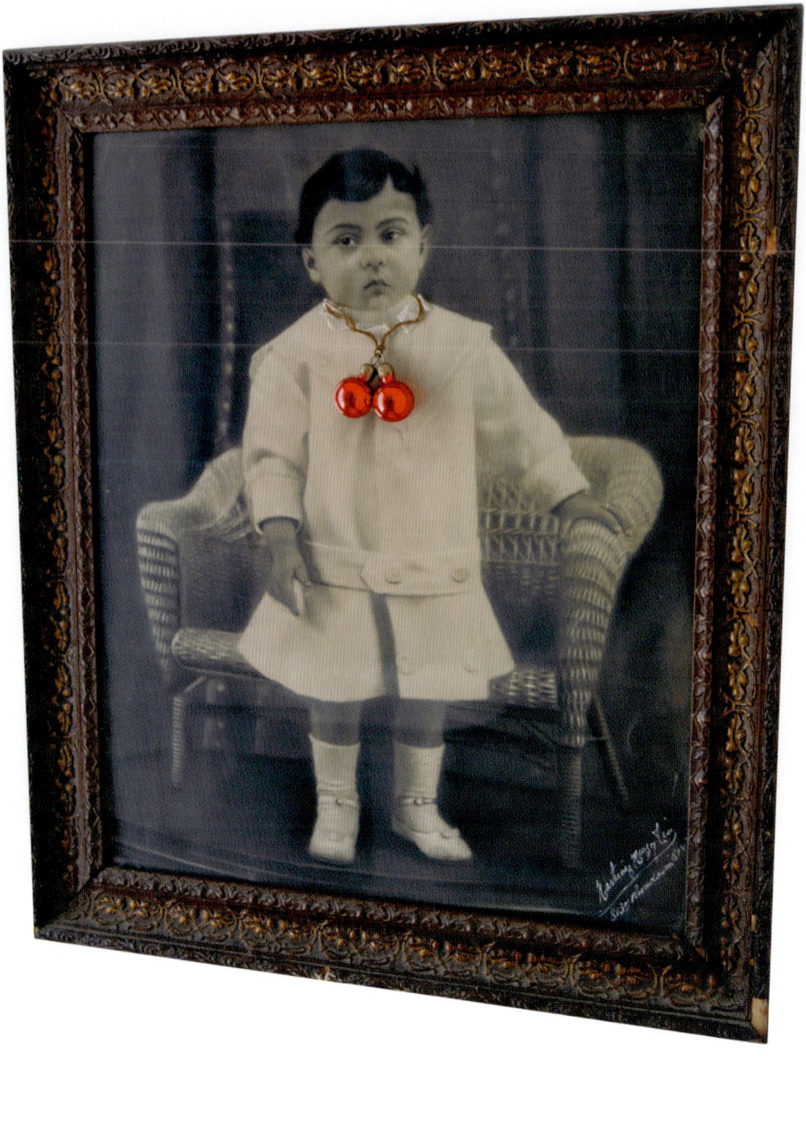

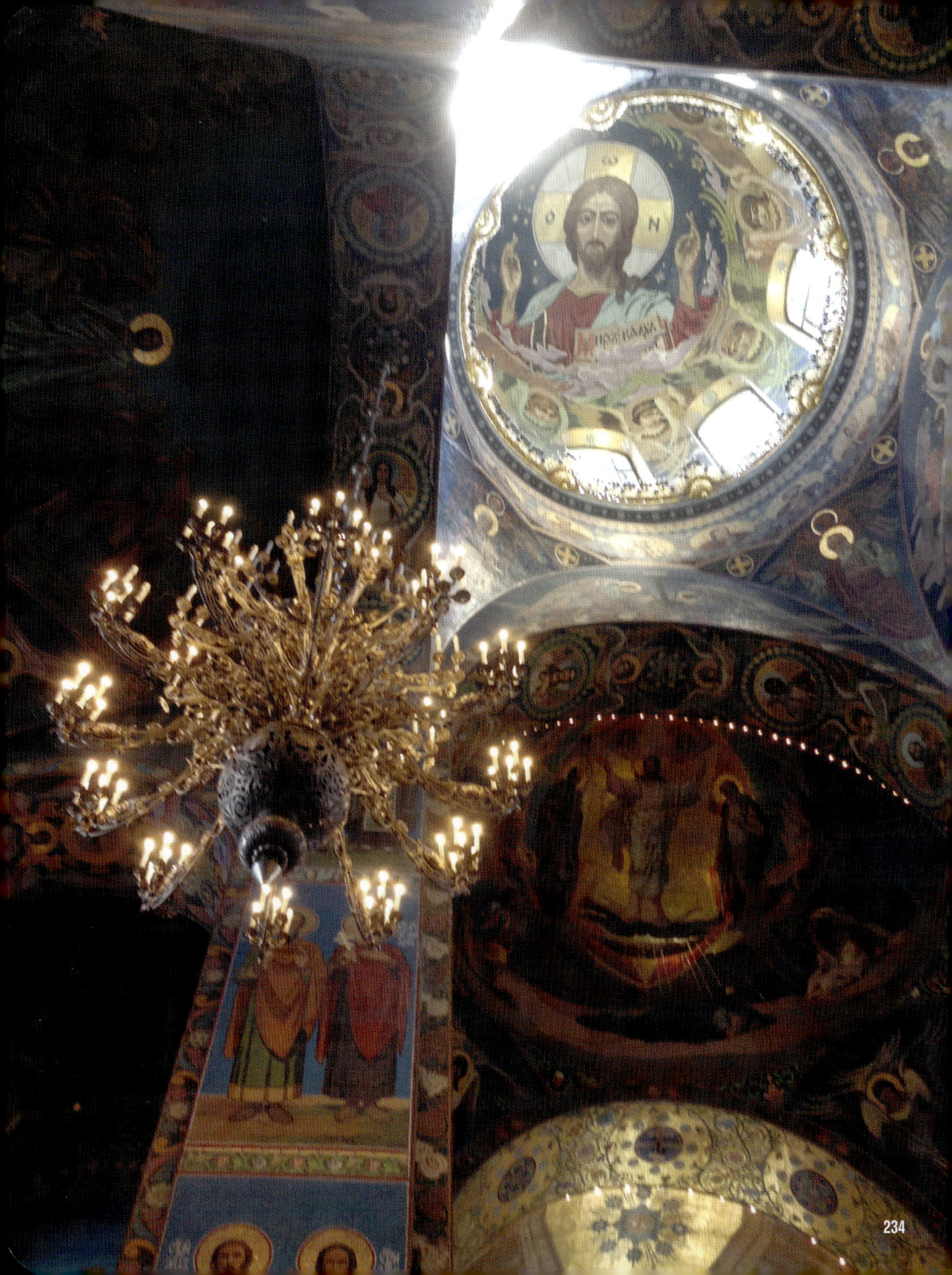

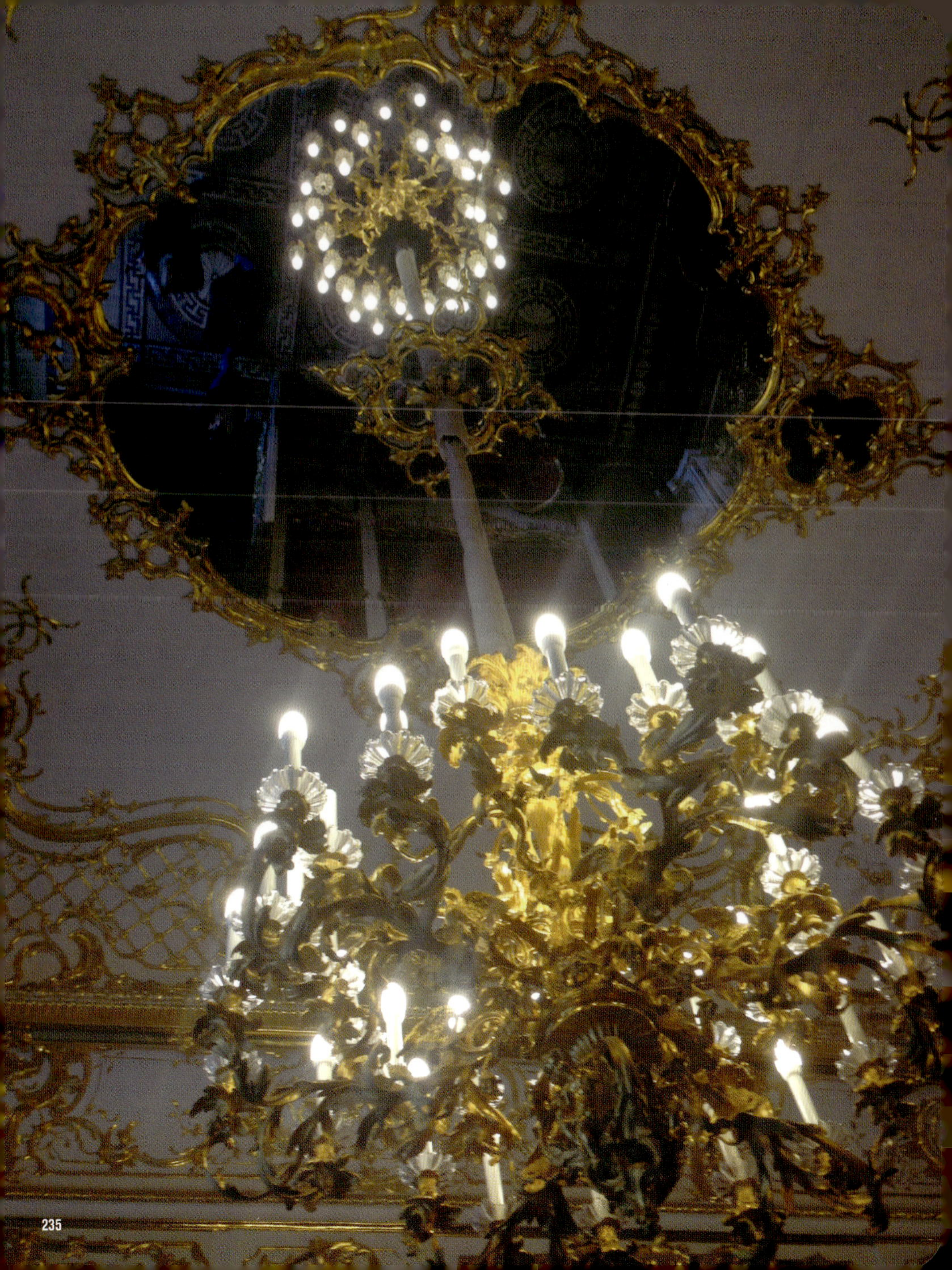

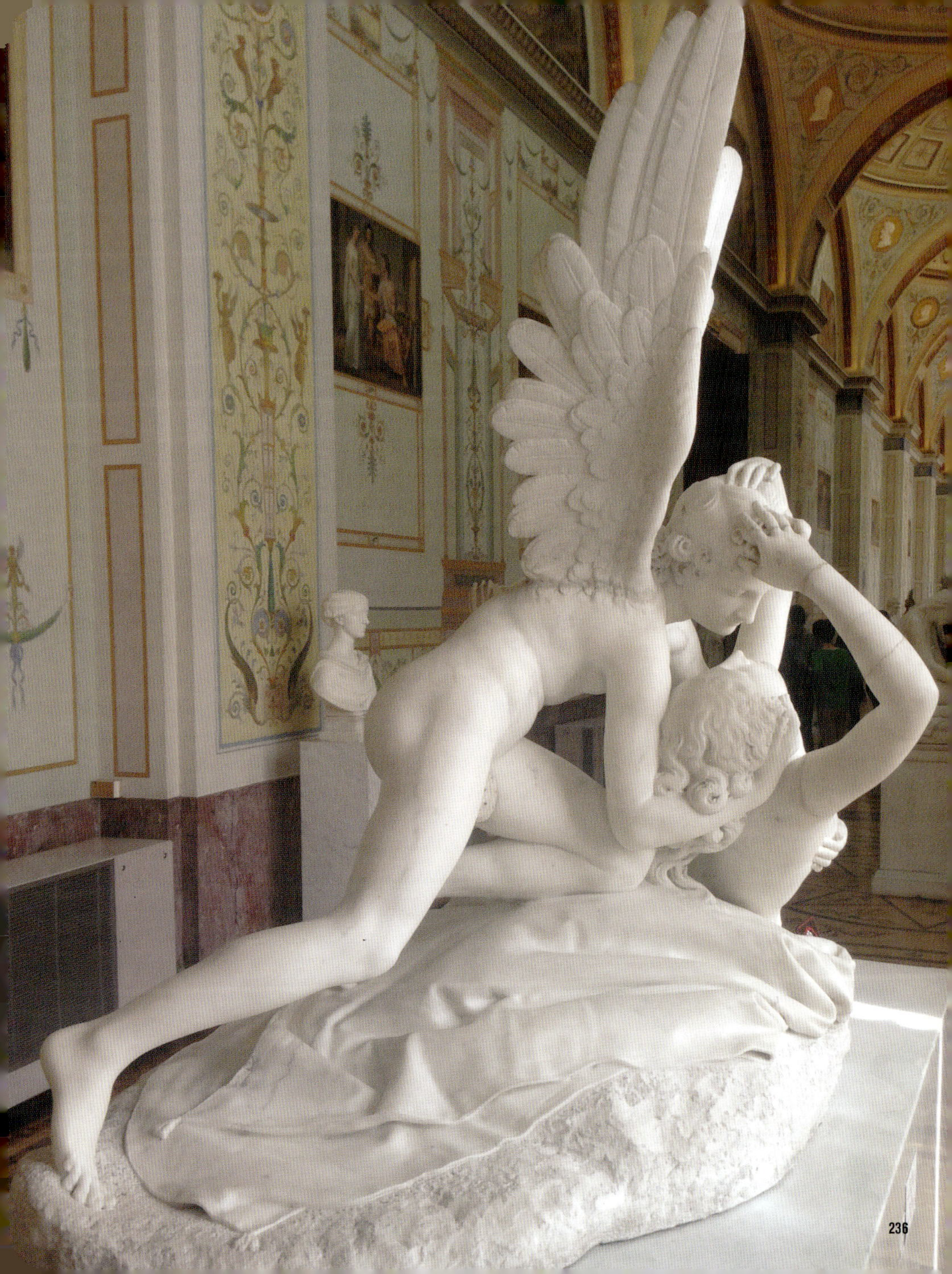

APPENDICES

Index to Photographs

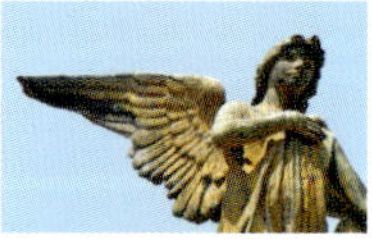
Rome, Italy

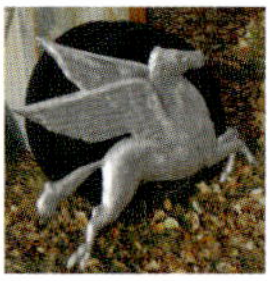
Madrid, New Mexico

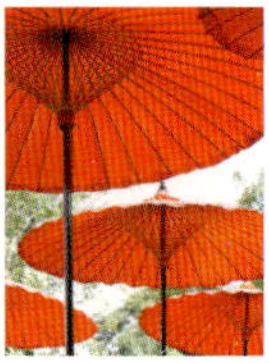
Beijing, China

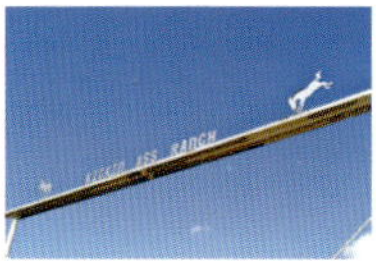
Somewhere in Idaho

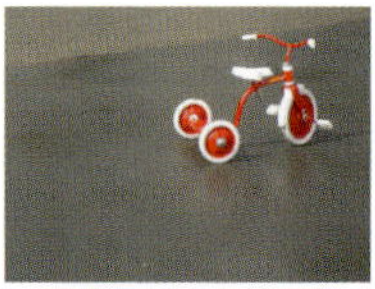
Helsinki, Finland

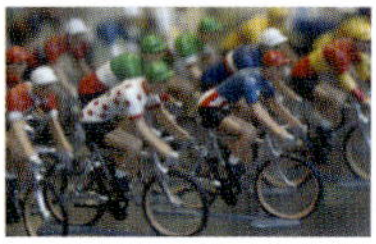
Paris, France

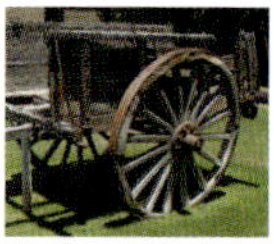
Hailey, Idaho

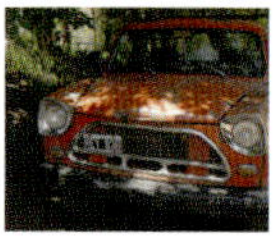
Mendoza, Argentina

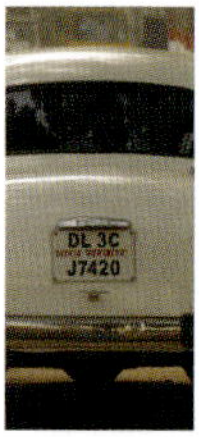

Delhi, India

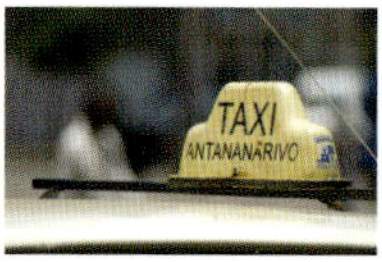

Antananarivo, Madagascar

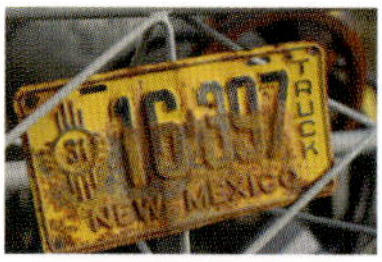

Santa Fe, New Mexico

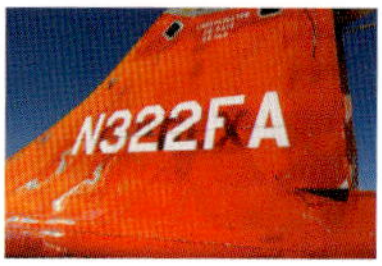

Tucson, Arizona

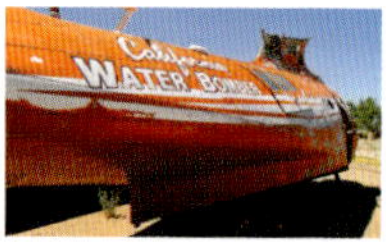

Tucson, Arizona

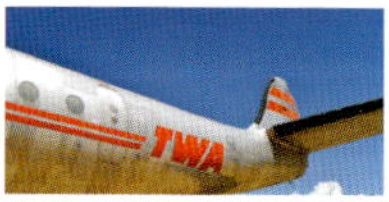

Tucson, Arizona

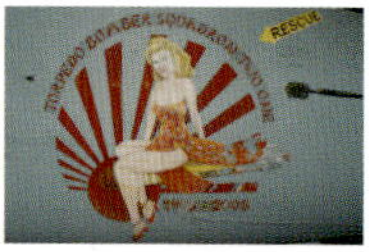

Tucson, Arizona

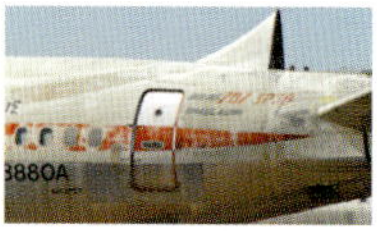

Tucson, Arizona

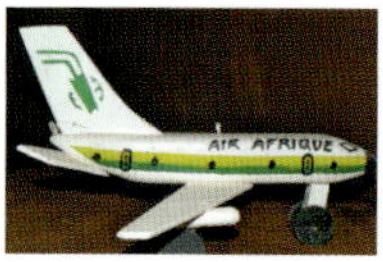

New York, New York

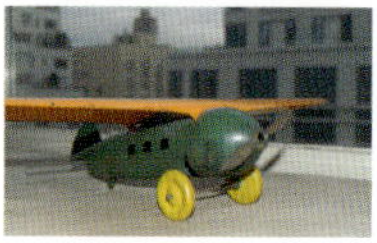
New York, New York

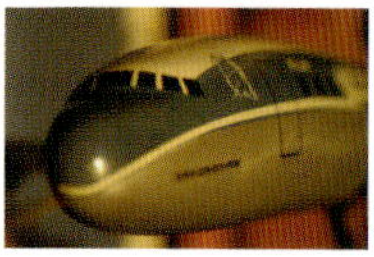
New York, New York

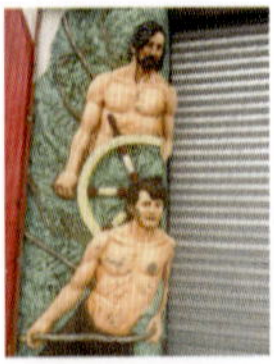

Buenos Aires, Argentina

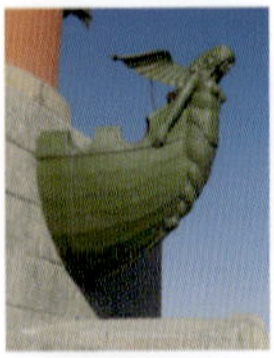

St. Petersburg, Russia

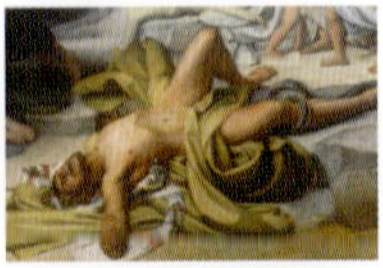

St. Petersburg, Russia

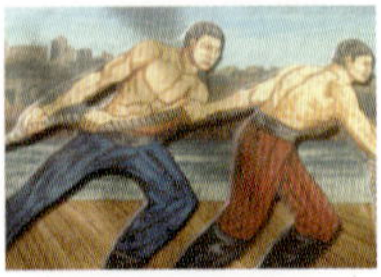

Buenos Aires, Argentina

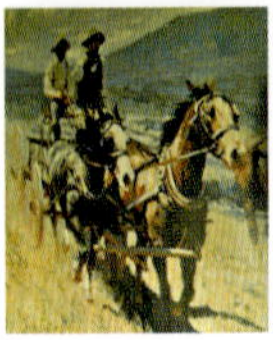

San Simeon, California

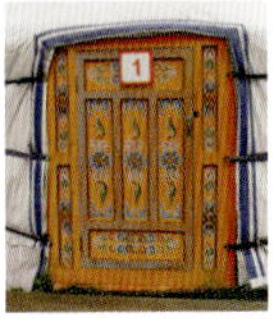

Lake Hovsgol, Mongolia

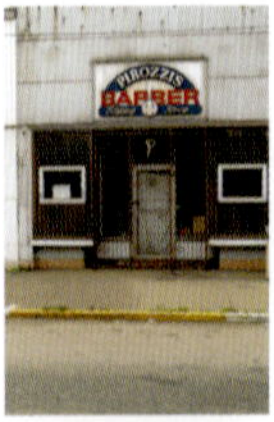

Braddock, Pennsylvania

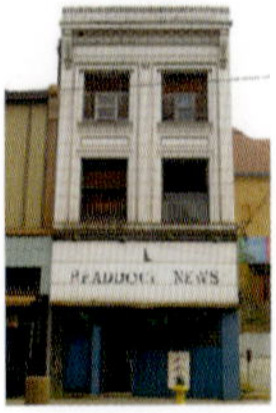

Braddock, Pennsylvania

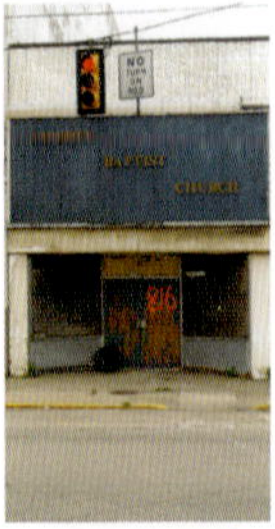

Braddock, Pennsylvania

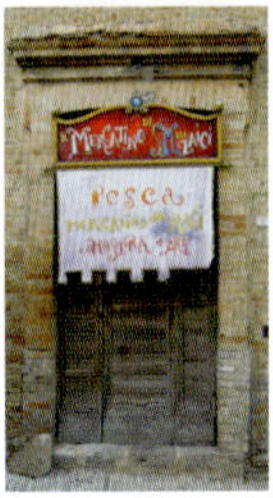

Perugia, Italy

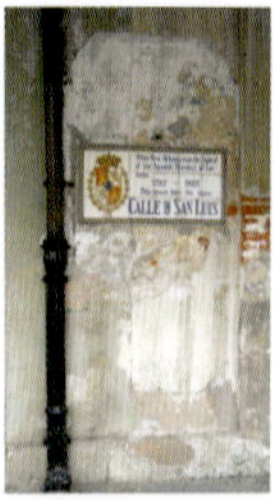

New Orleans, Louisiana

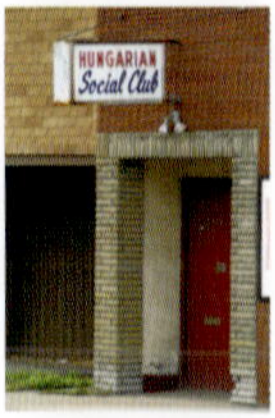

Braddock, Pennsylvania

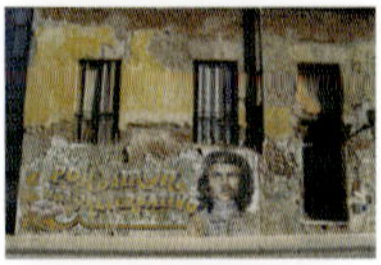

Buenos Aires, Argentina

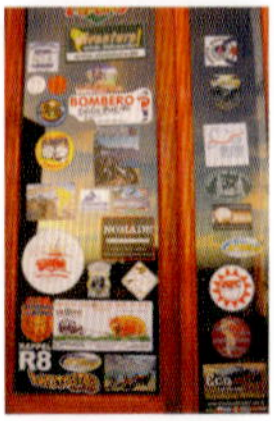

Ushuaia, Argentina

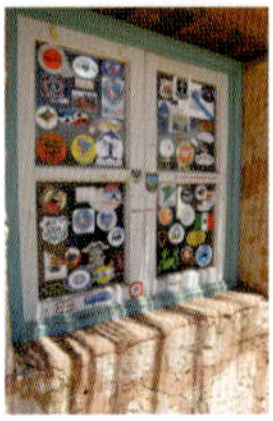

Ushuaia, Argentina

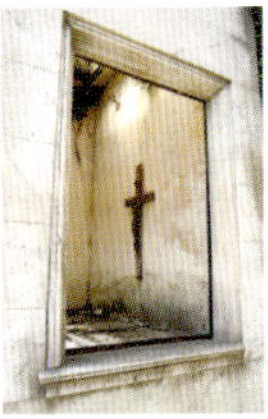
Buenos Aires, Argentina

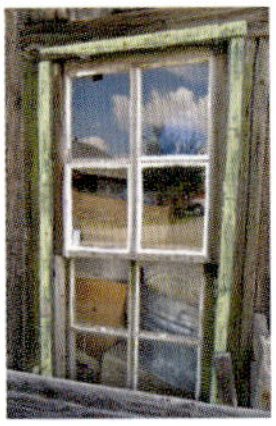
Hailey, Idaho

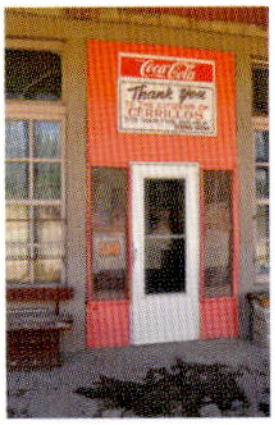
Los Cerrillos, New Mexico

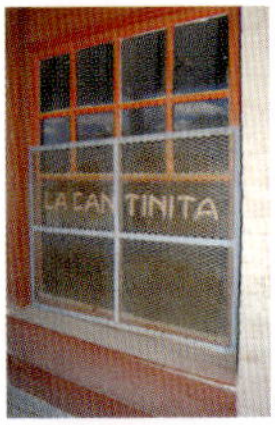

Los Cerrillos, New Mexico

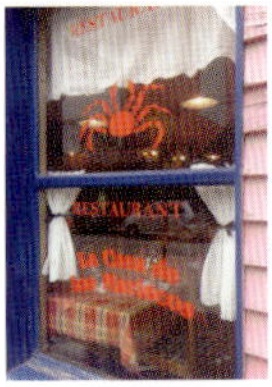
Ushuaia, Argentina

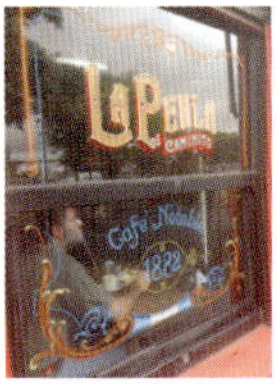
Ushuaia, Argentina

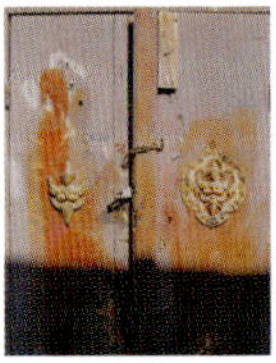
Luang Prabang, Laos

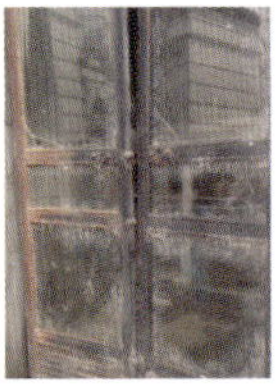
Buenos Aires, Argentina

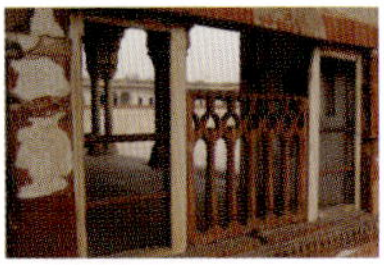
Delhi, India

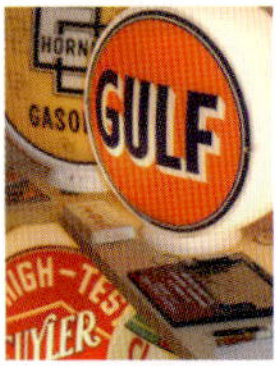

Santa Fe, New Mexico

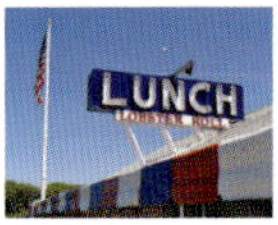

Amagansett, New York

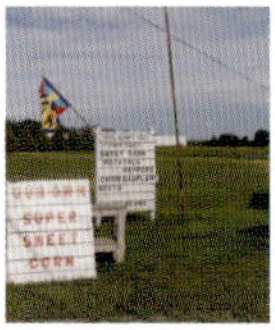
North Fork, Long Island

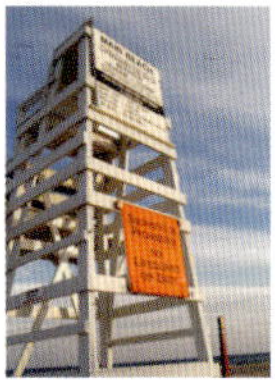
Easthampton, New York

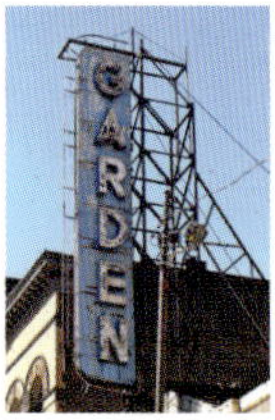

Pittsburgh, Pennsylvania

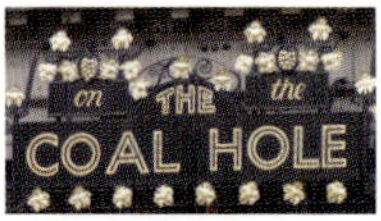

London, England

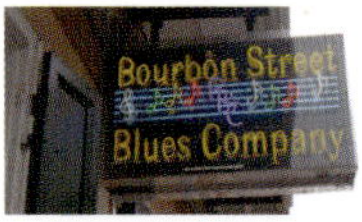

New Orleans, Louisiana

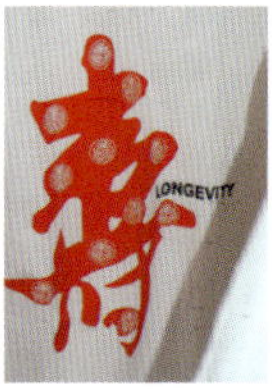

Beijing, China

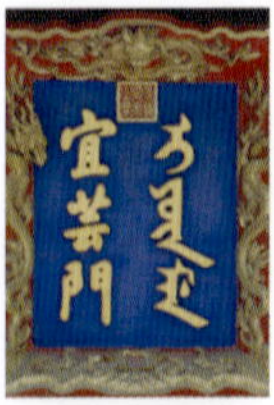

Beijing, China

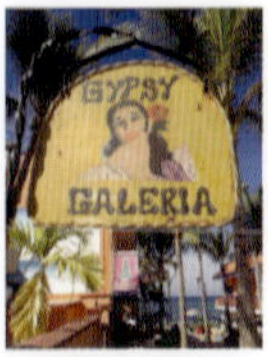

Sayulita, Mexico

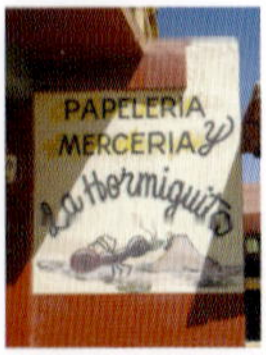

Perugia, Italy

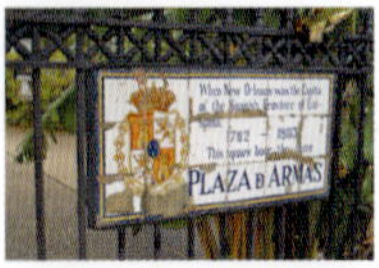

New Orleans, Louisiana

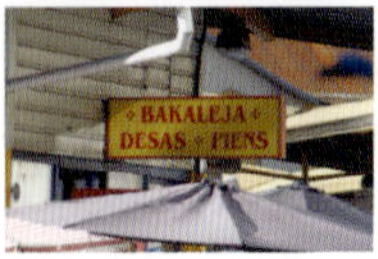

Riga, Latvia

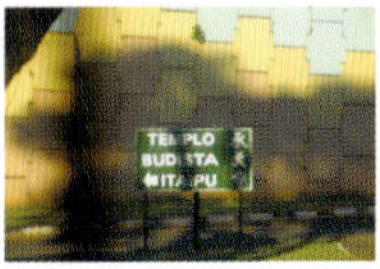

Shanghai, China

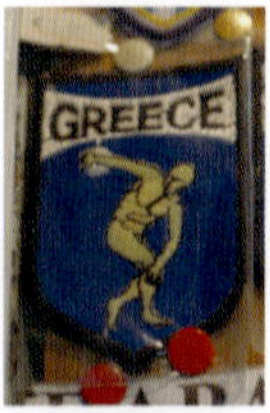

Delos, Greece

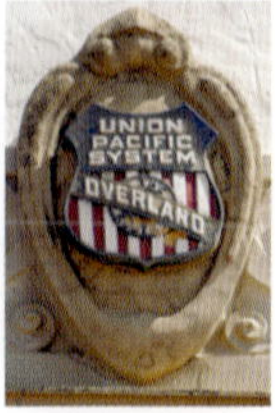

Stanley, Idaho

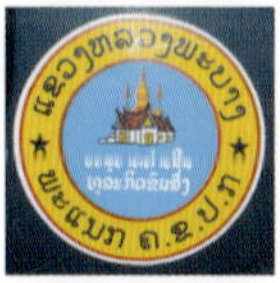

Chiang Mai, Thailand

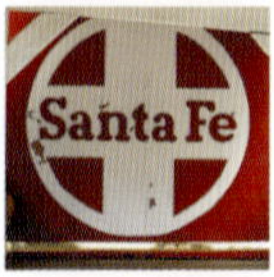

Santa Fe, New Mexico

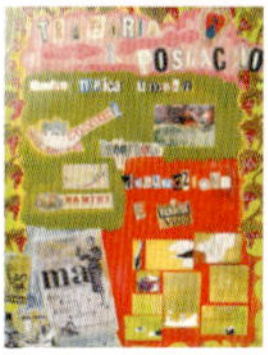

Somewhere in Umbria, Italy

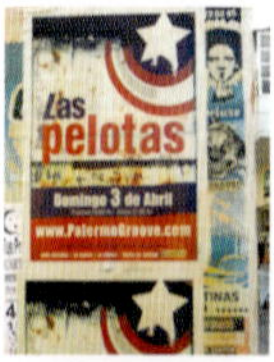

Buenos Aires, Argentina

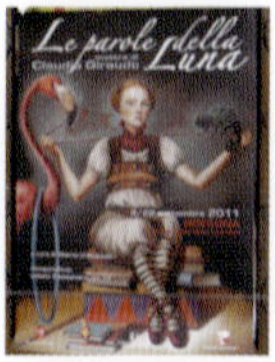

Umbria, Italy

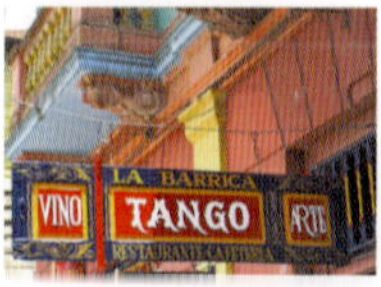

Buenos Aires, Argentina

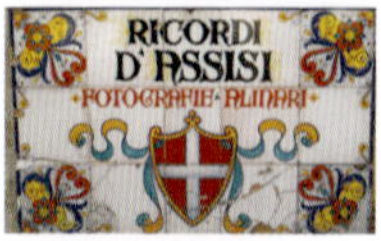

Assisi, Italy

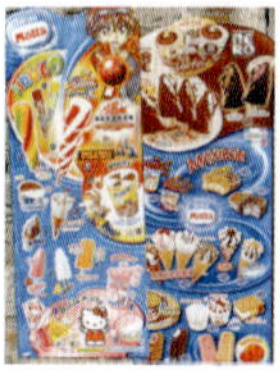

Umbria, Italy

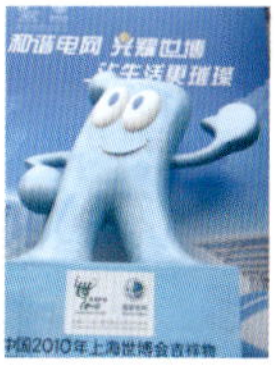

Shanghai, China

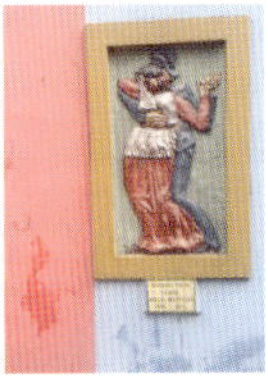
Buenos Aires, Argentina

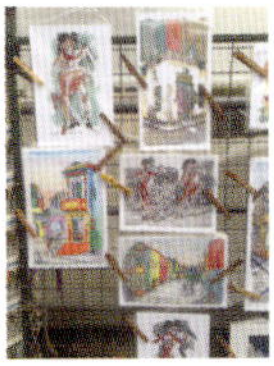
Buenos Aires, Argentina

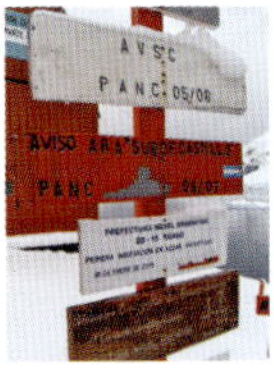
Antarctica

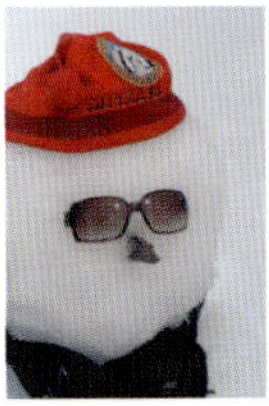
Antarctica

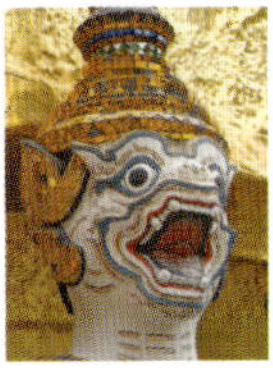
Bangkok, Thailand

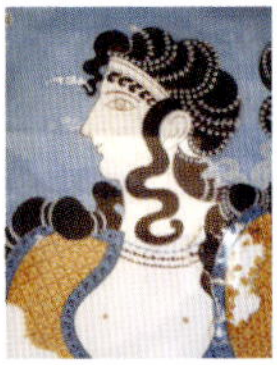
Delos, Greece

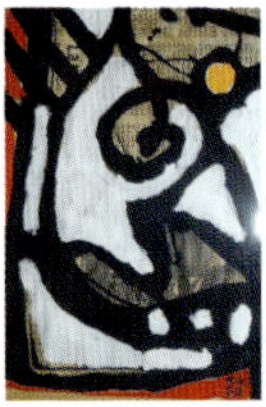
Paris, France

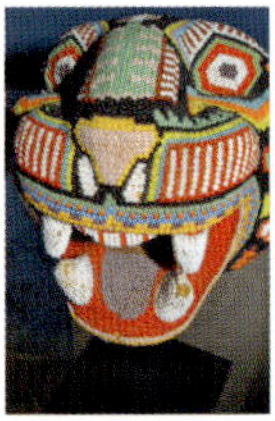
Oaxaca, Mexico

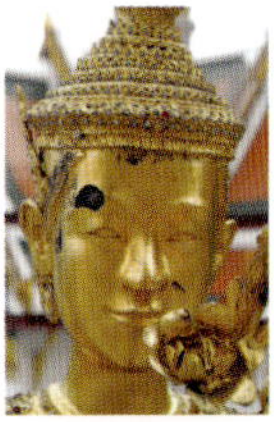
Bangkok, Thailand

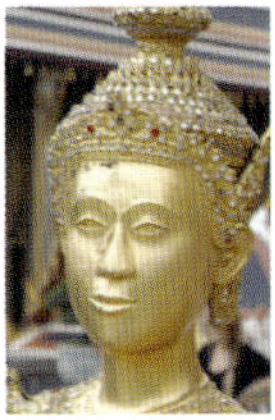
Bangkok, Thailand

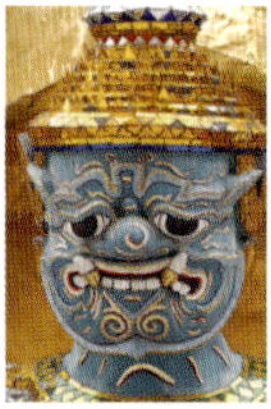
Bangkok, Thailand

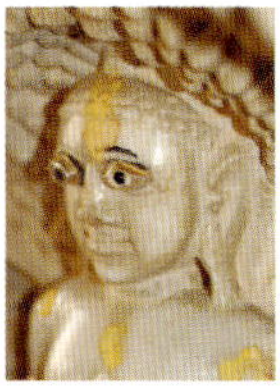
Siem Reap, Cambodia

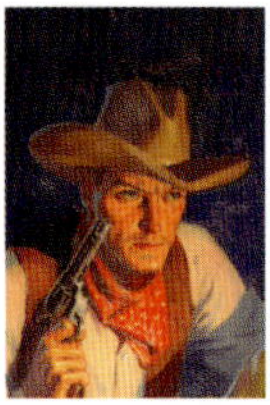
Santa Fe, New Mexico

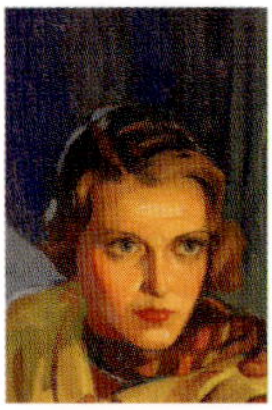
Santa Fe, New Mexico

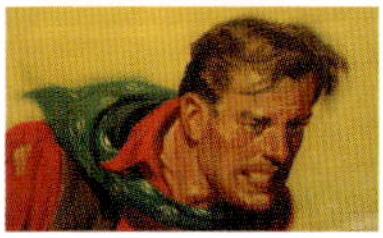
Santa Fe, New Mexico

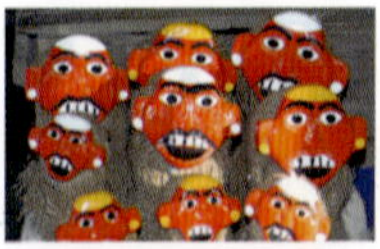
Luang Prabang, Laos

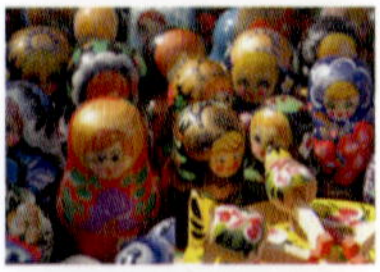
St. Petersburg, Russia

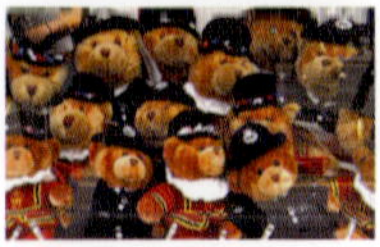
London, England

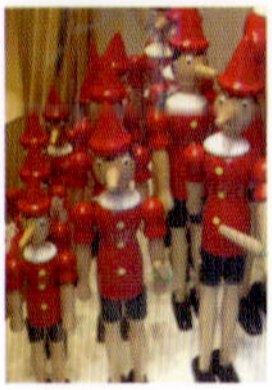
Cortona, Italy

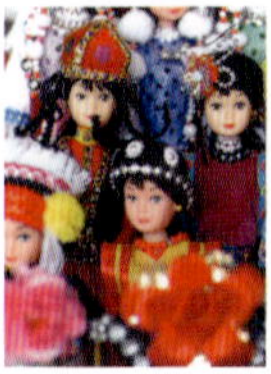
Beijing, China

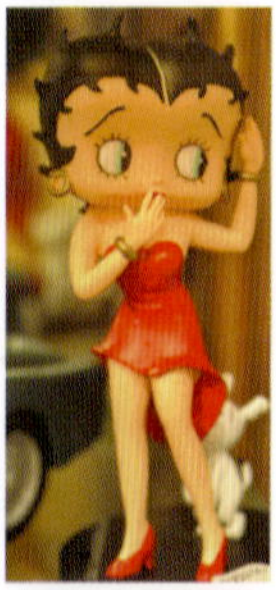
Paris, France

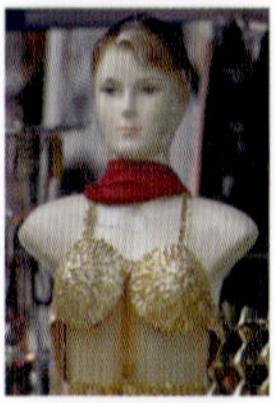
Oslo, Norway

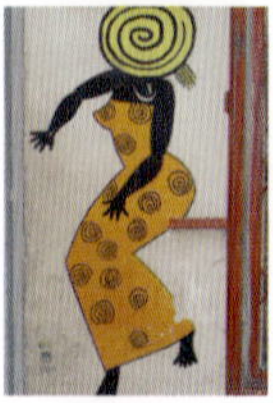
Madagascar

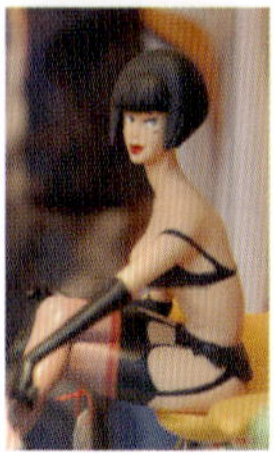
Paris, France

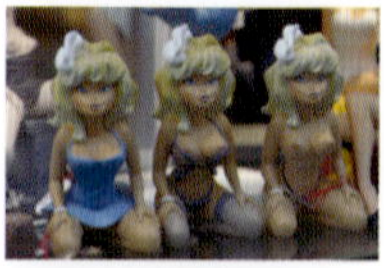
Paris, France

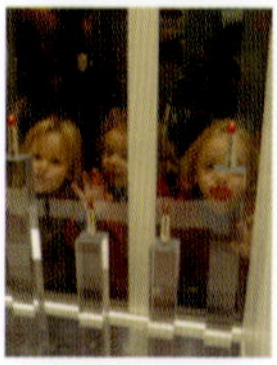
Paris, France

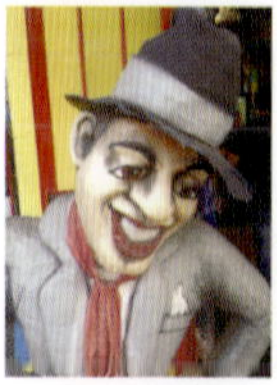
Buenos Aires, Argentina

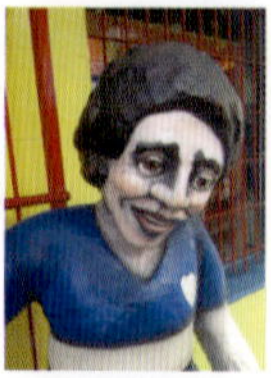
Buenos Aires, Argentina

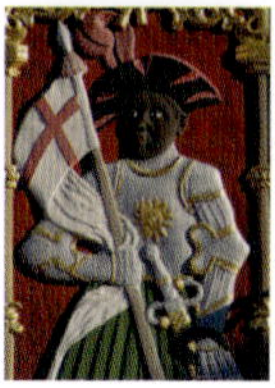
Unknown

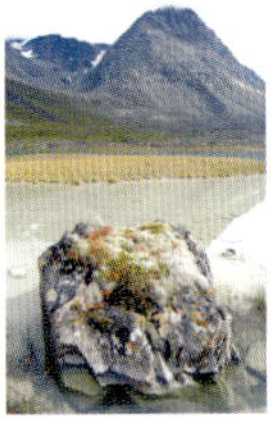
Above the Arctic Circle, Norway

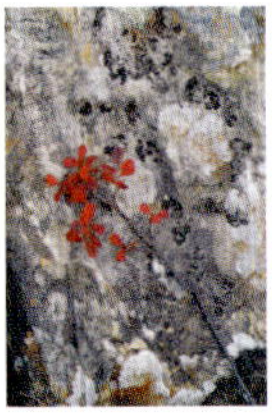
Above the Arctic Circle, Norway

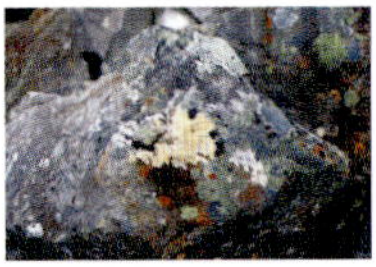
Above the Arctic Circle, Norway

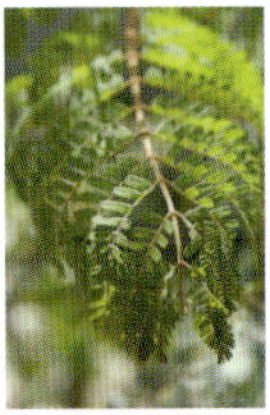
Sydney, Australia

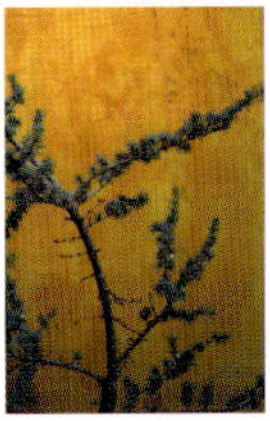
Taos, New Mexico

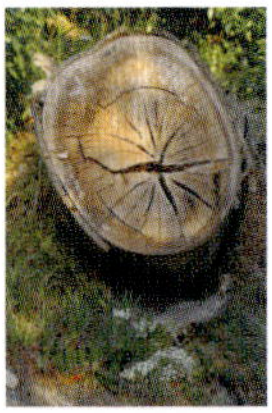
Above the Arctic Circle, Norway

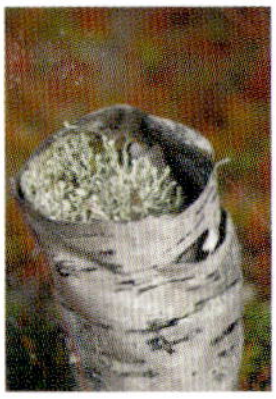
Above the Arctic Circle, Norway

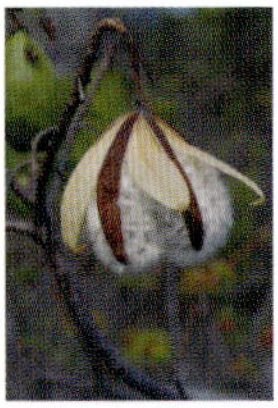
Lizard Island, Australia

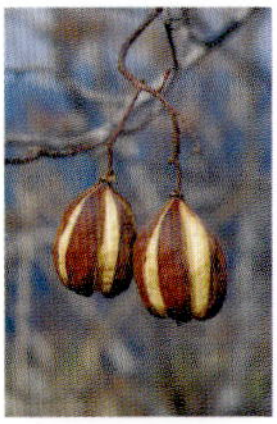
Lizard Island, Australia

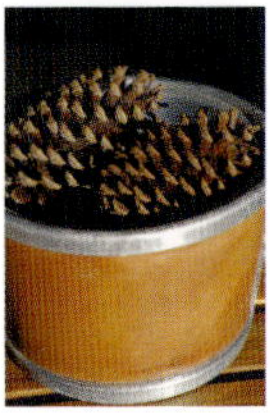
Water Mill, New York

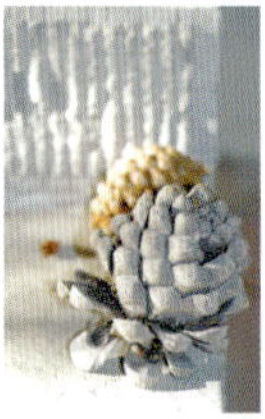
Water Mill, New York

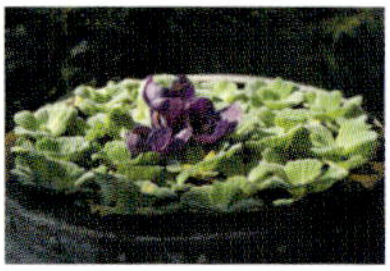
Bangkok, Thailand

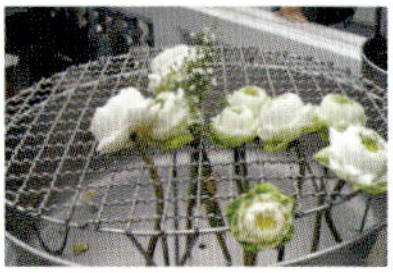
Bangkok, Thailand

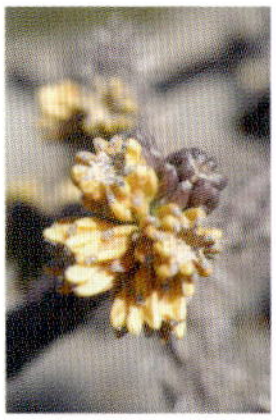
New Mexico

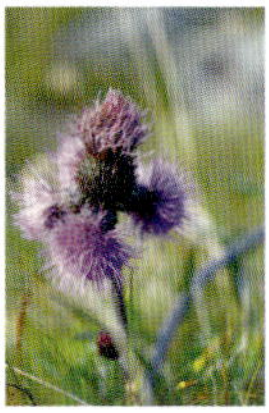
New Mexico

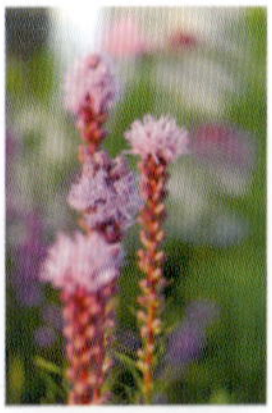

Southampton, New York

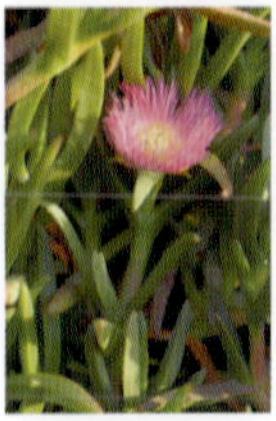

Southampton, New York

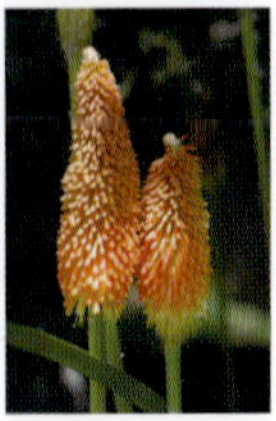

Southampton, New York

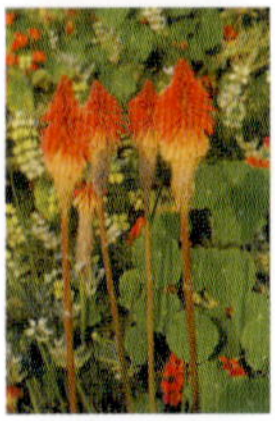

Southampton, New York

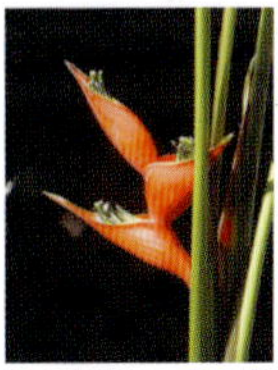

Bangkok, Thailand

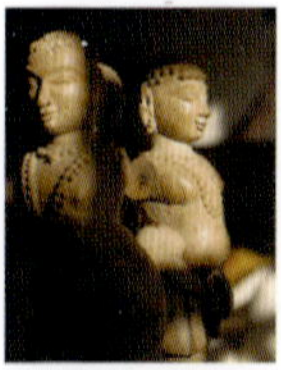

Siem Reap, Cambodia

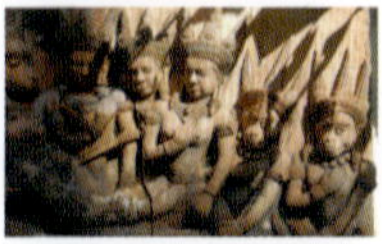

Siem Reap, Cambodia

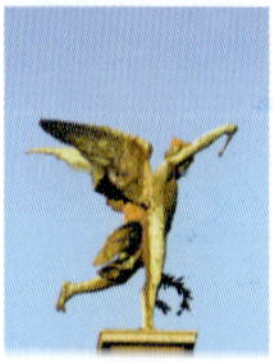

Rome, Italy

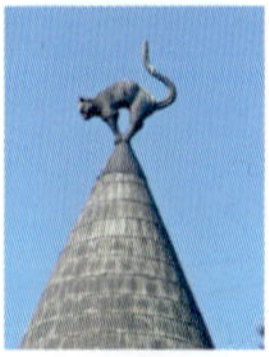

Riga, Latvia

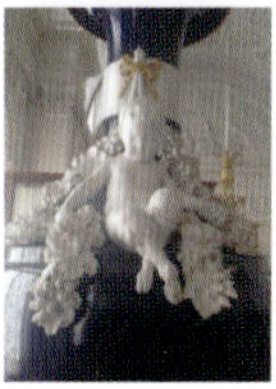

St. Petersburg, Russia

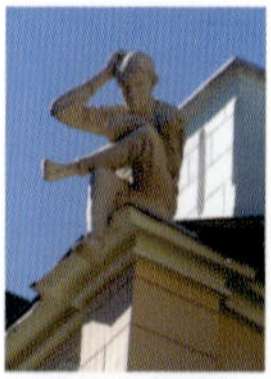

Oslo, Norway

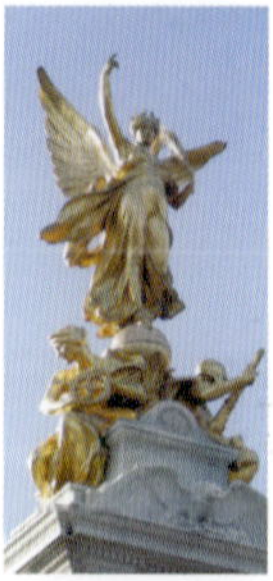

Paris, France

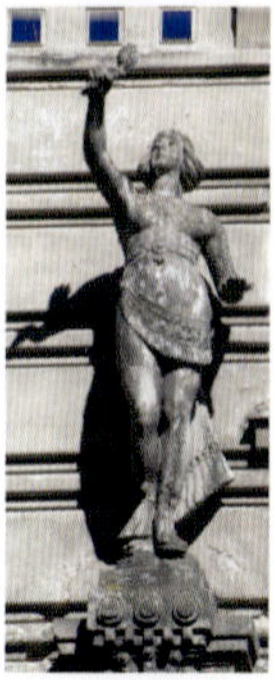

Riga, Latvia

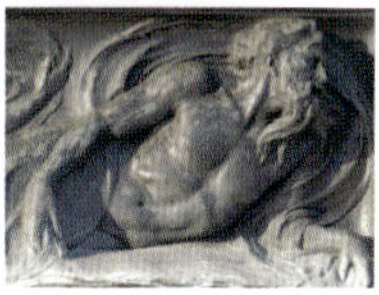

Rome, Italy

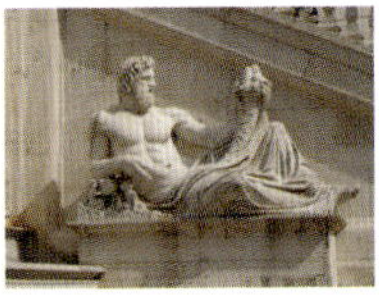
Rome, Italy

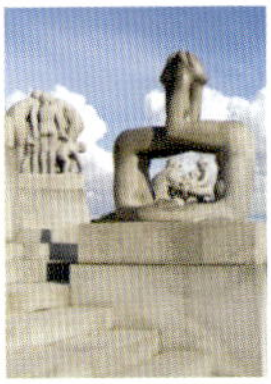
Oslo, Norway

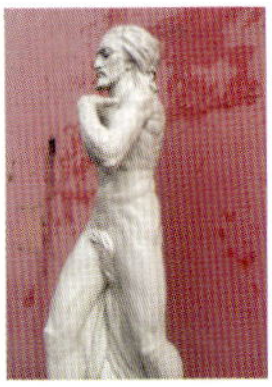
Buenos Aires, Argentina

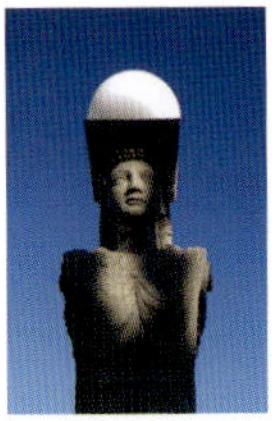
San Simeon, California

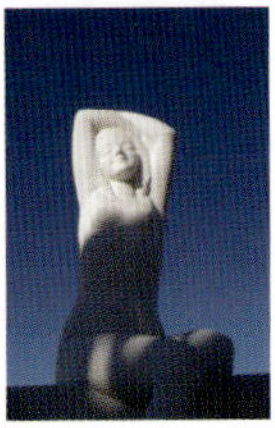
San Simeon, California

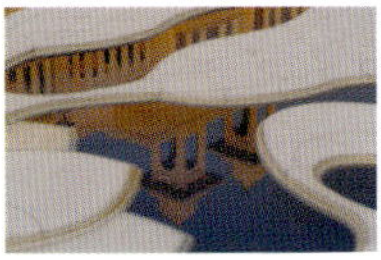
Jaipur, India

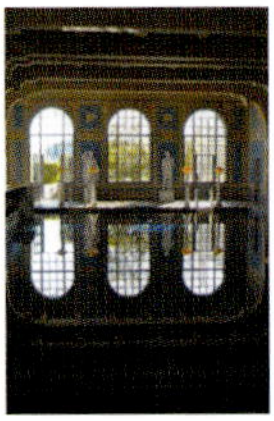
San Simeon, California

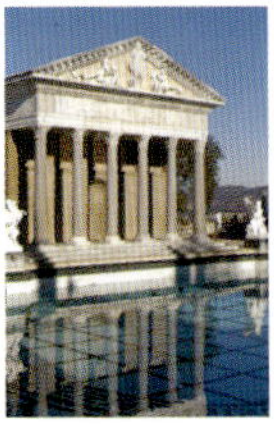
San Simeon, California

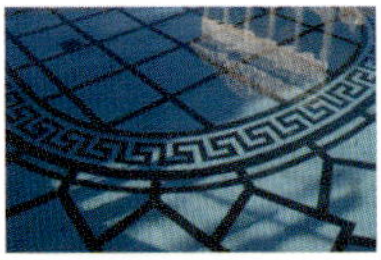
San Simeon, California

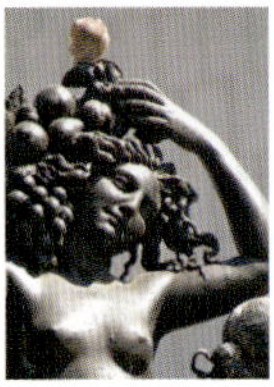
San Simeon, California

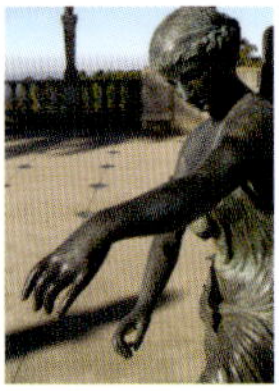
San Simeon, California

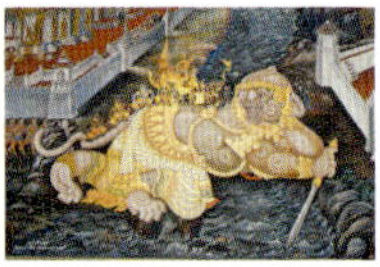
Luang Prabang, Laos

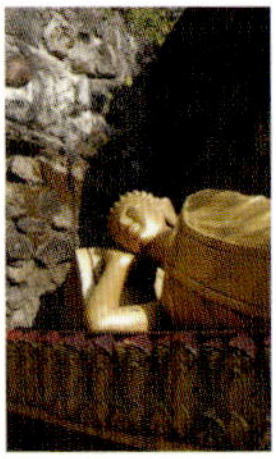
Luang Prabang, Laos

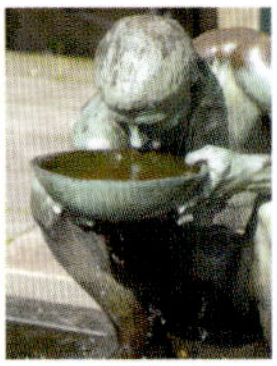
Oslo, Norway

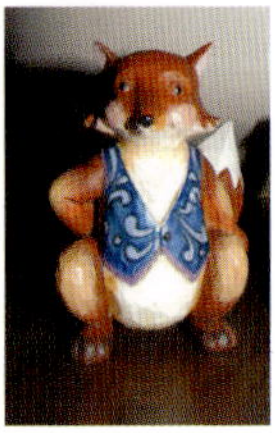
Florence, Italy

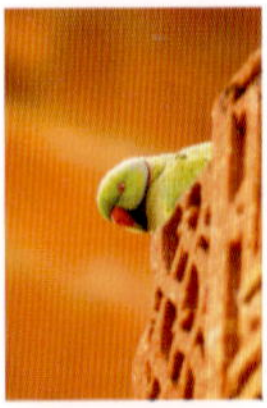
Jaipur, India

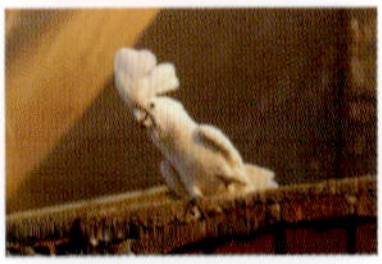
Sayulita, Mexico

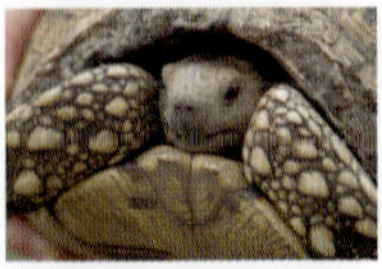
South Africa

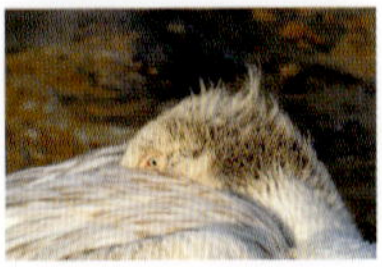
Mykonos, Greece

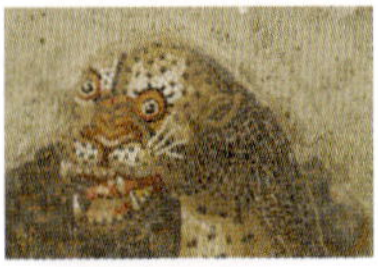
Delos, Greece

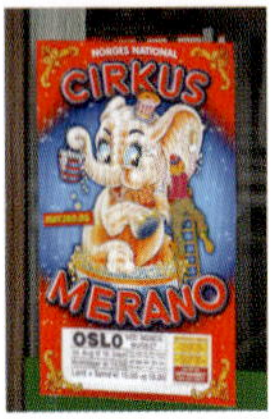

Oslo, Norway

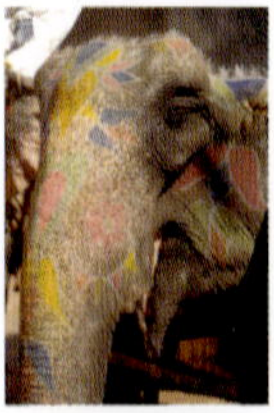
Jaipur, India

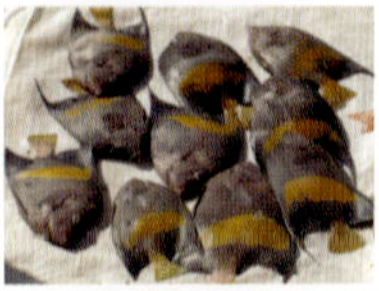
Nukubati, Fiji

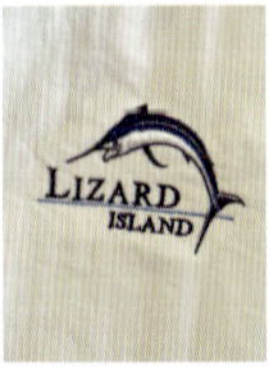

Lizard Island, Australia

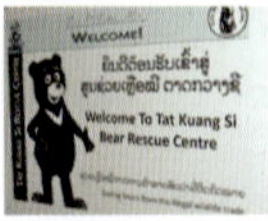

Chiang Mai, Thailand

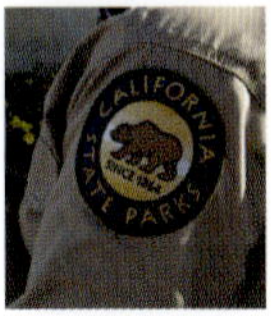

San Simeon, California

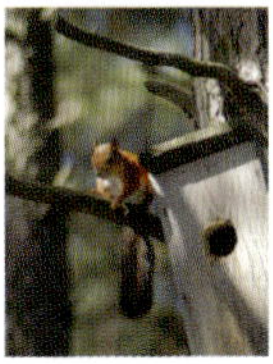
Sun Valley, Idaho

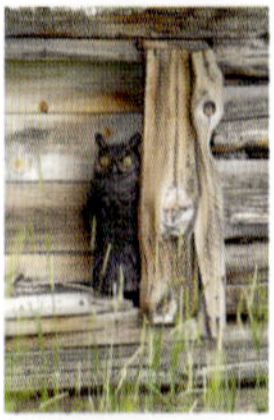
Hailey, Idaho

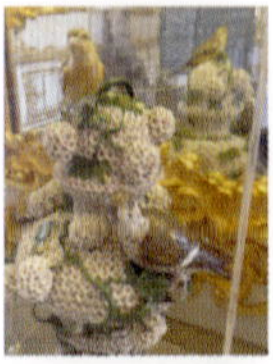
St. Petersburg, Russia

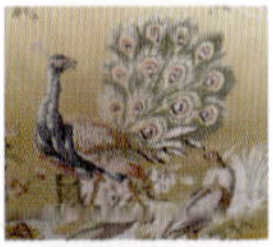
St. Petersburg, Russia

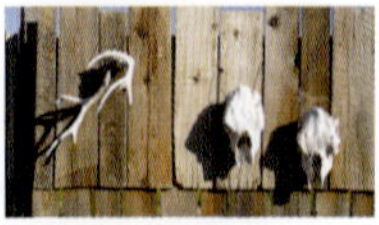
Santa Fe, New Mexico

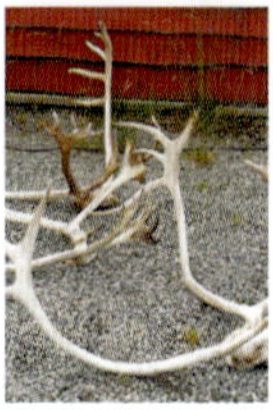
Santa Fe, New Mexico

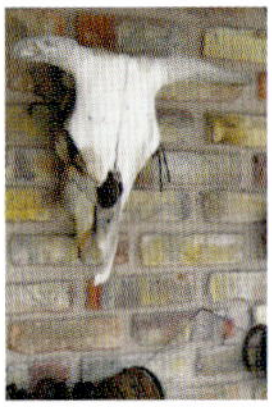

Santa Fe, New Mexico

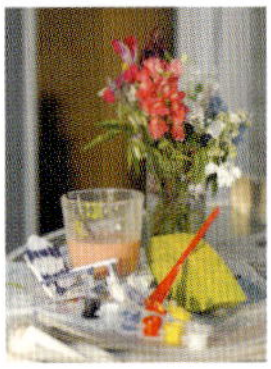

Southampton, New York

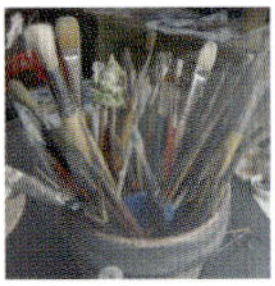

New Orleans, Louisiana

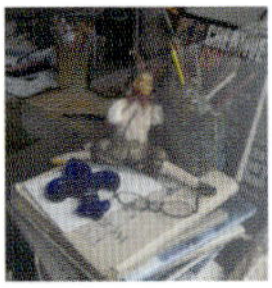

New Orleans, Louisiana

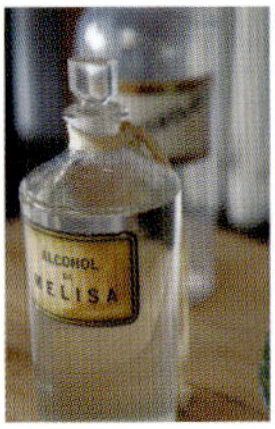

New Orleans, Louisiana

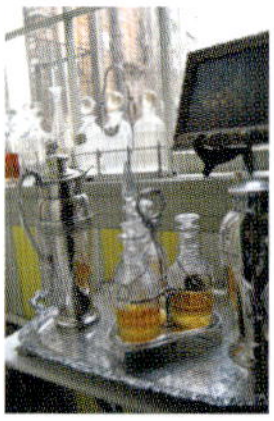

New Orleans, Louisiana

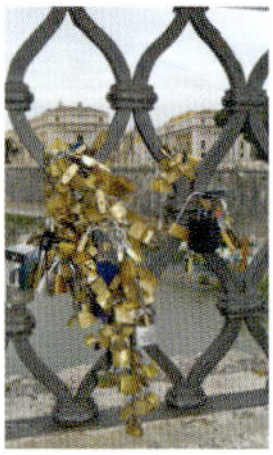

Paris, France

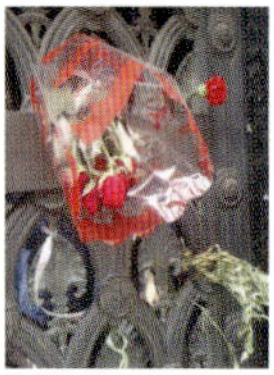

Paris, France

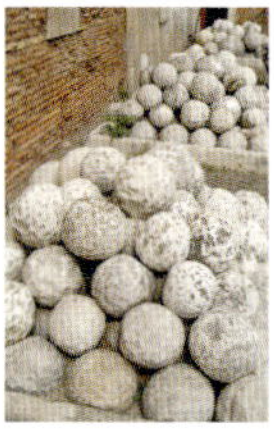

Athens, Greece

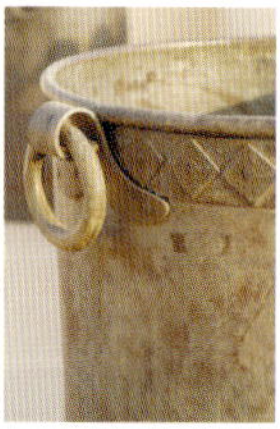

Athens, Greece

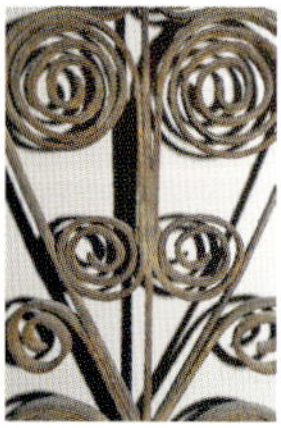

Charleston, South Carolina

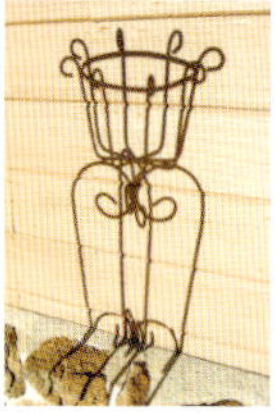

Charleston, South Carolina

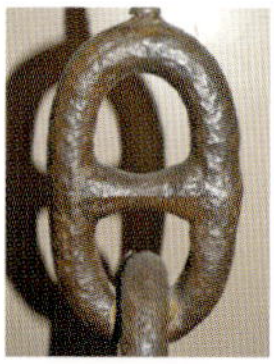

Zapallar, Chile

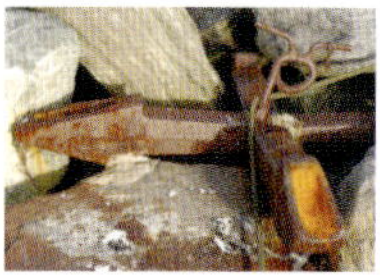

Zapallar, Chile

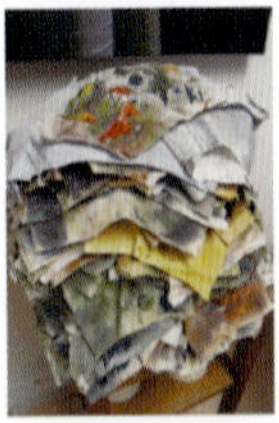

Santa Fe, New Mexico

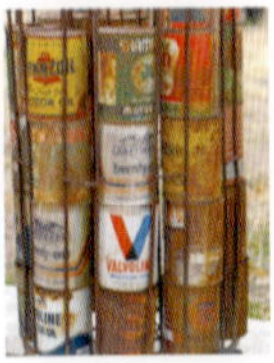

Santa Fe, New Mexico

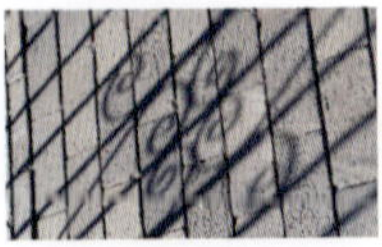

Charleston, South Carolina

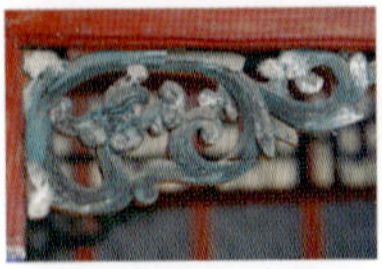

Beijing, China

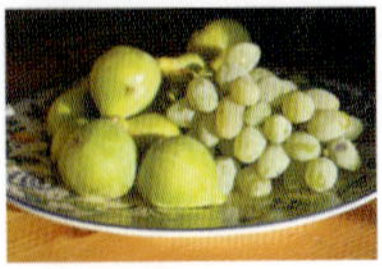

Tuscany, Italy

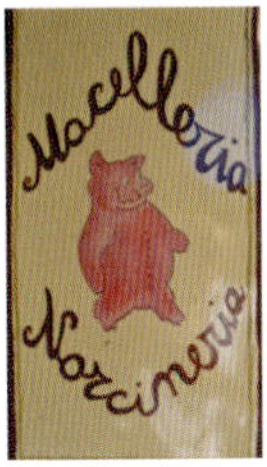

Florence, Italy

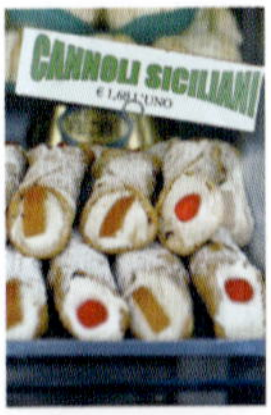

Florence, Italy

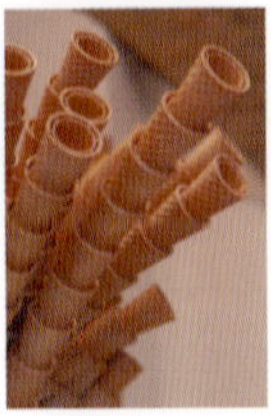

Above the Arctic Circle, Norway

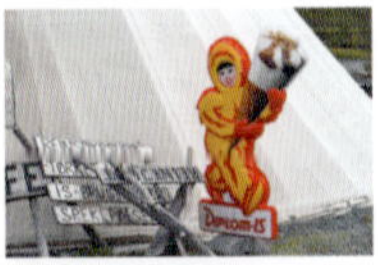

Above the Arctic Circle, Norway

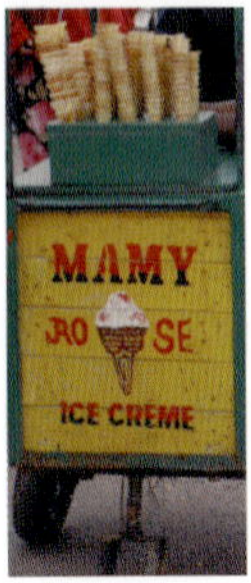

Tano, Madagascar

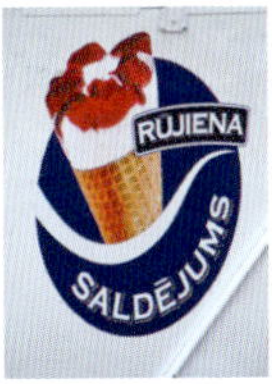

Tromso, Norway

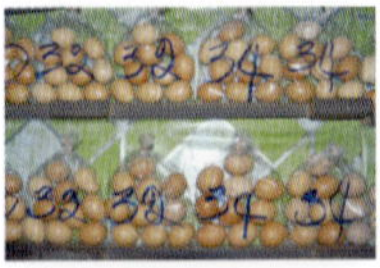

Luang Prabang, Laos

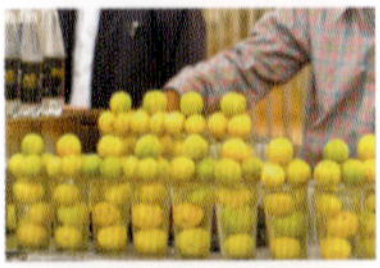

Luang Prabang, Laos

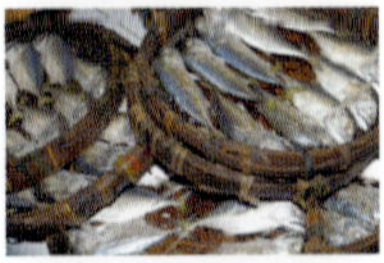

Luang Prabang, Laos

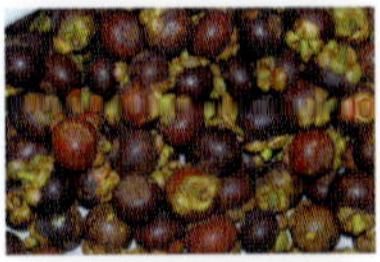

Luang Prabang, Laos

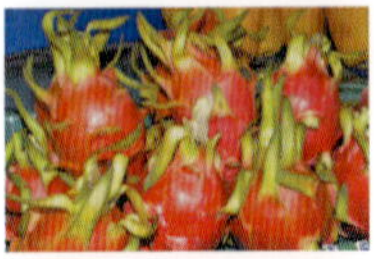

Luang Prabang, Laos

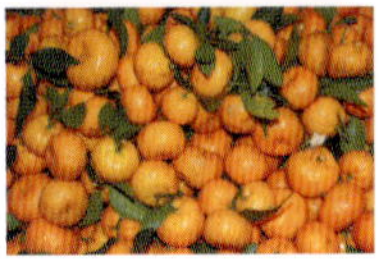

Luang Prabang, Laos

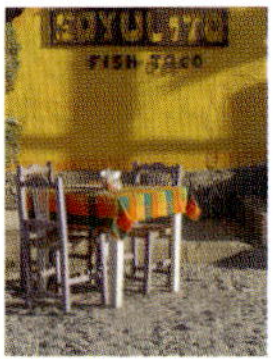

Sayulita, Mexico

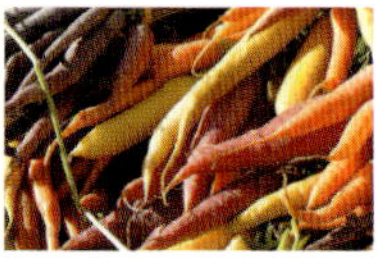

Sayulita, Mexico

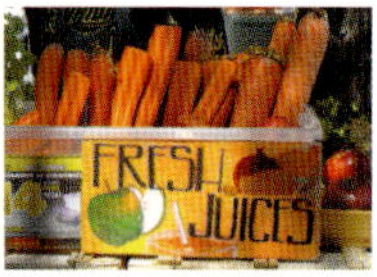

Sayulita, Mexico

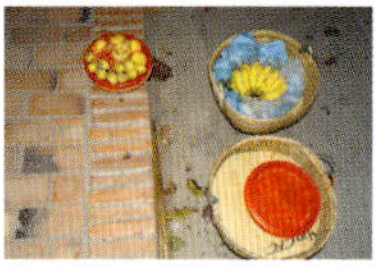

Luang Prabang, Laos

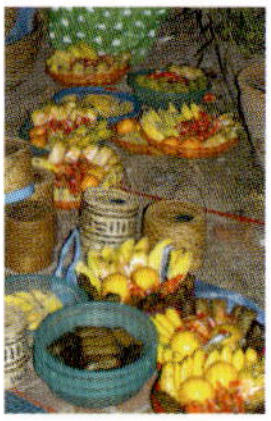

Luang Prabang, Laos

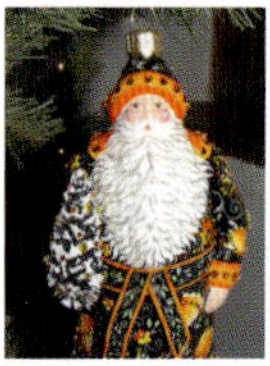

Stockholm, Sweden

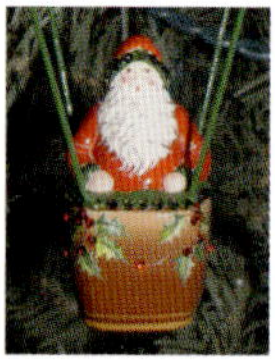

Stockholm, Sweden

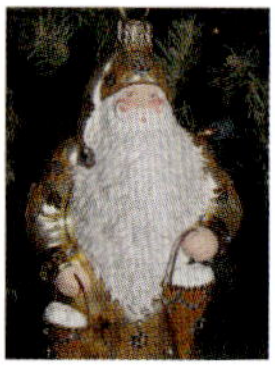

Stockholm, Sweden

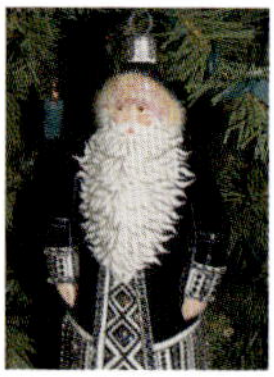

Stockholm, Sweden

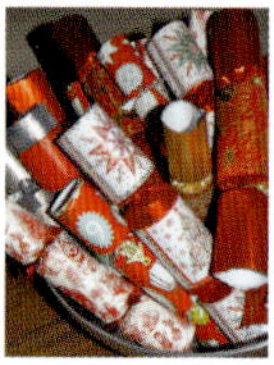

Stockholm, Sweden

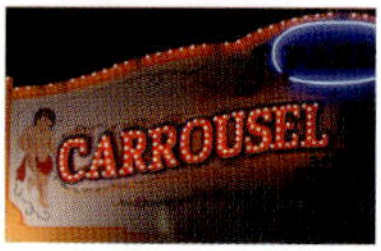

Paris, France

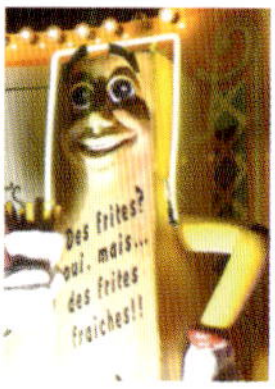

Paris, France

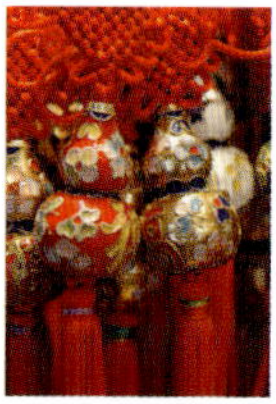

Shanghai, China

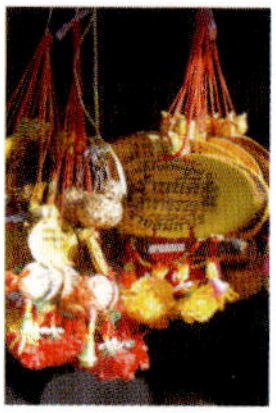

Bangkok, Thailand

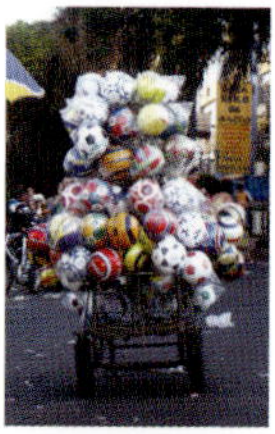

Paraguay

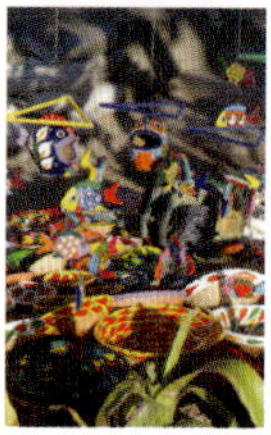

Taos, New Mexico

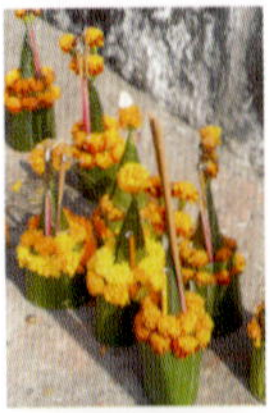
Bangkok, Thailand

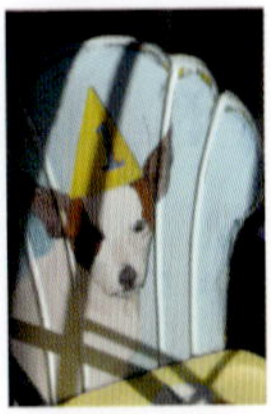
Kerrville, Texas

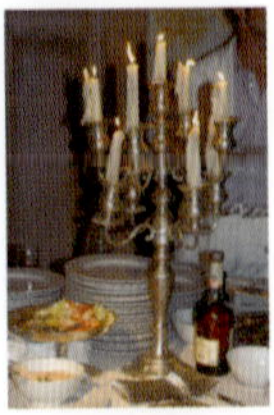
Puglia, Italy

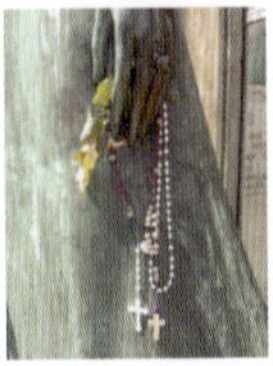
Buenos Aires, Argentina

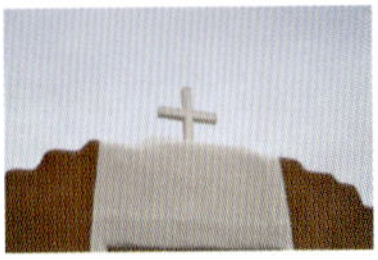
Taos, New Mexico

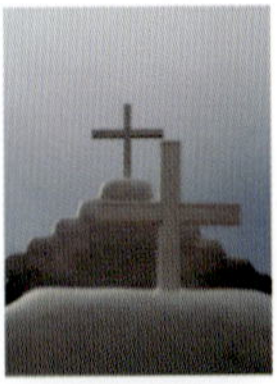
Taos, New Mexico

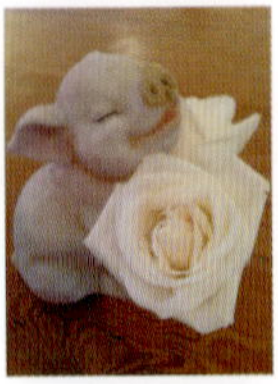
Buenos Aires, Argentina

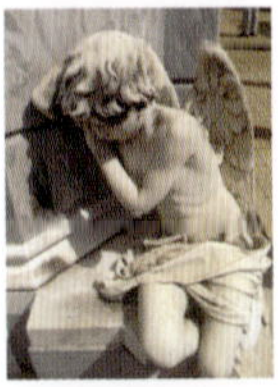
Buenos Aires, Argentina

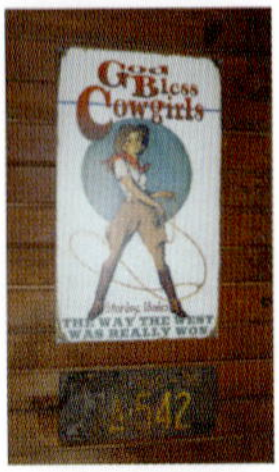

Stanley, Idaho

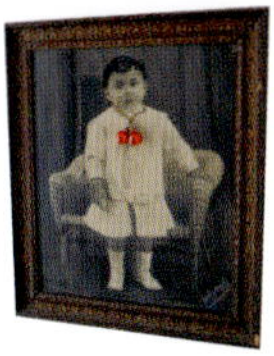
Mendoza, Argentina

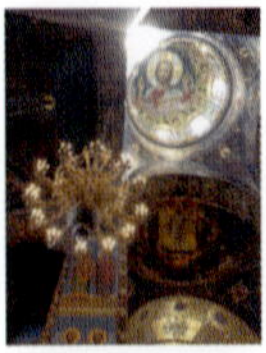
St. Petersburg, Russia

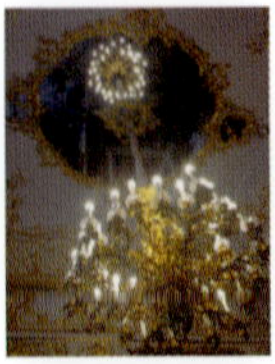
St. Petersburg, Russia

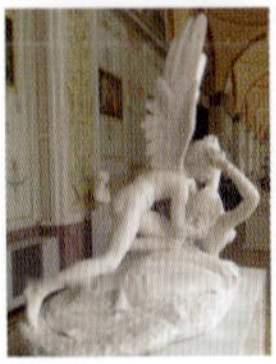
St. Petersburg, Russia

Acknowledgments

In our travels through life, there are many people who influence us along the way. In the beginning, it was my parents, my maternal grandmother, and my high school English teacher, Richard Price, who made words and reading more magical than I ever could have imagined.

Sometimes, we are influenced by neighbors, friends, brothers, sisters, and even strangers whom we meet on an airplane who make a comment that can change the course of our lives.

Over the years, there have been so many people who have helped me to shape who I am today. They are the ones I will cherish forever.

Like most families, mine has its ups and downs, but there is nothing like family. They are there through everything. To the members of my tribe, thank you for the support and love, especially to my parents, Nancy and Joe, who let me expand my wings at an early age and have been there all along, cheering me on. To Janet, Kate, Matthew, Debbie, Chris, Joe, Peg, Bobby, Shannon, Andy, Clint, Sean, Luke, Paul, Molly, David, Bobby, Nicolas, Emerson, and Kathleen: May you all continue to live well and embrace the details of what life can bring you.

To Tom, who all those years ago I met during a run in Central Park; who knew what richness it would bring to both of us. The list is endless, but thank you again and again.

Cap, Andy, Chris, Emily, Todd, Chris, Haideh, Penny, Jay, Amy, Jack, Tom, Bob, Martha: Who could have a better posse to run with, as we share life's experiences and build memories that fill us to the brim? To Sade, Keith, Adam, Susie, Joel, Pamela, Steve, and others who fill out the circle of friendship.

We spend a lot of our time with work colleagues, and I have been fortunate to know so many interesting and accomplished people in my career. Thank you to Frank, Gil, Steve, Mark, Cathie, David, Ellen, Jeff, Deb, Judith, and so many others.

To Fran, 30 years of experiences together. You are family to me.

Without Jacqui, I never would have met the one and only Marta Hallett, who has been a trusted publisher, adviser, and friend. Thank you for our shared love of words and pictures and for giving me the ability to share my work.

Thanks to Liz Trovato for her creative design, and to the team at Glitterati.

The people in our lives are the details that make us who we are. Celebrate them. Stay close and closer to them every day.

Other Glitterati Titles by Michael Clinton

American Portraits: 100 Countries (2010)

Global Faces: 500 Photographs from 7 Continents (2007)

Global Remains: Abandoned Architecture and Objects from 7 Continents (2011)

Global Snaps: 500 Photographs from 7 Continents (2005)

The Globetrotter Diaries: Tales, Tips, and Tactics for Traveling the 7 Continents (2013)

Wanderlust: One Hundred Countries, A Personal Journey (2006)

Wanderlust: One Hundred Countries, A Personal Journey, Limited Edition (2012)

About the Author

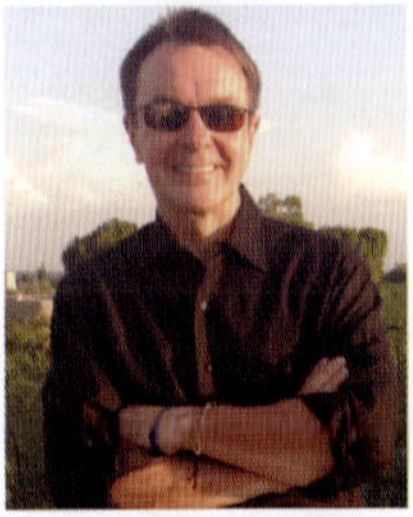

Michael Clinton is President and Publishing Director of Hearst Magazines. His responsibilities include oversight of 20 publications, including *Harper's Bazaar*; *Marie Claire*; *O, The Oprah Magazine*; *Seventeen*, and *Esquire*. Clinton also serves on the Board of the Hearst Corporation and is the Chairman of the Magazine Publishers of America. He is a Trustee of the International Center of Photography and is the Founder and President of the non-profit organization Circle of Generosity. He lives in New York City and Southampton, New York.